The Texas Pan American Series

BOLÍVAR

MEMORIAS DEL
General Daniel Florencio O'Leary
NARRACIÓN
·
ABRIDGED VERSION

Translated and Edited by
Robert F. McNerney, Jr.

AND THE WAR OF INDEPENDENCE

UNIVERSITY OF TEXAS PRESS · AUSTIN AND LONDON

The Texas Pan American Series is published
with the assistance of a revolving publication
fund established by the Pan American Sulphur
Company and other friends of Latin America
in Texas. This English translation was originally done for the Sociedad Bolivariana de
Venezuela with the approval of the Venezuelan
government.

International Standard Book Number 0–292–70047–4
Library of Congress Catalog Card Number 70–137997
© 1970 by the University of Texas Press

Printed by The University of Texas Printing Division, Austin
Bound by Universal Bookbindery, Inc., San Antonio

To the memory of a great Bolivarian scholar

VICENTE LECUNA

TRANSLATOR'S FOREWORD

I

Biographical Sketch

A native of Cork, Ireland, where he was born near the beginning of the nineteenth century—the exact date has never been satisfactorily determined[1]—Daniel Florencio (Florence) O'Leary arrived in the New World early in 1818 as a cornet in a cavalry corps recruited in the British Isles. After a relatively brief stay at Achaguas in the Apure region, O'Leary returned to Angostura[2] where he was assigned to the Guard of Honor and met Bolívar for the first time. This meeting marks the beginning of a lifelong friendship between these two men from different worlds.

During the remaining years of the war of independence, O'Leary distinguished himself as a soldier in decisive battles fought in Venezuela, New Granada, and Ecuador, and performed valuable missions as Bolívar's personal envoy in areas as widely scattered as Jamaica, Panama, Peru, and Chile. His close association with Bolívar as a member of the general staff, first as an aide and then as chief aide, gave him an excellent opportunity to become well acquainted with that great leader and with the march of events in all theaters of the war.

After the war the Liberator continued to send O'Leary, now a colonel, on important missions: to Venezuela in 1826 to talk to General Páez about the state of affairs there; to Ocaña in 1828, soon after his marriage to the sister of General Soublette, to report on the proceedings

---

[1] A very likely date is February, 1800, as claimed by his family.
[2] The name is now Ciudad Bolívar.

of the great convention; and to Peru as a peace envoy that same year. The outbreak of hostilities prevented him from reaching Peru, and he subsequently played an important role in the Colombian victory at Tarqui early in 1829, which brought him a promotion to the rank of brigadier general. Later in the same year he successfully put down a rebellion in Antioquia. Appointed minister to the United States by Bolívar, O'Leary was never able to assume this post because his services were then needed as head of an army on the Venezuelan border and the appointment was subsequently revoked by General Mosquera, the new president. Near the end of the year 1830 this loyal aide, standing in the cathedral of Santa Marta, watched in sorrow as the remains of the great man of the revolution were lowered into a humble grave.

A few months later, after an insurrection took place in Cartagena, O'Leary was ordered into exile. He went to Jamaica, where he was joined by his wife and three children. These two years of exile, though far from pleasant, gave him an opportunity to arrange his papers and the documents acquired from Bolívar's archives, to seek more information from his comrades and friends, and to write the greater part of his *Narración*.

After he and his family were able to return to the mainland in 1833 and establish residence in Caracas, O'Leary began what might be called the European phase of his life. He spent the next six years in England and on the Continent, as secretary of the Venezuelan legation seeking recognition of Venezuela's independence in England and Spain, and as chargé d'affaires to the Holy See in an unsuccessful attempt to arrange a concordat. There was time, too, for a visit to his native Ireland to see his family after an absence of seventeen years.

Upon his return to Venezuela in 1840, O'Leary resumed his diplomatic career, this time as acting British consul in Caracas and Puerto Cabello. It must have been especially gratifying to him to be able to take an active part in the ceremonies surrounding the removal of Bolívar's remains from Santa Marta to Caracas. In the year 1844 he became British consul general in Bogotá, a post he held for eight years. When his health began to fail toward the end of this period, he decided to seek a more complete diagnosis of his ailments in Europe.

Accompanied by two of his nine children, whom he was to place in a French boarding school, O'Leary set out for the Old World in July, 1852. After being assured in London that he was organically sound, he went to Paris and Rome before returning home by way of the United States with his son Simón. Despite the favorable diagnoses, little time remained to him after his return to Bogotá. He died quite suddenly on February 24, 1854, apparently the victim of a cerebral hemorrhage. His funeral took place the following day in the cathedral with full diplomatic and military honors. Many years later, in September, 1837, his remains were removed to the Panteón de los Héroes in Caracas, where they were given a final resting place near those of the immortal hero whose glorious career he had recorded for posterity in his *Memorias.*

II
The Writer

Shortly before his death Bolívar expressed the wish that General O'Leary write the story of his life, and it would seem that he chose the man pre-eminently qualified to record his lifelong struggle for freedom. The active role O'Leary played in the war of independence as soldier, diplomat, and chief aide-de-camp of Bolívar gave him an excellent opportunity to become well acquainted with his subject and to evaluate Bolívar's career in the light of the stirring events of this period of Spanish American history. In addition, the very fact that O'Leary came from a distant land enabled him to view these events with a certain amount of detachment.

The combination of a wealth of material, an able writer, and a dedicated historian imbued with the desire to present an authenic record of the Liberator's accomplishments resulted in a monumental work, the thirty-two–volume *Memorias del General O'Leary,* which was published in Caracas by his son Simón Bolívar O'Leary between 1879 and 1888. This work is still considered to be one of the most important sources of reference material for all students of this fruitful period of Spanish American history. It should be noted that the three volumes of the *Narración* are the only part that can be properly called the memoirs of General O'Leary. The other twenty-nine volumes, compiled by O'Leary, are made up of the correspondence of distinguished men with Bolívar, documents, and letters written by Bolívar.

III

The Present Edition

This edition is an abridgment of the first two volumes of my unpublished translation of the entire edition of the *Narración* published by the Venezuelan government in 1952 under the able editorship of Dr. Pedro Grases. With the approval of the Venezuelan government, the translation was done under the auspices of the Sociedad Bolivariana de Venezuela. The first two volumes of the work carry the life of Bolívar up to November, 1826. Worthy of note is the fact that I was able to use O'Leary's own original text in English for a large part of chapter one of the present edition. The part of his original manuscript discovered after an exhaustive search indicates that he started writing the work in English and then continued on in Spanish.

There is reasonable justification for excluding the third volume of the *Narración* from an abridged edition. The first two volumes contain the part that General O'Leary left written and ready for the press. The third volume, or *Apéndice*, contains journals, notes, and correspondence found among O'Leary's papers, which, as Dr. Pedro Grases suggests, undoubtedly would have been the basis for carrying the life of the Liberator up to the time of his death.

Most of the limited number of footnotes to be found in this edition are followed by the signature of their author. Those with the abbreviation "Ed." were added by me as editor. The other ones are from among those included in the original edition by O'Leary's son, Simón Bolívar O'Leary, and from among those included in the 1952 edition by Dr. Pedro Grases and by Dr. Vicente Lecuna. All the others, unsigned, are O'Leary's own. (A number of O'Leary's notes referring to letters or documents have been omitted.)

It may well be evident from what has already been said that this abridged edition of my translation is intended primarily for the general reader interested in Spanish America and for collateral reading in colleges and universities rather than for historians and specialists in the Spanish American field. Many readers will be afforded their first opportunity to view the life of the Liberator and the war of independence through the eyes of a very competent historian who had firsthand knowledge of his subject and who had himself played a prominent role in many of the events described.

The maps for this edition, used here by permission of the Sociedad Bolivariana de Venezuela, were done by Dr. Vicente Lecuna for his *Crónica razonada de las guerras de Bolívar* (1950). The illustrations are taken from publications of the Academia Nacional de la Historia, Caracas, and the Sociedad Bolivariana, from the 1952 *Memorias,* from *Bolívar, forjador de la libertad,* and from *Cartas del Libertador,* and are used by permission.[3]

I wish to express my appreciation to the Venezuelan government and to the Sociedad Bolivariana de Venezuela for the opportunity afforded me to prepare this edition for the English-speaking world. It gives me great pleasure to be able to mention here that the encouragement and the wholehearted cooperation of the late Dr. Vicente Lecuna and Dr. Cristóbal L. Mendoza proved invaluable in clearing the way for the translation. To my good friend and colleague, Dr. E. Edward Flynn, goes my deepest gratitude for the part of the translation that he generously undertook and for his many helpful suggestions after reading the entire manuscript. Also, I am very grateful to Señorita Esther Barret de Nazarís, secretary of the Fundación Vicente Lecuna, for her many valuable observations concerning the translation. I should add, however, that the final responsibility for the translation, as well as for the abridgment, rests with me. And, in conclusion, I want to thank my wife Mary for the countless hours she spent typing the manuscript and reading proof.

ROBERT F. McNERNEY, JR.

Holy Cross College
Worcester, Massachusetts

---

[3] *Memorias del General Daniel Florencio O'Leary, Narración* (Caracas: Imprenta Nacional, 1952); *Boletín de la Academia Nacional de la Historia,* Caracas, nos. 122, 128, 184; *Revista de la Sociedad Bolivariana de Venezuela,* nos. 44, 47; José de la Cruz Herrera, *Bolívar, forjador de la libertad,* edición auspiciada por el Ministerio de Relaciones Interiores (Caracas: Imprenta Nacional, 1957), Ediciones de la Sociedad Bolivariana de Venezuela; Vicente Lecuna, ed., *Cartas del Libertador,* mandadas publicar por el Banco de Venezuela, vol. II (1802–1830) (New York: The Colonial Press, Inc., 1948).

PREFACE

From the time of my arrival in America, early in the year 1818, I began to gather data and documents related to the war of independence and to the life of the extraordinary man who directed it. I gathered them at first with the idea of sending to my parents and friends in Ireland the impressions of my trip to regions unknown to them and to me. From the beginning of my career I had the good fortune to merit the friendship and confidence of my illustrious Chief. It was a mutual friendship and confidence that lasted while he lived and until I, broken-hearted and with my face bathed in tears, saw his mortal remains lowered into a humble grave in the cathedral of Santa Marta. During the campaigns in Venezuela, New Granada, Quito, and Peru, I assiduously collected documents and was actively aided in this undertaking by my comrades-in-arms, especially Antonio José de Sucre, Tomás de Heres, José Gabriel Pérez, José Domingo Espinar, and, above all, Pedro Briceño Méndez. As time passed and the collection of documents grew, I thought about using them to write the life of the Liberator. Many important papers were lost in the course of the campaigns, because the marches were strenuous in those days, and it was not always possible to carry even the baggage of the general staff. I succeeded, nevertheless, in saving the greater part of what came into my hands. After the death of the Liberator and the destruction of his great work, I retired to Jamaica; there I devoted myself to arranging the papers and to writing my memoirs. The Liberator's executors gave me his archives; and Carlos Soublette, Bartolomé Salom, Rafael Urdaneta, Juan José Flores, Mariano Montilla, Tomás de Heres, Jacinto Lara, Belford H. Wilson, and many other friends of mine gladly sent information at my request. My intention was to publish, during my residence on that island, the material that I had assembled. Since it was based on my documents and very respectable authorities, it would help to confound Bolívar's detractors, both in America and in Europe.

In 1835, accompanied by General Soublette, I visited General Pablo Morillo in La Coruña. When the latter learned that I was occupied in writing the life of his old rival, of whom he was a great admirer, he gave me many documents taken by the royalists on the battlefields of Venezuela. The most important of the documents that I have collected are Bolívar's letters and those from the various military leaders and prominent people who wrote to him. These letters set forth the principal events of the war and of political life. I have tried to collect the greatest possible number of them, but, in spite of my efforts, there are unfortunately many gaps in this correspondence that it is regrettable not to be able to fill. Some of these letters may seem trivial, but I have kept them, for all of them—some more, some less—are a reflection of the glorious period of the war of independence.

DANIEL F. O'LEARY

Caracas
July, 1840

CONTENTS

Translator's Foreword ix
Preface xv
Introduction 3
Chapter One 8
Chapter Two 22
Chapter Three 32
Chapter Four 45
Chapter Five 59
Chapter Six 72
Chapter Seven 87
Chapter Eight 99
Chapter Nine 116
Chapter Ten 128
Chapter Eleven 143
Chapter Twelve 157
Chapter Thirteen 168
Chapter Fourteen 185
Chapter Fifteen 203
Chapter Sixteen 220
Chapter Seventeen 236
Chapter Eighteen 253
Chapter Nineteen 271
Chapter Twenty 287
Chapter Twenty-one 302
Chapter Twenty-two 312

Chapter Twenty-three 322
Chapter Twenty-four 329
Chapter Twenty-five 340
Chapter Twenty-six 354
Index 369

ILLUSTRATIONS

Frontispiece: Simón Bolívar. Portrait by Gil de Castro, kept in Caracas. (Boletín de la Academia Nacional de la Historia, Caracas, no. 128.)

Following page 172:

Daniel Florencio O'Leary
Proclamation of War to the Death
José Francisco Bermúdez
Francisco de Paula Santander
José Antonio Páez
Rafael Urdaneta
Pedro Luis Brión
Santiago Mariño
Crossing of the Andes, 1819
Treaties for an Armistice and the Regularization of the War
Carlos Soublette
Antonio José de Sucre
Meeting between Morillo and Bolívar

MAPS

Theater of War, 1812–1813 33
Aux Cayes Expedition, 1816 100
Theater of the Carabobo Campaign, 1821 . . . 192

Bomboná Campaign, 1822 210
Pichincha Campaign, 1822 214
Junín Campaign, 1824 256
Ayacucho Campaign, 1824 266

Bolívar and the War of Independence

THE QUESTION that is most frequently asked now, and that is difficult to answer, is what the Spanish Americans have gained from independence. Many of those who have been faithful friends of the revolution are discouraged by the present state of affairs. Should it surprise us that there have been such different results in North and South America? It is not to be wondered at that Colombia is still struggling against the evils of ignorance, corruption, and ancient, deep-rooted prejudices. On the other hand, ideas of liberty are gradually prevailing in all classes of society. The friends of South American independence in Europe should frankly agree that their limited knowledge of the circumstances led them to expect more than they should have. I am presenting some observations on the physical and social state of Colombia and a sketch of the revolution that will serve as an introduction to the historical events set forth in the narrative of my residence here since 1818.[1]

In Spanish America, as we know, agriculture was the principal source of wealth. The result was that although many landowners were dispossessed during the vicissitudes of the revolution, very few, at least among the natives, lost their property completely. Also, natural simplicity and a common way of life helped them to survive the reverses of the revolution. The way of life of the lower classes was naturally related to that of the upper classes. These people went about barefooted and rudely dressed, or hardly dressed at all, on the hot plains. They had little need to fear the political fluctuations, and they made very few sacrifices when they took their places in the ranks of the soldiers of independence. Patience amidst privations and indifference toward the comforts and even the necessities of life were virtues familiar to them because of their very habits and even because of the very apathy and indolence peculiar to their character.

The geography of Colombia is an important part of its history. When we behold 2.5 million inhabitants spread out over a territory of more than 112,376 square leagues, we can readily imagine how easy it is to defend and how difficult to subjugate. The influence of geographical location on the fate of Colombia must also be examined in regard to its political consequences and its relationship to the social order. The great Andes chain divides various population groups that differ in origin, in customs, in feelings, and in education. Most of the inhabitants of the warm regions are Negroes, or descendants of Africans, whereas the downtrodden Indian race makes up the mass of the population of the *mesetas* or cold regions. The Creoles of pure Spanish extraction are separated from the Africans by racial pride and from the Indians by the pride of dominion; but, at the same time, they regard each other with mutual aversion, though there is no reason for it other than the difference in habits resulting from the difference in climate. This explains the rivalries between Venezuela and New

---

[1] As used here, Colombia really means the Greater Republic of Colombia, a union of Venezuela, New Granada, Quito, and Guayaquil, which later became the republics of Venezuela, Colombia, and Ecuador. —Ed.

Granada, between Cartagena and Bogotá, and between Quito and Guayaquil, all of which have been so fatal in the annals of the revolution. Communication between the highlands and the lowlands was difficult, and it was the policy of the Spanish government to favor this social isolation.

It was the especial object of Spanish policy to foster ignorance among the Americans by shackling the intellect. The commercial regulations had for their object the preservation of the monopoly of trade for the mother country. It would be difficult to speak with sufficient disparagement of the administration of justice or to give an adequate idea of the corruption of the judges. Under this unjust and oppressive system the South Americans were reduced to a political nonentity, and the masses remained totally indifferent. But the revolution of the English colonies of North America, soon followed by the great French Revolution, made it impossible to check the spread of the brilliant theories that then appeared. And as time went on, the ancient abuses became more frequent and therefore furnished new reasons for complaint.

It was not, however, the eloquence of Picornell, the generous efforts of Gual and España, the suggestions of Picton, the injudicious attempt at invasion by Beresford, or the adventurous spirit of Miranda that would overthrow Spanish dominion in America.[2] That vast structure had too deep a foundation and was supported by columns of too much strength to yield even to such sturdy blows. It was the disloyalty of the evil sons of Spain that first awakened in the Americans an awareness of the injustice with which they were being treated.

In 1808, when Captain General Juan de las Casas ordered the city council of Caracas to recognize the Supreme Junta, this body obeyed his commands. Such was still the force of habit and such the power of the legitimate sovereign in Venezuela that the arbitrary decision was respected without protest, though there was no military force to sup-

---

[2] Juan Picornell, Manuel Gual, and José María España promoted a conspiracy against the captain general of Caracas in 1797. Sir Thomas Picton, governor of Trinidad, encouraged the inhabitants of the Spanish Main to rebel. General William Carr Beresford invaded Buenos Aires in 1806 with one thousand British troops. Francisco de Miranda was one of the earliest and most active Venezuelan patriots. —Ed.

port it. Some ardent spirits, however, resented the conduct of the government and endeavored by indirect means to weaken its authority and to counteract its measures. Among these, Bolívar was the most conspicuous. At a cottage that he owned on the banks of the Guaire, some of the principal citizens used to meet to discuss the state of affairs and to consider the best means of obtaining justice for their country or at least a relaxation of the rigorous policy by which it had hitherto been governed. The idea of establishing independence was also broached at these meetings. Though earnestly urged by Bolívar and a few who like him had long cherished the project, it does not seem to have been acceptable to the majority, even of those who exhibited the most discontent. The only result was a presentation to the captain general of a petition requesting the institution of a junta to protect the rights of Ferdinand VII. Las Casas not only refused to heed this moderate request but, regarding all the petitioners as criminals, submitted them to a special tribunal, which sentenced some to temporary banishment, others to imprisonment, and the majority to house arrest.

Las Casas was superseded by General Vicente de Emparan, who arrived at La Guaira on May 17, 1809. He had the folly to declare that his will was the law, thus creating many enemies and estranging his friends. Among the latter were Fernando Toro and Simón Bolívar, whom he had known in the Peninsula. They urged him to grant the institution of a junta to protect the rights of Ferdinand, but he was inexorable. When a plot to overthrow him was divulged to the captain general, he separated several officers from the battalion of Aragua and banished to their estates a few of the other accomplices, among whom was Bolívar. When news of the sad state of the mother country became known not long thereafter, it was evident that measures had to be adopted to save Venezuela from the catastrophe that threatened or had befallen Spain. On April 19, 1810, the captain general was deposed, and the municipal government, moved to action more by the fiery Canon José Cortés Madariaga and other restless spirits than by the will of the people, disowned the authority of the regency and established a government that would exercise authority in the name of the legitimate king, Ferdinand VII.[3]

[3] After Napoleon occupied northern Spain in 1808, he compelled Ferdinand VII to

Thus began the revolution that was to result in the emancipation of the Spanish colonies in America from the mother country. In the course of these memoirs it will be seen how long and costly was the struggle and how many were the errors committed, but it will also be seen that, although there were blunders and even crimes to deplore, the display of valor, unselfishness, and patriotism not only makes one forget these crimes but also proclaims the virtues of the American people.

---

abdicate. The Supreme Junta of Spain and the Indies, first established in Seville, appealed to the colonies for loyalty and support. Subsequently, a committee of regency, formed in Cádiz in 1810, claimed the authority of Ferdinand VII and issued a call for a *cortes*, or parliament, but many colonial liberals protested against the lack of adequate representation. —Ed.

I N ORDER NOT TO INTERRUPT a series of intimately connected events, I have up to this point barely introduced on the scene a personage who, although he has already taken an active part in those events, is to absorb in the course of my narrative all the interest of the drama. His name—SIMÓN BOLÍVAR—was the standard of South American independence.

The family of Bolívar, originally Spanish, had been established in Venezuela since the conquest, and at an early period thereof had obtained wealth and distinction. Don Simón de Bolívar, one of the paternal ancestors of the illustrious subject of these memoirs, was delegated by the colonial government of Venezuela in the year 1589 to acquaint Philip II with the state of the colony and to solicit the royal protection in its behalf. On his mission to Spain he pleaded warmly for the rights of America. Another member of the Bolívar family purchased the seigniory of Aroa, a fertile region in the province of Caracas, famous since that early period for its rich copper mines. The letters patent, dated in Madrid, August 21, 1663, say that the ownership of the mines of Cocorote with all their dependencies was granted to Don Francisco Marín de Narváez[1] and his successors for the sum of forty thousand pesos. Shortly before the revolution the Bolívar family was granted the titles of Marqués de Bolívar and Vizconde de Cocorote, but these titles were never assumed by the member of the family who had a right to use them.

Don Juan Vicente Bolívar, who held a high office in the Treasury Department and afterwards became colonel of the regular militia of the Valles de Aragua, married Doña María Concepción Palacios y Sojo,[2] a lady of noble and wealthy family, who was known for her beauty and gentle nature as well as for her sound judgment and keen mind. Four children were the fruit of this union, Juan Vicente, María Antonia, Juana, and Simón. Simón was born at his father's residence on the Plaza de San Jacinto in the city of Caracas on the night of July 24, 1783. On July 30 the newborn infant was baptized in the cathedral of Caracas by Dr. Don Juan Félix Jerez y Aristeguieta, his near relative, who, with the assent of Don Juan Vicente, the child's father, and contrary to the wishes of the godfather, Don Feliciano Palacios, gave him the name of Simón. Both he and the father had a presentiment that the child would one day become a more famous man than the first of the family who bore the same name. Be this prediction as it may, the truth is that from the moment of his birth fortune smiled upon him. On the very day of the baptism he received from Don Félix Aristeguieta, his relative, the valuable gift of an estate that at that time produced an annual income of twenty thousand duros.

[1] Don Francisco Marín de Narváez, father of Doña Josefa María Narváez, married to Licentiate Don Pedro de Ponte Andrade, parents of Doña María Petronila de Ponte, married to Don Juan de Bolívar y Villegas, parents of Colonel Don Juan Vicente Bolívar, married to Doña María Concepción Palacios, parents of His Excellency the Liberator, Simón Bolívar. (Taken from the family genealogical tree.)

[2] The correct name is María Concepción Palacios y Blanco.—Pedro Grases.

Six months thereafter Aristeguieta died, and Don Juan Vicente followed him to the grave before two years had elapsed. The irreparable loss was of serious consequence to the sons, whom the father had intended to send to Europe in order to give them a better education than they could acquire at home. The mother would have realized his wishes had not her father vehemently protested against the idea of sending his grandchildren to live among foreigners and exposing them to the dangers of heresy, for foreigner and heretic were synonymous in Venezuela during that period. In order to remedy this disadvantage as much as possible, she provided them with the ablest instructors their native city could afford. Since she survived her husband by only five years, the guardianship of the little orphans devolved upon their maternal uncle, Don Carlos Palacios, who was too indulgent to exact from them much attention to their studies.

From his earliest years Simón exhibited proofs of strong, natural penetration, a retentive mind, and quick apprehension, but he was more addicted to gymnastic exercises, in which he excelled, and to boyish amusements than to study. In his disposition he was affectionate and generous but irritable and impatient of restraint or contradiction, owing, no doubt, to the overindulgence of his guardians and tutors. He preferred listening to the conversation of persons of more advanced years rather than talking with boys of his own age.

Under the direction of Don Simón Rodríguez, a man of various and extensive attainments but of an eccentric turn of mind, Bolívar became acquainted with the rudiments of Spanish and Latin grammar and of arithmetic and history. But his progress did not correspond with the abilities of his tutor and his own admirable facility of comprehension. The want of application notwithstanding, Rodríguez professed a high opinion of the talented boy, whose imagination was lively, if not poetic. He was often struck with the originality of the boy's observations. Despite his ungainly appearance and his stern manner, he completely gained the affections and confidence of Bolívar by entering with seeming earnestness into the boy's childish affairs.

Rodríguez entertained the most extravagant notions regarding religion, totally at variance with the Christian faith. Though he had the prudence to refrain from arguing with his pupil on such subjects, it is too true that he also abstained from teaching him those sublime principles of the Christian faith that are the best and the most unerring rules of life. Nevertheless, being a philanthropist, he never neglected to instill into the mind of his pupil the most wholesome and liberal social doctrines. Before Bolívar was fourteen years of age he had to part company with his tutor, who had been implicated in a conspiracy to depose the captain general and to change the system of government. With his abode, Rodríguez changed his name and assumed that of Samuel Robinson, so that, he said, he might not be reminded of his former servitude.

The tutor who replaced Rodríguez was Don Andrés Bello, scarcely two years older than Bolívar but already known as an eminent scholar and man of culture. It would not seem, however, that the pupil's application increased with the change of masters. As he grew up, he became addicted to field sports, and he spent the greater part of his time at one of his estates, where he paid some attention to agriculture. The beauty and boldness of the scenery awakened in him a love of nature that grew with his years and afforded him the most refined and purest enjoyment, compensating him for other pleasures of which he was deprived because of the nature of his occupations in later life.

In 1797 he received a commission as ensign in the regiment of militia of Aragua, which his father had commanded. At the beginning of the year 1799 his guardian decided to send him to Spain to pursue his studies. He left La Guaira on January 19, 1799, as a passenger on board the *San Ildefonso,* a Spanish ship of war commanded by Don José Uriarte y Borja, who had volunteered to take charge of the young traveler. At Veracruz, where it touched for the specie it was to take to Spain, the ship was delayed because Havana was blockaded by an English squadron. Bolívar availed himself of this delay to visit Mexico City. He was delighted with that fine capital and more so with the attention he received from Viceroy José de Asanza and from Judge Guillermo Aguirre, at whose house he resided during his week's stay, thanks to a letter of introduction from an uncle of the judge in Caracas. General Miguel Ricardo de Alava, who was then in Mexico and met Bolívar at the viceregal palace, told me that one day, when the conversation turned to the French Revolution, the young Venezuelan advanced opinions whose boldness astonished the hearers and would have caused the viceroy great displeasure had they been uttered by a person of riper years or more extensive acquaintance in the country.

After its departure from Veracruz on March 20, the *San Ildefonso* stopped at Havana for only forty-eight hours before continuing on to Spain, where it arrived in May, dropping anchor at Santoña. Bolívar proceeded immediately to Bilbao and thence to Madrid, where he was met by his maternal uncle, Don Esteban Palacios, to whose care he had been consigned. This gentleman was the intimate friend and companion of Don Manuel Mallo, who at this period shared with Manuel Godoy the affections of the lascivious consort of Charles IV and consequently enjoyed great influence at the Spanish court.[3] Born in Caracas, Mallo was attached to his countrymen, and Bolívar was kindly received by him. Many tempting offers were made to Bolívar, should he be inclined to enter public life. Happily for him, he had already perceived the disadvantage of a defective education, and he decided to mix with society as little as possible. In order to make up for the time he had lost, he sought competent tutors and applied himself to the study of mathematics, languages, and the ancient and modern classics. Days and nights were spent by him in reading, not without causing some alarm to his friends, lest his intense application to his studies should impair his health.

Among Bolívar's acquaintances in Madrid was the Marqués de Uztáriz, in whom he thought he beheld one of the sages of ancient times. For the pleasure of his company he used to leave his books, deeming that from Uztáriz's conversation more was to be gleaned than from their pages. Uztáriz must have obtained great influence over Bolívar's mind, for Bolívar always took pleasure in remembering him and spoke of him with veneration. The feasibility of separating South America from the mother country was a topic on which these friends frequently argued, and on such occasions the elderly Uztáriz, though

---

[3] Godoy, the favorite of Queen María Luisa, became the principal minister of Charles IV in 1792. After signing the treaty of Basel with the French in 1795, he was known as the Prince of Peace. In 1808 he was interned in France with the Spanish king and queen. —Ed.

not hostile to the idea, urged the difficulty attending the undertaking with such sound reasoning as would have dampened the ardor of his young companion had he been possessed of less profound convictions.

Bolívar sometimes consented, though not without reluctance, to accompany Mallo to court and to the royal seats in the vicinity of Madrid. On some of these occasions he was an unwilling witness to the depravity of María Luisa, who paid her favorite's expenses with a liberal hand. More than once, when Bolívar was with him, she entered his apartment. Such a lack of decorum on the part of the august lady was hardly calculated to inspire sentiments of respect and loyalty, and it is therefore not strange that the friend of the virtuous Uztáriz turned his back upon the palace.

At the home of the Marqués de Uztáriz, Bolívar became acquainted with the young lady who was to be his wife, and he soon fell in love with her. Doña María Teresa Toro, the only daughter of Don Bernardo, brother of the Marqués del Toro, was not beautiful, but her gentle nature and her accomplishments made her attractive. She was a few years older than Bolívar,[4] who, ardent in all his impulses, was as passionate a lover as he was an affectionate friend. In Teresa he beheld, according to his own expression, "a jewel of inestimable value, without a flaw." His passion was requited, and he was soon accepted as Teresa's betrothed. But the father demanded that the marriage be deferred for some time on account of Bolívar's youth, for he was only seventeen years old.

When Don Bernardo and his family went to Bilbao in the autumn of 1801, Bolívar felt this absence deeply. Shortly after their departure, however, an incident took place that led him, too, to withdraw from the capital. While passing through the gate of Toledo on horseback one day, he was detained by order of the minister of finance. The alleged pretext was that he was violating the ordinance that prohibited wearing a large quantity of diamonds without a permit. The real reason was the jealousy of the Queen, who, aware of the intimacy between the American youth and Mallo, thought that she might be able to find indications of some amorous intrigue of her favorite among

---

[4] She was almost two years older than he. —Vicente Lecuna.

Bolívar's papers. Refusing to submit to a search, he drew his sword and threatened to punish the first one who approached him. Thanks to the intervention of some of his friends, who were passing at the time, the matter was settled, but nothing could induce him to remain longer in Madrid. Having obtained a passport, he took the road to Bilbao and rejoined the object of his affections toward the end of the year. But he was able to enjoy this very much desired companionship for only a short time, because Don Bernardo was obliged to return to the capital. Bolívar then decided to pay a short visit to Paris before his marriage. He arrived there at the beginning of 1802, a time when great events were taking place in that city.

Bonaparte, with his transcendent genius, had crowned his reputation by restoring peace to France. Bolívar was a witness of the rejoicings that marked the ratification of the treaty of Amiens, but it was Bonaparte himself who was the main object of his curiosity, for the head of the Republic was then the theme of universal admiration. Recalling the degraded state in which he had left a neighboring nation and attributing its decay to the corruption of monarchical institutions, Bolívar concluded with youthful haste that a republican government alone was capable of ensuring the happiness of the people. During this period he became a decided republican, and thereafter he always adhered to his strong republican convictions.

Hastening back to Madrid, Bolívar remained there no longer than was necessary for the celebration of his marriage. Toward the end of May, 1802, he became the husband of Doña María Rodríguez del Toro, and they left immediately for La Coruña, where they embarked for La Guaira. The voyage of the youthful couple was pleasant and quick, and their reception at Caracas was everything they could have desired. Now that he was entirely his own master, Bolívar chose to retire to his country residence, where his energetic nature would find an outlet in work that would be both pleasant and profitable. In later years he loved to recall this period of his existence; he deemed it the only perfectly happy and calm one he had had in his checkered career. According to his own account, he rose early, superintended the work at his estate, indicated the improvements to be made, took a great deal of exercise on foot and on horseback, and devoted himself to study during the heat of the day and part of the evening. Thus, in the society of a beloved wife, he enjoyed a few months of unalloyed bliss, but the serene endearments of home and the pure joys of domestic life were not reserved for him.

His wife was attacked by fever, which terminated her existence in five days. An orphan at the age of seven, he was a widower at nineteen. His grief on this occasion bordered on despair, and had it not been for the tender solicitude of his brother, he too would have died. Since he could no longer bear to reside among the scenes of his former bliss, he decided to travel in order to give another direction to his thoughts. Notwithstanding the happiness he had enjoyed in the short space of his wedded life, he always counseled his unmarried friends to remain single.[5]

In the autumn of 1803, Bolívar again embarked for Europe and, after a long and tempestuous voyage, reached Cádiz toward the end of the year. Business more than mere curiosity detained him in Cádiz for some weeks, at the end of which he hastened to Madrid to mourn with Don Bernardo their mutual loss. He felt greatly relieved after his visit and long remembered it, often speaking of it with pleasure. Shortly after his arrival, a municipal order published in consequence of a scarcity of provisions obliged all foreigners who were not permanent residents to leave the city. Accompanied by his friend and countryman, Don Fernando Toro, he set out in the spring of 1804 for France.

After a short sojourn in southern France, Bolívar repaired to Paris at the beginning of May. As on the occasion of his first visit, notable events were taking place in that capital. The whole organization of the country had been reformed under Bonaparte, and he had established the Consulate for life. Now he was about to assume the title and scepter of Charlemagne. Bolívar's sentiments at this moment were far different from those he had entertained on leaving France two years previously. Napoleon was no longer, in his opinion, the symbol of liberty and glory, no longer the object of his political devotion. As

---

[5] In our judgment, this is an exaggeration. We believe that he gave this advice to some of his aides in order not to lose them, as happened with Marcelino Plaza and, in the long run, with Andrés Ibarra. —Vicente Lecuna.

Bolívar himself expressed it, "He became emperor, and from that day I regarded him as a hypocritical tyrant." In his mind, it would have been more magnanimous on the part of his hero, and more useful to mankind, to establish a great social example and to subdue the world by the force of reason and civilization than to retrograde, as he had done, in his glorious career and to abandon the sublime mission with which the genius of liberty had entrusted him.

The imprudence of Bolívar in not concealing his sentiments at a time when the secret police were active all over Paris more than once endangered his personal safety. Whenever political affairs were discussed in his presence, he never failed to declaim against the fickle character of the French people and the usurpation of Napoleon. His vivacity, frankness of manner, and romantic generosity of spirit won for him the friendship of a lady whose salon was the meeting place at that time for the most distinguished members of Parisian society. She was Mme Dervieu du Villars (Fanny Trobriand y Aristeguieta), who always remained an enthusiastic friend of Bolívar, whom she called her cousin. When the Spanish ambassador invited Bolívar to join his suite to witness the ceremony of the coronation, Bolívar refused the invitation and spent the entire day in his house.

The society to which his birth, circumstances, and connections gave him access afforded him frequent opportunities of meeting some of the most distinguished men of the day. Their conversation, his own taste, and the advice of his old friend and tutor, Don Simón Rodríguez, who had joined him in Paris, induced him to devote a portion of his time to the cultivation of letters. Metaphysics became his favorite study, and skeptical philosophy, it is to be regretted, made a deep impression on his mind. Helvetius, Holbach, and Hume were among the authors to whom Rodríguez directed his attention. Bolívar admired the stern independence of Hobbes, notwithstanding the strong monarchical bias of his writings. But the speculative opinions of Spinoza had more attraction for him, and to them, perhaps, may be traced the foundation of some of his own political ideas. Yet despite his own leaning to skepticism and the consequent irreligion into which he fell, he always believed it necessary to conform to the religion of his fellow citizens.

Among the illustrious men whom Bolívar met at that time were the

celebrated Baron Alexander von Humboldt and Aimé Goujaud Bonpland, who had lately returned to France from their trip to America.
Humboldt professed a sincere regard for those countries, and he
admired the ardor with which Bolívar advocated the necessity of
separating Spanish America from the mother country. When directly
questioned by Bolívar as to the capability of the Spanish colonies for
self-government, he replied that, in his opinion, they had arrived at
political maturity but that he knew no one qualified to direct the enterprise of their emancipation. However flattering this opinion may have
been to the colonies, it certainly was not well founded. Jefferson, a
better politician than Humboldt, judged Spanish America with less indulgence at a later period.

As for Bonpland, he frequently encouraged Bolívar in the enterprise, assuring him that the revolution would produce children worthy
of her. The amiable disposition of this celebrated naturalist and the
interest he evinced in the future fate of America awakened in the mind
of Bolívar the warmest sympathy, and he made Bonpland a tender of
half his income if he would consent to establish himself in Caracas. It
will be seen in the course of these memoirs how constant Bolívar was
in his friendships and how zealous he was in behalf of some of those
whose names I have already mentioned.

It was now the month of March, 1805, and Napoleon was about to
go to Milan to be crowned King of Italy. Bolívar, who had long been
desirous of visiting that classic country, determined to avail himself of
the present favorable circumstances. His health was rather impaired
from the sort of life he had led for the preceding ten months. He left
Paris in the company of Rodríguez, and, after a few days of rest at
Lyon, they proceeded on foot, traveling in easy stages on the advice of
Rodríguez, who said that it was the only way to restore the health of
his pupil. Though very tired when they reached Chambéry, they were
still determined to pursue their plan. After a short stay in the capital
of Savoy, they continued on their way, charmed with the wild, picturesque aspect of the country, which reminded them of the bolder and
grander scenery of the country in which they had passed their boyhoods.

By the time Bolívar reached Milan his health had improved more
than might have been expected. What pleased him was the grand

military spectacle that took place on the plains of Marengo. There, besides the troops, was assembled an immense concourse of people eager to behold the hero on the field of the most celebrated of his victories. The triumphal entry of Napoleon into Milan was no less splendid than the Piedmont festivities, nor was the ceremony of the coronation of the King of Italy less dazzling than that of the Emperor of the French. Yet, gorgeous and imposing as this ceremony was, Bolívar, though a witness of it, could not divest himself of the feelings that had prevented him from attending the one in Paris. He found more pleasure in surveying the noble city and in visiting its delightful suburbs.

From Milan he proceeded to Venice, tarrying some days on the route. In his childhood he had dwelt among scenes as beautiful as those about Desenzano on Lago di Garda, but as yet they were not consecrated by illustrious deeds. He stayed only a short time in Verona, Vicenza, and Padua, but long enough to admire in each of these cities some monument of antiquity or some new object of art that attracted his attention. So exaggerated an idea had he formed of Venice, from which the provinces in which he was born derive their name, that it disappointed him, notwithstanding the city's matchless beauty and unique position. He next visited Ferrara and the coast of the Adriatic, and proceeded thence by way of Bologna to Florence. That fair city, the Athens of Italy, filled Bolívar with admiration and respect, but it was the contemplation of her eminent statesmen and historians that aroused his greatest enthusiam. There he became acquainted with the language of these savants and studied some of their more celebrated works, from which he imbibed many a wholesome maxim. But his admiration of Tuscan writers did not extend to Machiavelli, against whom he entertained the vulgar prejudice that has rendered the name of that great and much injured patriot synonymous with political craft and crime. So strong was this prejudice that neither an intimate acquaintance with his various literary productions and the incidents of his checkered career nor time itself sufficed to modify it.[6]

[6] While in Cartagena a few months previous to his death, Bolívar called on me one day, and, finding on my table a volume of a new edition of Machiavelli's works, he observed that I might occupy my time better than in reading them. We thereupon en-

From Florence, Bolívar proceeded to Rome by the Perugia route, making occasional short stops at some of the classic spots with which that favored portion of Italy abounds. The delight he experienced during the progress of his tour increased to enthusiasm when he grew near to the Eternal City. The remembrance of the heroic epochs of Roman history, which the sight of the Capitol conjured up, created in his bosom hopes for the future. Full of the determination to realize them, or at least to endeavor to do so, he hastened to the celebrated Monte Sacro, to which Sicinius had conducted the plebeians of Rome when they were exasperated by the exactions, the injustice, the arrogance, and the violence of their patrician rulers. On Monte Sacro the wrongs of his own country flashed across his mind, and he knelt down and made that vow of whose faithful accomplishment the emancipation of South America is a glorious monument. This vow was much spoken of in Rome at the time, but the Spaniards living there little imagined that it was more than the expression of youthful ardor called forth by the associations attached to the spot on which it was pronounced.

I have heard Bolívar himself and many of the people who were then in Rome relate these details and also describe the episode that occurred a few days afterward in the Vatican and that created a greater sensation than the Monte Sacro incident. Bolívar accompanied the Spanish ambassador to the Vatican in order to be presented to Pius VII. Advised by the ambassador to kneel and kiss the cross on the shoe of the pontiff, Bolívar refused to comply. The Pope, perceiving the surprise and embarrassment of the ambassador and conjecturing the cause, said gently, "Let the young man from the Indies do as he pleases." Then, extending his hand, he allowed Bolívar to kiss his ring, which he did in a most respectful manner. The Pope, aware of his being a native of South America, addressed some questions to him and seemed gratified with the replies he received. On leaving the Vatican, the ambassador reproached Bolívar for not having conformed with the etiquette of the papal court, to which he replied, "The Pope must have little respect for

___

gaged in a conversation regarding the merit of these works. Finding that Bolívar was intimately acquainted with every production the new edition contained, I asked him if he had read it recently. He replied that he had never read a page of Machiavelli's works since he left Europe twenty-five years before.

the symbol of Christianity if he wears it on his sandals, whereas the proudest sovereigns of Christendom affix it to their crowns."

After visiting Naples, Bolívar returned to France with Rodríguez and shortly afterwards underwent the pain of separating from this old and loyal friend, who did not want to accompany him on his return to Caracas because he still dreaded Spanish persecution. Bolívar left Paris alone, coming back by way of the United States, and reached Caracas at the end of 1806, too late to take part in the insurrection that it was believed was going to take place in connection with General Miranda's expedition.[7] He returned preoccupied with the thought that he so ardently cherished and with his mind filled with a resolute and mortal hatred of everything Spanish. Young Hannibal, swearing eternal enmity against Rome, nursed less hatred toward the enemies of his country than did Bolívar toward the oppressors of his.

When Captain General Emparan arrived at the beginning of 1809, he heard that various officials and prominent persons in Caracas were seriously trying to establish a government in Venezuela like those that had been formed in Spain as a result of the imprisonment of Ferdinand VII, and that among them was Bolívar. He privately advised Bolívar, as a friend, to leave the capital for some time, which he did. The young man sometimes expressed his opinions in a frank and imprudent manner, and he had even gone so far as to propose a toast to the independence of America at a banquet attended by Emparan. This incident and his previous conduct made the local government suspicious, but its tolerance toward him and other young men of Caracas certainly does not reveal a tyrannical government.

A feeling of delicacy that does him much honor—his friendship with Emparan—was the cause of his not having taken an active part in the events of the nineteenth of April.[8] While the conspirators were seizing the authorities in the capital, Bolívar was at his estate in Los

---

[7] On August 2, 1806, an expedition of five hundred volunteers led by General Miranda landed in Venezuela and promptly occupied the city of Coro. When the inhabitants did not respond to the call to rise up in arms, Miranda decided to withdraw and disband the expedition. —Ed.

[8] On April 19, 1810, the municipal government deposed the captain general and established a government to exercise authority in the name of Ferdinand VII.—Ed.

Valles del Tuy, from where he followed with much interest the march of events. Upon receiving news of what had happened in Caracas, he hastened to offer his services to the new government. Aware of his determination and his activities, the government granted him the rank of lieutenant colonel in the infantry militia, in which he already held the rank of captain, and entrusted him at his own request with the important mission of informing the British government of the new circumstances. Though the junta acceded to this request, it did so reluctantly, for many of its members, as well as several other individuals who had taken an active part in the movement, had no kindly feelings for him. Since he offered to pay the expenses of the mission and there was no money in the treasury, they necessarily had to accept his generous offer, giving him as a companion Don Luis López Méndez, in whose experience and capabilities everyone had more confidence.

CHAPTER TWO

EARLY IN JUNE Bolívar left Caracas carrying credentials and instructions from the junta. With him on the trip were his fellow commissioner Luis López Méndez and Andrés Bello, who was acting as secretary to the mission. Immediately after his arrival in London a month later, he requested and obtained an interview with the Marquis of Wellesley, who was at that time the secretary for foreign affairs. He delivered a letter from the junta that stressed His Britannic Majesty's efforts to save Spain, the desire of the inhabitants of Caracas to maintain the integrity of their territory for the sovereign to whom they had sworn allegiance, and the need for the protection and help of Great Britain in the struggle against the French usurper and in the efforts to restore the reign of order and liberty.

The instructions from the junta made no reference to independence, for that word had not yet been pronounced. Although the idea of independence may not have displeased the British government, the able English diplomat realized that there was no reason for compromising the good name of his government by causing the colonies to rush headlong into something they would do of their own accord. He promised them protection against France and the mediation they requested.

One of the principal objects Bolívar had in mind when he requested the London mission was to induce General Francisco de Miranda, who was living there, to return to Venezuela in order to make his military skill and experience available to the American cause. Bolívar believed that he was more fortunate than Humboldt, having found in Miranda the man happily destined to accomplish the splendid project of emancipating South America. The members of the junta did not share this opinion and gave Bolívar to understand that he should not encourage Miranda to return to Venezuela in the existing circumstances. But since Bolívar was singularly devoted to the country's best interests, he took the course he considered best in a matter of such great importance. He pleaded with Miranda to continue cooperating in the cause for which he had already suffered so much. Though age and the hardships of a strenuous life had taken their toll, the old man welcomed the proposal as presented so enthusiastically by Bolívar, and he gladly accepted it without hesitation.

Bolívar devoted the moments he was able to steal from his pressing duties to a diligent and assiduous study of British law. So great was his admiration for English institutions that he made up his mind to introduce them into his own country if he ever gained sufficient influence, though with allowances for differences in climate, customs, and age-old prejudices. We shall see later how tenaciously he adhered to this decision.

Accompanied by General Miranda, he boarded the sloop of war H.M.S. *Sapphire,* which the English government had placed at his disposal, and on December 5, 1810, he reached La Guaira.[1] His ideas

---

[1] It is a well-known fact that Miranda left England after Bolívar. —Pedro Grases.

were so much out of harmony with the policy of the junta and the turn taken by affairs in his absence that, after reporting on the mission entrusted to him, he retired to the country in order to hide his feelings of mortification and sorrow. General Miranda, who shared his friend's feelings, was received coldly, but the junta soon conferred upon him the rank of lieutenant general. At a later date Pao de Barcelona elected him representative to the congress that had been summoned the previous June and that met March 2, 1811, in the name of Ferdinand VII. Juan Escalona, Dr. Cristóbal Mendoza, and Baltasar Padrón were chosen to exercise the executive power.

The junta established in Caracas lacked the vigor and energy essential to every political revolution. The mistakes they made were due wholly to their inexperience. As for the members of Congress, they were so dazzled by the results of the North American revolution that they thought nothing would be easier than to follow the same rules that had guided the patriots to the north. Since a misguided spirit of tolerance prevailed in the acts of the executive council, nothing was done during the first nine months to oppose the intrigues of the supporters of Spain, who were very busy preparing a counterrevolution. It was regarded as a violation of the rights of man to try to subjugate by force the provinces that had remained loyal to the old system.

The executive council did not seem to foresee the obstacles that would necessarily arise to hinder the government's progress. They made no arrangements to repel possible attacks by the Spanish party, and not even the blockade decreed by the regency was enough to awaken their suspicions of the imminent danger confronting them. Neither did they take any steps to guard against foreign enemies or machinations from within. But it was not only the government's apathy that prudent men lamented. What they and the real friends of South America foresaw was that, if the spirit presiding over Venezuela's destiny saved her from the wily snares of the Spaniards, anarchy would inevitably prevail with the spread of the principles then in vogue.

Bolívar, whose political ideas had been tempered and matured by study and reflection, viewed with distress the storm that was rising over his beloved homeland, but he could do nothing to avert it because his compatriots either feared his impetuosity or, as I heard him say himself, regarded his ideas as the ravings of a delirious mind. The trained and penetrating eye of Miranda saw in these ideas the flashes of a genius thirsty for glory.

Even though I am obliged to anticipate my narrative, it will not be amiss at this point to relate the steps that the British government had taken to effect a reconciliation between the regency and the colonies. The regency accepted the mediation proposal made by the St. James Cabinet but exacted conditions so obviously unacceptable that it was deemed useless to propose them to the dissident provinces. Another effort was made by the English government in the form of a new proposal. The principal articles were cessation of hostilities on both sides, general amnesty for the Americans, renewal of the rights granted them by the regency and more ample representation in the Cortes by deputies elected by a more popular vote, free trade with the reservation of some advantages for Spain, equal rights for Americans and Spaniards in the elections for high government positions in the colonies, and recognition of the regency by the colonies.

However moderate these conditions may appear, and even though they had the powerful backing of Great Britain, they were unanimously rejected by the Spanish deputies when submitted to the Cortes. On the other hand, they were accepted with equal unanimity by the Americans, in spite of the fact that the latter had been appointed by the regency. The behavior of the Cortes on this occasion was highly favorable to the American cause, for the mean spirit revealed brought disapproval from the most ardent friends of the Peninsula.

The blockade, though mostly harmless in itself, did give courage to the supporters of Spain throughout Venezuela. They planned conspiracies at their secret meetings in the principal cities, and, even though the government received ample notice of their existence and of their intentions, it did nothing to oppose their designs. The impunity with which it treated the Spanish agents only urged them on to new machinations.

Some time had already passed since the opening of Congress. Among its members were individuals of wealth, talent, and respectability, but this was not sufficient to destroy a system based on age-old prejudices. If this task is difficult everywhere, it was much more so in

South America, where the natives had not taken part in public affairs and were hardly known in their home districts. It was even more difficult in those places where the government representatives had everything to lose and nothing to gain by a change, and where an ignorant clergy, who confused loyalty with fanaticism, enjoyed a powerful influence that they used to stifle every new system.

Congress also had to struggle against other obstacles of a different nature. Those who had supported the revolution were not in agreement about the way to direct it. A patriotic society antagonized the moderate party supporting the executive council by taking upon itself the right to discuss and pass on the measures adopted by the government. The European Spaniards remaining in the country maintained an active correspondence with the authorities of Maracaibo, Coro, and Guayana, and hindered the plans of the revolutionaries by promoting and encouraging disunity among them.

In the month of June there came to light a vast conspiracy extending throughout the whole of Venezuela. The excitement resulting from this crime against the state enabled the supporters of independence to further the plan most dear to them. On July 5, 1811, Congress decreed, though not unanimously, the birth of a new nation; it signed a declaration of independence, which stated that "her united provinces are and should be henceforth, in fact and by right, free, sovereign, and independent states. . . ." On the thirtieth of the same month, in a vigorous and well-written, though somewhat exaggerated, manifesto, Congress announced to the world the reasons that had induced the Venezuelan people to separate from the mother country.

Strangely enough, this daring measure did not intimidate the leaders of the counterrevolution to which I have alluded. Alarming news was received from Valencia, where the conspirators had called on their allies in Coro for aid. A force was immediately organized to march against the rebels, and command of this division was given to the Marqués del Toro, an outstanding patriot who had taken a very active part in the revolution. Bolívar asked for and obtained service as a volunteer in these forces. The Marqués attacked the Spaniards in their positions, was repulsed with small losses, and had to retire to Maracay, from where he informed the government of what had happened and of his decision to wait there for the reinforcements he had requested. This action marks the beginning of a war whose acts of heroism and of cruelty, almost unparalleled in history, make it worthy of a place among the most famous ones.

Scarcely had news of the defeat reached Caracas when terror and consternation seized everyone's mind. All eyes turned toward Miranda, but since his advice had been disregarded at other times, he charged the government with a lack of foresight. "Where," he asked, "are the armies that a general of my rank can command without compromising his dignity and his reputation?" He did, however, accept the command of the expedition, exacting as a condition that Bolívar should not be in it. After his arrival in Venezuela he and Bolívar had had some differences of opinion on policy. Miranda pleaded in favor of the old Spanish residents who remained in the country, but Bolívar was of the opinion that they should be expelled until Spain recognized the state of independence. Since the militia battalion from Aragua, in which Bolívar was a colonel, was to form part of the forces under Miranda's command, Bolívar expressed to the government in energetic terms the injustice of acceding to a humiliating condition that could be attributed only to mean personal motives. The government heeded his just complaint and succeeded in having Miranda withdraw a proposal that did so little honor to his generosity, but he nonetheless did not want to give Bolívar even the lowliest command. If the Marqués del Toro had not taken him as his aide-de-camp, Bolívar would have had to make the campaign as a private in the ranks.

The capture of Valencia on August 12 ended this short and glorious campaign, in which Bolívar gave proof of bravery and of that energy and ability to make quick decisions which so well fitted him for leadership and gave him such great distinction in later periods. Miranda sent him to Caracas with the report of the surrender of Valencia. In spite of the suspicion and distrust with which Miranda regarded Bolívar, he had to confess his merit and to commend him for his conduct in the first action under fire. It won for Bolívar the rank of full colonel. This period marks the beginning of his prestige and influence in the army. In the course of time this influence exceeded all bounds, and he kept it to the last, in spite of the great reverses meted out to him by fate.

The leniency of the government in dealing with the leaders and agents of this latest conspiracy produced unexpected results. It cooled the ardor of even the most zealous advocates of independence and proved very trying to Bolívar, for he was of the opinion that once the shooting started the battle should be fought to the end. He regarded the halfway measures adopted by the government as worse than useless, because they did harm without setting things right. Another reason for his uneasiness was his feeling of disappointment over the shattering of the hopes he had based on Miranda's great talent, vast knowledge, and remarkable experience. The inability of the general to accomplish the results envisioned by these hopes became increasingly evident to Bolívar from day to day. The truth is that Miranda, though born in Caracas, was a stranger to his own countrymen and did not overlook their failings. But he was still regarded as the man most capable of directing public opinion and the course of the revolution.

With order re-established, outwardly at least, Congress applied itself to organizing the country. The federal system was the one most favored by the delegates from the provinces. The majority of the middle class was indifferent and incapable of judging what it did not understand, whereas the masses were satisfied with any form of government giving them hope of relief from their heavy burdens and freeing them from the dangers to which the disorganized state of the country exposed them. After some discussion the federal system was adopted. Even though the new constitution did follow the American one slavishly in some respects, it differed radically from that famous document in others. Miranda protested against the constitution on the grounds that the powers were not in the proper balance and that it was not adapted to the people, habits, and customs of the country.[2]

The appointment of three individuals to exercise the executive power still further weakened a system that was naturally weak. When

[2] This constitution, based on a rather exaggerated idea of the rights of man, allowed the provinces a large measure of self-government but did not give the executive

Valencia was selected as the seat of the central government, the other large cities felt slighted. Another even more mistaken measure, and one with more serious consequences, was the issuance of paper money. Every day there arose new obstacles that the government, despite all its efforts, could not overcome. The rather mild and benevolent nature of its policy was incompatible with the character of the struggle, but it refused to be intimidated in the discharge of its duty. At that time plans were made for the capture of Coro, and a division marched on Guayana from Barinas.

But these warlike plans were frustrated by a terrible calamity that could not have been foreseen or prevented. On the afternoon of March 26, 1812, Holy Thursday, an earthquake made a shambles of the principal cities of Venezuela. Its effects in Caracas were frightful. As if fate had allied itself with the spirit of evil to make the destruction inevitable, almost all the inhabitants of the city were in their homes or in the churches at the time of the earthquake. Statistics show that the earthquake victims in Venezuela numbered 120,000. Furthermore, the moral consequences that Venezuela had to lament were even more irreparable than the material damage.

Among a fanatic and ignorant people the most trivial events can be interpreted in a manner suited to the purposes or interests of those whom the masses are accustomed to respect. Unfortunately for the cause of independence, the clergy, who exercised great influence in Venezuela and were opposed to the revolution, pretended to see in the terrible calamity that had devastated the country the scourge with which Divine Providence was punishing the rebellion. The most subversive doctrines were preached, and new punishments were asked of Heaven for those who did not repent immediately and who refused to recognize the justice of the divine vengeance. Since both the revolution and the earthquake had happened on a Holy Thursday, this coincidence was insidiously adduced as proof that Almighty God had chosen that date to show his anger. Though the authorities were given ample notice of the seditious acts of the clergy and the dangerous

---

branch of the central government sufficient power for prompt and decisive action. —Ed.

tendencies of their talks, they were so overwhelmed with fright that they did nothing to check these outbursts.

Bolívar kept his presence of mind amidst the general consternation. Ignoring the entreaties of his friends, who feared for his life, and without stopping to consider the growing fury of the populace, he hurried to the central square, where the mad frenzy of an excited monk had attracted a large number of the terrified devout. In an imperious tone of voice Bolívar commanded him to stop immediately. While the resolute expression on his countenance and the severe tone of voice that he assumed astonished the frightened crowd surrounding him, they served also to provoke the indignation of the fanatical preacher, who in his turn threatened the intruder with the wrath of Heaven if he persisted in interrupting his preaching. The ominous muttering of his listeners indicated a readiness on their part to serve as the instrument of the holy wrath being evoked. Bolívar, immediately recognizing the critical situation into which he had thrust himself and realizing that a retreat would only give encouragement to the superstition and increase the influence of the clergy, unsheathed his sword and, leaping onto the improvised pulpit, pulled the monk down from it. Dragging him away, he threatened him with immediate death if he resisted. Heartened by his example, some soldiers standing nearby helped him to disperse the crowd. This resolute action checked for the time being the terrible consequences of popular discontent stirred by fanaticism and encouraged the government to take suitable steps to put an end to the excitement caused by the imprudent and harmful zeal of the clergy.

Bolívar showed great concern for his fellow men and a strong spirit of patriotism as he worked furiously to support the efforts of the government and the police. He pointed out the immediate necessity of making bonfires out of the beams from the fallen houses in order to burn the corpses of the unfortunate victims. Indefatigable in his generous efforts to save those threatened by the ruins, he ranged from one end of the city to the other. Notwithstanding his heroic spirit of self-sacrifice, for which no reward would have been adequate compensation, there were some who resisted his efforts to save them from the danger of death. Acting as though they were rooted to the spot where they had fallen on their knees and as though they were blinded by a badly understood sense of duty, they beat their breasts with religious fervor, heedless of the debris that fell about them. There they remained, unmoved by his pleas and even cursing him for daring to interrupt their prayers, and there they perished.

Words cannot describe the wretched state of Caracas for some time after that catastrophe. Hunger and disease added to the desolation caused by the earthquake. People from all walks of life, urged on by that part of the clergy whose zeal is limited to berating private vices, did their best to placate God's wrath with the most scrupulous observance of certain precepts of the Church. But however much public morality gained this way, the cause of independence lost ground from day to day. The lone efforts of Caracas to revive the dying flame of patriotism were not supported by the interior provinces, because the sinister machinations of the fanatical element attained success for lack of opposition. What is more, the people, seeing their hopes thwarted, already felt discouraged. Liberty as a political panacea had turned out to be a Pandora's box.

CHAPTER THREE

S UCH WAS THE STATE OF VENEZUELA when an officer of the Spanish navy outlined a plan to overthrow the new government. The
province of Coro had almost single-handedly continued to defy the
forces of the Union with an energy that does great honor to José
Ceballos, who ruled there in the name of the regency. At this juncture
Domingo Monteverde, a brevet captain in the Spanish navy, volunteered his services to the governor of Coro. Impressed by his ve-
hemence and aware of his energy, the governor proposed him to
Captain General Fernando Miyares as leader of the forces. On March
10, 1812, Monteverde left Coro at the head of a force of 230 men,
and, after entering Siquisique, he was joined by Juan de los Reyes
Vargas, an influential Indian who had been a captain in the patriot

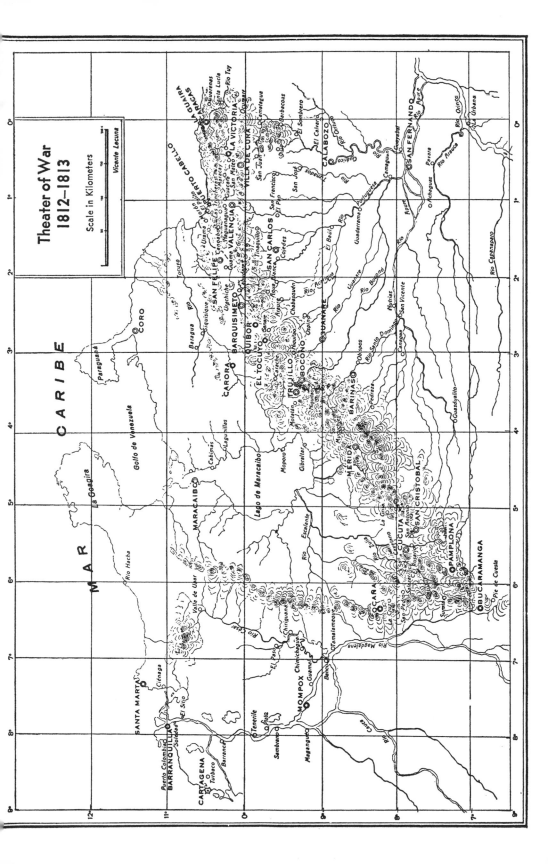

Theater of War
1812–1813

Scale in Kilometers

Vicente Lecuna

forces and had been induced by Andrés Torrellas, a priest from the town, to betray the patriot cause. When he heard about the damage wrought by the earthquake, Monteverde made plans to defeat the patriots. He occupied Barquisimeto without resistance, because the troops quartered there had perished in the earthquake. Since his small army already numbered one thousand men and public opinion was in his favor, he decided to penetrate far into the interior, despite orders from Ceballos to stop at Barquisimeto.

As soon as the government learned that the Spanish forces were on the move, it brought into play all its resources to advance to meet them. Once again Miranda was singled out as the man of the hour to save the country, and he was appointed generalissimo with dictatorial powers. At that time the independent forces amounted to seven thousand men in all branches. The flower of Venezuelan youth gathered around the veteran in command, eager to distinguish themselves in defense of their country. None was more eager than Bolívar, but Miranda assigned him to command the fort of Puerto Cabello[1] instead of using him in active service as he had requested. Bolívar saw that the idea was to keep him away from the scene of the fighting, and he felt displeased and hurt as he set out for his appointed post.

Meanwhile, Monteverde was advancing rapidly through the territory of the Union. San Carlos fell into his hands on April 25, following the defeat of the republican troops who attempted to defend it. This was the most important victory won by Monteverde up until that time. It was not, however, victories or material strength that helped him most, but rather the decision of the people to favor the royal cause. After a few days of rest at San Carlos, the Spanish leader advanced toward Valencia, which Miranda had already evacuated, and occupied it on May 3. Up to this point his army's march seemed more like a military parade than an advance of troops taking part in a war.

The situation of the patriots was quite different in these critical

[1] O'Leary says that Miranda appointed Bolívar commandant of the fort of Puerto Cabello, or that he assigned him to command there, but the post that he actually gave the Liberator was that of political and military commandant and assistant director of national revenue of the fortified city of Puerto Cabello and its district. —Vicente Lecuna.

moments. With a depleted treasury and a dissatisfied populace, it was difficult enough to supply the army. In addition, Miranda's haughty manner offended the soldiers and caused discontent among the civilians. If he had boldly attacked Coro, counting, as he could have, upon superior naval forces, the campaign would undoubtedly have had a different outcome. Meanwhile, bands of robbers, led by chiefs chosen from their ranks, had risen in rebellion on the Calabozo plains. East of Caracas the slaves had taken up arms at the instigation of the supporters of Spain and were threatening the capital.

When Miranda, with an army vastly superior in numbers, kept the Spaniards in a constant state of alarm by means of false attacks, Monteverde lost confidence and began to fear that he had advanced too far inland. He asked the governor of Coro for help, which did not surprise Ceballos. Ceballos entered Valencia with a small reinforcement on May 30, intending to resume command of the army, but Monteverde, whose vanity and ambition kept pace with his good fortune, advised him to return to his governor's post. The prudent Ceballos followed this advice.

After two unsuccessful attacks on Valencia, Miranda withdrew to La Cabrera, a strong position commanding the road to Caracas. Monteverde made three assaults on Guaica Pass but was repulsed each time, and with considerable losses the third time. His situation became more critical every day, but once again fortune smiled on him. When a traitor revealed a poorly guarded short cut, Monteverde executed a flank movement that completely disrupted Miranda's plans and led him to decide to fall back to La Victoria.

Although the country was in a state of dire distress and only a victory over Monteverde could save Venezuela, Miranda would not risk a battle. Monteverde finally tried to break through the La Victoria defenses, but he was repulsed with even greater losses than those suffered at Guaica. Miranda, however, did not even attempt to take advantage of the discouragement produced in the enemy army. Monteverde withdrew to Maracay to gather together his scattered forces. Both royalists and patriots have declared that if Miranda had pursued the Spanish forces as they withdrew, he would have ended the campaign with a complete victory over Monteverde. Miranda was of a different mind, however, and believed it impossible to stem the tide of popular opinion.

The singular good fortune accompanying Monteverde from the beginning of his daring enterprise helped once more to save him from the dangers surrounding him in such a dire situation. Several political prisoners from among the leaders of the July revolution of the previous year were confined in the dungeons of Puerto Cabello. Two influential people among them, Francisco Inchauspe and Jacinto Iztueta, managed by means of generous promises to induce their guards, Francisco Vinoni and another officer named Pedro Carbonell, to betray their trust and set them free. Making the most of a moment on June 30 when the commandant of the fort, Ramón Aymerich, had gone into the city to receive orders, they seized the garrison in the King's name and directed the batteries on the city.

It seems fitting to state here that from the time he took command of the stronghold of Puerto Cabello, Bolívar had pointed out the danger of keeping so many important prisoners there, in view of their talent, their influence, and the wealth of many of them. For six days he held off the rebels and the enemies outside. Finally, after he had been reduced to the last extremity by the number of casualties among the troops and by a lack of ammunition, and after he had tried in vain to persuade some officers to help him in a bold attack to regain the fort, he had to retreat along the coast and go on board a brig that had succeeded in leaving the bay at the start of the uprising. On the following day, July 7, he reached La Guaira along with seven officers, one of whom, Colonel José Mires, left immediately for general headquarters. On the fourteenth Bolívar wrote to Miranda from Caracas a detailed report of the downfall of Puerto Cabello, which he ended with these words: "As for me, I have done my duty, and although the city of Puerto Cabello has been lost, I am blameless and have saved my honor. Would that I had not saved my life but had left it, rather, under the debris of a city that ought to be the last refuge of the liberty and honor of Venezuela!"

The unfortunate loss of Puerto Cabello decided the fate of the country. Monteverde, however, did not dare to risk a new battle, so great was the state of dejection into which he had fallen after the last repulse. It was in these circumstances that Miranda, who still had in La Victoria a superior force of five thousand well-armed and well-equipped soldiers, decided to enter into negotiations to end the campaign. It would appear that he had become convinced that the declaration of independence had been premature, because the people of Venezuela were not ready to govern themselves. One must confess with complete impartiality that Miranda acted through conviction and according to the dictates of his conscience.

An agreement was signed and ratified by both chiefs on July 25, 1812. By virtue of this pact the lives and property of the patriots were protected, a complete amnesty for political crimes was granted, and passports were offered to those wishing to leave the country. Under the terms of the capitulation Miranda took leave of the army and returned to Caracas, but doubt concerning Monteverde's good faith led him to decide to leave the country before the latter occupied the capital. He went, therefore, to La Guaira with the intention of embarking immediately for Curaçao.

The San Mateo pact met with marked disapproval in many quarters, especially among the military. Since Miranda's subordinates believed that the capitulation left them free of all restrictions, they proceeded to criticize his conduct bitterly and even reached the point of accusing him of being a traitor. Bolívar was one of the most indignant and vociferous, and his despair knew no bounds when he read the general order announcing that the army had ceased to exist. He looked upon it as a terrible sentence that condemned his country to servitude and dishonor.

Bolívar viewed Miranda's decision to leave the country without awaiting Monteverde's arrival in Caracas as a step that would expose his fellow citizens to all manner of evils. He used all his influence, though in vain, to induce some of the principal leaders and officers of the army to reassemble the various scattered bodies of troops, to notify Monteverde of their decision not to comply with the San Mateo pact, and to make an immediate effort worthy of their cause. If their attempt failed, they would withdraw to Barcelona and Cumaná, where they could build up their forces.

Bent on preventing Miranda's departure, Bolívar moved on to La

Guaira, where, together with Colonels Mires and Miguel Carabaño and Commander Tomás Montilla, he approached Dr. Miguel Peña, the governor, and Colonel Manuel M. Casas, the military commandant of the port, both of whom had already entertained the same idea. With their approval he put his plan into practice. It was limited to seizing Miranda and obliging him to remain in the country, in order to exact from Monteverde the faithful fulfillment of the articles of capitulation. But the military commandant of La Guaira, anxious to make peace with the victor even at the cost of his honor and of the safety of his friends, handed Miranda over to the enemy.

Some time after his arrest and imprisonment in the fort, Miranda was moved to Puerto Cabello for eight months and then taken to Puerto Rico. He was finally sent to Spain, but his sufferings did not end there. His protests and complaints against the cruel treatment he had received were of no avail. Instead of receiving the liberty he was hoping to attain, he was confined in closer quarters. Burdened with chains in La Carraca, he continued to suffer until his death in 1816. He died a martyr to the cause he had embraced from his youth. Whatever his faults may have been, posterity should do justice to the sincerity of his patriotism, and nobody can deny him his notable talents and vast knowledge. While he governed in Venezuela, his greatest fault consisted in not understanding the nature of his compatriots and in not adjusting himself to the circumstances.

During the San Mateo conferences Captain General Miyares arrived in Puerto Cabello and notified Monteverde that he was marching immediately to the general headquarters. Monteverde answered the first notice from Miyares by congratulating him upon his return to the country, but, once in Caracas, he informed him in no uncertain terms that he would not give up his command until the King's decision was known. In his speeches and conversations he declared his intention of carrying out religiously what had been agreed upon in the San Mateo pact, but he alarmed the city on August 1 by imprisoning several of the most distinguished citizens among those who had become involved in the revolution. Two days later he reiterated his solemn promise in a proclamation full of words of consolation for all.

So sincere did Monteverde appear to be that there arose new hope of a reconciliation, but he was not the man required by the circumstances. Made more vain by his rapid and easy success, he just was not able to understand and follow the policy suited to the occasion. His weakness was his excessive gullibility and a mistaken idea of loyalty. Among the clever schemers surrounding him were many of his countrymen, natives of the Canary Islands, who were accusing people of imaginary conspiracies. Honorable and sincere men among the royalists rejected such charges as false, but in his rash way Monteverde not only scorned their wise warnings but even welcomed the suggestions of the evil advisers.

On August 14 armed bands spread through the city and its suburbs, and some of the principal citizens were arrested without warning. In many cities of the interior the same steps were taken simultaneously and carried out with barbarous cruelty. Many respectable citizens of Caracas were set up in stocks and exposed to the mockery of the brutal soldiery and the jeers of the lowly mob. Other persons were forced from their homes, tied to the tails of horses, and dragged off to the dungeons of La Guaira. Still others among the prisoners were sent to Puerto Cabello, put into chains, and shut in the filthy dungeons of that fortress. Eight outstanding patriots were sent to the Peninsula. In a letter to the regency Monteverde referred to them as "these eight monsters who are the underlying cause of all the evils and troubles of America."

So great was the terror and consternation caused by such wild and savage behavior that the inhabitants fled to the wilderness by the hundreds. Others requested passports in order to leave the country, but even this small privilege was allowed to very few. Bolívar was one of the privileged ones. He planned to go abroad to seek a way to redeem his country from servitude and punish the treacherous Monteverde. With these thoughts in mind, he appeared before Monteverde to ask for a passport, in accordance with the capitulation. On hearing his name, the royalist leader accused him of having shot two Spaniards at Puerto Cabello, to which Bolívar replied that, since they were spies, the laws of war authorized him to deal with them in that way. Monteverde pretended not to pay any attention to the answer and added, "You have done a great service in arresting Miranda, and that makes you worthy of the King's favor." "Since that was not my intention when I seized General Miranda," Bolívar retorted, "I have no right to the merit you wish to attribute to me. The reason for my conduct is quite different. I considered him to be a traitor to my country." These words offended Monteverde, who had not been accustomed to being contradicted since his arrival in Caracas. He refused him the passport, and Bolívar most likely never would have obtained it without the friendly intervention of Francisco Iturbe, the acting secretary of the Spanish leader. Yielding to his pleas, Monteverde grudgingly agreed to grant it. In a communication sent to the president of the Congress in session at Cúcuta in 1821 requesting that Iturbe's property not be confiscated, Bolívar himself refers to this episode and shows how grateful he was for the generosity of his friend Iturbe.

Immediately afterward Bolívar went to La Guaira, and on August 27 he embarked for Curaçao on the schooner *Jesús, María y José,* the first ship leaving the port. Because of an irregularity in the ship's papers, the Curaçao customhouse attached his baggage, in which he was carrying some jewels and all the cash he had on hand. This misfortune did not detain him, however, longer than the time necessary to look for a way to move on to Cartagena, the stronghold of New Granada, where the fight for the American cause was continuing. He sacrificed his personal property as less important than the public welfare, although he could easily have gotten it back if he had taken time to declare his obvious rights to it. This trait of unselfishness is characteristic of Bolívar. Though frequently reduced to absolute poverty in the course of his public life, he never avoided a financial sacrifice, and many times he paid for state services out of his own private purse. His liberality was often governed more by his generous feelings than by the amount of his resources. With money borrowed in his own name, he took along some other penniless leaders and officers who like himself had left Venezuela and were in Curaçao. They were all useful to the cause of independence during the war.

Cartagena was then the capital of the province of the same name and the seat of its government, which was headed by young Manuel Rodríguez Torices. When Bolívar arrived in that city about the middle of November, 1812, he met many of his compatriots who had also escaped the anarchy of Venezuela and the vengeance of the Spanish authorities. In Cartagena the arrival of these officers was regarded as a definite sign of the intervention of Divine Providence in favor of that state, which was in dire danger. There was a lack of officers in Cartagena, and those whom misfortune now brought to its shores were among the most distinguished ones of the ill-starred Venezuelan army: José Félix Ribas, uncle by marriage and intimate friend of Bolívar, the Spaniard Cortés Campomanes, who was following the flag of freedom, Antonio Nicolás Briceño, the intrepid Carabaños, the Montillas, and others.

Bolívar lost no time preparing the way for the acceptance of his plans. In fiery and eloquent language he informed the people of Monteverde's treacherous violation of the San Mateo pact. He also published a memorial addressed to the citizens of New Granada. This document contains the political principles he followed so consistently during his public life and is proof of the correctness of his views concerning the revolution, even in those earliest days. In it he deplores Venezuela's fatal adoption of the system of tolerance, the opposition to raising an army of well-disciplined troops, the establishment of the federal system of government and of popular elections in an infant state beset by factional strife, and the unfortunate effects of the earthquake. He concludes with a plea for a united effort to liberate Venezuela before reinforcements arrive from Spain. This memorial helped to further the cause of independence in Cartagena because it was read with great eagerness by all the factions. As for Bolívar, he was admitted into service as a full colonel and appointed inspector of the militia.

It was not long after his arrival in Cartagena that, active as always, he wrote to some of the principal people of Bogotá, requesting them to support his views concerning Venezula and exhorting them to preserve the closest unity in their deliberations. He addressed a similar message to the General Congress of New Granada gathered at Tunja. These letters brought a wonderful response in favor of both the writer and the cause for which he was pleading. The energetic style and the unyielding patriotism apparent in every sentence struck a sympathetic note in all those who read them and aroused a keen interest in his person.

At that time there were gathered in New Granada men of great talent motivated by the purest principles of honor, justice, and patriotism. Conspicuous among them for his influence and ability was Don Camilo Torres. So profound was the impression made on that noble soul by the vehement eloquence of the illustrious expatriate that he did everything in his power to bring to the attention of others the conviction he held of the soundness of Bolívar's plans. As we shall see later, support from Torres not only helped these plans immensely but also proved very valuable to Bolívar personally.

The Cartagena government gave Bolívar command of a corps in the division headed by Colonel Pierre Labatut, who had rendered useful service to the province by defeating the enemy and driving him from towns on the west bank of the Magdalena River that, though insignificant in themselves, enabled the Spaniards to interrupt river navigation and keep the opposite bank in a constant state of alarm. Labatut, who did not appear very much inclined to contribute to Bolívar's reputation, assigned him to the command of the detachment located in the town of Barranca, with strict orders not to move from there. This assignment, made with malicious intent, was accepted reluctantly by Bolívar. Confident of his own strength, he decided to take on his shoulders a tremendous load of responsibility, counting on the brilliance of his daring enterprise to excuse the offense he was going to commit.

Bolívar decided to dislodge the Spaniards from the fortified town of Tenerife in order to open up the river. After assembling a force of two hundred poorly armed men and the necessary riverboats, he started up the river in the greatest secrecy. Caught by surprise, the Spaniards abandoned the position, leaving behind all their military supplies and boats. Continuing up the river, he reached Mompox on December 27 and was unanimously acclaimed military commander of the district. Having augmented his forces with volunteers from the leading families, he occupied El Banco and went on to defeat the Spaniards at Chiriguaná on January 1, 1813. Thereafter he seized Tamalameque by surprise and occupied Puerto Real and Ocaña without any enemy opposition. Thus ended the campaign that freed the Upper Magdalena region and cleared the way to the interior of New Granada, which had been cut off by the Spanish ships on the river. Labatut's complaint to

the provincial government about Bolívar's insubordination was ignored. On the other hand, Bolívar received praise from Torices and
the grateful recognition of Cartagena for the services he had just
rendered. Everything seemed to favor Bolívar's noble plans. Later on
we shall see how the misfortunes and dangers threatening New Granada also helped his plans.

When Monteverde advanced toward the center of Venezuela, Don
Ramón Correa, the military commander of Maracaibo, invaded the
province of Mérida and routed the patriot troops, which enabled him
to occupy the valleys of Cúcuta and to threaten Pamplona and Ocaña.
Though he did not attempt to take Pamplona, his very presence in
Cúcuta kept the patriots in a constant state of alarm. Bolívar was in no
position at the moment to go to the aid of Colonel Manuel Castillo,
the commander of the province of Pamplona, but he did request orders
from the government of Cartagena, emphasizing the need to increase
his forces. In the meantime he exerted himself to the utmost to obtain
what was needed for the liberation of Venezuela. During this period
he showed himself to be as strict and energetic a disciplinarian as he
was an active and daring leader in battle. His prompt action in appre-
hending fugitives and employing stern measures saved his division
from the dissolution threatening it and won for him the lasting respect
and love of his subordinates. Then, after returning to Mompox, he
visited all the places under his jurisdiction on both banks of the river
to collect the arms and ammunition left behind.

Having been granted the permission he had requested, Bolívar
started out with four hundred men for Cúcuta on February 9, 1813.
They followed the frightfully rugged route leading through Salazar
de las Palmas. Thirty miles from Ocaña the ascent begins abruptly, and
this spur of the great cordillera presents extremely bad going, made
even worse by the frequent storms. All the soldiers were from the burning hot climate of Cartagena and Mompox, and their sufferings were
intensified because they were not used to the cold and the penetrating
mountain air. There were so many hardships that only Bolívar's inspiring leadership kept them plodding along. They were able to reach
Salazar without any opposition, thanks to a skillful stratagem that led
the commander of a detachment of one hundred men, stationed on an

impregnable height called La Aguada, to march back to Salazar and beyond. After giving his weary troops some rest, Bolívar was able to go as far as San Cayetano, on the banks of the Zulia River some ten miles from Correa's general headquarters, without any major loss or any real opposition. In this town he received the Pamplona reinforcements of about one hundred men, including some cavalrymen and some horses for a cavalry picket he had formed.

At dawn on February 28, Bolívar crossed the Zulia River and marched on San José, the capital city of the rich valleys of Cúcuta. Correa, who mistakenly concluded that he had only the vanguard before him, attacked Bolívar, who made up for his numerical inferiority with the advantages gained from the mastery of several heights. The battle lasted four hours and ended with the complete defeat of the Spaniards. Correa received contusions and almost fell into the hands of the victors, but he managed an orderly withdrawal because the patriots were so exhausted that they could not continue the pursuit. The next morning Bolívar followed him as far as San Antonio, a town on the north bank of the Táchira River, a small stream dividing Venezuela from New Granada.

This victory had splendid results. It freed New Granada from the invasion threat; it gave confidence to the patriots of that country; it renewed the hopes of the patriots in Venezuela; it gave the soldiers a respite from their many hardships; and it filled the public coffers with the rich booty of more than a million pesos in merchandise that the Spanish merchants of Maracaibo had accumulated in Cúcuta in the belief that Correa would subjugate the viceroyalty right up to Sante Fe.[2] The valleys of Cúcuta, which received immediate benefit from this victory, are the northern gateway to New Granada.

[2] This statement is completely erroneous. The booty from Cúcuta produced only 33,306 pesos up to April 6, in addition to the reward given to the troops. At a later date 10,000 pesos were realized from the remaining confiscated goods. With respect to this, consult *Memorias*, XIII, 173, 207, and 220; and Vicente Lecuna, *Crónica razonada de las guerras de Bolívar,* I, 16.—Vicente Lecuna.

CHAPTER FOUR

N OW LET US SEE what the situation was after the occupation of
Venezuela by Monteverde. The inexcusable blunders made during his administration exasperated the inhabitants so much that reconciliation became impossible and, in addition, caused reprisals that made
this war more ferocious than any other in the annals of civil strife. The
shameless violation of the pact, which committed Venezuela once
more to Spanish misrule, gave rise to countless injustices and excesses
and produced a general feeling of distrust. Although the upper
classes were the particular targets of this vengeance, the others did not
escape scot-free. A ray of hope brightened the dark clouds of despotism
for a moment after the Cádiz Constitution had been ordered promulgated as the fundamental law of the land,[1] but when Monteverde

---

[1] This constitution, commonly called the Constitution of 1812, was proclaimed by

finally authorized its publication, he did so only with the intention of manipulating it to suit his fancy. The reign of terror continued, with its accompaniment of violence, injustice, and lawlessness. Commerce, industry and agriculture suffered perforce amidst the general distress. In a word, only two classes existed in Venezuela—the oppressed and the oppressors, the Americans and the Spaniards. But in justice to the latter I should make it clear that among them were many honorable men who deplored the ignominy that Monteverde's conduct and his violation of a solemn pact had heaped upon their country.

After the victory in Cúcuta, Bolívar renewed his correspondence with all those who could further his plans, and he did not miss the opportunity to paint in the most vivid colors the conduct of the Spaniards in Venezuela, as well as the policy they undoubtedly would follow in New Granada should they carry out the invasion as planned. He had this end in view when he addressed letters to the president of the General Congress of the Federal States of New Granada and to other very influential members of the government. These letters full of characteristic traits, reveal an intimate knowledge of the human heart. Bolívar begins by describing the extreme ease of subjugating Venezuela and the advisability of this step. Overcoming then, little by little, the scruples that such a daring enterprise must have aroused, he receives from these prudent men a halfhearted consent hedged in by many provisos. Once he has their consent, however, he reveals the dangers surrounding the undertaking and the disparity between the means at hand and the magnitude of the task. This disparity would disappear, he says, if the leader of the army had unlimited authority. His ideas and suggestions are worthy of a first-rate politician and an able soldier, and his foresight was crowned with success.

During these negotiations with the Granadine Congress, Bolívar had other worries that gave him many anxious moments and even led him to request his separation from the army, not once, but many times. Shortly after he established his headquarters in Cúcuta, there arose a difference of opinion, which started over a point of etiquette, between

---

the Cortes of Cádiz. Enunciating the doctrine of popular sovereignty, it gave little authority to the king. Real power resided in the Cortes. The rights and liberties of all Spanish subjects were recognized. —Ed.

him and Colonel Castillo. When Bolívar was on his way to Cúcuta, Castillo had helped him all he could, but, once the danger was past, Castillo treated him as a rival rather than as a friend because he became convinced that he had been slighted, though there was no justification for this belief. If at the beginning of this stormy quarrel Bolívar was not entirely blameless, justice obliges me to state that if the friendly advances he made to Castillo on more than one occasion had been returned in a like spirit, there would have been a reconciliation. When Bolívar was given the post of commander in chief of the two divisions with the rank of brigadier general, Castillo became his subordinate, which only increased his bitterness. The dispute spread little by little and finally brought about a split in the army. Among the serious and deplorable consequences of the unfortunate disagreement was the regrettable division between Venezuelans and Granadines, which never disappeared completely.

Bolívar was overjoyed to receive the permission of Congress to march into the provinces of Mérida and Trujillo. After New Granada added a few auxiliary troops, the army prepared to go into action divided into two groups, with the vanguard under Colonel Castillo and the other group under Colonel José Félix Ribas. Castillo delayed for some time before carrying out his orders to attack Correa in La Grita, but he finally marched and was able to defeat the enemy on April 13, 1813. Leaving his vanguard division in La Grita, he returned to Cúcuta and wrote a letter of resignation to the president, which certainly did not displease Bolívar. Some officers who supported Castillo and his opinions followed his example, and the whole division would have fallen apart if the general in chief had not energetically destroyed the spirit of insubordination undermining the discipline of the army, which was already down to five hundred men on account of desertions and illness. This was a critical period for Bolívar, but his faith never left him. It was at that time that Colonel Rafael Urdaneta wrote to him the following words: "General, if two men are enough to free the country, I am ready to go with you."

Since in spite of Castillo's retirement the division at La Grita, now commanded by Major Francisco de Paula Santander, a devoted follower of Castillo, continued to show signs of discontent, Bolívar and his staff left Cúcuta for La Grita. He happened to arrive just as the troops were being assembled in what appeared to be quite suspicious circumstances. Addressing Santander, he ordered him to march, but the latter replied that he was not ready to obey. "March immediately," Bolívar answered in a severe and peremptory tone of voice. "There is no choice. March! For either you will shoot me or I will certainly shoot you." The division left, but Santander offered flimsy excuses for remaining in La Grita and did not rejoin the division. Thus it was that Bolívar got rid of two influential leaders whose intrigues had for the moment lost him the confidence of his subordinates and dampened the enthusiasm of the troops.

It was at about this time that the Congress of the Granadine Union appointed a commission to help Bolívar in every way conducive to the success of the campaign. As he had wisely pointed out, there would be difficulty in communicating with him at so great a distance. The prompt decisions of this commission would facilitate the development of his plans. On May 17 he left La Grita for Mérida, and, upon his arrival in the capital of the province on May 23, he re-established the government that had been overthrown as a result of Monteverde's invasion. This step naturally increased his popularity, and all the people vied with each other in furnishing him the supplies needed by his troops. The enlistment of young men swelled the ranks of the army.

The enthusiastic celebration in honor of the arrival of Bolívar and his army was dampened by the sad news of the tragic death of Colonel Antonio Nicolás Briceño, who was shot in Barinas by the Spanish commander of that province, Lieutenant Colonel Don Antonio Tizcar. Briceño had accompanied Bolívar to Cartagena, and later to Cúcuta. Unable to control his impetuosity or his thirst for vengeance, Briceño decided to lead some of his men into the province of Barinas and stir up a rebellion there, despite the efforts of his friends to dissuade him. Defying the orders of his superiors, he marched to San Cristóbal, published a proclamation in which he declared his intention to give no quarter to the Spaniards, and invited the slaves to rise against their masters. He translated his dire threats into action by having two Spaniards beheaded. Before he reached Guasdualito, he was surprised, defeated, and captured by the Spanish commander José Yáñez. Yáñez took him to the city of Barinas, where, after a mock trial, he was shot as a rebel. All the other prisoners suffered the same fate. This event was one of the immediate causes of the declaration of war to the death.

In addition to the news of these executions Bolívar received daily reports of savagely cruel murders committed by Spanish officers in different parts of Venezuela. All these atrocities made him so indignant that on June 8, 1813, he issued a strongly worded proclamation recalling the excesses of the Spaniards in America and declaring his intention of fighting a war of extermination. He soon gave orders for this terrifying declaration to be put into practice. Posterity will pass judgment on whether or not it was necessary or just.[2]

After placing the government of Mérida in the hands of the proper authorities, Bolívar continued his triumphant march. When the army reached the town of Macuchíes, a Granadine officer, Captain Hermógenes Maza, sacrificed the first victims of American vengeance. On June 14, Bolívar took possession of the city of Trujillo, the capital of the province of the same name, and made the same changes in the government that he had already made in Mérida. In a proclamation addressed to the Venezuelans on the day after his arrival, he repeated the solemn declaration of the war to the death; but he did offer a general amnesty to all Spaniards who would help to re-establish the Republic of Venezuela, and he pardoned all Americans who had betrayed the cause.

No one will deny that this declaration had the stamp of frankness. Bolívar could have imitated the conduct of the Spaniards, making treaties only to violate them and issuing pardons to attract the unwary, only to shut them up later in dungeons or force them into exile. All this and much more he could have done, but there was no room for hypocrisy in the man. He preferred to face the charge of cruelty rather than to cover himself with the mask of deceit. Political expedience prompted this decree and dire necessity required that it be carried out. We do not venture to judge whether the benefits gained from inde-

[2] Opinion is still divided. Some writers have condemned the proclamation of the war to the death as an act of terrorism that could not be justified, but many others consider it a legitimate reprisal made necessary by the many Spanish atrocities and the Spanish laws prescribing death for anyone bearing arms against the King. —Ed.

pendence were worth the bloodshed involved, but there are, indeed, reasons for believing that it never would have been attained in Venezuela without the terrible measure to which Bolívar had to resort.

The ranks of the patriot army were notably increased with the addition of Americans captured from the enemy, deserters from the enemy ranks, and the volunteers who appeared from all quarters to enlist. But since the instructions from Congress prevented Bolívar from making the most of his victories, and since he was unable to provide subsistence for the troops, the only choice he had was to undertake a withdrawal or to strike a blow worthy of the cause he was defending. His enterprising spirit and the prospect of nothing but dishonor in a withdrawal led him to choose the second alternative. Evading the government's orders, he took upon himself the responsibility of advancing into the interior of Venezuela.

From the statements of some prisoners taken by Colonel Atanasio Girardot, Bolívar was able to fathom Monteverde's plans for taking New Granada. A considerable force assembled in Barinas under the command of Don Antonio Tizcar was to invade the provinces of Trujillo and Mérida, cut the patriot army's lines of communication, and send superior forces against it from all sides. Bolívar therefore decided to attack Tizcar himself. To prevent leaving Trujillo exposed, he spread a rumor that the whole patriot army was marching westward. At the same time he ordered Colonel Ribas to advance rapidly by way of Boconó with four hundred men to surprise the enemy before the latter discovered the route of the main body of troops.

Near the end of June Bolívar left Trujillo and crossed the mountain range to the fertile Barinas plains by a route as rough and dangerous as the one between Ocaña and Cúcuta. This daring and rapid march disconcerted Tizcar when he learned to his surprise that Bolívar was already four leagues from his headquarters, between him and Caracas. He barely managed to evacuate Barinas, leaving behind in his haste all his military supplies and provisions. He tried to cross the Apure River at Nutrias when he heard that Colonel Girardot was drawing near, but the inhabitants rose in rebellion and forced him to embark almost alone for San Fernando. The valuable booty taken included tobacco worth more than 200,000 pesos, but even more valuable to the patriots were the arms and ammunition that fell into their hands.

Meanwhile, the daring Ribas was carrying out his mission with the zeal and energy that characterized his short but glorious career. On the Niquitao heights he attacked the division commanded by Don José Martí and won a decisive victory, despite the favorable position occupied by the enemy and the superiority of its forces. Four hundred American prisoners were added to the ranks of the patriot army, all the Spaniards were put to the sword, and all the enemy supplies were seized by the victor. Having occupied the city of El Tocuyo on July 18, Ribas marched on Barquisimeto and completely defeated the forces of Colonel Francisco Oberto at Los Horcones after a short but very bloody struggle remarkable for the bitterness of the feelings on both sides. Ribas went on without stopping, crossed El Altar Mountain, and on July 30 joined Bolívar, who had already occupied San Carlos. At this time Bolívar once more addressed the Spaniards and Canary Islanders, urging them to give up the struggle.

On the same day that the army was reunited, Bolívar marched against the royalists under Colonel Julián Izquierdo. The following day, July 31, 1813, he attacked them on the savanna of Taguanes. After a bloody combat in which all the enemy infantry perished, his patriot forces had the good fortune to win the most complete victory of the whole campaign. Monteverde scarcely had time to flee from Valencia to Puerto Cabello, leaving the road to Caracas open. In their hurried flight the scattered royalists committed all kinds of outrages and acts of vengeance, which brought on reprisals.

On August 2, Bolívar occupied Valencia amidst the enthusiastic cheers of the inhabitants. After assigning Girardot to watch the enemy at Puerto Cabello, he went on toward Caracas, where the greatest confusion now reigned. At a meeting of the authorities and the principal Spaniards, Brigadier General Antonio Fierro, the governor of the city, pointed out the inadequacy of the garrison and asked for advice. They unanimously agreed to ask the victor for a capitulation guaranteeing the life and property of the Spanish subjects and a pardon for past acts. Fierro, as fainthearted as the resolution itself, appointed a commission to meet with Bolívar, who received them with the greatest courtesy immediately after his arrival in La Victoria. When the Spanish negotiators requested recognition of the Cádiz Constitution, Bolívar answered that the people would choose the form of government best suited to them. He granted amnesty, but with the condition that the city and province of Caracas, as well as the port of La Guaira, would be turned over to the patriot authorities. The capitulation was to be presented to the governor on the following day for his ratification within twenty-four hours. In his letter to Fierro, Bolívar said, "The terms of this capitulation shall be faithfully observed, to the ignominy of the treacherous Monteverde and to the honor of the American name."

Proud of having obtained such favorable conditions, the deputies returned to Caracas, but their surprise was great when they discovered that the acting captain general, many of the authorities, and a large number of Spaniards had fled and embarked at La Guaira. This ill-advised and imprudent step could have had terrible consequences, for it cruelly endangered the lives of thousands of Europeans abandoned to the vengeance of an angry populace.

The Spaniards have not missed an opportunity to complain bitterly about Bolívar's conduct and have pictured him as a man of bloodthirsty, cruel, and vindictive character. Future generations, however, will examine the history of the revolution impartially and will, in justice, absolve him of such charges. Every act of violence authorized by him was provoked by the conduct of the Spaniards. They violated treaties, practiced deceptions contrary to honor and decency, and sacrificed countless victims. Though I sincerely accept the philosophy that teaches us that the path of virtue alone leads to liberty, I must confess with sorrow that we rarely see a people win their independence through virtuous means. In such cases we can excuse up to a certain point those who, prompted by desperation, commit acts of violence contrary to their better natures. Inexorable necessity, even more than policy, forced Bolívar, as I have said, to consent to those terrible reprisals.

The members of the city council had no other recourse than to place themselves at the mercy of the victor. With this end in view, a deputation returned to report to Bolívar the flight of the captain general and to implore him to make haste, since his presence in Caracas was necessary to protect the lives and property of its inhabitants. Fierro's conduct gave him the right to take the sternest measures, but he chose to present the matter to Monteverde. Protesting against the untimely flight of Fierro, he sent the same commissioners to Puerto Cabello to demand the ratification of the terms as stipulated.

The welcome given Bolívar in Caracas was extremely flattering, for the rejoicing of his fellow citizens exceeded all bounds. The city remained almost deserted, because its joyful inhabitants went out to meet the victor, who entered his native city on August 6, 1813, amidst the cheers of a grateful people.

During the course of the events I have just related, others of equal importance were taking place in the eastern part of Venezuela. The rest of Venezuela had been subjected to the same evil measures that had exasperated the inhabitants of Caracas after the occupation of the city by the royalist troops. So terrible was the persecution of the patriots—especially in Barcelona, Cumaná, and Maturín—that many of them left the country or sought refuge in the more isolated sections.

Outstanding among those who carried abroad the memory of their country's misfortunes were Santiago Mariño, José Francisco Bermúdez, Manuel Valdés, Antonio José de Sucre, and Manuel Piar. The unfortunate exiles did not find in Trinidad the hospitality one usually finds on British soil. Sir Ralph Woodford, then governor of the island, thought it his duty to harass them at every turn.

A mere handful of these patriots (for there were barely forty-five of them) decided to liberate Venezuela, even though they had no money or supplies. They did know, however, that

> Within that land was many a malcontent,
> Who cursed the tyranny to which he bent.
>
> (Lord Byron, *Lara,*
> Canto 2, stanza 8)

They also knew that hundreds of patriots would come to join their ranks. On the night of January 13, 1813, they landed on the coast of Güiria under the orders of Mariño, a person of great influence in the eastern part of Venezuela. Their noble undertaking flourished, and they saw their fondest hopes realized. The brave exploits of Mariño, Bermúdez, Valdés, and Piar made their names fearful to the Spaniards. The first one to feel the weight of their vengeance was the bloodthirsty Francisco Javier de Cerveriz[3] who was forced to hide shamefully in Guayana. Monteverde fled from Piar to Maturín. On August 3, Cumaná had to open its gates to receive Mariño.

Thus, in the short space of six months, Venezuela was free, except for the provinces of Guayana, Maracaibo, and part of Barinas. Six hundred patriots had sufficed to crush six thousand royalists; but the day of real peace was still very far away, for Venezuela had yet to undergo all the calamities that follow in the path of war:

> New havoc, such as civil discord blends,
> Which knows no neuter, owns but foes or friends.
>
> (Lord Byron, *Lara,*
> Canto 2, stanza 8)

It had yet to see its whole territory converted into a vast charnel house in which the victims sacrificed in the name of liberty and loyalty would be heaped.

The commissioners sent by Bolívar to Monteverde, in order to request the ratification of the capitulation granted to Fierro, made repeated attempts to obtain passports from the Spanish leader so that they could go to Puerto Cabello to discuss the entire matter with him, but all their efforts were fruitless. They did, however, receive two replies from him informing them that all negotiations were null and void and that he could not pay heed to any proposal not aimed at placing the provinces under the legitimate authority. It is useless to comment on this strange conduct, which left to their fate more than four thousand innocent European Spaniards. Monteverde knew only too well that his own excesses and the crimes perpetrated by his bloodthirsty subordinates gave the victor good reason for reprisals. The declaration of war to the death must have removed any doubts on that score. What is more, he had seen the manifesto issued by Bolívar in which the latter generously offered to spare the lives of the Spaniards in return for the ratification of the capitulation. Despite everything he remained unmoved.

---

[3] A Spanish officer who served under Monteverde. —Ed.

Although the Spaniards had been defeated in all their encounters with the patriots, the latter were still far from being in peaceful possession of the country. In these circumstances Bolívar did not consider it wise to re-establish the federal government in Caracas. In the above-mentioned manifesto he said: "Nothing shall make me forget my first and only aims: your liberty and glory. An assembly of outstanding, upright, and wise men should be formally convoked to discuss and authorize the form of the government and the officials who are to run it in the critical and extraordinary circumstances surrounding the Republic." This manifesto was received enthusiastically by all classes of society. Bolívar's popularity was so great that the proclamation he addressed to the people on August 11 was all that was needed to bring in contributions from everyone according to his means.

Bolívar had a personality admirably suited to the dangerous undertaking of freeing his country. Young, active, brave, and unselfish, he devoted his life and all his thoughts to this end. He was the first to blaze the trail to be followed and to attempt through his eloquent writings to arouse in others the sentiments that he professed. The obstacles arising at every turn would have discouraged anyone with a less zealous nature or with less profound convictions.

After occupying the capital and conferring with educated and influential people, Bolívar organized the political government according to the plan presented by Don Francisco Javier de Uztáriz.[4] He appointed three individuals of recognized ability to help him as secretaries in the dispatch of public business. One of his first acts was to invite foreigners to settle once more in the country, with a guarantee of the same privileges granted to the native-born. The Spanish government had promoted the most absurd prejudices against foreigners.[5] During the few days he spent in Caracas he issued several decrees and regula-

---

[4] Uztáriz was a prominent patriot, later a victim, together with his entire family, of a royalist massacre in Maturín in 1814. His plan, aimed at the incorporation of the Venezuelan provinces into the Granadine Union, provided for the exercise of executive and legislative power by the general in chief (Bolívar) until the end of the war. —Ed.

[5] The American seaports were closed to the subjects of other nations, and foreigners were presented as enemies of the established religion. —Ed.

tions for the benefit of commerce and agriculture, which had suffered enormously since 1811.

In the eloquent answer he gave to the governor of Barinas, a decided advocate of federalism, Bolívar explained very clearly the reasons that led him to recommend the new system of government just adopted, the only one, according to him, that could save Venezuela in the existing circumstances. He pointed out that the only powerful and respected nations were those with a strong central government, that nations had won respect only through the concentration of power, and that without a supreme authority there could be no order or strength in the administration of Venezuela.

Local measures did not, however, absorb all of Bolívar's attention, nor could the exigencies of war distract him from a vast political project that he had conceived during his exile and that was always on his mind. It was nothing less than the union of Venezuela and New Granada into a single republic. The Spanish policy of prohibiting communication between sections and fostering rivalries, even between cities, had produced deeply rooted prejudices that were, perchance, one of the causes of the prolongation of the struggle and of the bloodthirsty character it assumed. Here we find too the origin of the discord that has grown with independence and of the tendency of the new states to make war on each other for the most trivial reasons. Bolívar's efforts were directed toward the destruction of this evil. When he informed New Granada of the brilliant results of the campaign, he took advantage of the very favorable opportunity to emphasize the usefulness and importance of his favorite project. But new and terrible calamities prevented its immediate realization.

More urgent business required Bolívar's presence elsewhere. The arrival of reinforcements from the Peninsula, consisting of a division of thirteen hundred men commanded by Colonel José Miguel Salomón, brought new courage to the royalists in Puerto Cabello. The impatient and restless Monteverde decided, despite Salomón's opposition, to attack the besieging forces. As Girardot's division withdrew under orders from Bolívar, who had already arrived on the scene, the enemy vanguard followed in hot pursuit. On September 30, 1813, at Bárbula on the Valencia road, the Spanish troops were defeated, and they suffered great losses as they were pursued to Las Trincheras, where Colonel Salomón and the newly arrived troops had taken positions. After a lively show of stubborn resistance, this force was obliged to seek refuge in Puerto Cabello, which was then besieged once more by Colonel Luciano D'Elhuyar. General Monteverde was badly wounded in the fighting at Las Trincheras.

The victory at Bárbula was bought at a very high price—with the death of the gallant Girardot, the idol of the army. Bolívar was deeply moved by his death, for he was very fond of him. The honors decreed in his memory show the army's great respect for him and also the eagerness on the part of Bolívar to win the friendship of the Granadine people and at the same time to foster the spirit of emulation in the army by awakening a desire for honorary awards and honorable mention in the military annals of the country.

After Bárbula and Las Trincheras, General Rafael Urdaneta marched with a division to protect the western part of Venezuela, which was exposed to enemy raids, for they still controlled Coro and Maracaibo. Another force under Colonel Vicente Campo Elías, a European Spaniard serving the Republic, was sent to Calabozo, a city located on the Upper Llano.

Before leaving to take Girardot's heart to Caracas to be enshrined in the cathedral, Bolívar once more appealed to Monteverde in the name of human kindness. He was reluctant to enforce a cruel law that condemned to death a large number of Spaniards shut up in the dungeons at La Guaira. The inflexible Spaniard, governed by a false sense of honor, refused to rescue them from death. The generous intercession of the English governor of Curaçao led Bolívar to make another proposal to the Spanish leader concerning the exchange of prisoners. Don Salvador García de Ortigosa, a Spaniard and a priest, acted as envoy on this occasion, but all his arguments and pleas were in vain. In his second letter to the governor of Curaçao, Bolívar referred to Monteverde's unjustifiable detention of Ortigosa and to the cruel practices of "these barbarians," despite all his efforts to be generous. Another attempt was yet to be made to save these victims from the death to which Monteverde had abandoned them.

When Bolívar returned to Caracas on October 13, 1813, the municipality called a meeting of prominent citizens in order to reward the meritorius conduct of the general in chief in a manner befitting his modesty and spirit of self-sacrifice. The assembly conferred upon him the rank of captain general and the magnificent title of Liberator. Bolívar's reply on this occasion was couched in the simple language of modesty, which is all the more fitting for the speaker when his exalted position and his deeds allow him the use of more pretentious language.

Shortly thereafter Bolívar instituted the Order of Liberators, thus providing an incentive for glorious deeds without compromising republican principles and without burdening the treasury. The distinction was so highly prized that the honorable insignia was considered to be the highest award to which a soldier could aspire. In the beginning this honor was conferred on only a few. The founding of this order proved that Bolívar did not aspire to any distinction he was not ready to share with his comrades-in-arms. He could have monopolized the glory and the rewards for victory, but, being both generous and diplomatic, he shared the laurels with those who had helped him to win them. Never, indeed, had it been more necessary to put into play the energy and strength of the Republic and to adopt all those measures prompted by prudence and public policy, because the royalist forces, like the legendary monster that multiplied itself after each blow, reappeared in greater numbers after their defeats, in one part or another of the vast territory of Venezuela.

CHAPTER FIVE

THE VAST PLAINS OF VENEZUELA offered a safe place of refuge for the royalist troops after their reverses. The invincible natives of the Apure region had not yet decided for independence, and the fleeing leaders were well received in San Fernando, the principal city of that region. It was easy for them to promote small uprisings, which the patriots dreaded on account of the nature of the terrain and the class to which the instigators belonged.

Of all the monsters produced by revolution in America or elsewhere, José Tomás Boves was the most bloodthirsty and ferocious. At the outbreak of the revolution he enlisted in the patriot forces, and it is said that he went over to the royalists following some slight or insult. After obtaining command of a guerrilla troop, he carried on irregular warfare, and his daring exploits attracted the *llaneros,* who were eager to fight under a leader rough and ferocious like themselves. Though rebellious toward his superiors, Boves exacted the blindest obedience from his subordinates. He became notorious about the time of the earthquake. The swiftness of his movements was surprising; the destruction that he caused was distressing. He was incapable of showing pity, and neither sex nor age nor profession could shield his victims. He looked like a kindly person with his blond hair, big brown eyes, and fair complexion. Tall and well-built, he could endure the greatest hardships. Such was the chief of the bandits who now gathered to invade the province of Caracas, which was then bearing the entire brunt of the war.

The eastern section of the Republic had been separated politically since the occupation of the area by General Santiago Mariño, who had assumed the title and authority of dictator in September, 1813. Bolívar proceeded very carefully, in order to seek in every possible way to bring about a union of all the provinces under a central government. He therefore invited Mariño to come to Caracas but had to join his army before the interview could take place.

Colonel Campo Elías had succeeded in clearing the whole Calabozo region of enemies, but his brutal severity and rigorous application of reprisals put the cause of independence in an unfavorable light on the llanos. Urdaneta's division had to stop near Barquisimeto when confronted by superior forces commanded by Colonel José Ceballos. General Bolívar joined the division with a small reinforcement and attacked the enemy on November 10, but he was forced to retire to San Carlos. After assembling a larger force, he drove the enemy from the heights at Vigirima. But Colonels Yáñez and Ceballos succeeded in putting a larger force than ever in the field following their meeting in the town of Araure, which is on the plains between San Carlos and Guanare. It was here, on December 5, 1813, after being reinforced by the troops of Campo Elías, that Bolívar forced them to fight. When the battle situation became very dangerous, Bolívar placed himself at the head of the select troop of cavalry held in reserve and launched a sudden attack on the enemy cavalry, which did not venture to stand up under the blow. Thus it was that he won one of the most important victories achieved by patriot arms up to that point.

The royalist losses in this battle were considerable. The American prisoners were incorporated into the patriot ranks. Most of the Spanish forces were, in fact, made up of Venezuelans, which grieved Bolívar more than a little. Almost immediately after the victory he addressed a proclamation, dated December 7, from his headquarters at San Carlos to his misguided fellow countrymen, offering a full pardon to all provided they presented themselves within a month's time at any of the patriot camps. The invitation was ignored, as such appeals generally are in civil wars. The enemy continued to recruit troops from among the inhabitants of the country, and American blood continued to be shed by American hands. Some of America's native sons were the most stubborn enemies of independence during the long struggle that followed.

After some divisions had marched westward again on Calabozo, Bolívar started back toward the capital for the purpose of giving up the supreme authority. Since he knew that only a strong central authority was capable of fostering the revolution, he had kept in his own hands the authority conferred upon him by victory and popular assent. There were many, however, who begrudged Bolívar his superiority, despite the purity of the intentions that motivated his conduct. Rather than point out the injustice of their accusations, he chose to offer incontestable evidence of his republican principles. On January 2, 1814, he convoked an assembly of the magistrates and the people and had his secretaries give an exact account of all the acts of his public administration. In his address to that body he stated that his desire to save them from anarchy had forced him to accept and retain the sovereign power, and that all he wanted was the honor of continuing to fight their enemies without having to hold an office which not a few of them could hold with distinction. This address was greeted with loud applause from the immense gathering that filled the spacious hall and the avenues leading to it. Then the governor spoke in praise of the leader who had rescued Venezuela from the dreadful yoke that had oppressed her; he concluded with the proposal that General Bolívar should con-

tinue in command. Replying with that easy, gifted eloquence he possessed, Bolívar declared that his fellow soldiers were the true liberators.
After reminding them that a victorious soldier earned no right to rule
his country, he asked to be relieved from a task beyond his strength.
Several other distinguished people present pleaded unanimously for
a dictatorship, and Bolívar finally declared that he would accept the law
that circumstances imposed upon him, but that he would act as the
trustee of supreme authority only until the present danger ceased.
There was not a single vote opposed to the unlimited confidence placed
in Bolívar. However dangerous such a step might seem, he was given
absolute power. Considering the critical situation of Venezuela in that
exceptional period, we must agree to the imperious necessity of the
measure. Later on we shall see that the crown of dictatorship encircling
Bolívar's brow soon became a veritable crown of thorns for him.

Don Manuel Cagigal, a suave, popular Spaniard who was more of a
politician than a soldier, had succeeded Monteverde in the captaincy
general of Venezuela after Monteverde had been removed from command at Puerto Cabello on October 28 of the previous year.[1] A man
of Cagigal's ability could have done much good for the country in
1812, but the criminal work of destruction was too far advanced for
any remedial measures to be effective. The monsters spawned by the
revolution were now opposed to submission to an authority they had
helped to create but had come to regard as obtrusive. The result was
the reign of anarchy and confusion in all parts of the Spanish territory.

The eastern and western sections of Venezuela were united by identical principles, but each one recognized a distinct government and
each one acknowledged a leader who had been the immediate author
of its emancipation. The Constitution of 1811 had really expired with
the occupation of the country by Monteverde, and not even a semblance
of the old bond of union remained. Coro and the important provinces
of Guayana and Maracaibo, key points in Venezuela, were in Spanish
hands. The Puerto Cabello stronghold worried the patriots because
they had to employ a large force to maintain the siege. Furthermore,
Colonel Yáñez had been able to recruit a force large enough to take

[1] Monteverde was unable to continue in active command after his jaw was shattered in the battle of Las Trincheras on October 3, 1813. —Ed.

the offensive and clear the patriots from Barinas. There was nothing prosperous about the state of the Republic at the beginning of 1814.

On the coast to the west of Caracas the ferocious Francisco Rosete made his appearance and spread terror and desolation. At the same time another enemy leader and his wild hordes were darkening the southern skies. It was Boves, whose numerous followers, atrocious deeds, and terrifying name made him the most formidable enemy of all. He and his swarm of thieves and murderers were this time threatening Valencia and Caracas after having devastated the whole area from the banks of the Orinoco to the vicinity of the Valles de Aragua. On that march of over a hundred leagues he destroyed all the towns along his route and put to death the inhabitants whose sex or infirmities prevented them from joining his ranks. And his opponents were not the only objects of his implacable anger, for death was the punishment meted out to those of his followers who showed the slightest sign of commiseration at the sight of the sufferings of the unfortunate victims.

After Boves defeated Campo Elías at La Puerta, a singularly fateful battlefield for the patriots during the course of the war, Bolívar assembled all available troops and took up a position on the estate at San Mateo that he had inherited from his parents. Boves soon appeared, ready for battle, with seven to eight thousand of his barbarous soldiers. Meanwhile, Ceballos appeared in person before Valencia, after he had obliged the patriots to abandon the siege of Puerto Cabello; and Rosete threatened Caracas, after he had put to the sword three hundred defenseless inhabitants of Ocumare who had gathered in a church in the belief that this sanctuary was inviolable. General Juan Bautista Arismendi[2] rushed with a small force to check the savage Rosete; but his force was destroyed, and he was very fortunate to escape. The valor and good fortune of Ribas redeemed this defeat, for he routed Rosete.

In an extreme effort to force the San Mateo position, Boves showed no regard for the lives of his deluded, savage proselytes, and he often exposed his own life with a bravery that would have done honor to a better cause. But his own prowess and the courage of his troops could not match the stubborn resistance and most heroic valor displayed by

---

[2] Arismendi had been the first governor of the island of Margarita after a successful patriot rebellion. —Ed.

the San Mateo defenders. Campo Elías, extremely courageous and scornful of danger, fell mortally wounded. His own followers mourned his loss, but not so his own countrymen, who thoroughly detested him because of the way he persecuted them. But his reckless, dashing courage was eclipsed at San Mateo by the noble sacrifice that will make the name of young Captain Antonio Ricaurte immortal forever. Assigned with twenty-five men to guard the military stores in a building on a hilltop, Ricaurte ordered his subordinate to take the men down to reinforce the main body, which was being hard pressed. When the enemy troops approached, in the belief that he had decided to surrender, he applied a lighted fuse to a box of powder and blew up the building. He and the attackers died together in the ruins.

Bolívar decided to withdraw to Valencia when he found himself hemmed in on all sides by Boves' troops, with no prospect of reinforcements. After withdrawing without loss, he forced Ceballos to raise the siege of Valencia. Meanwhile, the gallant Ribas advanced on La Victoria and defeated Boves there on February 12, 1814. This barbarian once more retired to the llanos of Caracas to rebuild his shattered forces with slaves and fugitives, who were attracted to the banner of death by his terrifying name.

When Bolívar reached Valencia, he signed the order condemning to death the Spanish prisoners shut up in the dungeons at La Guaira, but only after having offered to exchange all of them for one single patriot, a Spaniard named Colonel Jalón.[3] This terrifying order, which only dire necessity could have wrung from Bolívar, was occasioned by the frequent provocations, the unprecedented cruelty toward the Venezuelans, the burning of cities and plantations, the murder of harmless citizens, the many contemptible refusals of proposals for the exchange of prisoners, and, finally, the discovery of a conspiracy to free the Spanish prisoners in conjunction with the enemy march on Caracas. Eight hundred hapless victims were sacrificed in Caracas and La Guaira, under orders from General Arismendi, on February 14–16, 1814.

I have related the causes of this lamentable bloodshed, and I have denounced the horrible excesses that provoked it; but I do not intend

[3] Jalón was exchanged later for Captain Miramón, a prisoner at La Guaira.

to defend the measure by offering as an excuse the nature of the reprisals or by adducing proof of its absolute necessity. It is to be regretted that the sword of retribution cut down the innocent and the guilty indiscriminately. No one more than the Dictator himself regretted the tragic necessity of that sentence. The proclamation concerning the war to the death and the execution of the prisoners caused the greatest indignation among the royalists against the person and reputation of Bolívar. They pictured him as a bloodthirsty, cruel, and relentless man. "Of all princes," said Machiavelli, "it is impossible for the new prince to avoid the title of cruel." Bolívar had to bear this reproach.

When the conquistadores first came to America, they resorted to crime and human bloodshed in order to establish their power; blood and crime were the means they used three centuries later to maintain their tottering power. The nature of the South American had undergone a surprising change during that long interval. He was no longer the humble, gentle Indian of the sixteenth century who was incapable of resistance. Nothing remained in him of the aborigine but the memory of his sufferings and the awareness of injustices. From his European ancestors he had inherited the courage to avenge these wrongs.

The success of Ribas at La Victoria gave Venezuela a brief respite, but by March the formidable Boves was once more besieging the San Mateo position, which Bolívar had occupied again. The Spaniard set out after General Mariño as soon as he received news of his approach from the east to help Bolívar. Their encounter at Bocachica on March 31, 1814, resulted in heavy losses on both sides; consequently, Mariño countermarched to La Victoria and Boves withdrew toward Valencia. Boves suffered numerous casualties as a result of the measures taken by Bolívar to prevent a retreat, but he was able to join Ceballos, who had come out from around Valencia to support him. Now that the siege of this city was lifted, Bolívar quickly reorganized his forces and re-established the siege of Puerto Cabello. Boves returned to the llanos of Calabozo, the inexhaustible source of his rough warriors, and Ceballos withdrew to San Carlos, where he was hoping to meet Cagigal.

Though the province of Caracas had been reduced to a state of dire poverty, Bolívar worked tirelessly to reorganize the army and to obtain means to defray the great expenses of the war. His noble generosity in putting his entire inheritance at the service of the state induced others to follow his example, thus making it possible for the government to satisfy the unceasing demands of the public creditors. But, although the moral consolation of gaining independence, sooner or later, sustained the upper class of society, it meant very little to the unambitious masses. Consequently, it became increasingly difficult to find the necessary replacements to fill the gaps in the units caused by casualties.

By merging the divisions of Generals Mariño and Ribas and adding troops from the Puerto Cabello division and from new levies, Bolívar managed to form a considerable force capable of opposing General Cagigal, who was advancing with an army superior in numbers and completely equipped. It is hard to believe that by the month of May the royalists could appear on the borders of Caracas with the largest and most powerful army they had ever been able to organize. But it must be remembered that the peculiar nature of the country favored them in their withdrawals, that the people were accustomed to obeying them, and that the hope of getting some of the inevitable booty served as an inducement to them. Bolívar decided to go out to meet the royalists before they penetrated to the heart of the province. Without wasting a moment's time, he marched with the united forces of Cumaná and Caracas, which had the most gallant and popular leaders of the Republic to spur them on. On May 28, 1814, the two armies came within sight of each other on the savannas of Carabobo. The battle began at once, and the patriots won a most signal victory, leaving the field littered with enemy corpses. Cagigal, Ceballos, and a few cavalrymen managed to escape in the direction of Barquisimeto and Coro. Soon thereafter Bolívar returned to the capital, where his presence was required for the conduct of civil affairs.

It seemed only natural to hope that this decisive setback at Carabobo would discourage the royalists, but Boves once more threatened the Republic with his hordes. Bolívar had no choice but to face them, despite the fact that the only troops on hand capable of facing Boves' *llaneros* were those of General Mariño. The same field where Campo

Elías had been defeated was to be the scene of a new victory for Boves. The battle at La Puerta, with the existence of the Republic at stake, was waged with a tenacity unusual even in that period of veritable slaughters. Unable to resist the formidable charges of the cavalry from the llanos, the patriots suffered complete defeat on June 15, 1814. Bolívar, Mariño, and a few others managed to get back to Caracas over different routes with a total of eight hundred to a thousand men. Boves occupied the fertile Valles de Aragua and cut communications between the capital and the garrison of the stronghold of Valencia.

Words fail to describe the discouragement occasioned by this unexpected blow. It seemed impossible to think of prolonging the struggle without the slightest hope or probability of success. A decision was taken at a council of war to have Mariño hurry back to the region where his authority was recognized, in order to raise troops and prepare it for an attack. Meanwhile, Bolívar was to continue to oppose the enemy as much as possible and then withdraw toward Barcelona. He did not hesitate to come to a decision to march to the East; there was reasonable hope of obtaining reinforcements and returning shortly, since the provinces of Cumaná and Barcelona offered the advantages of an abundance of cattle and a population definitely in favor of the cause of independence. With these ideas in mind, he wrote to Colonel Juan Escalona, who commanded the stronghold of Valencia, ordering him to defend it at all costs until he returned with help.

Boves had meanwhile sent a division to occupy Caracas while he himself marched on Valencia. The inhabitants of the capital fled by the thousands, for what was uppermost in everyone's mind was the terrifying idea of falling into the hands of Boves. When Bolívar heard that Boves was marching on Valencia, he assumed that the division threatening the capital could not be as strong as was said and that a sudden attack would succeed in re-establishing the morale of his troops. With this hope in mind, he set out on July 6 and came across the enemy only a few leagues from Caracas, but he was repulsed with considerable losses. This debacle decided the fate of the capital, which he evacuated on the following day, along with the troops he had managed to save and those who had come by sea from the siege of Puerto Cabello. They were followed by a large number of unfortunate people who did not stop to think of the almost insurmountable difficulties involved in this decision. When the royalists occupied the city and ransacked the houses, they found nothing of military value, because Bolívar had previously sent to Barcelona everything belonging to the government.

Hunger, hardships, disease, and the constant fear of being overtaken by the enemy conspired to make the lot of the hapless refugees horrible to an extreme. People accustomed to the pleasures of a comfortable life could hardly stand such great hardships, and many died every day. Bolívar himself told me that he saw mothers pull their young babies from their emptied breasts and hurl them, with horrible curses, over a precipice. These sufferings went on for twenty days until the unhappy wanderers reached Barcelona, where they were given help. Many of them succumbed later, victims of the diseases contracted on the way.

The troops brought from Caracas by Bolívar halted at the boundary of this province, where they were reinforced by recruits gathered by General Mariño in Barcelona and Cumaná. On August 17, Colonel Francisco Tomás Morales, Boves' second in command, appeared before the patriot headquarters at Aragua, which is protected by a river difficult to ford in the rainy season. When Bolívar received the fearful news that the enemy had forced his way across the river, the troops fell in quickly and went into action right away, but the outcome was fatal for the patriots. So great was the panic that seized the undisciplined recruits that they deserted at the mere sight of the enemy. After the defeat Bolívar made his way to Barcelona; he continued his withdrawal to Cumaná upon learning that the inhabitants were proposing to surrender the city to the enemy in the hope of saving it from pillage. The wretched survivors of the emigrant families from Caracas had arrived in Cumaná before him. When he reached the city on the night of August 25 and was informed of the absolute impossibility of reestablishing order, he had to agree, much to his sorrow, to the necessity of abandoning the place. Accompanied by General Mariño, he set sail, intending to land at some other point on the coast where he could assemble the fugitive patriots for a new attempt to save his unfortunate country.

Let us leave him for now on the tossing waves, which are a true image of his changing fortune, while we turn our attention to his inhuman antagonist, whom we left outside Valencia. This city is situated on a spacious, open llano to the west of the beautiful lake that bears its name and a little more than ten leagues from Puerto Cabello. After the battle of La Puerta, Boves laid siege to Valencia, but he was held at bay by the small garrison, which disputed every inch of ground with the most heroic tenacity. Even the savage Boves seemed to feel for a moment that such indomitable courage deserved some consideration, and he sent a truce envoy to offer terms of surrender to the city. A capitulation was arranged immediately, on July 8, and was ratified by Boves on the following day. The city was to be surrendered to the royalists with the express provision that the lives and property of the citizens and the garrison would be fully guaranteed.

Pretending not to be satisfied with the mere ratification of the treaty, Boves swore by the Sacred Host to fulfill religiously the promise he had made. The following day he invited the prominent citizens and the officers of the garrison to eat with him, and that same night he invited their wives to a ball. When the ladies arrived, he gave secret orders to his executioners for the death of the victims. An hour later all of them had been murdered. Meanwhile, the ladies continued dancing until midnight, and Boves joked with them about the absence of their loved ones. They came face to face with the stark reality of their misfortune when they returned to their homes. Since many patriots could not attend that banquet of blood, they were sought out the following day, and those who were found were put to death. We should look in vain through the annals of human depravity for incidents comparable in cruelty to those that took place in Valencia during the few days that Boves remained there.

Boves left Valencia for Caracas, where new victims were to be sacrificed to his insatiable cruelty. Although Cagigal had been appointed captain general, Boves obeyed no dictates other than those of his own fancy. When Cagigal promoted him to the rank of colonel, Boves returned the dispatch with the answer that he also made colonels. Arriving before Cumaná in the month of October, he managed to take it in short order. A thousand victims were slain in this city alone, including many of the unfortunate families who had migrated from

Caracas. Blood literally ran through the streets. Learning that Morales, his second in command, had been repulsed at Maturín on September 12 by General Bermúdez, Boves set out to join the advance guard division. On the way, he met Bermúdez's forces at Magueyes and succeeded in defeating them after an hour of fighting. Then he joined Morales and lost no time in going after the patriots who had withdrawn to Maturín.

A cleavage had unfortunately developed among the patriots at that time. Bermúdez believed it preferable to wait for Boves in the town of Maturín; but Ribas was of a contrary mind, and his opinion prevailed despite all opposition. Consequently, the army marched out, three thousand strong, and soon came across Boves at Urica, on December 5, 1814, with a force almost twice as large. There followed one of the bloodiest battles of that fateful period. Despite their heroic efforts under the inspiring leadership of Ribas and Bermúdez, the patriots were repulsed on all sides and unmercifully put to the sword. Very few managed to escape and return to Maturín. On that fatal battlefield the hopes of the free were buried, and the noble cause of independence was almost extinguished; but there was some consolation to be gained in this agonized state from the blow that brought the brutal Asturian to earth in the midst of victory and laid his crimes to rest. The name of Boves still causes fright and terror.

Colonel Francisco Tomás Morales, a native of the Canary Islands, succeeded Boves in the command of the conquering army at Urica. Like his predecessor, Morales had risen from lowly positions to high rank and to the power that he maintained through acts of terrorism and cruelty. Little remained to do of the work of extermination. Morales marched against Maturín, which Bermúdez attempted to defend with the three or four hundred infantrymen he had barely managed to assemble. After four hours of fighting on December 11, the city fell to the Canary Islander, with great losses. A large number of the inhabitants were brutally murdered by Morales' followers, who also boasted of having violated every woman in the place. The brave Ribas, who had shown such magnificent courage in his constant struggle for his country, fell prisoner after the battle and was shot and dismembered. By the end of January, 1815, the entire province was in the possession of the royalists.

The disaster at La Puerta was as fatal to the whole West as the other disasters were to the eastern sections. When Urdaneta learned in Barquisimeto about the defeat, he decided to march toward Valencia. Upon his arrival in San Carlos he received news of the magnitude of the loss and of Bolívar's march to Cumaná. After a careful study of the situation he decided that it was wise to withdraw to Mérida. This plan was not easy to carry out, for Barquisimeto and El Tocuyo had gone over to the royalist cause. Urdaneta had to fight Sebastián de la Calzada's forces at Macuchíes, two days' march from Mérida, and he was obliged to continue his withdrawal after suffering considerable losses. Finally, he passed the Táchira River and joined the troops of General Custodio García Robira,[4] who were quartered there.

[4] An outstanding Granadine patriot, executed in Bogotá by General Morillo in 1816. —Ed.

CHAPTER SIX

I T IS TIME FOR US to turn back to Bolívar. His hopes of landing on the coast and joining the fugitives and dispersed elements were shattered when he arrived in Carúpano and surveyed the scene, for the most complete anarchy prevailed, and every idea of submission to authority seemed to have vanished. Following this disappointment, he sailed for the island of Margarita, where he had no better luck. He set out to sea again with General Mariño, bound for Cartagena, where he arrived about the end of September, 1814.

And so it was that after having liberated Venezuela from the oppression of the unpredictable Monteverde in a short and glorious campaign, Bolívar eventually was forced by an unavoidable chain of events to abandon it to its fate and to seek refuge on other shores. I shall not maintain that his administration was perfect, but it is unquestionably true that the defects had their origins in general conditions or in abuses of which he was not aware and for which he cannot in any way be held responsible. Unselfish to an extreme in money matters, he attributed the same unselfishness to others, but he was deceiving himself. When he discovered his mistake, he went to the other extreme and distrusted others even when there was no reason for the slightest suspicion. Many of his subordinates were mercenary, even to the point of exasperating the people with their rapacity. Unfortunately, these abuses under whose weight the people suffered never came to the attention of Bolívar in time.

The lucrative posts distributed with more liberality than prudence in the first period of independence were abolished by Bolívar. In his government merit alone served as a recommendation in the distribution of public posts. Illicit commerce was prohibited under the severest penalties. With commerce free from the impediments that had obstructed it, foreigners were invited to settle in the country. General Bolívar sought most earnestly to remove the deep-rooted suspicion of foreigners that Spanish policy had spread among the natives. His superiority over his compatriots in this respect is indisputable.

As a soldier, Bolívar displayed most unusual talent. The campaign that rescued Venezuela from Monteverde's grasp deserves special praise as the initial effort of an inexperienced warrior. His rapid and skillful movements were surprisingly successful against experienced adversaries who commanded troops very superior in numbers and discipline and who had at their disposal all the resources of the country. In years to come the astounding episodes of that memorable campaign will be regarded as fables or historical exaggerations. Very few have possessed to such a high degree as Bolívar the gift of inspiring noble sentiments and laudable enthusiasm in the hearts of others. Evidence of this is found in the funeral honors for Girardot and in the institution of the Order of Liberators.

When we see Bolívar forced to take the defensive, his efforts are not less praiseworthy. Even though attacked simultaneously at different points, his attention was not thereby distracted from the enemy he had to keep pinned down in an almost impregnable fortress situated in the heart of the territory that was the source of his supplies. Despite the never-ending intrigues of the royalist party, he defeated the Spaniards in several encounters. Whenever he suffered a reverse, he replaced his losses with astounding celerity and went on to score new victories. Though finally abandoned by fortune and defeated, he revealed to the very end a strength of character that enabled him to rise above every disaster.

The secret of the success of the Spaniards is not hard to discover. Bolívar's superior ability always triumphed while Ceballos and Cagigal conducted the war on equal terms with the patriots. But it was morally impossible to oppose the force of the hurricane unleashed by Boves against unhappy Venezuela, for he proclaimed principles completely destructive of society and broke the bonds that united it. To check the diabolical course of the career of this perverted soul, it would have been necessary to invoke the spirit of evil. No human power could have done it.

One of the principal charges made against Bolívar by his political enemies is his opposition to the re-establishment in Venezuela of the government overthrown by Monteverde in 1812. There were a thousand reasons for opposing this step, but the most persuasive one was the natural weakness of the federal system in the face of the uncertain state of the country and the necessity of concentrating all the power in order to oppose the unceasing efforts of the royalists. In 1813, as during his whole career, General Bolívar heeded the advice of his friends, but he almost always made up his own mind. If the people around him had spoken frankly of the abuses that were being committed and of the complaints that they heard, I am certain that he surely would have corrected the evils and paid due attention to the reasons for the complaints. I have before me a letter written to Fernando Peñalver nine years after these events, in which the accuracy of my assertion is corroborated. In this letter Bolívar says that he would never forget the excellent advice of Peñalver; he recalls that in the year 1813 Peñalver alone told him the pure and unadulterated truth without the slightest admixture of flattery. Worthy, indeed, of governing a free people is the man who cherishes such sentiments, who remembers after so long a period of time the advice of a friend without distinctions or rank, and who recognizes how right he was in having told him the truth, even when that truth included, perchance, reproaches against his conduct.

Bolívar received a resounding welcome in Cartagena. Months before, the Chamber of Deputies of the state had decreed a vote of thanks for his services in Venezuela. Soon after his arrival he wrote to the president of the Granadine Congress, explaining the causes that had contributed to the ruin of Venezuela and announcing that he would soon appear before him to give an account of his actions. At that time Cartagena was torn by civil strife, with the state divided into two parties: the moderate one composed of wealthy citizens and headed by José María García Toledo, the extremist one bitterly opposed to the European Spaniards and headed by the brothers José Gabriel and Juan Antonio Piñeres. The same Colonel Castillo who had opposed Bolívar in Cúcuta belonged to the Toledo party. Both political factions made overtures to Bolívar, but he decided to march into the interior to join General Urdaneta and his division. Following a joyous welcome in all those places which had been the scene of some of his previous victories, he met Urdaneta in Pamplona and accompanied him to Tunja, where he met with a very gratifying reception, despite the intrigue carried on by individuals who insisted on blaming him for Venezuela's misfortunes.

Great changes had occurred in this country during Bolívar's absence. Some provinces had proclaimed their independence from the Spanish crown, and most of them had formed a confederation. The government established was not, however, the most suitable one to direct a nation divided into factions and threatened by a foreign enemy. The invasion of Popayán by Juan Sámano in 1813 checked the disturbances that had arisen because of differences between the government of Cundinamarca and the federal Congress.[1] Consequently, General Antonio Nariño marched at the head of the troops of the Union and won

---

[1] Sámano was a royalist colonel at the time. After the Spanish reconquest of New Granada in 1815–1816, he was appointed viceroy. —Ed.

the victories of Palacé and Calibío over Sámano.[2] After crossing the formidable Juanambú River, Nariño was taken prisoner on the streets of Pasto, and his troops disbanded.

After the departure of Nariño, Cundinamarca was governed by Don Manuel Bernardo Alvarez, an elderly man of little ability, strictly honorable in private life but a fanatic in religious matters, with the same prejudices as his predecessor concerning Congress. This province refused to accept the Union even after all the other provinces had sanctioned it. The forces that Urdaneta had saved from the ruin of Venezuela enabled Congress to employ the imperative tone to which its sovereign character gave it a right, and the arrival of General Bolívar could not have been more opportune. Since the demand made on the government of Cundinamarca did not bring a favorable reply, Bolívar had to march there. On arriving before Bogotá on December 8, 1814, he informed Alvarez of the object of his mission in a courteous and most eloquent letter. The refusal of Dictator Alvarez in his reply to recognize the government of the Union left no alternative but to use force. Alvarez had used every means within his power to further his obstinate resolution to defend the city, including criminal accusations directed against Bolívar and the Venezuelan troops and a declaration that they were excommunicated from the Church. Of all the measures adopted by him, the one that caused the most indignation was that of inviting the European Spaniards to take up arms, but it cannot be denied that he was innocent of treason.

On December 10, Bolívar attacked the city, and on the eleventh he pushed the garrison back to the main square. The city capitulated on the following day, and he occupied it immediately. The government of Cundinamarca recognized the government of the Union, but the obstinacy of Alvarez and his followers had cost a great deal of bloodshed. It was impossible to effect a reconciliation between the people and the soldiers, for fanatic clergymen had taught the people to regard the soldiers as enemies of God. Even though the ecclesiastical authorities

[2] Nariño was president of Cundinamarca, whose capital was Bogotá. He was opposed to the confederation and its congress, preferring a strong central government. —Ed.

lifted the excommunication, it was not possible to avoid its fatal consequences. For this reason Bolívar wrote to the administrators of the archdiocese to point out how humanely he had acted toward the people of Cundinamarca, to protest against the pastoral letter in which he and the army had been accused of coming to attack religion, and to request that they make an attempt to restore his reputation by means of a pastoral letter truly worthy of their ministry.

The victory won by Bolívar caused great satisfaction in Congress and the general government, and it was celebrated with great rejoicing throughout the country. His reward for these services was a vote of thanks and the highest military rank in the Republic. In spite of everything, however, Bolívar was not absolutely satisfied with his victory, because he had a dreadful foreboding that the Spaniards residing in the capital would continue to fan the fire of discord. He proposed that Congress should adopt the most rigorous measures against the principal instigators in order to frighten the royalists, but Congress considered conciliatory measures to be preferable to harsh ones. When José Fernández Madrid indicated to him the desires of Congress, Bolívar replied: "Tell Congress that it will be obeyed but that some day it will have cause to repent. It is inevitable that this country will soon be occupied by the Spaniards, but it does not matter, for I shall return."

The resources now at the disposal of the government enabled Bolívar to think once more about the emancipation of his country, which could be attempted once the independence of New Granada had been established and the common enemy had been driven out of its territory. For the purpose of furthering this plan he strove with the greatest perseverance and his characteristic eloquence to convince both the members of Congress and the heads of the departments of its usefulness. When the seat of the government was transferred to Santa Fe about the middle of January, 1815, Bolívar had an opportunity to complete his military preparations rapidly. On the twenty-third, the day of the inauguration of the government in the capital of the Republic, he delivered a notable address, in which he reviewed the difficulties encountered in America on the road from slavery to freedom, swore that he would carry the banners of New Granada to the utmost bounds of the areas subjected to tyranny, and urged the establishment of supreme courts and the organization of a national treasury.

While Bolívar was carrying forward his preparations for the march to Santa Marta, Colonel Castillo published a libelous attack in Cartagena, blaming him for the loss of Venezuela and accusing him of shortcomings and crimes of the most serious nature. This accusation, based on the most unworthy motives, bothered Bolívar, who was too sensitive by nature to this kind of attack. The government did not take the charge seriously. In a letter remarkable for its prophetic note, the president of the Congress, Camilo Torres, gave him the most complete satisfaction and approved his conduct, but no matter how satisfactory the declaration may have been, it failed to counteract the harmful influence of Castillo's handiwork. In a country where prejudices against foreigners, including natives of Venezuela, are so strong, nothing more was needed to awaken the passions of the populace. Since the plan that now absorbed the government's attention had to do with the provinces on the coast, where Castillo enjoyed a certain amount of influence, the direct consequences were foreseen. No one was more anxious to prevent them than Bolívar. We shall soon see the regrettable results that came from his generous conduct at the beginning of the unfortunate disagreement that occurred.

General Bolívar proposed the assignment of a corps to occupy Santa Marta and Río Hacha so that it could be built up with recruits from these provinces and march from there to Maracaibo, from where an invasion of the interior of Venezuela would be easy. He thought that two thousand men, the number in the corps then under his immediate orders, would be enough to carry out the first part of his plan. The government acceded to his plan, and not a moment was lost in carrying it out. To overcome a scarcity of arms and supplies, the federal government decided to order the authorities of the state of Cartagena to place a given quantity of arms and ammunition at the disposal of General Bolívar. The Cartagena troops should necessarily obey him as captain general of the Union and commander in chief of the expedition against Santa Marta. Bolívar sacrificed his personal interests for the public welfare and tried indirectly to effect a reconciliation by proposing the promotion of Castillo to the rank of brigadier general. He even went to the extreme of resigning his own command, with the hope of removing every reason for misgivings. The promotion was granted, but his own resignation was not accepted.

On the way to the coast after leaving Bogotá on January 24, 1815, General Bolívar learned of Castillo's efforts to obstruct the expedition. He also learned that Castillo had marched against Cartagena with the ostensible purpose of overthrowing the government, of which one of the Piñereses was a member. Recognizing the difficulties of his position, Bolívar earnestly implored the government to exert every possible effort to remove the obstacles that were being placed in the path of his activities. The government appointed Dr. Juan Marimón y Enríquez, a canon of the cathedral of Cartagena and deputy from that province to Congress, to serve as mediator. He was a man of limited intelligence, somewhat shy by nature, not at all scrupulous morally, and not well suited for the delicate task with which he was entrusted.

In the meantime, Bolívar continued his expedition and, after dislodging the enemy from Ocaña, reached the city of Mompox, where he was received with very fervent demonstrations of popular approval. There he learned of the complete collapse of the party headed by the Piñereses and of the exile of the two brothers and many of their most active supporters. He also learned that they had been succeeded in the government by Dr. Pedro Gual, a highly intelligent Venezuelan, through whose intervention the gates of the city had been opened to Castillo. Finally, he learned that Don Juan de Dios Amador, a well-to-do merchant who was beloved by everyone in the country, had replaced Gual in the office of state executive by virtue of a new election.

All Bolívar's efforts to obtain arms, ammunition, and troops proved futile, as did his attempts to induce Castillo to forget his resentment. Castillo recognized Bolívar as captain general, but he instructed the minor officials not to obey orders that did not emanate from the provincial government. At the same time he withdrew the detachments placed in the towns on the west bank of the Magdalena and removed everything that might be used for offensive and defensive operations. He finally succeeded in making Bolívar feared, if not hated, and in arousing hatred among the people against the troops, who were coming, he said, to take their land from them and to plunder their homes. At one point he agreed to meet Bolívar, but he did not appear, offering inane excuses for his absence. This naturally offended Bolívar's pride and irritated his friends.

By this time Dr. Marimón had arrived in Cartagena after a meeting with Bolívar in Mompox, at which he had appeared to be in agreement on all points with the general and had promised to settle the matter satisfactorily. But shortly after leaving the general's headquarters he began to disseminate the most shameful accusations against him. What was even less consistent with his responsible position of mediator was the fact that upon his arrival in Cartagena he became the agent for the proposals of the provincial government, which were suggested by the personal enemies of Bolívar. Then the government of Cartagena asked Bolívar for recruits and a considerable sum of money. Under these conditions Castillo offered to furnish eight hundred rifles with the necessary ammunition and to join, with his troops, in the liberation of Santa Marta.

Bolívar had already advanced as far as Barranca when he received these proposals. In his reply he stated that it was morally impossible for him to accept the terms in view of the sad state of the army and the gradual deterioration of his financial resources. Forty days were consumed in this exchange of notes, without any practical result other than increased antagonism on both sides. Urged on by his subordinates and other persons with unselfish motives, he determined to move near to the city. With his army reduced to almost half its effective strength, it would have been insane to attempt the subjugation of Santa Marta. Colonel Tomás Montilla, the bearer of the communication announcing this final decision to the governor of the province, was grossly insulted by the boisterous populace after he entered Cartagena, and he barely managed to escape with his life. The authorities of the city refused to reopen negotiations with the general in chief or to answer his last note. They let him know, however, through his agents, that the water had been poisoned in the environs of the city and in the reservoir of La Popa. The purpose was to terrify, not to kill.

Since all hope of a friendly settlement had disappeared, the general in chief summoned a council of war, which agreed that it was absolutely necessary to approach the city and to lay siege to it. General Bolívar agreed to this proposal in a moment of extreme annoyance, apparently forgetting that he lacked the means to reduce a city as strong as Cartagena and that he was going to give the lie to his previous protestations of peaceful intentions. Before moving from Turbaco, he detached a small force to occupy the part of the province that supplied the city. Meanwhile, Castillo was not idle, for he had taken effective measures to guard against a surprise move. Various proclamations produced the desired result: the inhabitants of the rural sections began to hold back provisions from the Union troops and then showed uncompromising hostility toward them. Bolívar's situation was extremely difficult when on March 26, 1815, he decided to approach the city. On that same day he informed the general government of what had happened, in a detailed account that described the acts of disloyalty committed by Castillo and other members of the faction. He also reported the decision made at a council of war to attack Cartagena lest the Republic and the army perish. His concluding words were a request that another general be appointed in his place, "for I am more willing to mount the scaffold than to continue in command."

On March 27, Bolívar established his headquarters in the monastery of La Popa, which became very difficult to supply with water and provisions because of the steady fire from Fort San Felipe, from the city, and from the gunboats on Tesca Lagoon. In these adverse circumstances he again resorted to negotiations, but to no avail. The provincial government insisted that he withdraw to Ocaña with only the Venezuelan troops, leaving the Granadine soldiers in Cartagena. In the meantime the royalists took advantage of the situation and kept advancing, occupying the territory left undefended. Both sides seemed inclined to listen to the voice of reason when it was learned that a Spanish expedition under the command of General Pablo Morillo had arrived on the island of Margarita.[3] A meeting held by Bolívar and Marimón aroused hopes of a quick reconciliation, but Castillo made a sally from the city on the following day and had to be repulsed. The

[3] General Morillo, who had distinguished himself in the Napoleonic wars, arrived from Spain in 1815 with more than ten thousand veteran troops. His mission was the pacification of America, and he had the official title of Pacificator. —Ed.

besieged had been constantly defeated in all their encounters with Bolívar's troops, but these partial triumphs had served only to weaken both factions. Bolívar never provoked hostilities, and during that unfortunate struggle he invariably distinguished himself by deeds of the most chivalrous unselfishness, whereas only hatred and vengeance animated his rival.

Shortly thereafter it was learned that Barranquilla and Mompox had fallen into the hands of the royalists. As a consequence of this news the negotiations were resumed, resulting in a meeting held between the leaders of both factions. It was finally stipulated that Bolívar would leave by sea to attack Santa Marta and that Castillo would immediately proceed against the royalists who had occupied Mompox and the towns on the west bank of the Magdalena. Then Castillo changed his mind, with his customary malevolence, and informed the general in chief of the Union that he preferred to direct the attack against Santa Marta himself. Bolívar agreed, but then new difficulties arose. It was apparent that hatred was inspiring all the movements of Castillo and that his only aim was to frustrate the plans of his liberal adversary.[4] Bolívar finally determined to quit the army and the country rather than give further impetus to civil war. Twice he had presented his resignation to the general government, and twice it had been refused. He offered the same resignation to the federal commissioner on April 24 after suggesting the march to Santa Marta or against the enemy who had invaded the interior of Cartagena.

The choice between abandoning the country at a moment of great danger or witnessing the destruction of his army was torturing the heart of a man with the noblest motives, but the base jealousy of Castillo left no other road open to him. On May 7 he assembled the Union officers to inform them of the decision he had made. They heard it with sincere regret, and, in proof of their affection for him and the confidence they had in him, they unanimously decided to share his fate.

[4] It seems clear from the historical record that Castillo opposed Bolívar at every turn because he considered Bolívar an intruder and an adventurer who was undercutting him on his home ground and who was employing reckless military strategy contrary to his own ideas on the subject. Another factor was Castillo's provincialism against Bolívar's nationalism. —Ed.

Immediately afterward Bolívar wrote to the commissioner general to inform him of his decision and to request that those officers who so wished be allowed to withdraw from the army and leave the country.

Two days later Bolívar embarked in an English warship for Jamaica, where he arrived on May 13, 1815, accompanied by his private secretary and faithful friend, Pedro Briceño Méndez, but not by the other officers because, lacking resources, they were deprived of the privilege of accompanying him into his voluntary exile. Before embarking, he took leave of his valiant companions with an affectionate and eloquent address, in which he spoke of the grief caused all of them by having to fight against their brothers on two occasions and of his great regret over not being able to accompany them in the continuing struggle for freedom. Complete vindication of his conduct is found in a manifesto he addressed to his compatriots from Kingston on July 10. In this manifesto he reviewed all the significant events that had occurred from the time of his second return to New Granada until he made the sacrifice of withdrawing from New Granada in order to save the country from anarchy.

During this eventful period the provinces of New Granada were reduced to a most deplorable condition. Civil discord had exhausted the physical strength of the country, and love of independence was now losing ground day by day. The army scarcely totaled five to six thousand men spread out through the very extensive territory, and it lacked arms, equipment, and ammunition. The elimination of taxes had made it necessary to have recourse to forced loans, which, poorly honored and more poorly paid, brought discredit to the new system and exasperated the people. All in all, the existing conditions could not have been more favorable for making New Granada the easy prey of an enemy determined to invade it, and this enemy was already knocking at its gates.

After assembling an army of five thousand men on the border, the royalists of Venezuela proceeded to occupy Mompox and to capture the ships at Barranquilla. Control of the Magdalena enabled them to cut off communication between Cartagena and the interior. Despite numerical superiority, the patriots of Cartagena were so divided that anarchy made all their strength useless. General Florencio Palacios, a relative and countryman of Bolívar, had succeeded him in command of the army of the Union. Unable to bring about the desired reconciliation with Castillo, he marched toward the interior of the province, determined to return to Santa Fe. After the failure of an attempted attack on Mompox, he eventually countermarched to Cartagena, where he arrived on August 24 with his force reduced to skeleton strength. Such was the result of the intrigues that drove Bolívar from the country at a time when his services were most needed. Castillo, the principal cause of the misfortunes, was destined to be ignominiously hurled from his high post, to see himself accused of treachery by his very comrades-in-arms, and finally to die on the gallows as a rebel against the King.

The Spanish expedition that sailed from Cádiz in February, 1815, landed on the eastern shore of Venezuela at the beginning of April. It was composed of 10,500 completely equipped men, most of whom had been chosen from among the finest of the Spanish infantry, and it was convoyed by a mighty squadron. Well directed, this army would have succeeded in bringing peace not only to the Spanish Main but also to the whole continent, and it would have assured the crown of Spain possession of the continent for many years. But Ferdinand was unfortunate in his choice of peacemaker. If exceptional military talents, extreme courage, and virile steadfastness had been sufficient for the task entrusted to General Don Pablo Morillo, the designs of the sovereign would undoubtedly have seen their fulfillment. What force and terror could accomplish had been accomplished in Venezuela by the bloodthirsty Boves. The pleasing and beneficent task of reconciling discontented subjects with their sovereign was what remained to be done; Morillo was not the right man for this.

Learning from Morales soon after his arrival that several leaders, among them Arismendi and Bermúdez, had taken refuge in Margarita and had succeeded in assembling some of the island people to oppose him, Morillo immediately set sail for the rebellious island, taking along Morales himself and the three thousand Venezuelan troops who made up his army. The brave islanders had no choice but to yield to Morillo, who offered them guarantees of life and property. Some of the patriots, including Bermúdez, evaded the vigilance of the squadron and succeeded in making their escape. The inhabitants were generally treated with kindness and suffered no molestation. This promising beginning of Morillo's undertaking was counterbalanced by the accidental explosion of the seventy-four–gun *San Pedro*. Over nine hundred men perished in this disaster, and the expeditionary army lost, in addition, all its clothing, a great quantity of ammunition, and half a million pesos.

Upon reaching Caracas, Morillo tried in his first proclamations to instill confidence in the inhabitants, but the measures he took at the same time gave the lie to his promises. His arrogant attitude offended particularly the colored people, who had become accustomed to the flattery of those who were in power, royalists or patriots. Many of them withdrew their support from him. To obtain money Morillo established a council of sequestration for the seizure of the property of all those who had directly or indirectly taken action in favor of independence, and he made no exceptions. More than two-thirds of the Venezuelan families were deprived of their property as a result of this edict. Reconciliation was now impossible, and all foresaw it thus: such extreme measures brought desperation even to the very partisans of the King, who realized that Morillo could subjugate the country but could not bring it peace.

After making arrangements for the preservation of peace in Venezuela, Morillo turned his thoughts to New Granada; he had already been informed of the serious dissensions there. Having organized his army, he set sail from Puerto Cabello on July 12, taking with him the major part of his forces. Soon after his arrival at Santa Marta he dispatched two columns to clear the banks of the Magdalena, to reinforce Mompox, and to occupy Ocaña and Antioquia. At the same time he gave orders to Colonel Morales to march by land to Cartagena with the advance guard. On his march Morales found the towns deserted, many of them reduced to ashes. Morillo actually began the siege on September 1, after landing the main force unopposed a short distance from Cartagena.

The stronghold was really in no fit state to resist the relatively strong army threatening it, because active measures to supply it were taken only after news had been received of the arrival of the expedition at Santa Marta. In view of the lack of provisions it was very unwise on the part of the government to permit men and women who were useless for service to remain in the city. Scarcely two months passed before hunger produced its cruel effects of illnesses and death; General Castillo was singled out as the prime cause. On October 17 he was deposed, and by the vote of the garrison General Bermúdez succeeded him. The gallant defenders of Cartagena were reduced to desperation after communications were cut between the city and the Bocachica forts at the entrance to the bay, and the inhabitants thus deprived of the meager subsistence derived from fish. Finally the government and the officers of the garrison resolved to evacuate the city. Early in December the troops filed along the beach, silent and sad, and boarded their transports, which were small, uncomfortable, and poorly equipped. After they set out to sea, a heavy squall scattered them, and the greater part of that unhappy emigration perished after having suffered the most horrible privations. Many of them, after they had victoriously combatted the waves, fell into the hands of the royalists of Cartagena and Cuba, only to lose their freedom and their lives.

On December 6, 1815, Morillo made his entrance into the city. In his official report he describes the state of the city in these words: "The city presented a most frightful spectacle. The streets were strewn with unburied corpses that polluted the air, and the majority of the inhabitants were plainly dying of hunger." Let it be said in justice and to the honor of the Spaniards, and I do it with satisfaction and sincerity, that even the common soldiers shared their rations with those unhappy people and comforted them in their misery. General Morillo applied the most humane and efficacious measures to relieve the suffering of those starving people and was solicitous in taking care of their most urgent needs. It is very gratifying, in the midst of the horrors of war, to be able to record deeds of this nature. Quite different, however, was the conduct of the barbarous and brutal Morales. He and his soldiers, almost all of whom were Americans, steeped themselves in the blood of those helpless people whom the fortunes of war placed in their hands in the forts and town of Bocachica.

CHAPTER SEVEN

I T IS NOW TIME TO RETURN to Bolívar, who, in sorrowful exile on the island of Jamaica, was bemoaning the fate of the fatherland. From the moment of his arrival in Kingston he devoted his hours of leisure to the interests of the fatherland. Though the most respectable inhabitants of this city were opposed to South American independence, they looked upon Bolívar as a sincere and ardent patriot who had made laudable sacrifices in his country's behalf. He did his best to convince them of the benefits to be derived from free trade with South America, and he succeeded in making many converts with his solid arguments. The news of the advantages gained by Morillo in Venezuela greatly affected him. In a confidential letter of May 19, 1815, to his friend Mr. Maxwell Hyslop he foresaw the possible re-establishment of the Spanish government from the mouth of the Orinoco to Quito and even to Buenos Aires. In his opinion, England could and should take a hand in the destiny of the hemisphere.

A Kingston newspaper published a letter written by Bolívar in September, 1815, in answer to one he had received from a gentleman who was taking a great interest in the cause of South America. The letter displays an intimate knowledge of the history of that area and its inhabitants. It is prophetic in many passages and refutes in great part, if not absolutely, the charges made more recently by a mean-spirited faction in an effort to tarnish the reputation of its author and take credit away from him.[1] The opinions that Bolívar expressed in this letter are those which governed his conduct up to the very end of his life, and the sequence of later events has demonstrated the solidity of the foundation upon which it is based.

Surveying the entire continent and its population, Bolívar declares that the tie that bound America to Spain has been severed because of misrule and that the whole New World is in motion and armed for defense, though the tyrants still have the advantage, especially in Peru and in Venezuela, where they govern a devastated land. Spain is now too weak to rule the new hemisphere, and Europe would do her a service by dissuading her from her rash obstinacy. The inhabitants of America, doomed to live a passive existence as serfs, have been kept in a state of infancy with regard to public affairs, trade, and relations with other people, all of which leaves them ill prepared for self-rule, especially under the federal system adopted initially in some regions. Existing circumstances make it impossible to organize the New World as a great republic, and it would be disastrous to establish American monarchies, though the larger areas will inevitably do so. America is divided by climatic differences, geographic diversity, conflicting interests, and dissimilar characteristics. Buenos Aires will probably have a central government dominated by the military, which will degenerate into an oligarchy or monocracy. If any American republic is to have a long life, it may well be Chile, where the spirit of freedom has never

[1] At the Convention of Ocaña in 1828 and thereafter, when Greater Colombia was being torn apart by dissension, Bolívar was accused by his enemies of fighting against disintegration from motives of personal ambition. —Ed.

been extinguished. Peru, on the contrary, will have much to do to re-cover her independence. Mexico may establish a republic with a strong executive maintaining his power for life, but also possible is a limited monarchy later degenerating into an absolute one. The states of the Isthmus of Panama will perhaps form a confederation, which may in time become the emporium of the world, with its canals strengthening commercial ties between Europe, America, and Asia. New Granada will unite with Venezuela, if they can agree to the establishment of a central republic. This nation should be called Colombia. Its govern-ment might have a president elected for life, a hereditary senate, and a legislature similar to the lower house in England. Coming to the close of his extraordinary analysis of the American scene, Bolívar sees an imperative need for union in order to expel the Spaniards and found a free government, and this union will come about only through sensi-ble planning and well-directed actions. When the American states gain strength and have the guidance of a liberal nation that will lend them its protection, they will "march majestically toward that great prosper-ity for which South America is destined."

Although Bolívar was at that time leading a secluded life and one of extreme economy, he was not spared many financial embarrass-ments. Some of his countrymen, lacking funds, were forced to seek them from him, and he supplied their needs with kind generosity. In a short time he found himself in very straitened circumstances, espe-cially mortifying for one who, born to wealth, had never known the want that accompanies the total lack of resources. If it had not been for his good friend Hyslop, he no doubt would have been reduced to the utmost wretchedness. However, he refused Hyslop's offers until all hope of receiving money from his friends on the continent had dis-appeared. Despite his own need, he willingly shared with his com-panions in exile the sum that Mr. Hyslop lent him, but since it was insufficient to relieve the want of the many whom he aided, he found himself still owing a small sum for his lodging expenses. When his landlady suspected that his money was becoming scarce, she flew into a rage and became so mean that he again had to appeal to his charitable friend in order to satisfy her demands. He immediately sought other lodgings, and, although it was Sunday, he was fortunate enough to find them. After having dinner at the home of a friend, he went to the new lodging house to spend the night, for he was determined not to go back to his old quarters, where so many annoyances had been his lot. This was a happy decision for him and for his country, because he would otherwise have fallen victim to the dagger of an assassin.

During Bolívar's absence from the house on that day, a compatriot named Félix Amestoy, who was on his way to Santo Domingo, had gone to say farewell to him; not finding him at home, he had decided to wait for him in his room. Overcome by drowsiness, he lay down in the hammock and soon fell asleep. At about eleven o'clock a young Negro named Pío came into the room. A former slave of Bolívar, to whom he owed his liberty, Pío was now in the service of Captain Rafael Páez, one of Bolívar's aides-de-camp. Thinking that the general was sleeping in the hammock, he approached cautiously and stabbed Amestoy. At his cries, the other residents of the house came running, but too late, for Amestoy had already breathed his last. Pío, without losing a moment, leaped through the window to the street; but his disappearance aroused suspicion, and on the following morning he was apprehended. Without hesitation he confessed that a Polish Jew had bribed him to assassinate General Bolívar and that for three months he had been carefully seeking an opportune moment to accomplish his purpose. Despite Bolívar's intercession in his behalf, the assassin was tried, sentenced to death, and hanged. The villain who had induced him to commit the crime succeeded in concealing himself at first and in leaving the island later without being discovered. This infamous attempt was attributed to suggestions made by General Morillo, but from the personal knowledge I have of the character of this man I am inclined to disagree with this opinion, which has, perhaps, no basis other than impassioned party spirit.

The advances of the royalists on the Spanish Main and the misfortunes of Cartagena saddened Bolívar even more than his own troubles. When the news of Castillo's removal reached him, he determined to set sail himself, hoping to evade the vigilance of the besieging squadron and to take supplies into Cartagena. After appealing to his compatriots to accompany him and obtaining the necessary funds from some business men, among whom Messrs. Pavageau and Hyslop contributed generously, Bolívar set out to sea on December 18, 1815, with arms and provisions in one of the ships belonging to Luis Brión, a rich and respected Creole of the island of Curaçao who had devoted himself and his fortune to the cause of South American independence. On the following day, by a most fortunate coincidence, he encountered a schooner coming from Cartagena, which gave him the details of the evacuation of the city. Had it not been for this meeting, he might in all probability have fallen into the hands of the royalists. Aware of the loss of Cartagena, Bolívar changed his course and sailed toward Haiti, resolved to seek the protection of the leader of the republican part of that island rather than return to Jamaica to drag out a miserable existence.

The recent events in France, which had deprived Napoleon of his throne and his freedom, destroyed the slim hope of aid that had seemed promising to some of the prominent men in America and had been harbored by the government of Venezuela as well as that of New Granada. The other continental powers of Europe either did not want to or were not able to aid the rebellious colonies or befriend them in their heroic efforts. Great Britain, satisfied with the great influence that she was called to exert on the South American continent, did not think the time had yet arrived to encourage the patriots or to give them the aid that in a not too distant day would incline the balance in their favor. And, finally, the United States had displayed a cold indifference with respect to the outcome of the conflict.

After much profound and serious consideration Bolívar finally decided to bring the refugees from Cartagena together at Port-au-Prince as an assembly point for operations against the Spanish Main. There they could at least count on a safe asylum from the persecution of the Spaniards. Actually, his hopes were not vain, for in Haiti a most flattering reception was accorded not only Bolívar, but many others of his compatriots and entire families who had taken refuge there, fleeing the vengeance of the royalists. President Alexandre Sabès Pétion himself, a man of generous feelings whose education was superior to that of the people of his class, went to great pains to make the expatriation of the unhappy emigrants bearable. From the time of his first meeting with Bolívar, he approved of his plans and favored his patriotic designs, offering him the support of the government of the Republic of Haiti as well as his own personal support. Upon learning that Bolívar was engaged in organizing an expedition, the fugitives from Cartagena who were arriving in Jamaica hastened to join him and enlist anew under the standard of such an illustrious leader.

Let us now follow Morillo on his march to the interior and cast a glance, if only a hasty one, at the condition of the Spanish Main while Bolívar, in Haiti, was establishing the basis of his future glory and of the emancipation of his country. After the occupation of Cartagena the Spanish general gave his full attention to the subjugation of the provinces of the interior of New Granada. With this in mind, he detached Colonel Miguel de la Torre with a strong division to join Sebastián de la Calzada and march with him on Santa Fe. In Santa Fe the news of Morillo's landing and his siege of Cartagena had filled everyone with great discouragement. The discovery there of two plots for the overthrow of the new system of government increased the discouragement, if that were possible. Although the plots failed, they caused greater restlessness and dismay in the entire country. Convinced of the weakness of the Union government, Congress approved in November, 1815, the reform that concentrated the entire authority in one single individual.

But while the patriots were discussing forms of government, the royalists were working with the vigor and speed that spell victory. Colonel Calzada, in command of the Fifth Division, invaded the province of Pamplona and defeated Urdaneta at Chitaga on November 30. The fall of Cartagena and the unimpeded march of the expeditionary army were frightful blows for the patriots of New Granada. While they were suffering the most profound depression, their enemies within, who were becoming increasingly bold, succeeded in winning over the lower classes in favor of the Spaniards.

After joining up with the reinforcements sent by La Torre, Calzada set out after the patriot division of three thousand foot soldiers commanded by General Custodio García Robira, which was in a position to block his path. In a battle fought on the paramo of Cachirí on the morning of February 22, 1816, Calzada won a complete victory, as was to be expected, considering the superior discipline of his troops. The slaughter of the prisoners after the combat was horrible. This action was fatal for New Granada, because it marked the end of the only army on which the government had fixed its hopes. The inhabitants declared themselves to be on Calzada's side and pursued the fugitives from the battlefield. The entire province of El Socorro was easily occupied, but the column under Colonel Francisco Warleta encountered fierce resistance before subduing the province of Antioquia. The province of El Chocó was also occupied.

The defeat of García Robira and the royalist army's march to the interior produced the greatest consternation in all the Union, particularly in the capital. Congress tried to restore order by appointing Dr. José Fernández Madrid as successor to the illustrious Camilo Torres, who had been in charge of public affairs since November of the previous year. Neither the eloquence nor the noble example of the new president could overcome opposition and apathy on the part of the people. His government was one in name only, for it lacked power and resources. Madrid was dragged along by the torrent that was bringing on the ruin of his country. The military element disobeyed him, and the people abandoned him. The division under the command of General Manuel Roergas de Serviez, a French officer who had won fame in the service of the Republic, withdrew to the llanos of Casanare, accompanied by many civilians. Madrid withdrew toward Popayán with a small unit called the Guard of Honor.

After Colonel La Torre occupied Santa Fe on May 5, 1816, only a short time was needed for the whole country to be reduced to submission. General Morillo, who entered the capital on May 26, did not approve La Torre's decree granting general amnesty to all those who swore allegiance to the sovereign. The policy followed by the Pacificator after subjugating New Granada merits the condemnation of all parties, for it was not only mistaken but cruel in the extreme. Those who had taken a major part in the revolution were sought out and brought before a military court, which condemned them to death before a firing squad. The noblest blood of the most illustrious sons of New Granada was shed at that time. In the minds of those who know Spanish America and the character of her sons, the conduct of Morillo in Santa Fe did more damage to the royalist cause than the most disastrous defeat. When he reoccupied the country, he could have destroyed the revolutionary spirit for many generations, but his excessive cruelty, exercised without distinction, produced the opposite effect. The evil influence of his tactless rule was not confined solely to New Granada but was extended to the entire continent. It did, however, affect Venezuela most immediately, and just when Bolívar was conceiving the gigantic task of freeing her, even though he could count on only the few fugitives assembled in Haiti who had been happily rescued from the universal destruction.

The whole country of Venezuela, which the cruelty of Boves and Morales had desolated, was in the power of the royalists from one end to the other. The wandering guerrilla bands of Pedro Zaraza, Manuel Cedeño, Andrés Rojas, and José Tadeo Monagas were scarcely aware of each other, scattered as they were over the broad plains. The forces left in strategic positions by Morillo were composed exclusively of his expeditionary troops. He had the wise good sense to take with him four thousand native soldiers, who were accustomed to the climate and the fatigues and trials of the irregular war that had taken place in the country during the campaigns of 1813 and 1814.

The island of Margarita was soon forced to revolt, driven on by the tyrannical conduct of its rulers. General Arismendi, mistrusting the intentions of Governor Urreiztieta, communicated his suspicions to his comrades, and the most implicated among them were able to flee to the woods in the interior of the island. Since Arismendi had great influence in Margarita, the alarm was soon sounded over the entire island, and the Spaniards remained masters of the deserted towns. Soon findings themselves able to take the offensive, the rebels forced their opponents to seek refuge within the fortified cities after several engagements. In these encounters the islanders displayed such heroic valor and performed such great feats that it would all sound like a remarkable fabrication were it not related by their enemies themselves. Such were the fruits of an evil government! Eternal praise to valorous Margarita, the Sparta of America and the humble home of simple fishermen. Now we see this tiny island, spurred on by desperation and inspired by patriotism, face 800 Spanish veterans, reinforced afterwards by 2,500 under José de Canterac,[2] and prepare itself, after hurling a proud challenge, to resist the powerful army of Morillo himself.

Inspired by the example of Margarita, the guerrilla units on the llanos of Venezuela redoubled their efforts. Zaraza harassed the towns of the Upper Llano with his surprise attacks and distracted the enemy's attention in that direction. Monagas and Barreto kept the royalists of Cumaná and Maturín in a constant state of alarm. Even though they were not always fortunate in their frequent encounters, their losses were insignificant and soon replaced, enabling them to reappear suddenly where they were least expected, thus keeping the enemy in constant turmoil. The effect of this type of warfare on regular troops is inconceivable, and only those who have had such experience can understand it. Victory itself does not inspire confidence, because on the following day it can be changed into defeat.

Morillo had fathomed Bolívar's plans. Before reaching Santa Fe, he had already taken the steps best calculated to thwart them, or at least to impede their execution. Morales received orders to march to Valencia to be on the lookout for any movement by Bolívar and to proceed to whatever point along the coast where he might try to make a landing. Salvador de Moxó, the captain general of Caracas, was given instructions to lend all necessary aid to the military leaders in the East, in order to repel the invasion. In addition to the garrisons of Puerto Cabello, La Guaira, Caracas, and those of the eastern cities, there were other bodies of troops on active duty: the division of Commander Rafael López in Barinas, which controlled the llanos there, and the units of Pascual Real and Juan Nepomuceno Quero, which were covering the plains from Caracas to Maturín.

Although in these notes I have not proposed to write the history of the war that ended in independence for the American colonies of Spain but to relate the events in which Bolívar took a direct part and to defend him against the unjust accusations of his enemies, it does not seem inappropriate to relate briefly what happened in Venezuela

---

[2] General Canterac was on his way from Spain to Peru, where he became one of the most outstanding royalist leaders. —Ed.

while Morillo was subjugating New Granada and Bolívar was preparing his expedition in Haiti.

After the defeat at Maturín and the complete occupation of the coast by the Spaniards, the few patriots able to escape the sword of Morales fled to the forests, where they led a precarious existence, fighting off the wild beasts and avoiding pursuit by the Carib Indians sent to hunt them down. Their valor seemed to increase with desperation, and they gathered under the orders of a leader of their choice, determined not only to protect their hapless existence but also to contribute to the emancipation of their country. Subsisting on roots and wild fruit and wearing nothing but loin cloths, they finally mustered their courage and sallied forth to seek provisions. When they received news of the existence of other groups like themselves, they sought each other out and joined forces. In this way the first guerrilla bands were formed. Though their only weapon was the *púa*, a sort of pike made from the wood of a poisonous shrub called *píritu*, bands like those of Colonels Parejo and Monagas quickly strengthened their ranks and made themselves feared by the royalists. An Indian named José Miguel Guanaguanay stood out because of his aggressiveness. He shortly became the terror of the llanos of Barcelona but finally succumbed at the hands of the royalists after accepting their promise that he and several of his captured friends and officers would be pardoned if he gave himself up.

The llanos of Barcelona were well suited to this sort of warfare because of the abundance of horses and cattle, and Monagas was able to assemble a sizable unit. It was not long either before the llanos of Cumaná also had a number of guerrillas. Stern measures did not suffice to exterminate the patriot bands, because the outrages committed by the Spaniards made their authority and their name so hateful that the few patriotic leaders who remained in the country preferred death to submission to the yoke of the King.

A complete victory over a sizable force at San Diego de Cabrutica afforded Monagas arms and ammunition and brought him the aid of the Indians nearby on the banks of the Orinoco. He was soon joined by Zaraza and Cedeño, but they had to disperse their band after being routed at Peñas Negras. In April, 1815, Monagas and his comrades entered Villa de Aragua in order to force the Spanish commander Don Salvador Gorrín to abandon the banks of the Orinoco. It was here that Monagas learned information of great importance about the state of the country, Morillo's forces, and his plans. After routing Colonel Juan José Rondón, who later abandoned the royalist ranks, Monagas crossed the Orinoco with more than a thousand men and appeared before Angostura, but Gorrín, who had also crossed the Orinoco, surprised the patriots, killing many and dispersing the rest.

Shortly afterward Cedeño and his small band crossed the Caura River in boats made of hides and marched over water-covered savannas. After Cedeño established himself in Caicara, there was a rapid increase in the number of guerrilla bands recognizing him. He soon found himself at the head of a thousand men scattered over a vast territory. But the only weapon these forces had was the pike, and they lived in complete ignorance of what was happening in the rest of the country. There were, indeed, bands of patriots in the provinces of Barcelona and Cumaná. Zaraza was harrying the royalists, and other leaders, like Barreto and Rojas, were roaming through the forests of Maturín, like Cedeño unaware of the existence of other groups.

After remaining hidden in the neighborhood of Angostura for three months, Monagas marched toward the Cuchivero River. Cedeño, fearful that Monagas would seek to wrest the leadership from him, not only refrained from helping him but even obstructed his advance. How many times were the efforts of those valiant leaders frustrated by wretched rivalries and jealousies! Only after coming to an understanding with Cedeño was Monagas able to cross to the north bank of the Orinoco and return to the point from where he had started out. He finally joined Zaraza, and the two leaders soon succeeded in augmenting their numbers with other groups wandering through those areas. But new quarrels arose again, for each leader claimed the command or at least wanted to remain independent of the others. When more reinforcements arrived under the command of Rojas, who had succeeded in driving the enemy from Maturín but had had to fall back when attacked by Colonel Rafael López, it was agreed that Monagas, assisted by a council, would direct operations.

At this stage Monagas received sealed documents from Bolívar notifying him of the latter's landing in Carúpano. Great was the rejoicing caused by this news, which spread rapidly throughout all Venezuela, bringing a ray of hope to the patriots and inspiring terror and dread in the royalists. But Monagas was unable to take advantage of the prestige that such welcome news gave him. In the severe winter, horses and cattle perished on the savannas for lack of pasture ground, and desertion diminished his ranks solely because the soldiers were destitute of clothing. It was therefore not difficult for the Spanish leader, Colonel Rafael López, to defeat him, since he had the greater resources of Aragua at his disposal. Following this disaster Monagas joined Francisco Vicente Parejo in the town of Micura, where he received communications from Manuel Piar in Maturín asking him for aid and offering him ammunition. While preparing to send him some men, Monagas learned of the march and difficulties of Gregor MacGregor.[3] Considering help for MacGregor to be more urgent, he marched to join him and arrived in time for the action at Alacrán, in which the patriots triumphed.

There are no words that can adequately commend the patriotism, the constancy, and the unselfishness of these leaders, who were worthy of the liberty they were struggling to win. Without arms, without clothes, and almost without subsistence, they did not count the number of their enemies before going out to meet them. Defeats did not dishearten them but seemed instead to strengthen their love for their country and their faith in the cause that they were defending.

[3] A native of the highlands of Scotland and a former captain in the British army, MacGregor had served under Miranda and had fought in New Granada before joining Bolívar. He was at this time conducting a successful retreat to Barcelona. —Ed.

CHAPTER EIGHT

N EAR THE END OF DECEMBER, 1815, as I have already said, Bolívar landed in Aux Cayes and went immediately to Port-au-
Prince, where Pétion received him with demonstrations of high esteem
and assured him of help in all matters pertaining to his authority. As a
matter of fact, arms and ammunition were given to him. Bolívar's
generous efforts and sacrifices in behalf of the unfortunate part of the
human race to which the population of that island belonged were well
known and admired. Foreign merchants living in Port-au-Prince, especially Mr. Robert Sutherland, also exerted themselves in his behalf.
During his entire lifetime Bolívar retained the fondest memory of this
gentleman and of Mr. Pavageau. A considerable part of the emigration
from Cartagena arrived at Aux Cayes on January 6, 1816, and during
the course of the month many others joined them.

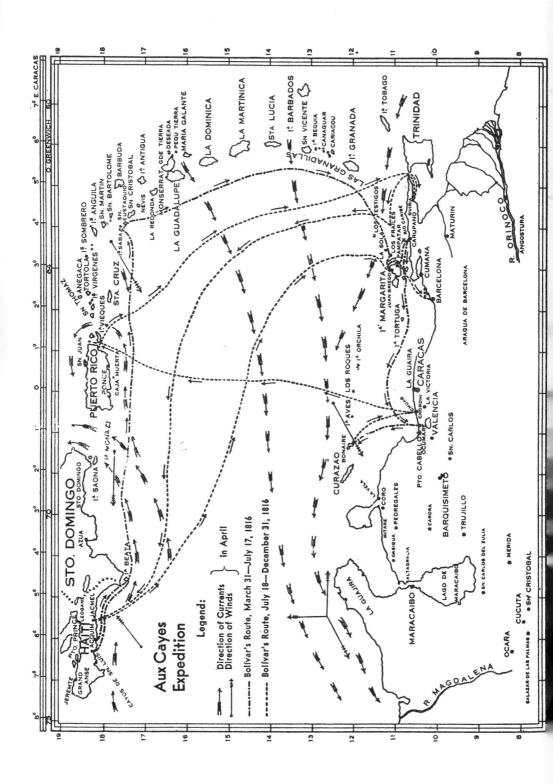

Aux Cayes
Expedition

Legend:

Direction of Currents } in April
Direction of Winds

Bolívar's Route, March 31—July 17, 1816
Bolívar's Route, July 18—December 31, 1816

After moving to Aux Cayes in February, Bolívar assembled the principal military leaders and the former civil authorities of New Granada and Venezuela to inform them of his plan. They did not hesitate to make a choice between this seemingly desperate project and the cruel alternative of leading a wandering and dishonorable existence in the Antilles. At a second meeting—attended by Brión, Mariño, Piar, Bermúdez, Luis Aury, Florencio Palacios, MacGregor, H. L. V. Ducoudray-Holstein, Marimón, the Piñereses, Don Francisco Antonio Zea, José Antonio Anzoátegui, Soublette, and others—Brión proposed that an expeditionary force be formed under the command of Bolívar, who would assume the supreme civil and military authority until a congress was convened. All those present at the meeting agreed to Brión's proposals except Aury, Bermúdez, and a few others, who withdrew from the expedition.[1] The preparations were made under the personal supervision of Brión, whose money and credit were used to procure the means of transportation.

On March 31 the flotilla of one brig and six schooners set sail with about 250 men, mainly officers, and a considerable quantity of arms and ammunition. During the crossing, a Spanish merchant vessel was seized. As they approached Margarita on the morning of May 2, they sighted a brig and an armed schooner of His Catholic Majesty off the islands of Los Frailes, and they succeeded in capturing them despite stubborn resistance. The Spanish commander, Don Rafael Iglesias, died in the engagement, and Brión was wounded. Leading its prizes of war, the patriot flotilla entered the harbor of Juan Griego on the island of Margarita on May 3.

General Arismendi, the governor, welcomed Bolívar and his companions and invited them to land. Bolívar had Arismendi call a meeting of the prominent inhabitants and authorities of the island in Villa del Norte, the latter's headquarters. This junta approved everything that had been decided in Aux Cayes, and it recognized Bolívar as Supreme Chief of the Republic and General Mariño as second in authority. On the eighth of that same month Bolívar issued a proclamation calling the attention of all Venezuelans to the beginning of the third period of

[1] They opposed unlimited authority for Bolívar, proposing instead that a three-man junta share authority with him. —Ed.

the Republic on Margarita, to the expeditionary force assembled under his command to terminate forever the dominion of the tyrants, and to the authorization given to them to name their deputies to Congress.

The Spaniards evacuated Asunción, the capital of the island, and withdrew into the fortresses of Pampatar, but Brigadier Juan Bautista Pardo refused to heed Bolívar's demand for surrender. Lacking the means to render his threats effective, Bolívar decided to make his way to the continent in order to establish contact with the bands operating in the interior and add them to his forces. Two days before his departure he announced to the inhabitants of the Spanish Main that he and his brave comrades were about to return to the mainland. After enlisting some recruits from Margarita, Bolívar embarked on May 25, and on the same day the flotilla set sail under the orders of Brión, now recovered from his wound.

Six days later the expedition reached Carúpano and, making a landing, forced the royalists to abandon the fort after they refused Bolívar's demand for surrender. The patriots found the town well stocked with provisions and in the bay a beautiful brig and a schooner, which they seized. Now that communications were open with Maturín and the interior, Bolívar directed his energies toward augmenting his forces. Mariño and Piar, well equipped with arms, made their way to Güiria and Maturín with a schooner and some *flecheras*.[2] They soon sent to Carúpano about two hundred Negroes with their officers, who were formed into the Güiria Battalion. But both leaders, despite orders to return to headquarters, remained on those shores. On June 12, Bolívar wrote to the English admiral at the base in Barbados and to the governor of Trinidad informing them of the arrival of the expedition on the Spanish Main. Anxious to dissipate the charges of bloodthirstiness that had been leveled at him, he told them that it was his intention to bring to a close the war to the death.

News of the landing soon spread all over Venezuela, alarming the Spaniards and inspiring confidence in the wandering bands of patriots. When General Tomás de Cires, the Spaniard in command in Cumaná, was informed of Bolívar's arrival, he started out for Carúpano. En-

[2] Large rivercraft. —Ed.

couraged by the repulse of the patriots by a strong detachment in La Esmeralda, Cires attacked Colonel Francisco de Paula Alcántara's outpost on the night of June 19 and forced it to fall back on the town. Bolívar, satisfied with having attracted the attention of the Spaniards to that point, left one hundred men with Mr. Brisel to observe the enemy and sailed with seven hundred men on July 1 for Ocumare, seven leagues to the east of Puerto Cabello. Landing on the fifth without opposition, he addressed to his compatriots a proclamation in which he declared that, for his part, the war to the death had ceased and that the slaves were free. "That unhappy segment of our brothers which has groaned under the miseries of slavery," he said, "is now free. Nature, justice, and policy demand the emancipation of the slaves. Henceforth there shall be in Venezuela only one class of men: all will be citizens." Never has power been used more nobly than the way Bolívar used it when he abolished that curse of civilization. But let it be said in passing that this declaration and his subsequent efforts in behalf of the African race brought upon Bolívar the enmity of many of his compatriots whose interests were affected by this unselfish act.

On July 7 Colonel Soublette left with three hundred men to occupy La Cabrera and to promote a rebellion in the Valles de Aragua. He was attacked by Morales, who had set out after the patriots with a strong force immediately after his arrival in Valencia from New Granada. Soublette fell back in good order to the hill of Los Aguacates and informed Bolívar, who assembled the two hundred men remaining in the port and started out to join him. At dawn on the thirteenth, Morales suddenly attacked Soublette. Bolívar arrived during the combat, but the reinforcements coming up with Anzoátegui were delayed by the difficulties of the terrain. After offering fierce resistance and losing a third of the division, the patriots had to abandon the field and fall back to Ocumare. This was not the worst, for Brión had had to leave port in order to secure provisions in Curaçao, leaving only two small merchant ships and the armed brig *Indio Libre* in the bay with Agustín Gustavo Villaret, the commodore of the squadron. At a meeting in town, the principal leaders displayed their anxiety for the safety of Bolívar. They said that together or in small groups they would make their way into the interior and join the guerrilla bands on the llanos.

Bolívar disapproved this proposal, for he was determined to follow the fate of his comrades-in-arms, and he gave orders to that effect.

That night when Bolívar went to the port to hurry the loading of the arms and ammunition, he found everything in the greatest confusion. All his efforts to establish order were of no avail. In the midst of all this, Isidro Alzuru, his aide, came to report that all was lost, that Morales was in the town, and that it was impossible to assemble the people. In these circumstances the only alternative left to Bolívar was to take refuge in the brig. Urged on by the men who surrounded him, he got into the launch and reached the brig when the cables had already been cut and it was setting sail. Bolívar had another reason for embarking—to save what was on board the ships, which Villaret, taking advantage of the confusion, was trying to appropriate.

Alzuru's story was false. Colonel Soublette had sent him to announce to Bolívar that the enemy was encamped in the woods a short distance from the town, that the camp was covered, and that he was only awaiting his orders and the return of Colonel Salom to begin the march to Choroní. Whatever it was, treachery or bewilderment, that caused Alzuru to act as he did, the truth has never come to light. This unfortunate officer went back to Ocumare and told Colonel Soublette that the Liberator had embarked before his arrival in the port and that Salom was still there, not knowing what to do because Villaret had departed, leaving on the beach some artillery pieces and several cases of arms and ammunition. That same night Alzuru left the patriots and was never seen again in their midst.

This event is one of those which have been most frequently used as a basis for criticism and calumny, but the testimony of Generals Briceño Méndez, Soublette, and Salom, who were important participants in all these actions, indicates that under the circumstances the only sensible course left open to the Liberator was to leave by ship. Furthermore, a bulletin from the headquarters division in the central section, dated in El Pao de Zárate on July 20, when Bolívar was far away, contains not a word of complaint, not a word of reproach against the man who, according to his enemies, had cowardly abandoned his comrades.

On July 15, Bolívar reached the island of Bonaire, where Brión joined him on the following day with the other ships of the flotilla. They went back together to Choroní in the schooner *Mariño*, but they found the town in the hands of the enemy, or pretending to be so. Bolívar then learned that MacGregor had marched on into the interior with the division. Since it was impossible to remain on Bonaire, and since there were not sufficient provisions for the trip to Güiria, he set sail with two small schooners, intending to land in some Spanish possession and provide himself with the provisions he needed. After several misadventures the crews of the schooners managed to obtain a few head of cattle, some rice, and corn on the island of Vieques, near Puerto Rico. Subsequently, on August 16, Bolívar arrived in Güiria, sustained by the hope of joining his comrades-in-arms.

Soon after he landed, however, Generals Mariño and Bermúdez disavowed his authority. The former sought power in order to exercise a command based on license and anarchy, whereas the latter, a man of no education and very unstable, considered himself slighted by Bolívar, who had opposed his joining the Aux Cayes expedition. Bolívar reproached them for their disobedience, but he realized that his presence in Güiria could provoke a civil war. He therefore resolved to make another sacrifice in behalf of the Union by leaving the country. He proceeded to embark immediately, but only after having had to draw his sword to defend himself against Bermúdez, who had pursued him to the beach. Once again on the high seas, Bolívar started for Margarita, but the presence of the Spanish fleet forced him to sail to Jacmel, from where he set out at once for Port-au-Prince. After being hospitably received by President Pétion for the second time, he remained there, completely devoted to his country's cause and making efforts to aid it once more. Let us leave him in the midst of these preparations and return to Ocumare, where his heroic comrades remained, plotting an enterprise that seemed impossible of accomplishment.

When he learned of the occurrences at the port and of the departure of Bolívar, Soublette sent Lieutenant Colonel Miguel Borrás to ascertain what had happened there and to hasten the return of Salom to his troops. The march to Choroní was begun on July 14. Not finding Bolívar at that port and having no news of him, the leaders met in council and assigned the command to MacGregor, who was attached to the expedition but without an official position. The division crossed the cordillera dividing the Valles de Aragua from the sea and routed a detachment that tried to oppose it. Driven back by a small force of Spaniards who had fortified themselves in Chaguaramas, MacGregor had the good fortune to meet Colonel Leonardo Infante with a cavalry squadron from Zaraza's guerrilla forces. In Quebrada Honda on August 10 Commander Quero overtook the patriot forces and attacked them, trusting in the numerical superiority of his division, but the result of the battle was not in his favor. Although MacGregor did not obtain a decisive victory, he was able to continue his withdrawal without interference.[3] His small force grew larger every day, and when he reached San Diego de Cabrutica, he was joined by three to four hundred men under Zaraza's command and shortly afterwards by Monagas' guerrilla band. When Colonel Rafael López attacked at El Alacrán, fortune again favored MacGregor, for López was completely routed. Three hundred of his men were taken prisoner in the battle, and a greater number were killed. MacGregor then occupied Barcelona, while Anzoátegui occupied Píritu, a small seaport nearby, where he seized a rich booty. General Manuel Piar, with a division, joined MacGregor's force in Barcelona and assumed the supreme command.

This admirable campaign was one of the most daring undertakings of the war of independence. In order to appreciate fully the magnitude of those operations, it would be necessary to have at hand a map of the country and to know the rough roads and the wilderness that the patriots had to traverse. In the meantime, Morales, indignant over the defeats that the Spaniards had suffered at the hands of those whom he characterized as a gang of fugitives, redoubled his marches and approached Barcelona. Piar and MacGregor went out to meet him, and at El Juncal, a short distance from the city, a battle took place whose result was also glorious for the patriots. Of three thousand royalists, only three hundred escaped with Morales.

The insult to Bolívar from the Güiria faction caused great distress among the patriots, and thoughtful men viewed it as a very likely source of disorders and misfortunes for the country. All the army

---

[3] Quero was thoroughly routed in Quebrada Honda. What MacGregor could not do was to pursue him.—Carlos Soublette.

leaders, and especially those of MacGregor's division, were convinced of the need for Bolívar's services, and they therefore decided not to recognize any supreme authority other than his. Since the people shared the same sentiments, a decision was reached to send a deputation to him with a request that he come back to direct the country's efforts. This mission was entrusted to Don Francisco Antonio Zea, who left immediately for Port-au-Prince. On the way he touched at Margarita, where Governor Arismendi and the inhabitants expressed their conviction of the need of Bolívar's assistance. Zea found Bolívar busy making preparations for the new expedition. Bolívar was delighted to learn of the good fortune of his comrades-in-arms. It was easy for him to blot from his memory the insults he had received at the hand of the Güiria faction. No one was quicker than he in forgetting an affront, especially when the country's cause or a political objective was at stake.

After receiving assistance from Pétion and being rejoined by Brión, Bolívar once more boarded ship at Jacmel for Margarita and arrived there on December 28. The Spaniards had already abandoned Pampatar, the only point on the island that they still held, and General Arismendi had just left for the mainland with three hundred men. After issuing a proclamation convoking a congress and confirming his previous declarations about the emancipation of the slaves, Bolívar went on to Barcelona, where he arrived on the last day of the year. The inhabitants of the city gave him a warm welcome.

His first care was to organize a provisional government, and he immediately took steps to restore hope to the people. Then he announced his arrival to the division leaders and impressed on them the need for union. He wrote to the émigrés in foreign colonies, appealing to them to return to their country and inviting them to cooperate with him in saving it. The situation of Venezuela in this period was distressing, but Bolívar spoke to all with unshakable confidence not only of victories in Venezuela but of "marching on Santa Fe and rich Peru." In a letter written on January 1, 1817, to the leaders of the division that had made the heroic withdrawal from Ocumare, he encouraged them to fulfill "the destiny that called them to accompany him to the farthest reaches of the American world."

The relatively few, poorly armed, and ill-clothed patriot forces were scattered over an immense expanse of territory, but they kept the royalist towns and authorities in a state of alarm. Most of the territory of the provinces of Barcelona and Cumaná was occupied by the patriots, because General Mariño had just had some successes in the interior. Moreover, General Piar had gained control of the towns of Barcelona on his way to Guayana. There were nearly fifteen hundred men with Piar at the beginning of October, 1816, when he marched toward the Orinoco with the intention of crossing it and undertaking the subjugation of Guayana in conjunction with General Cedeño. Overcoming innumerable natural obstacles and enemy resistance, Piar crossed the Orinoco and the Caura and continued his march toward Angostura. Meanwhile, General Páez occupied the llanos between the Apure and the Meta rivers, with two thousand *llaneros* under arms. Such was the situation of the patriots when Bolívar landed at Barcelona, and all the leaders recognized his authority except General Páez, who, without questioning it, did not accept it explicitly.

The cruelties committed in New Granada by Morillo, and in Venezuela by Moxó, the captain general of those provinces, had aroused the anger of all those who desired independence and of even many royalists who disapproved of their barbarous policy. Had not the *audiencia* of Caracas intervened,[4] Moxó would have continued his reign of terror until every family in the land had contributed at least one victim. This humane intervention had no effect, however, in the provinces, where his subordinates committed outrages that would be hard to believe were it not for the testimony of impartial eyewitnesses. After being defeated at El Juncal, Morales infamously took revenge on the unarmed civilians and filled the country with terror and blood. These outrages had an effect contrary to that expected by their perpetrators, for they made the patriots implacable in their hatred of the Spaniards and strengthened the resolution of those who were armed never to submit to their would-be executioners. Nevertheless, Moxó and the bloodthirsty Morales received a reward from their King, instead of the hanging they deserved.

At the beginning of 1817, Morillo commanded large, well-dis-

---

[4] The *audiencia* was a superior court composed of judges called *oidores* who represented the monarch in the administration of justice. —Ed.

ciplined forces, and he had in his power all the fortified places, all the principal cities, and almost the entire coast. His troops controlled most of the richest and most populated part of the interior. With the subjugation of New Granada completed, he had at his disposal the immense resources of that area. At that very moment a strong division commanded by Canterac was crossing the ocean on its way to reinforce him. His orders were obeyed without question by the royalists from Guayana to Guayaquil.

Bolívar's fondness for Caracas, or his exaggerated idea of the patriotism of its inhabitants and the resources it could furnish, caused many errors in his military career. On more than one occasion he postponed more important operations in order to seize it or help it. After his arrival in Barcelona he fell into the same error again when he decided to invade the province of Caracas with only seven hundred men, of whom four hundred were recruits. On January 5, 1817, he advanced on Clarines and attacked the town, but he encountered unexpectedly strong resistance. When some of his men to the rear mistakenly thought that they had been cut off, the troops broke ranks and fled. The remainder fell back with Bolívar and Arismendi to Barcelona. Neither did Mariño meet with success in his attack on Cumaná. Marching on the city, he demanded its surrender. Unable to intimidate its defenders, he decided to attack. On January 19 he took a house on the outskirts that the royalists had fortified, and he immediately made a reconnaissance of the enemy positions. Then he attacked the city, but he was repulsed with some losses and had to retreat to Cautaro the following day and immediately afterward to Cumanacoa.

Meanwhile, the Spaniards were not idle, for Pascual Real was marshalling his force of 4,500 men to capture Barcelona, and the royalist squadron was making ready for a joint operation. On the morning of February 8, 1817, Real occupied the city without opposition, because Bolívar had fallen back to the fortified convent of San Francisco while waiting for the reinforcements he had urgently requested of Mariño. Bolívar had only 600 poorly armed troops. The rest of the day was spent in skirmishes, and at nightfall Real, fooled by a ruse of Bolívar, withdrew to El Pilar. Due to this mistake, General Mariño was able to enter the city on February 11. A few days later men from the Spanish ships seized El Morro de Barcelona, hoping to establish communications with Real, but their battery on this promontory was taken after Bolívar ordered an attack on it. Meanwhile, the patriot *flecheras* forced the Spanish squadron to withdraw. After this disappointing royalist campaign, Real was relieved of his command, as was General Morales, who was second in command.

After the blockade of Barcelona was lifted, Bolívar decided to move to the province of Guayana to direct personally the operations in that sector, which was all the more necessary because of the great dissatisfaction provoked by General Piar's arbitrary decisions.[5] Bolívar wanted to evacuate Barcelona completely because he foresaw the misfortune that would threaten it, but the inhabitants and the city government were opposed to this plan. Leaving a small force of native soldiers, he also requested General Mariño to do everything possible to bolster the defense. Accompanied by fifteen officers and their orderlies, Bolívar left for Guayana on March 21. On the way they routed a band of royalists who were lying in ambush and reached the Orinoco without any further trouble. Bolívar and his secretary crossed the river in a small canoe, the only available craft, on the night of April 3, and he joined General Piar on the following day.

General Piar had established his headquarters near Angostura, and on January 18 he had made an unsuccessful assault on this well-protected city, which is built on a promontory jutting out from the river bank. Then he started out for the Missions of the Caroní River, but there were many desertions during this march, occasioned as before by Piar's intolerant attitude. It was imperative to occupy the Missions territory, the best cultivated part of Guayana, in order to deprive the enemy of supplies and provide subsistence for the patriot troops. The occupation of the Missions was accomplished almost without opposition during the month of February. The seven thousand native inhabitants, accustomed to obeying the Spanish Capuchins, regarded the patriots as enemies of God and religion, but once the monastic rule over them was removed, they quickly took up the cause of independ-

[5] There was much discontent among the officers of Piar's division because he had accused Mariño and Bermúdez of sedition and had ordered the arrest of officers who had expressed doubts about his Guayana expedition.—Ed.

ence. Though reduced to Angostura and the fortress of Guayana la Vieja, the enemy continued to control the Orinoco. Piar headed back toward Angostura when he learned near the end of March that the city had received a reinforcement of eight hundred men under the orders of General Don Miguel de la Torre.

It was at this point that Bolívar arrived on the scene. Upon learning that La Torre and Governor Nicolás María Cerruti had gone down the river with all the troops that could be spared from the city, he ordered Piar to march in pursuit of the royalists. Piar established his headquarters at San Félix on April 8, after deciding to wait for the enemy. La Torre attacked the patriots on April 11, and his force of fifteen hundred men was completely routed when our infantry made a frontal assault and the cavalry attacked it on the flanks and to the rear. Suffering only minor losses themselves, the patriots killed over five hundred of the enemy, captured a like number, and seized one thousand rifles and a large quantity of ammunition. Piar defiled the honor won with this victory by slaying 160 Spanish prisoners, including Governor Cerruti, in reprisal for the blood this leader had shed. After incorporating the American prisoners into his division, Piar returned with it to Angostura and made another assault on the city on the morning of April 25. It was no more successful than the one on January 18.

After giving his orders to Piar and making a reconnaissance of the city of Angostura, Bolívar had recrossed the Orinoco on April 7 with the intention of bringing to Guayana the forces that were to be assembled in Aragua under Mariño and of making that province the base of his future operations. But when he reached El Pao, he received two equally bad bits of news—the defection of Mariño with part of the forces of his command[6] and the loss of Barcelona with all the horrors that accompanied it.

Colonel Juan Aldama, who had taken over Real's command, had decided to capture Bolívar before engaging in any other occupation, but when he learned that his prey had escaped him, he entered Barcelona without opposition on April 5. Two days later he took the forti-

---

[6] A native of the East, Mariño had no desire to serve under Bolívar. He believed that leadership in this theater belonged to him. —Ed.

fied convent of San Francisco and encouraged his soldiers to slaughter not only the garrison but all the men, women, and children who had sought refuge there. Such a horribly bloody scene has rarely been equalled and rarely surpassed, not even during this terrible war.

The defection of Mariño added to the trials and tribulations suffered by Bolívar as a result of the Barcelona disaster, but it was consoling for him to know that very few troops and no outstanding leader went with Mariño. In El Pao the Supreme Chief met Colonel Francisco de Paula Santander and Lieutenant Colonel Manuel Manrique, who gave him information concerning the province of Apure that was useful to him later in his dealings with General Páez. When he reached El Chaparro, he joined the troops led by Bermúdez and went on with them to the Orinoco. After suffering many hardships during the crossing, they joined Piar's division before Angostura on May 2.

After making a reconnaissance of the city, Bolívar decided to draw the siege closer and let hunger take its toll. His principal aim at that point was to control the Orinoco. Since the small fleet of *flecheras* to be brought by Brión had not appeared, General Arismendi was designated to rush the construction of *flecheras* in the department of the Caroní River. Bolívar went there himself toward the end of May to prepare operations against the forts of Guayana la Vieja. During this same period a commission sent by him to General Páez brought its mission to a happy conclusion when Páez decided to recognize the authority of the Supreme Chief.

While Bolívar was directing all his policy toward the conservation of the union and was succeeding in making it work in Guayana, the spirit of discord was arising in Maturín to frustrate his aims and complicate the difficulties of his position. Upon leaving his comrades in Aragua, Mariño went to Cariaco. From there, he came to an understanding with Canon Cortés Madariaga, who had just arrived in Margarita after escaping from Spain, where he had been sent as a prisoner by Monteverde. It would be difficult to find in any country two men better suited to stir up trouble. Mariño had Cortés come to Cariaco and brought together a few distinguished citizens, old patriots who allowed themselves to be deceived by his intrigues. At a meeting on May 8, 1817, it was agreed that those present should reassume immediately all the powers of the government. The executive power was to be exercised by Don Fernando de Toro, Don Francisco Javier Mayz, and General Bolívar. Mariño would command the army and Brión the navy. Asunción would be the provisional capital of the Republic. These were the resolutions of the Congress of Cariaco! After twelve days of rule in Asunción, the members of this government abandoned the island, for none of the people obeyed them and the announced invasion by Morillo frightened them. Thus ended this farce, which, though ridiculous, did do some harm, inasmuch as the pernicious example spread throughout the country.

When Bolívar received news of these happenings, he sent Generals Rojas and Tomás Montilla to Cariaco to notify the instigators that he did not recognize the meeting of the miniature congress or its decrees. He was at the Missions, busy with the arrangement of the administration of the country and with the development and discipline of the army units. It was he who was the organizing genius in all the country's conflicts. Meanwhile, Mariño persisted in his defection, but he had only some six hundred undisciplined troops. General Urdaneta, Colonel Antonio José de Sucre, and many other leaders who had previously obeyed him left his headquarters and went to Guayana to place themselves under Bolívar's orders.

In these circumstances, Piar, who was dissatisfied with his secondary role after having arbitrarily exercised complete authority for so long, began to show his displeasure. A native of Curaçao, he had embraced a military career soon after the revolution broke out, and he had served in the East under General Mariño, distinguishing himself by his personal courage. But his restless and unruly spirit was always very much in evidence. When Bolívar entrusted the organization of the Missions to Reverend José Félix Blanco, Piar pretended to see an insult to his rank in this appointment. Bolívar removed Blanco from his post in order not to wound Piar's vanity, but nothing could satisfy Piar. After obtaining permission to leave the country, he devoted himself to plotting Bolívar's destruction. Aware of his intrigues, Bolívar tried to bring him back to the path of reason by writing him friendly letters couched in conciliatory terms.

Referring to his own origin, which he had through vanity tried to hide until then, Piar made friendly gestures toward the colored people for the first time.[7] Then he moved to Bermúdez's headquarters near Angostura, where he continued with his machinations. Fortunately, everyone recognized the real reason for his antipathy, and he did not find followers anywhere. It was feared, however, that he might succeed in corrupting the troops, some of whom were accustomed to obeying him. To forestall this great evil, which might cause a slave or race war, Bolívar isued an order for his arrest. No sooner had the order been communicated to Piar than he left Angostura and, adding desertion to his crimes against the state, fled toward the eastern provinces. Bolívar sent General Cedeño after him, with orders to take him to Angostura to be court-martialed.

While this was going on, military operations continued in their course. A flotilla capable of opposing the enemy's had already been launched successfully on the Orinoco, and Brión had just appeared with eight ships, some of which were brigs and some schooners, and five well-armed and well-manned *flecheras*. The cities of Angostura and Guayana la Vieja were reduced to dire straits. Bolívar had his headquarters three leagues away from the latter city on a sugar plantation called Casacoima, which is about a league away from the Orinoco on one of its branches. On July 4 he and the members of his general staff came close to losing their lives or being captured after they had heard cannon shots being fired at some patriot *flecheras* and had gone to the river to find out what had happened. Cut off from their only exit by some men from enemy gunboats who had landed up the river, the Liberator and his companions were able to save themselves by plunging into the flood waters from the Orinoco and making their way toward their house, a quarter of a league away.

Having exhausted all his provisions and suffered the effects of hunger and disease, La Torre evacuated the city of Angostura on July 17. General Bermúdez occupied the city the following day. The fall of the city of Guayana la Vieja occurred on August 3. Several ships of the convoy led by La Torre fell into Brión's hands, along with much war matériel and considerable plunder.

[7] Piar's father was a native Spaniard from the Canary Islands, his mother a mulatto from Curaçao.—Ed.

Now master of Guayana, Bolívar believed that the independence of his country was assured. The possession of that province opened communications to the whole interior of Venezuela by way of the Orinoco and its large tributaries. It also gave him a port where foreign goods could be received and means for the development of trade. The conquest of Guayana was equally advantageous to him abroad, for the importance of this province had always been exaggerated on account of the old legends and the memory of El Dorado. Bolívar was able to make use of these advantages and thereby increase his resources. All the branches of the administration received the impetus needed for their development.

CHAPTER NINE

L ET US NOW CONSIDER the operations of Morillo, whom we left in
Santa Fe about the middle of the previous year. Having reduced
the provinces of New Granada to the yoke of the King, he re-entered
Venezuelan territory in January, 1817. He was not completely aware
of the progress of the insurrection. General La Torre, who had preceded him, met an unexpected enemy on January 28, when thirteen
hundred *llaneros* under General Páez appeared at Mucuritas to engage him in battle. After defeating La Torre's cavalry, Páez set fire to
the grass, thus forcing the royalist infantry to break ranks. The dense
clouds of smoke enabled La Torre to retreat with the infantry to the
tree cover along the banks of the Apure, and he was able to join
General Morillo soon afterward. When they reached San Fernando,
Morillo received more detailed information about the growth of the

insurrection and about the agitation among the people caused by the arbitrary behavior of some of his lieutenants. Although his position was not at all promising, he knew that the superiority of his army and the material resources at his command gave him great advantages over his opponents.

While in San Fernando, Morillo decided to head an expedition against Margarita, assigning La Torre to the defense of Guayana. This decision to concede more importance to Margarita was a great mistake, motivated principally by the hatred Morillo professed for Arismendi. After fortifying San Fernando and taking measures to ensure the safety of the province of Barinas and the llanos of Caracas, Morillo left for the province of Barcelona to take command of Aldama's division. At about this time the expedition of 2,600 men under General Don José Canterac had arrived off the coast of Cumaná from the Peninsula. Once in the city of Barcelona, Morillo sailed to Cumaná and immediately dispatched forces against Cariaco, Cumanacoa, and Carúpano under the orders of Commander Francisco Jiménez, who was able to take these towns easily because of the dissension among the patriots. Following this success, Morillo sent this column against Güiria and put garrisons in the cities and towns occupied by the royalists on the east coast. This done, he set sail from Cumaná for Margarita with the divisions of Canterac and Aldama, which amounted to 3,000 men. The convoy reached the port of Guamacho on July 14, 1817.

From the beginning Morillo encountered a resistance he was far from expecting. The royalists suffered heavy losses in their first clash with the patriots. When Morillo offered to forget the past if the inhabitants submitted and threatened them with extermination if they did not, Colonel Francisco Esteban Gómez, the commander of the patriot forces, rejected his offers and scorned his threats. Gómez pulled his main force back toward the interior but left small bands to harass the royalists on the way. Morillo occupied Porlamar and Pampatar, but he suffered heavy losses both on the march and in camp. Convinced that he needed more troops, he wrote to the continent for reinforcements. His attack on Asunción, the capital, which is located at the center of the island in rough terrain, was repulsed, and he was forced to withdraw to Pampatar. Turning next to the port of Juan Griego at the northern end of the island, he was able to take it on August 8 after a bitter struggle in which the royalists paid dearly. He tells us himself that the people of Margarita "were endowed with superhuman bravery, possessed of the strength of giants."

When Morillo received news of Bolívar's complete subjugation of Guayana and of the threat to the province of Caracas, he had a specious pretext for abandoning the island, of whose complete reduction he already had reason to despair. While busy with the evacuation, he did not fail to leave traces of the rage that had seized him as a result of the discredit brought on his army. The territory was laid waste, the means of subsistence were destroyed, and blood was shed needlessly. He abandoned the island on August 17, 1817, and arrived in Caracas at the beginning of September. When he issued an amnesty in honor of the marriage of Ferdinand and Isabel de Braganza, the Venezuelans once more scorned his false promises. In justification of Morillo, however, if such behavior can be justified, we should not forget that he was acting in accordance with the orders of his sovereign. After provisioning the army and mobilizing the various operational units, he moved on to Calabozo and established his headquarters there. Then he decided to take some of his troops and move along the north bank of the Apure, with the hope of finding Páez and preventing him from joining Bolívar, whom he supposed to be coming up the Orinoco for this purpose.

Once the province of Guayana was completely liberated, Bolívar was confronted with an administrative chaos. The vast territory required a progressive administration if some advantage was to be gained from it. It was also necessary to organize the army and establish order and discipline. But what was most imperative was to put an end to the arbitrary behavior of the division leaders.

The right of reprisal would have permitted the complete confiscation of the possessions of the wealthy people of Angostura who had emigrated with La Torre, but the decree that Bolívar issued on September 3 favored the rights of the wives and dependent children of the royalist émigrés. Only the third and fifth parts of what the fathers could assign in their wills were to be liable to confiscation. This measure was indeed harsh, but the state of the treasury made it indispensable. Although it is true that the nation profited little from the confiscations, Bolívar should not be blamed, for he had only the public welfare in mind when he promulgated the decree.

One of Bolívar's first concerns was also the creation of courts for the administration of justice with sufficient independence and freedom. At the same time he established municipal government in Guayana. Since the soldiers had hitherto served without pay and without any incentive other than glory, he ordered that some national property be divided among them according to their rank and services. Spiritual needs likewise merited special consideration. Since the death of the bishop of Guayana had left the diocese without a head, Bolívar convoked the ecclesiastical chapter to appoint a vicar-general.

Having made these and other provisions required by the urgent needs of the country, he created a Council of State to draw up the government regulations most urgently needed in the various branches of the administration. This council was composed of high-ranking civil and military authorities. Although the council's functions were limited and purely advisory, the whole country welcomed its creation. It inspired confidence in those who had emigrated from the country since 1815 to escape royalist persecution. Confident of security and guarantees in their native land, they hastily returned to Angostura.

I have already told the story of how Piar, his designs thwarted, fled from Angostura upon learning of the order for his arrest and went to the province of Cumaná. Convinced that further toleration of abuses on the part of the leaders would lead to the destruction of the country, Bolívar decided to test the stability of his government. He therefore sent General Cedeño with a cavalry escort in pursuit of Piar, who now had under his command some troops in Maturín who, unaware of his desertion, had consented to obey him. After he explained to the troops the object of his mission and they expressed their willingness to obey the Supreme Chief, General Cedeño was able to arrest Piar, despite his refusal to submit. After being taken to Angostura, Piar was immediately tried as a deserter, a rebel, and a traitor before a court-martial, which, after a careful observance of all the proper legal procedures, unanimously condemned him to death. Despite the warnings of those who feared a military insurrection, Bolívar approved the sentence and signed it, for he realized that the welfare of the Republic depended to a great extent on the resolution of the existing crisis. The sentence was carried out on October 16, 1817, and Piar died very bravely. It is likely that he believed right up to the time of his death that Bolívar would not dare to have him shot. Some leaders regretted his sad end but recognized the justice of the sentence. Everyone reproved his behavior after reviewing his life.

Bolívar's firmness assured the future of the Republic. The proclamation with which he announced this event is an eloquent monument of tender sentiments, good judgment, and moral values. After speaking of the important services that General Piar had rendered to the Republic and of the high position that would have been entrusted to him, the Liberator went on to state that Piar had been planning on a civil war that would inevitably have brought about a state of anarchy and the sacrifice of his own comrades and brothers—in effect, opening the grave of the Republic with his own hands. This could not be tolerated. Bolívar's final words touched on the confidence that the soldiers should have in him as their leader and comrade-in-arms. General Mariño undoubtedly deserved the same fate as Piar, except that he was less dangerous, and a single example was enough.

Neither Mariño's defection nor Piar's trial distracted Bolívar from the important business of the war. On September 25 he sent Bermúdez to the province of Cumaná with the order to form cavalry and infantry units. The fact that he conferred the government and commandancy general of that province upon a man who had done him so much harm does great honor to Bermúdez and also reveals the generosity of Bolívar. Monagas was sent to Barcelona with instructions to gather troops and harass the royalists, and General Zaraza was to form another unit in the regions of Chaguaramas and San Diego de Cabrutica. General Páez, who was defending the Apure line, was to hold himself ready to join his forces with those of Bolívar, who was planning to go up the Orinoco as far as the Pao River, meet Monagas and his cavalry, and then join forces with Zaraza's brigade in order to operate against Morillo in conjunction with Páez. The scarcity of rifles and ammunition did not daunt the patriots, for the infantrymen armed themselves with arrows and lances. The cavalry soldier rarely carried any weapon other than the lance.

Before leaving Angostura, Bolívar appointed a Council of Government and delegated to it part of his authority for the conduct of business during his absence. He also installed the Council of State that I have already mentioned. In the course of his address to the nineteen members, he spoke of the functions of the Council of State as a legislative body with limited power and of the appointment of a Council of Government as a central authority for foreign affairs and as the provisional executive power in case of the death of the supreme chief. After the installation of the latter body, which was headed by Brión, Cedeño, and Zea, Bolívar departed for Zaraza's headquarters on November 21.

After being joined by the brigade under General Pedro León Torres, Zaraza fell back, in accordance with the Liberator's orders, when he learned that La Torre was coming after him and was already near. On November 22 Colonel Julián Montes de Oca arrived to notify him of the approach of the Supreme Chief and to order him to withdraw slowly in the direction of Santa María de Ipire. Either because of an involuntary error or because of a desire to win a victory by himself, Zaraza deviated from the route assigned to him and ran into the royalist division at the ranch of La Hogaza. In a battle there on December 2, 1817, the patriot infantry was almost completely wiped out after being abandoned by the cavalry, which had been outflanked. The losses in men and ordnance supplies were considerable, much greater than those of the royalists.

Even though this disaster upset all of Bolívar's plans, he was far from being disheartened. After dispatching officers from San Diego de Cabrutica to round up the scattered elements, he left the command of his troops to General Pedro León Torres and went down the Orinoco back to Angostura. He found the city in an alarming state of confusion, and it cost no little effort to calm the panic-stricken inhabitants. Redoubling his activity and ably aided by his subordinates, Bolívar formed and equipped a new expeditionary force in less than three weeks. Though poorly armed and hardly trained at all, it had the advantage

of being commanded by veteran leaders and officers who were enthusiastic about the cause they supported. Before starting out, Bolívar
informed his lieutenants of his new campaign plan and gave each one
of them detailed instructions. Bermúdez was to head the troops that
Mariño, apparently repentant and ready to obey again, had placed at
the disposal of the government, to add to them by new levies, and to
harass the enemy on the coasts of Güiria and Cumaná. Meanwhile,
Zaraza was to form a cavalry unit in the province of Barcelona in order
to threaten the province of Caracas and divert Morillo's attention in
that direction. Páez, who was then outside San Fernando de Apure,
an important but poorly fortified stronghold in the possession of the
Spaniards, received orders to have his division ready to begin operations but to avoid all serious contact with the enemy.

Leaving Angostura on December 31, Bolívar joined forces with
the division of General Monagas at the mouth of the Pao River. While
the troops crossed the Orinoco and continued overland toward Caicara,
Bolívar and his general staff continued by water toward the same
point. Joined by Cedeño in Caicara, he marched to La Urbana, where
the whole army crossed the Orinoco on January 22–24, 1818. Concluding a laborious march of three hundred leagues, with many river
crossings, he and his men joined forces with the Apure troops on the
last day of the month. The Apure leader, José Antonio Páez, had
presented himself to Bolívar the previous evening at the ranch of
Cañafístolo. The force led by Bolívar amounted to nearly 3,000 men,
of whom 2,000 were infantry. The cavalry was armed with lances,
and only 1,400 of the infantry had rifles, the rest having bows and
arrows. The division of General Páez consisted of 1,000 horse and
250 foot soldiers.

Bolívar and Páez saw each other for the first time at Cañafístolo. It
will not be amiss to make a brief sketch of this distinguished commander who will occupy henceforth a prominent place in these memoirs. General José Antonio Páez, then about thirty years old, was a
powerfully built brown-haired man of medium height with a tapering
waistline. The expression of his lively dark eyes indicated a cautious
person who was not very trusting. In the presence of educated people
he was reticent and even timid, but among his inferiors he was loqua-

cious and fond of telling rough jokes. His complete lack of education left him unacquainted with even the most elementary technical terms of the military art, but he never would have become an expert commander anyway, for the slightest contradiction or emotional stress, even in battle, would throw him into violent convulsions that were followed by physical weakness and depression. On the other hand, he had no equal as a fearless and resourceful guerrilla leader. Though not cruel, he was careless of human life, sometimes shedding blood needlessly. He was ambitious for power, for absolute power, the power to abuse and to satisfy his whims. This ambition and covetousness were his dominant passions. He succeeded in acquiring extraordinary influence over the *llaneros,* who made up his army. Lax in military discipline, he tolerated their fondness for plunder. Such was the Apure leader.

After spending four days in San Juan de Payara, Bolívar began the march with the army. When they reached the banks of the Apure, the squadron had not yet arrived, despite the instructions given to it, and there were no other vessels available for the troop crossing. This lack was soon remedied by Colonel Francisco Aramendi and fifty of the Húsares de Apure, who plunged into the water, riding bareback, seized an enemy gunboat and three unarmed boats on the opposite side, and brought them back. While the troops were crossing the Apure, Bolívar sent an envoy to Colonel Quero of the San Fernando garrison, offering him an honorable capitulation. The valiant colonel rejected this offer and a stronger ultimatum, replying in few words that he was determined to do his duty. Since Bolívar knew that the stronghold would have to surrender shortly, he allowed it to await its fate and marched on Calabozo in the hope of surprising Morillo, who, according to his spies, had fortified himself in that city with better than two thousand men. After surprising some royalist detachments and capturing an outpost, Bolívar and his army took up a position before Calabozo, which is located between the Guárico and Orituco rivers in the midst of an extensive savanna.

Morillo, who had thought that Bolívar was still in Guayana lamenting the defeat suffered at La Hogaza, hurried at once to Calabozo when he learned of the approach of the patriot forces. Having arrived there on February 10, 1818, he was making ready to help defend it when he himself was surprised at his headquarters on February 12. Remaining calm, he quickly made his plans and prepared to face the danger. His aim was evidently to save his outlying units by having them move toward the city at the moment of the appearance of the patriot army, which, in its turn, was maneuvering to cut them off. The patriots put to flight a body of Spanish hussars who came out to their left and overwhelmed two companies of the La Unión Regiment, which tried to cover the retreat. Morillo, who had hurried in person to direct this operation, owed his life only to the speed of his horse. The Castilla Battalion was more successful, for it was able to take refuge in the city with few losses. As soon as it did so, Morillo shut himself up in the city with the rest of the infantry, leaving three hundred dead on the field. The patriots did not lose more than thirty men between dead and wounded. Generals Cedeño, Monagas, and Páez distinguished themselves by their fearlessness and the success with which they led their respective columns in the struggle. Calabozo was the first battlefield on which Bolívar and Morillo met.

On the following morning Bolívar sent Major Silvestre Palacios to the Spanish leader with a note and the prisoners taken the day before. In this note Bolívar once more proposed the termination of the war to the death and pointed to the return of all prisoners as evidence of his generosity. He urged Morillo to take advantage of the mercy of the patriots at this moment when he was pinned down in Calabozo. Morillo did not answer this note.

Since there was no pasture land nearby for the horses, Bolívar marched at noon on the thirteenth to El Rastro, a small town three leagues north of Calabozo, leaving a regiment of hussars under the command of Colonel Guillermo Iribarren to watch the city. The following night Morillo decided to abandon the city and go by way of La Uriosa to the west bank of the Guárico River, seeking to reach El Sombrero twenty leagues away on the Caracas road. It was a daring project that never could have been carried out without cavalry, which he lacked, if Colonel Iribarren had done his duty and watched his movements carefully. This was not the only case of carelessness on the part of the cavalry leaders in this campaign or in the previous ones. Their lack of discipline and their fondness for plunder frequently made their cooperation of dubious value and always proved very embarrassing to their general in chief.

When Iribarren discovered on the following morning that the city had been abandoned by Morillo and a large part of the population, which was royalist in sympathy, he reported the event to headquarters without ascertaining the route taken by the enemy. This negligence led Bolívar to return to Calabozo instead of taking the crossroad to La Uriosa, where he could have arrived at the same time as the royalists. He immediately started in pursuit of the enemy. The advance patrol of the cavalry overtook the enemy in the afternoon, but Morillo continued his withdrawal without paying any attention to the large number of stragglers being taken prisoner. The following morning he took up positions near the town of El Sombrero, and his forces offered vigorous resistance when attacked by the patriot infantry, which was by now almost completely exhausted. Continuing the withdrawal after nightfall, Morillo finally gave the army a day of rest on the twenty-first in San Sebastián de los Reyes, after he had reinforced it with units brought by La Torre and Aldama. Leaving a strong garrison in Villa de Cura under General La Torre and placing others in various towns of the Valles de Aragua, Morillo went with the rest of the army to Valencia to await the arrival of the division that was operating around Barinas under the command of Calzada. From Calabozo to the seventeenth his army suffered eight hundred casualties, while Bolívar's losses consisted of a hundred casualties in the action at El Sombrero.

If Bolívar's march from Angostura and his surprise attack on Morillo constituted, in the opinion of a Spanish historian who has consulted only hostile accounts, "a most brilliant enterprise," it cannot be denied that Morillo deserves the highest praise for his difficult retreat. The rapidity of Bolívar's movements in the pursuit is also worthy of admiration. Leaving to the chronicler of military events the decision as to the relative merits of both chiefs, I claim the vote of the philosophical historian in favor of the republican, who paused in the moment of victory to end the atrocities that dishonored the war being waged. He himself set the example when he renounced the right of reprisal and returned the prisoners. And one of his first concerns immediately after the occupation of El Sombrero on the morning of the seventeenth was to order the leaders who were operating away from headquarters to show respect for the lives of the prisoners. In an official letter to Colonel Antonio Rangel he said: "Humane considerations have led me to suspend the declaration of the war to the death."

After the action at El Sombrero, Bolívar sent ahead a squad of cavalry to harass the enemy; but he desisted from an active pursuit because the cavalry could not be used effectively in the mountainous country where Morillo had taken refuge and the infantry was badly spent after the long march across the sun-scorched plains. On February 18, Cedeño and Páez countermarched to Calabozo with most of the cavalry in order to remount it. Two paths were open to Bolívar: to return to Calabozo or to advance as far as Ortiz on the edge of enemy territory. He was very much in favor of this second course of action because the Ortiz position offered many advantages for military operations against the Valles de Aragua, San Carlos, or Valencia. But since Cedeño and Páez raised so many objections to this plan, he had to yield and decided to countermarch, after he had proceeded as far as the Corozal ranch. Páez then proposed to return with his division to press the siege of San Fernando, which was completely unnecessary because the stronghold was on the point of surrendering or being abandoned. Bolívar had to consent to this, however, because the Apure troops were a contingent from a confederate state rather than a division of his army, and they wanted to return to their homes.

Accustomed to exercising his despotic will and opposed to any subordination, Páez would not bow before an authority that he had so recently recognized. Bolívar, on the other hand, was too wise and diplomatic to arouse the violent and impetuous feelings of Páez. According to General Briceño Méndez, Bolívar yielded because his authority at that time had no guarantee or basis other than the will of each main commander of his army. In no way did Bolívar show his genius and diplomacy so much as in maintaining union and not compromising his authority. His singular behavior in this respect is the greatest encomium that can be given to his ability and talent.

After securing subsistence for the troops and issuing orders for Zaraza to join the army without delay, Bolívar went to the towns of

Guardatinajas and San José de los Tiznados with the object of pacifying that district, raising a corps of cavalry, and obtaining definite information about the movements of the royalist division of Calzada. The great lack of rifles prevented the building up of the infantry, which had lost a great many men as a result of the casualties suffered during the campaign, the departure of the Apure Battalion for San Fernando, and continual desertions. So great was this latter evil, which was not limited solely to the infantrymen, that the complete dissolution of the little army was feared. This consideration more than any other led Bolívar to recommence his operations in enemy territory. He believed that it was better to perish in the glory of combat than to come to an ignominious end while inactive. This decision was strengthened by the reports from the spies about the enemy's movements. Before marching, however, he wrote to General Páez, recommending the greatest speed in his operations and his prompt return to the army. "We shall not," he said, "obtain a decisive advantage until we are all together working as a single unit."

The soldiers should not be blamed for their desertion. The war had no attraction for them, for they had scarcely any clothes, they received no pay, and they were poorly fed. Though the generals and the officers also lacked comforts, this did not enter into the calculations of the soldiers, nor did it remedy their situation. During operations there was hope of improving their lot, but none when they were in quarters.

M OVING OUT ON MARCH 3, 1818, the army reached the ranch of
San Pablo two days later. On the way it was joined by General
Monagas with a brigade of cavalry. Bolívar assembled a council of
generals in order to determine their opinions concerning future operations. Some, like Urdaneta, were of the opinion that they should gain
complete and secure possession of all of the llanos, thus being able to
count on all the *llaneros*, who, as was known from experience, served
only those who were masters of the llanos. Others, like Cedeño, were
of the opinion that they should advance to the Valles de Aragua, and
this opinion prevailed.

Taking the best and most direct route to the Valles de Aragua, the
patriot army occupied Villa de Cura and then went on to take Maracay,
La Victoria, and other towns to the north of the lake. Bolívar set out

with the infantry to attack La Torre, but, while he was preparing to do so, he learned from intercepted messages that the royalist army had already moved toward him with three divisions from both sides of the lake. Fortunately, the weak resistance that Monagas was able to offer with his cavalry and the Angostura Battalion checked Morales, the leader of the enemy advance guard, and covered the retreat ordered by Bolívar.

Continuing the withdrawal and marching with little rest, the army fell back until Bolívar ordered it to take up positions in the valley of Semen, which was named after the brook flowing through it. There, on March 16, 1818, the royalists repeatedly attacked the patriot forces, but the latter maintained their positions and repulsed the attacks. Bolívar, accompanied by Monagas and a small cavalry escort, personally directed the movements, traversing the entire line and taking command at all points threatened by the enemy. The outcome was doubtful until Colonel Genaro Vásquez and some squadrons of cavalry received orders to dismount and charge the enemy column with their lances. They charged with such daring that the enemy column became disorganized and took to flight. Enemy dragoons held in reserve checked the pursuit by the patriots momentarily, but the rout became general after they were charged by Monagas' cavalry. The fleeing royalists and the pursuing patriots came upon a Spanish division, which arrived at that moment from Villa de Cura to snatch from Bolívar the victory won at so great a cost. Bolívar and his officers had to retreat after attempting to assemble the scattered elements in spite of the cowardly flight of the cavalry. During the pursuit Morillo was wounded by a patriot trooper's lance. Correa assumed command and continued the pursuit as far as San Juan de los Morros, where he halted and remained for two days until La Torre replaced him.

Both sides suffered heavy losses in this bloody conflict. Bolívar lost almost all his infantry and war matériel, and his papers and those of the general staff fell into the hands of the victor.[1] Among the wounded were Generals Urdaneta, Valdés, Torres, and Anzoátegui. Despite the reinforcements that reached them so opportunely on the battlefield,

---

[1] Many of these papers were given to General O'Leary by Morillo in La Coruña in 1835.—Simón B. O'Leary.

the Spaniards could not prevent Bolívar from reorganizing his forces. The perseverance and activity of this renowned chief grew in the face of adversity and commanded the respect of the enemy. Withdrawing by way of Ortiz and El Rastro, he arrived in Calabozo on March 20 with what was left of his army. Leaving it there in camp, he set out with his staff and a cavalry escort to join Cedeño and Páez. Páez had occupied San Fernando and had also forced the surrender of the fleeing garrison, which after a heroic defense had abandoned the stronghold.

Meanwhile, General La Torre was marching with most of his forces along Bolívar's route. After being joined by Colonel Rafael López, he went on until he was only a short distance away from Calabozo, but he ordered a rapid countermarch to Ortiz when he learned that Bolívar had been joined by Cedeño and Páez and was marching to meet him. Believing that he was beyond the reach of Bolívar, whom he supposed to be tired from the campaign and discouraged by his reverses, he sent López toward El Pao and had other units march to the Valles de Aragua.

After Páez and Bolívar met in San Pablo and the latter was informed of the approach of La Torre, he started out without losing a moment. He would have surprised the enemy had La Torre not received a warning from Calabozo about the army's movement. On March 24, Bolívar marched on Ortiz to attack the enemy, who occupied strong positions near the town with 1,500 infantry and 150 horse. Since the patriot infantry was decidedly inferior in numbers and discipline, his efforts to dislodge the enemy proved futile, and he had to fall back to the ranch of San Pablo after a struggle lasting six hours. La Torre, on his part, hurriedly returned to the Valles de Aragua, abandoning his wounded and prisoners.

Bolívar remained in San Pablo until March 29, taking steps to augment the infantry and destroy the guerrilla bands that were devastating the area. He sent General Soublette to Guayana to obtain arms and ammunition and send them to headquarters, for the lack of these was not only paralyzing operations but had also prevented the pursuit of La Torre. When he arrived in San José de los Tiznados on March 30, he learned that the enemy was assembling a large body of troops in

El Pao. To prevent this, Bolívar ordered General Páez to march there immediately. Though it was his intention to carry the fight to that region, he had to put aside his plan in order to attend first to the organization of the llanos of Caracas. Upon his arrival in Calabozo he sent out officers to enforce martial law in the towns of the department and dispatched others to destroy the enemy guerrilla bands and bandits. The latter leaders won temporary advantage over the factions they encountered, but they did not succeed in exterminating them. Bolívar marched from Calabozo to El Rastro and then went on to San José de los Tiznados, where he remained until April 16, assembling the various detached squads. He sent General Cedeño with a column of cavalry to protect the operations of Colonel Ambrosio Plaza, for he supposed that Colonel Rafael López must be nearby.

On April 16, Bolívar stopped at the ranch called El Rincón de los Toros, a league and a half from San José. Colonel López, who was moving upon this town with the aim of surprising him, forced a captured soldier, who turned out to be the assistant of Father Prado, Bolívar's chaplain, to reveal the size and location of the patriot forces and the place where Bolívar and his staff were sleeping without a guard. Shortly afterward a sergeant who had just deserted told López the countersign. Captain Don Tomás Renovales volunteered to go with eight chasseurs from Burgos Battalion and try to capture Bolívar. Proceeding cautiously and in complete silence, he came across Colonel Santander and answered correctly Santander's "Who goes there?" When Santander heard that it was "a patrol looking for the Supreme Chief," he called Bolívar, who had fallen asleep despite his presentiment of danger. Upon hearing his name, Bolívar jumped from his hammock and, as though guided by instinct, went over to his horse, which was saddled and close at hand. He was about to mount when a volley was fired at the hammocks by the chasseurs. The volley wounded the horse and killed the chaplain and Colonels Galindo and Salcedo.

Starting at once for the camp, Bolívar moved away from the area, without a hat or jacket, when he encountered some fleeing soldiers, for he assumed that all was lost. López had led his cavalry in an attack on Zaraza, who, caught by surprise, took to flight with his men after receiving word of Bolívar's death. His flight with his men threw the infantry into confusion. Bolívar had not gone far when he came across the troops and some other leaders. Commander Fernando Serrano refused him his horse and would not even allow him to mount behind him, but a trooper later offered him his unsaddled mule. As Bolívar approached the mule, he received a kick that slightly damaged his leg. At this point Commander Leonardo Infante rode up on the horse of the enemy leader, who had been killed in the struggle. Dismounting, he insisted that Bolívar should accept it and save himself.

Almost all of the patriot infantry with Bolívar at El Rincón de los Toros perished, as did Commander Silvestre Palacios. Other outstanding officers fell into the hands of the enemy and were shot later, as will appear farther on. Accompanied by the dispersed troops he had overtaken on the road, Bolívar reached Calabozo on April 17. Ever active and persevering, and even more so after meeting with reverses, he decided to take over the leadership of the division led by Páez that was attacking San Carlos. He and his general staff arrived in Guadarrama on the twenty-fourth, but then he went to San Fernando because he had not received news from Páez. Immediately afterward he started out with infantry and cavalry reinforcements for the division led by Cedeño, whom he had put in charge of the defense of the llanos, which were again threatened by General Morales. But his robust constitution had finally reached the breaking point after so many hardships, so much watchfulness, and so much mental and physical effort. In the town of Camaguán, while marching to Calabozo, he was overcome by extreme weakness and fever, which obliged him to return to San Fernando on May 3.

Since the division under Real had fallen back to Valencia when threatened in El Pao by the movement of General Páez, Morillo sent General La Torre with all the troops he had at hand to reinforce him and ordered General Correa to join him on the way to El Pao. They joined forces in San Carlos on April 30. The royalist army amounted to more than three thousand men, infantry for the most part. On May 2, General Páez appeared on the llano of Cojedes, some leagues to the west of San Carlos, with a smaller force that was strong in cavalry but inferior to the enemy in infantry. His advance patrol lured the enemy to the plain that he had selected beforehand as a field on which his

horsemen could match the renowned Spanish infantry. The bloodiest battle of that terrible campaign was fought there, with great losses on both sides, though both sides claimed victory. Páez lost almost all his infantry, which, commanded by Anzoátegui, fought, as always, with admirable courage. He had to return to Apure to reorganize, but the enemy did not dare to follow him. Withdrawing slowly, he entered San Fernando on May 21. Many of La Torre's officers were wounded or killed, and he turned his command over to Correa when he himself was wounded.

Elated over the outcome of El Rincón de los Toros, Morillo ordered Morales to march with the troops he had organized and occupy the llanos as far as Calabozo. With this force he occupied Calabozo, and on May 20 he attacked Cedeño at El Cerrito de los Patos, to which the latter had withdrawn after evacuating the stronghold. Cedeño's small infantry force was smashed after a heroic resistance that was not supported by his numerous cavalry, which had fled in cowardly disorder. The remnants of the division then recrossed the Apure. Cedeño should have avoided this encounter, because Bolívar had dispatched Captain Aldao with messages ordering him to withdraw to San Fernando.

Thus ended the campaign of 1818 in this part of Venezuela, with more honor for the patriots than for their opponents, who once more occupied their old positions. Now recovered from his wound, Morillo devoted himself to repairing his losses, making new levies, and organizing the recruits. I have already made mention of the note in which Bolívar proposed to Morillo the regularization of the war. The latter considered it an insult, though he did, when wounded, order General Correa to respect the lives of the prisoners taken in the battle of Semen. Scarcely had Morillo recovered his health when he once more resorted to cruel warfare, even though he had authentic proof of Bolívar's generosity in the papers taken at Semen, which contained orders to leaders operating away from headquarters. Despite such unequivocal testimony of the good will of his opponent, Morillo committed the barbarous act of shooting prisoners taken in the campaign. This atrocious provocation did not, however, lead Bolívar to vary his conduct.

In the meantime, the dissension of Mariño and the lack of resources had paralyzed the operations that Bermúdez was assigned to direct in the East. After entering Maturín on April 26, Bermúdez wrote to General Mariño, inviting him to join him. Though Mariño refused to obey the government, he offered to cooperate against the common enemy, and it was agreed that he would move on Cariaco while Bermúdez attacked Cumaná. But this division of command, which weakened both bodies of troops, was fatal to the outcome of the campaign. On May 10, Mariño occupied Cariaco, and at Cautaro on the twenty-fourth he defeated a column that was trying to harass Bermúdez's rearguard. Bermúdez unsuccessfully attacked the bridgehead protecting the entrance to Cumaná. On May 30 the enemy sallied forth from the city, attacked Bermúdez in his positions at the port of La Madera, and routed him completely after a stand that cost the aggressors dearly. He withdrew with the scattered elements to Cumanacoa and from there to Angostura, while Mariño was obliged to fall back to Maturín.

Bolívar arrived in Angostura on June 5, 1818, and immediately devoted himself to reforming the administration in order to correct the imperfections to which it was subject and to protect industry. Though busy with civil affairs, he still found time to attend to the very important business of the war and to the prompt repair of the army losses in the last campaign. A brighter future loomed at last. Arms and ammunition were beginning to arrive from England, where misfortune always arouses sympathy, and some skeleton units were also coming from there, despite the prohibition contained in the Prince Regent's proclamation of November 27, 1817.[2] The government of the United States, which had hitherto regarded the sufferings of the South Americans with cool and aloof indifference, also showed signs of growing interest in their cause.

In view of these resources and this promising outlook, Bolívar broadened his plans. He decided to take advantage of the favorable circumstances by undertaking the liberation of New Granada, thus depriving Morillo of the abundant resources he was obtaining from that area. After serious deliberation he decided to send Francisco de Paula Santander to take command of the guerrilla bands that were scattered

---

[2] British subjects were forbidden to take part in the disputes between the king of Spain and the persons who exercised authority in certain provinces of America. —Ed.

throughout Casanare and to form a sizable division in that province. A native of New Granada who started his military career in the early days of the revolution and who had already been promoted to brigadier general, Santander was the most competent of all the Granadines at headquarters to fill the post. An excellent judge of men, Bolívar did not make a mistake in his choice. After being provided with arms and ammunition, Santander left for Casanare on August 26 with some officers, most of whom were Granadines. He carried with him a proclamation to the Granadines in which Bolívar told them that Spain was approaching her end and that Venezuela was marching to free them, aided by war-hardened foreigners. His final words were a prophecy that was to come true very soon: "The sun will not have completed the course of its present cycle without beholding in all your territory the proud altars of liberty."

Bolívar was then giving thought to a political measure of the greatest importance—the convocation of a congress. Though realizing that the time for successful deliberations had not arrived, he knew that the measure would serve to throw the common enemy off balance and to disarm rivals who detested him personally, even though they pretended to fear his power. Fernando Peñalver, a friend who enjoyed his unlimited confidence, urged him to put the idea into practice before he started the campaign he planned to undertake. To obviate the many difficulties standing in the way, it was decided that elections should be held in the free parishes and in the army divisions and that five deputies should be elected for each province, whether free or partly dependent on the army. There would also be five for Casanare, even though this province was Granadine territory. The decree convoking the congress for the next January 1 was published September 24 on this basis, and the heads of the provinces and of the divisions were ordered to enforce it.

Meanwhile, recruiting was being rushed, and preparations were being made for the campaign. The occupation of Güiria on the Gulf of Paria by General Bermúdez, with the cooperation of Admiral Brión, contributed to the campaign plan that Bolívar had conceived at that time. His intention was to assemble an army corps in the East and lead an attack on the whole eastern coast that would be coordinated with the operations of Cedeño and Páez. This plan was too complicated to be carried out in such a vast country lacking resources and means of communication.

Having determined, nevertheless, to make the plan work, Bolívar crossed the Orinoco on October 24 and headed for Cumaná. The lack of harmony between the division chiefs and their rash haste upset his plans. An attempted surprise attack on Río Caribe by Bermúdez proved to be disastrous. Then, on November 3, while on his way to Mariño's headquarters, Bolívar learned that the latter, contrary to his orders, had left to attack Cariaco and had been repulsed with great losses. Mariño had already been fully pardoned and had become reconciled to the government. As in the previous year and for like reasons, Bolívar now saw his plans disrupted at the very moment when everything was ready for their execution. He immediately returned to Maturín, conferred there with Mariño, appointed Bermúdez to the command of the troops that were to operate in the province of Cumaná in conjunction with Admiral Brión's fleet, and, finally, ordered these forces to raid the coast and draw the attention of the enemy in that direction. Mariño was assigned to the province of Barcelona to cover Angostura in case the royalists should attempt to fall on it suddenly. Once these provisions were made, Bolívar started for Angostura, where he arrived on November 11.

The mediation requested by Ferdinand VII of the great powers gathered together in the Congress of Aix-la-Chapelle did not alarm Bolívar,[3] but gave him instead one of those opportunities that he knew so well how to use to arouse the sympathy of Europe. The declaration published by him in the name of the Republic on November 20 was directed to this end. Summing up the steps taken by Venezuela since the year 1810 to put an end to the disagreements existing between her and the mother country, and boasting of her ability to maintain her independence, he concluded the declaration with a reaffirmation of the state of independence. This declaration was really no more than a vain

---

[3] The Quadruple Alliance (or Holy Alliance), composed of Russia, Austria, Prussia, and England, had been organized in 1815 to preserve "the tranquillity of Europe." Nothing came of Ferdinand's request for mediation or intervention in 1818.—Ed.

boast, but it did satisfy national pride and inspire confidence both at home and abroad.

After the campaign in the province of Caracas ended in May, Morillo devoted himself with his usual energy to the task of enlarging and training his army. Since he had in his possession the richest and most populous provinces of Venezuela and was master of the immense resources of New Granada, he did not have to overcome the obstacles facing his opponent at every step. But his situation was not devoid of troubles, and he showed admirable vigilance and perserverance in his tireless efforts to eliminate them. Bolívar did not serve his country with more loyalty than did Morillo his king. During the rainy season he visited the different points serving as winter quarters for the divisions that were to operate under his orders in the next campaign and supplied them with provisions. When the rains stopped, these divisions proceeded to Calabozo, where a body of seven thousand men assembled in December under La Torre. A fall from a horse kept Morillo in Caracas.

While the enemy was concentrating his forces in Calabozo, Bolívar embarked at Angostura on December 21 and proceeded to the mouth of the Pao River, where he was joined by a squadron of cavalry under the English Colonel James Rooke and by 459 infantry led by Monagas. After reinforcing these troops in Araguaquén with others from Cedeño's division, he marched with them and joined forces with General Páez at San Juan de Payara on January 17, 1819.

I shall now interrupt my account to relate an incident of the middle of the year 1818 to which I owed in large part the esteem and friendship shown me thereafter by General Bolívar. In the month of March of that year I arrived in Angostura with the rank of cornet in the Húsares Rojos, a corps commanded by Colonel George Elsom that was part of the expedition formed in London by Colonel Wilson. Shortly after our arrival we received orders to continue to headquarters, which were then on the Apure llanos. We went up the Orinoco, but fate would have it that we should arrive after the unsuccessful campaign of the first months of that year, when the dispersed elements and fugitives from the battle that had been fought were returning to San Fernando. Bolívar had just left for Angostura. On the day following his departure, General Páez reviewed the assembled forces in Achaguas. In this review our corps occupied the place of honor to the right of the line, undoubtedly as an expression of respect for our showy uniforms, which contrasted with the rags and the seminakedness of the hardy, brave *llaneros*. A few days after the review Wilson invited the general in chief to dinner and showered him with servile adulation during the course of the country-style banquet. Páez welcomed it as just praise for his merits. That same afternoon it was agreed that Wilson and the Apure leaders present would proclaim General Páez captain general of the army on a certain day of the following week. On the afternoon of the appointed day the aforesaid leaders met, each one bringing along as many *llaneros* as he could gather. The proposed farce got under way after the *llaneros* exhibited their extraordinary skill in horsemanship and the handling of the lance on the broad savanna to the east of the town. Páez was greeted with cheers and enthusiastic applause when he appeared with an escort of thirty or forty leaders, officers, and aides-de-camp. The act proclaiming him captain general was presently read. After more cheers and further exhibitions of agility on the part of the cavalry, the leaders signed the act. Páez, quite naturally, was delighted with the British auxiliaries. Before nightfall, however, someone approached him to warn him that he had done wrong. After reflecting on what had transpired, he decided to send the act to Bolívar.

In the meantime, Wilson had offered in the grand manner to bring him a large corps of thousands of men, which he would raise in England. Páez gave him permission to go to Angostura and supplied him with letters of recommendation for Bolívar. Upon his arrival in that city, the castles he had built in the air collapsed, for Bolívar, warned beforehand of his intrigues, had him arrested and taken to the fortress in Guayana la Vieja, where he remained until he left the country after his discharge from the army. At that time Páez received a reprimand in a letter from the Liberator, informing him of the arrest of Colonel Wilson for his serious crime and ordering him to send the act and other documents so that all legal formalities might be observed in Wilson's trial.

Disgusted with what I had witnessed in Achaguas and with the barbarous slaughter of prisoners, most of whom were Americans undoubtedly forced to serve in the royalist ranks, I requested my discharge from the corps in which I was serving and permission to return to Angostura. I obtained it with some difficulty, and I had to sell most of my equipment to make the trip. Upon my arrival in the capital I asked to be placed in a Creole corps, since I was anxious to learn Spanish. Acceding to my request, General Soublette, chief of the general staff, assigned me to the corps then being organized by General Anzoátegui. It was at that time that I met the Liberator. Although the sketch of him that I copy below was written many years after that period, he changed so little in his physical appearance and in his moral character that it differs little from the person who received me kindly in 1818 and approved my conduct.

Bolívar had a high, rather narrow forehead that was seamed with wrinkles from his early years—a sign of the thinker. His eyebrows were heavy and well shaped, his eyes black, bright, and piercing. On his long, perfectly shaped nose there was a small wen that annoyed him greatly until it disappeared in 1820, leaving an almost imperceptible scar. His cheekbones were prominent, his cheeks sunken from the time that I met him in 1818; his mouth was ugly, his lips rather thick; the distance between his nose and mouth was notable. His teeth were white, uniform, and beautiful, and he took the greatest care of them. His ears were large but well placed. His hair was black, curly, and of fine texture; he wore it long between 1818 and 1821, when it began to turn grey, after which he wore it short. He had side-whiskers and a mustache, both rather blond, and he shaved them off for the first time in Potosí in 1825. He was five feet six inches tall. His chest was narrow, his figure slender, his legs particularly thin. His skin was swarthy and rather coarse. His hands and feet were small and well shaped—a woman might have envied them. His expression, when he was in good humor, was pleasant, but it became terrible when he was aroused. The change was unbelievable.

Bolívar always had a good appetite, but no one could equal him in the capacity to endure hunger. Though a real connoisseur of good cooking, he found pleasure in eating the simple and primitive dishes of the *llaneros* and the Indians. He was very temperate. His favorite wines were Graves and champagne, but not even at the times when he was drinking most did I ever see him take more than four glasses of the former or two of the latter. At table he himself filled the glasses of guests seated beside him.

He took a great deal of exercise, and I have never known anyone who could endure fatigue so well. After a day's march, enough to exhaust the most robust man, I have seen him work five or six hours, or dance as long with the enthusiasm that he had for this diversion. He slept five or six hours out of the twenty-four. Whether in a hammock, on a cot, on a cowhide, or wrapped in his cloak on the ground out in the open, he slept as well as he would have on soft feathers. If he had not been a light sleeper, quick to awaken, he never would have escaped with his life at El Rincón de los Toros. Not even the *llaneros* excelled him in keenness of vision and fineness of ear. He was an expert in the handling of arms and a most skillful and daring horseman, though rather awkward-looking on horseback. Extremely fond of horses, he personally supervised their care and would visit the stables several times a day, whether on a campaign or in a city. He dressed with great care and kept himself very clean, taking a bath every day, and as many as three daily in regions where the heat was intense. He preferred country to city life. He detested drunkards and gamblers and, even more, gossips and liars. He was so loyal and gentlemanly that he would not allow others to be discussed unfavorably in his presence. To him friendship was a sacred word. Trustful to an extreme, if he discovered deceit or betrayal, he never forgave the one who had abused his confidence.

His generosity was really extraordinary. Not only would he give away whatever he had, but he would also run into debt to help others. Prodigal with what was his own, he was almost miserly with public funds. At times he may have inclined his ear to praise, but flattery angered him.

He spoke much and well; he had the rare gift of conversation and liked to tell anecdotes about his past life. His style was rhetorical and correct; his speeches and writings are full of daring and original metaphors. His proclamations are models of military eloquence. Elegance of style, clearness, and terseness are evident in his dispatches. He did not forget even the most trivial details in the orders that he communicated to his lieutenants: everything was calculated and foreseen by him.

He had the gift of persuasion and was able to inspire confidence in others. To these qualities are largely due the astounding triumphs achieved by him despite conditions so difficult that a man without his natural endowments and mettle would have become discouraged. A creative genius par excellence, he obtained resources when none seemed available. Always great, he was greatest in adversity. "Bolívar was more to be feared after defeat than after victory," his enemies used to say. Reverses made him rise above himself.

In the dispatch of civil affairs, which he never neglected, even when on campaigns, he was as skillful and prompt as in all other phases of his life. Swinging himself in a hammock, or walking up and down, usually with long steps—for his restless nature precluded repose—with his arms crossed or with his left hand grasping the collar of his coat and the forefinger of his right hand on his upper lip, he would listen to his secretary reading official correspondence and the innumerable petitions and personal letters addressed to him. As the secretary read, he would dictate his decisions regarding the petitions, and, as a rule, these decisions were irrevocable. Then he would start dictating—to as many as three amanuenses at a time—official dispatches and letters, for he never left a letter unanswered, no matter how humble the person who wrote to him might be. Though he might be interrupted during dictation, I never heard him make a mistake or get confused on resuming the interrupted sentence. When he did not know the correspondent or the petitioner, he would ask a couple of questions, but this happened very seldom because, gifted as he was with a prodigious memory, he knew not only every officer in the army but also all the officeholders and persons of note in the country. A great judge of men and of human affections, he realized instantly for what sort of work each man might serve, and very rarely did he turn out to be mistaken.

He read much, despite the scant time for reading that his busy life allowed him. He wrote little in his own hand—only to members of his family or some intimate friends—but he almost always added a line or two in his own handwriting when he signed what he had dictated. He spoke and wrote French correctly, and Italian quite well; as for English, he knew only a little, barely enough to understand what he was reading. He was thoroughly versed in the Greek and Latin classics, which he had studied, and he always read them with pleasure in good French translations.

Attacks directed against him in the press made the deepest impression on him, and calumny irritated him. Though a public figure for more than twenty years, he was never able, because of his sensitive nature, to overcome this susceptibility, rare indeed among men in high position. He had great regard for the sublime mission of the press as a guardian of public morals and as a curb on passions, and he attributed the greatness and the moral standards of the English people to the skillful use made in England of this civilizing agency.

CHAPTER ELEVEN

IT WAS IN THE MIDDLE of January, 1819, that Bolívar established his headquarters in San Juan de Payara and assembled there the divisions of Páez, Anzoátegui, and Cedeño, which gave him a total of 3,400 infantrymen and 1,000 cavalry. Though these forces were very inferior to the enemy in point of numbers, he planned to attack the enemy suddenly near Calabozo before the latter had even the remotest idea of his arrival in Apure. The divisions were about to march when he unexpectedly received word from Angostura of the arrival of troops recruited in England by Colonel Elsom and of the impending arrival of another considerable force under the command of Colonel James T. English. He immediately decided to return to Angostura in order to hasten the installation of the Congress and effect the prompt incorporation of the newly arrived auxiliaries into the Army of the

West or Apure. He consequently turned over the command of the army to Páez, promoting him to major general and giving him instructions to remain on the defensive.

At intervals during the trip to Angostura, while reclining in his hammock or on board the *flechera* that carried him down the majestic Orinoco, Bolívar dictated to his secretary his famous address to the Congress of 1819 and the constitution that he was preparing for the Republic. Upon his arrival in the capital on February 8, he set the date of February 15 for the installation of the Congress. At noon on that day he submitted to the Congress his plan of a constitution and delivered his address in a clear voice that, however, betrayed his excitement. In his initial remarks he expressed his relief over being able to return to the representatives of the people the supreme power entrusted to him. Reviewing the peculiar situation of America, he declared that the threefold yoke of ignorance, tyranny, and vice made it especially difficult to establish the rule of law in a free democratic society. He proposed a hereditary senate, a strong president, an independent judiciary, and a fourth power, or moral power, to watch over the education of youth and promote national enlightenment. Near the end of his address he made a fervent plea for the absolute freedom of the slaves and for the union of New Granada and Venezuela into a single state.

Some passages of Bolívar's address even moved the audience to tears. Rarely does one see a leader relinquish, in the moment of victory, the authority conferred upon him and hand it back to the people after having fought so hard for their independence amidst all kinds of suffering. When he concluded, he invited the members of Congress to choose a presiding officer, and the majority of the votes were for Zea. Congress immediately recognized and confirmed all the ranks conferred by the Supreme Chief. When Zea continued to point out the need of approving the reappointment of General Bolívar, the latter interrupted him to say that he would never again accept an authority that he had sincerely renounced forever. Having said this, he departed, leaving, as he himself would have it, "my personal enemies buried alive in the Congress of Venezuela."

In the plan of a constitution that General Bolívar submitted, he concentrated the executive power in one person to be elected by popular vote every four years. The legislative power was exercised by the hereditary Senate, modeled after the British House of Lords, and the House of Representatives, similar to the one in the United States. The first senators would be elected by the Constituent Congress. The judiciary was independent, and judges could be removed only by formal indictment. The most notable part of the plan was the introduction of a fourth power entrusted with the supervision of the moral standards of the citizens. He requested the establishment of trial by jury, the liberty of the press, the most explicit guarantees for civil liberty, and the complete abolition of slavery. He carefully avoided mention of religion, because he had the good sense to respect the ancient prejudices of a people reared on all the errors of the most crass superstition. Whatever may have been the errors of the plan, they were the errors of a great soul always favorably disposed toward what was just.

When the matter of the election of a president was taken up on the following day, there was absolutely unanimous agreement on the necessity of having Bolívar continue in the supreme command. Consequently, he was appointed to this high office, and Francisco Antonio Zea to the vice-presidency. The people of Angostura received the news of the appointments with the greatest enthusiasm, but when the deputation designated by Congress communicated them to Bolívar, he repeated his decision not to accept the presidency. When the principal citizens of the capital pleaded with him to accept, he stated that it would be impossible for him to preside over the destiny of the infant state in the dual role of first magistrate of the people and leader of the army, since he could not at one and the same time attend to the conduct of the civil administration and direct military operations. Congress removed this difficulty by authorizing the vice-president to act as first magistrate in the absence of the president. Bolívar therefore had to agree to assume the important duties of the high office to which he was called by virtue of the fervent wishes of the people and the army.

The Congress then directed its attention to the specification of the duties and prerogatives of the executive. In addition to the usual prerogatives, he was given supreme command of the armed forces and authority to raise troops and admit foreigners into the service of the Republic. After the establishment of the judicial power and the declaration of an amnesty for political crimes, the political code presented by Bolívar was discussed judiciously and in detail. The plan was adopted with very few alterations after six months of debate. The most important change was, in fact, that concerning the Senate. The hereditary clause was rejected, but it was voted that the senators, once elected, should serve for life.

During his stay in Angostura, General Bolívar had the satisfaction of witnessing the arrival of some of the foreign volunteers, whose bravery on the battlefield would merit no little praise, for on more than one occasion it would be a deciding factor in victories for the cause that they had come to uphold. He learned at the same time that another unit of English's division was landing at Margarita and that he could count on this force to attract the attention of his tireless rival toward the coast, which had been left exposed at more than one vulnerable point after the invasion of the llanos. He sent General Urdaneta to the island of Margarita to organize this unit and take advantage of the circumstances. After completing the arrangements required by the new system of government and giving the necessary instructions to the various corps that were engaged in irregular warfare in the provinces of Cumaná and Barcelona, Bolívar set out on February 27 to join the Apure army.

One of the most memorable campaigns of the war of independence is about to begin. Morillo crossed the Apure at the San Fernando crossing on January 24, 1819, had a small fort constructed there, and went on to occupy San Juan de Payara, which General Páez had evacuated before crossing the Arauca at El Caujaral. When Páez learned that Morillo had also crossed the Arauca toward the headwaters of the river, he had to order Anzoátegui to withdraw with the infantry and artillery to La Mata Casanareña and then continue the withdrawal to the Orinoco. Páez decided to stay within sight of Morillo and make the most of the advantage afforded him by his cavalry and his thorough knowledge of the terrain. The Spaniards occupied El Caujaral on February 5 and spent three days making it defensible and assuring communications with San Fernando. However prudent these measures might have been, they were to be of little avail against the enterprising and tireless *llaneros*, who, knowing the area intimately, were constantly spying on the Spaniards, surprising their detachments, intercepting their communications, and keeping them, in short, in a constant state of alarm.

Morillo continued his march on February 9, following the path of the patriot infantry, with Páez, ever watchful, observing him near at hand. When the *llaneros* were pursued by the Spanish cavalry, they would quickly and resolutely plunge into the swampy sections or *morichales* of the rolling country. The enemy, unaware of the peril, would follow them and encounter certain death. As the patriot infantry withdrew, the cavalry set fire to the savannas to deprive the enemy of forage, and thus it was that Morillo encountered only hunger and devastation on his march from Arauca to Cunaviche. A few days of these trials were sufficient to convince Morillo that it was absolutely impossible for him to subdue the *llaneros* or to match them on their own ground. Aware that the patriot infantry was beyond his reach and that his army would inevitably perish in that hostile wilderness, the Spanish general determined to retrace his steps. Executing the withdrawal with the dash and skill that had distinguished his advance, he recrossed the Arauca without any losses on February 25 and then went on to San Juan de Payara. After reinforcing the garrison at San Fernando, he marched on Achaguas, the capital of Apure, which he occupied on March 8. He was planning on fortifying the principal towns of Apure and inducing the inhabitants to return to their homes before the rainy season started. He had *flecheras* constructed to give him control of the rivers, and he kept his cavalry busy rounding up cattle. In short, he omitted nothing that would contribute to the security and comfort of the army under his command.

At about this same time Bolívar was coming up the Orinoco, accompanied by a foreign battalion of three hundred Englishmen under the command of Major John Mackintosh. On March 11 he joined the infantry of General Anzoátegui, which was encamped in Araguaquén, close by where the Arauca enters the Orinoco. The arrival of the president was greeted with the most enthusiastic demonstrations of joy by the entire army and especially by the infantry, who had hitherto played a major role in the trials as well as in the glories of the campaign, marching for long distances without even a drop of water and subsisting on unsalted beef of the poorest quality provided by the *llaneros*, who looked with marked disdain upon the foot soldiers. The order issued for an immediate march was greeted as a signal of victory and the termination of their sufferings. General Páez, at the head of his victorious cavalry, joined the infantry in Cunaviche. The army crossed the Arauca at El Caujaral and headed for Morillo's headquarters. Páez had so exaggerated the latter's losses that the president calculated that his force would not exceed his own in numbers and would be suffering from lowered morale.

But since Páez was unwilling to change his original successful plan of operations, Bolívar decided to attack an enemy unit quartered at La Gamarra, a ranch located about five leagues from Achaguas. On the morning of March 27 he surprised the enemy outposts, but the royalists put up a stubborn resistance, favored by their excellent position. While the patriots were waiting for reinforcements, the Spaniards crossed the Apure in canoes and effected their retreat in good order and almost without loss. General Páez fell victim during the action to some kind of an attack of epilepsy, from which he unfortunately suffered. This unexpected reversal blasted Bolívar's hope of surprising Morillo, but on the following day he approached Achaguas, intending to induce the Spanish leader to abandon the town in order to weary him with marches and countermarches. This move had the desired effect, for Morillo assembled his troops and came forth against Bolívar. The latter very wisely avoided a battle and took up positions on the south bank of the Arauca. The Spaniard encamped opposite.

On April 2, Páez was ordered to make a reconnaissance of the enemy positions. Choosing 150 of his finest lancers to accompany him, he crossed the river at a point above the royalist camp and set out at full rein toward the enemy. When Morilla saw this move, he judged that the whole patriot army had crossed the river. He advanced with his cavalry and some infantry to meet Páez, but the latter began a withdrawal and continued it until he had drawn the cavalry pursuing him away from the main force. Then, wheeling about suddenly, he fell upon them with such speed that he obliged them to retreat to their infantry and artillery, slaying all those who offered the least resistance. Páez's column had very few casualties in a combat as glorious as it was unequal. Morillo's losses were rather heavy, more than 400 dead and wounded. Bolívar rewarded the gallant *llaneros* by bestowing upon them the star of the Order of Liberators of Venezuela and issuing an eloquent proclamation in which he extolled their feat of arms and predicted that what they had done at Las Queseras del Medio was but the prelude of what they would henceforth accomplish.

General Morillo broke camp on April 4 and countermarched to Achaguas, where he concentrated his forces. It would be tedious to enter into the details of the advantages obtained in the numerous engagements of this campaign between the patriot guerrilla bands and the Spanish troops, although there were some real prodigies of personal bravery that well deserve the honor of being mentioned in the history of the country. During his stay in Achaguas, Morillo could not maintain rapid communication with San Fernando, although he did put the latter stronghold in an excellent state of defense against any sort of unexpected attack. It was necessary to protect the couriers with strong pickets of infantry and cavalry, and even these were not always sufficient to accomplish that purpose.

When Morillo withdrew toward Achaguas, Bolívar marched for several days along the bank of the Arauca, and on April 8 he crossed with the infantry and some poorly mounted squadrons to the south bank for the purpose of rounding up cattle. A picket of carabineers discovered that the whole Spanish army was encamped on the very ranch toward which the patriots were making their way. A brief skirmish ensued between twenty troopers led by General Páez and an escort accompanying Morillo, who was surprised to see indications of the enemy's approach, even though he thought then that it could be only a guerrilla band. When Páez and his men withdrew, Morillo came to a halt, suspecting that it was part of a ruse. It was greatly to the advantage of the patriots that Morillo did not follow Páez and discover the main force. Even a withdrawal would have been risky against forces four times larger and supported by excellent cavalry.

When Bolívar realized that his opponent was not even remotely aware of his movements, he gave orders to Anzoátegui for a countermarch. It can be said that a continued series of successes marked the military and political career of Bolívar from that fateful day. After an arduous march and another crossing of the Arauca, the cavalry and the infantry moved over the very savannas that they had previously burned in order to deprive the royalists of forage. It is very difficult to give a complete idea of the sufferings of the patriots on their marches over these sun-scorched plains. Despite everything, not even a single complaint was heard from that brave army, which was inspired by the example and steadfastness of the general in chief, who led the same life as the soldiers.

During these marches Bolívar arose at daybreak and visited the various units, encouraging them as he went. Accompanied by his staff, he followed the army, dismounting at midday to bathe whenever it was possible. After lunching like the others on meat alone, he dictated his orders and dispatched his correspondence while swinging in his hammock. When the troops had eaten their short ration, they continued their march until they found a place to camp, whether in a small wood or in the open fields. Bolívar was then thirty-five years old and at the height of his physical and mental powers. We who accompanied him during that period—at the time I was aide-de-camp to General Anzoátegui—can bear witness to his incomparable activity and his vigilance, not only in regard to the fate of the Republic, but also in regard to that of the very least of his soldiers.

On April 12 the army came to a halt on the banks of the Arauca at the Caraballero ranch in order to give the infantry a much-needed rest and to enable the president to take care of the great amount of business that had accumulated during the campaign. The royalists, in the meantime, had returned to Achaguas, where the *llanero* cavalry kept them in a constant state of alarm. On the twenty-first the patriot army crossed the Arauca once more and moved toward Nutrias in order to threaten Barinas and thus force Morillo to abandon his position in Achaguas, which afforded him all manner of supplies. At this juncture the royalists, fearful of the approaching rainy season, determined to evacuate not only Achaguas but also that entire region of the Apure that had been so fateful to them. Morillo crossed the Apure on May 1.

Aware of this move, Bolívar planned to pursue one of Morillo's divisions, but it was necessary, first of all, to remount the cavalry and to round up cattle in case the patriots should have to take up winter quarters in Barinas. He therefore set up camp in Rincón Hondo, where there was an abundance of pasture and meat, and he ordered Páez to assign some cavalry units to harass the enemy's rearguard and to round up horses for the coming operations. During this interval Colonel Jacinto Lara arrived at headquarters from Casanare, with official communications in which Santander informed the president of several victories won by him over a Spanish division that had crossed the Andes and descended to the plains of Casanare. He also reported that the mistaken policy and oppressive measures of the Spanish authorities had exasperated the people of the trans-Andean provinces to the point of rebellion. In his reply on May 18, Bolívar praised Santander for his success in repulsing the enemy division and thanked him for preventing an invasion.

Bolívar immediately realized the advantages to be gained from a successful invasion of New Granada. He also considered the favorable circumstances that could facilitate that operation: the rainy season was beginning, the enemy in Venezuela had withdrawn into his winter quarters, and the royalist army in New Granada considered itself to be safe from any invasion. He thought, too, that public opinion would be favorable to the patriots' operations. From these premises he concluded that despite the initial difficulties such a campaign could not fail to result favorably for the cause of America.

After having obtained a brief rest, the infantry broke camp at Rincón Hondo. The president hastened to carry out the preparations necessary for the operations that were to be undertaken. He was particularly attentive to Páez, for nothing could be done without the aid of the *llaneros*, who were so devoted to their native soil that they were unwilling to leave it, especially in view of the hardships they and their families had suffered. Páez was convinced, or seemed to be convinced, of the accuracy of Bolívar's observations concerning the difficulties involved in maintaining an army in Barinas during the rainy season or in having the infantry spend the winter in Apure, and he appeared to be satisfied with the importance of the plan. Though Bolívar had not sounded out the other leaders, he did not expect any opposition on their part.

On May 23, while on the way to El Mantecal, Bolívar called a council of war of the army commanders. Present at it were Soublette, Anzoátegui, Briceño Méndez, Cruz Carrillo, Iribarren, Rangel, Rooke, Plaza, and Manrique. The invasion of New Granada was decided upon in a tumble-down hut in the deserted village of Setenta, on the banks of the Apure. There was no table in that hut, nor even a chair, other than the skulls of the cattle a royalist guerrilla force had slain not long before to feed its troops. Seated on these skulls, which the rain and the sun had bleached, these leaders were to decide the fate of America. Bolívar explained his plan for surprising the enemy occupying New Granada. To accomplish it, he would invade by way of Cúcuta with the divisions of Páez and Anzoátegui, while Santander would create a diversion through Casanare. Although this was not his real plan,[1] he nevertheless charged all present with absolute secrecy, which none of them failed to observe. They all approved the plan.

From El Mantecal, which they reached that very afternoon, Rangel departed with a letter for Páez informing him of the plan just adopted, and at the same time an emissary left to deliver to Santander the order to remove the obstacles that stood in the way of this extensive plan. On the twenty-sixth, Bolívar also sent to the government of Angostura an explanation of his plan. He emphasized the importance of speed and the element of surprise in taking advantage of the favorable conditions in New Granada. In order to avoid old rivalries, General Mariño would be summoned by Congress to exercise his legislative functions, while General Bermúdez would assume command of the Army of the East for operations in the eastern sector of Caracas and an attempt at taking the city of Caracas and the Valles de Aragua, should the enemy move westward. General Urdaneta's division, operating independently, would come to the Apure and send military supplies to Casanare. Dur-

---

[1] Bolívar was really planning to march himself toward Casanare and to send Páez and his division by way of Cúcuta. The Casanare route to New Granada was much more difficult; fearful of desertions and protests, Bolívar did not reveal his real plan until the army was on its way. —Ed.

ing the president's absence the vice-president would assume all necessary military authority for the direction of the campaign in eastern
Venezuela. To Bermúdez, Urdaneta, Mariño, and Brión he gave the
same detailed instructions, in which nothing was overlooked, nothing
left to chance. Not for a moment did Bolívar doubt the success of his
undertaking.

When the army began its march on May 26, it was composed of
four infantry battalions, totaling thirteen hundred men, and three
cavalry squadrons of eight hundred men. The rainy season began precisely on that very day, but the army nonetheless displayed the greatest
optimism. In Guasdualito the army's destination was published in the
general order, and the vice-president was informed of the true plan
of the campaign in the official communication of June 3. Bolívar told
him of his decision to march with the infantry to Casanare instead of
going to Cúcuta. While he and General Santander occupied Chita,
General Páez would take the valleys of Cúcuta, thus diverting the
enemy's attention. He would remain in command of the entire combined army inside New Granada, and Páez would return from Cúcuta
within fifteen or twenty days to direct operations as the situation might
require. Meanwhile, the major part of the cavalry, operating in two
divisions, would lay siege to San Fernando and make incursions against
the enemy in Barinas.

Then Bolívar dispatched his final orders to General Páez, without
whose cooperation he feared that the undertaking might fail. These
orders were explicit and detailed, providing for a number of contin-
gencies. Marching toward Cúcuta, Páez was to cut the enemy's communications with Venezuela, establish communications with Bolívar,
and send some units to Mérida. If the enemy should come after him,
Páez was to join Bolívar or withdraw if necessary. If Morillo should
decide later to march to New Granada, Páez was to seize the province
of Caracas and the capital and then move rapidly westward to close
in on the enemy from behind. In case Morillo should keep his troops
in Venezuela, Páez was to combine operations with the Army of the
East and also press the attack on Barinas and San Fernando, without
committing all his forces unless Morillo should make an all-out effort.
I have dwelt on this matter because later on there were many who

tried to excuse the disobedience of Páez or to attribute to themselves the glory of having conceived the plan that Bolívar so successfully executed.

On June 4 the division crossed the Arauca and entered the province of Casanare. The rain had set in with unusual intensity and was falling in torrents, flooding the savannas. For the crossings it was necessary to construct cowhide boats, both to prevent the ordnance supplies from getting wet and to transport those soldiers who did not know how to swim. The troops marched for a week with the water up to their waists, having to camp in the open at places not covered by the water. The only protection the soldier had was a wretched blanket, but he did not even use that to cover himself, so eager was he to protect his weapon and his ammunition. On June 11 the division, now in the most miserable condition, reached Santander's headquarters in Tame, where it at least gained some relief in the form of a little salt and a few bananas to be added to the ordinary ration of meat.

The army was composed entirely of young men who were not greatly affected by the cares of life or its hardships and perils. The president himself was never heard to complain of weariness, not even after arduous exertions and long marches, during which he often helped in the loading and unloading. When it was a question of the general welfare, no task was too lowly for Bolívar. Second in command was General Soublette, the chief of staff, then twenty-nine years old, who was united to Bolívar by bonds of blood and friendship. In the whole course of the war he always occupied positions of trust. I have already spoken of Santander, the commander of the vanguard division, whose able performance of his assignment in Casanare was recognized by the government in expressions of satisfaction. General José Antonio Anzoátegui, the commander of the division designated as the rearguard, was born in Barcelona in 1789. His extraordinary valor and fearlessness earned for him the esteem of Bolívar and of his companions, despite his surly and unpleasant disposition. He hated Santander with his heart and soul, but out of respect for General Bolívar he concealed this profound dislike as far as he was able. Colonel Rooke, who was in command of a brigade in Anzoátegui's division, had a personality dia-

metrically opposed to that of his commander. Pleased with everyone
and with everything, and especially with himself, he seemed to be
satisfied with the life he was living and not at all indifferent to it.
Such men were the principal commanders of the small army with
which Bolívar accomplished the emancipation of one of the most important sections of Spanish America. Among the corps commanders
and the subordinate officers there were many young men who distinguished themselves in that memorable campaign and won honors during the course of the war.

After the pacification, which is the word used by the Spaniards to
indicate the subjugation of a country through the extermination of its
prominent men, New Granada was subjected to all the horrors of the
most intolerable despotism of the military system. Morillo's orders were
carried out by Juan Sámano, a bloodthirsty tyrant who had all the
prejudices and bad habits of old age without having succeeded in
acquiring the experience that it gives. Promoted to viceroy, he became
proportionately more cruel when he found himself with a higher rank
and in possession of the power he was seeking. The natives and the
wealth of that unfortunate country were used to bind the chains of
Venezuela, its sister nation and ally.

A Dominican friar and a woman rose up to defend the honor of the
country. Father Ignacio Mariño abandoned his habit and his rosary,
put on the uniform of the warrior, and was the first to display valor as
a soldier under the banner of rebellion. The story of Policarpa Salavarrieta is simple as well as pathetic. She loved her country and, the better
to serve it, gave her heart to a youth who belonged to the party seeking
independence and who, for this reason, had been sentenced to serve
as a private in the Spanish army. Through him Pola succeeded in brib-
ing some royalist soldiers, who deserted at her suggestion. The flight
was discovered, and her sweetheart was apprehended while carrying
important documents that were to be handed over to the patriot chiefs
in Casanare. These papers revealed the complicity of Pola, and the two
of them, along with the other deserters, were tried and condemned to
death by a court-martial. Although a pardon was offered to Pola, there
was no human consideration that could induce her to betray her ac-

complices, and Sámano was barbarous enough to order the immediate execution of the sentence. She met her death before a firing squad in the main square of Santa Fe on November 14, 1817.

The Granadine people bemoaned the death of their heroine, but they showed no sign of a desire to avenge her, for terror had completely extinguished the flame of patriotism. A few guerrilla attacks in the northern provinces were the only protest, weak but honorable, against the oppressors. If Bolívar's genius had not conceived the project that he accomplished so skillfully, New Granada would have had to mourn for a long time the loss of her liberty and to curse the apathy of her sons.

CHAPTER TWELVE

AT THE TIME WHEN BOLÍVAR was massing his army in Tame, the royalists had four thousand perfectly equipped men stationed in garrisons along the northern frontier and three thousand in the garrisons of Santa Fe and other cities in the interior and on the coast. In view of these formidable forces and the natural obstacles offered by the terrain, Bolívar's plan would seem like a foolish fancy, had it not been that he relied more on the resources of his own genius than on the material strength of his army.

From Tame to Pore, the capital of Casanare, the whole route was flooded, being, as Santander describes it, "more like a small sea than solid ground." On June 22, 1819, the gigantic Andes, considered impassable in this season, loomed ahead of the patriot army, presenting what seemed to be an insurmountable barrier. For four days the troops struggled upward from mountain to mountain, with the ascent made even more difficult by the incessant rain and the ever increasing cold. Feeling helpless in the face of such extraordinary difficulties, the *llaneros* became convinced that only crazy men could keep going at temperatures that benumbed their senses and froze their bodies. Many of them, in fact, deserted because of these conditions. Few horses survived the five days' march, and the dead ones obstructed the path. Bolívar alone remained steadfast amidst the hardships. His presence and his example cheered the troops, and they redoubled their efforts when he spoke to them of the glory that awaited them.

On June 27 the advance guard dispersed a royalist force of three hundred men occupying a formidable position before Paya, a town in the cordillera. Overjoyed by this victory, the troops recovered their former vigor, now thinking that their troubles were almost over. Since it was no longer possible for Bolívar to continue to hide his movements from the enemy, he felt obliged to address a proclamation to the inhabitants. Announcing the arrival of the liberating army, an army of friends and benefactors, he urged them to turn against the Spaniards and to have no fear of those who had come to free them. He managed to have this proclamation introduced and circulated in the province of Tunja, where it had the double effect of awakening in the inhabitants thoughts of the injustices suffered and a desire to avenge them. The persecuted patriots made ready to help the army in every way possible.

After a few days of rest the army renewed its march on July 2, following a road that would take them across the paramo of Pisba. Considering it impassable, the Spaniards had neglected to defend it, and this is precisely why Bolívar chose it. At many points the way was completely blocked by huge boulders and fallen trees or by washouts caused by the constant rain. After a terrible night, during which it was impossible to keep a fire going, the army struck out across the paramo itself, a bleak and uninviting desert area devoid of all vegetation because of its height. That day the cold, penetrating air proved fatal to many soldiers, most of whom were almost naked. During this day's march my attention was drawn to a group of soldiers who had stopped near the place where I had sat down, overwhelmed by fatigue. One of them informed me that the wife of a soldier of the Rifles Battalion was in labor. The following morning I saw the same woman with the newborn baby in her arms, and apparently in the best of health, marching along behind the battalion, having already walked two leagues over one of the worst paths of that rugged terrain. The following night was even more horrible than the previous ones, and many soldiers perished as a result of their sufferings and privations.

As groups of ten to twenty men started down from the paramo, the general congratulated them and expressed the hope that the campaign might soon be over. On July 6, Anzoátegui's division reached Socha, the first town of the province of Tunja, where they received a very hospitable welcome from the people of the town and the surrounding countryside. But while the troubles of the soldiers lessened, the General had more and more matters to occupy his attention. Great soul that he was, Bolívar refused to be daunted by the many shortcomings. His first concern was to assure subsistence for the troops and to get them ready to face the royalists. He sent Colonel Lara to round up as many mules as he could, before going out to collect the arms and ammunition left behind and to bring in the stragglers and the sick. He also sent out agents to collect horses and to bring in livestock. A hospital was set up. Spies were sent out in all directions to gather information about the enemy and to spread exaggerated reports about the size of the patriot army. Nothing was left undone in the way of taking all the precautions dictated by prudence.

The royalists were greatly surprised when they heard that they had an enemy army in their midst, since it seemed incredible to them that Bolívar would undertake operations in the face of so many obstacles during a period of the year when few risked even the shortest trips. The general belief was that the body of troops that had reached Paya was the division from Casanare. José María Barreiro, the commander in chief of the third Spanish division, had his camp in Sogamoso, a central position where he had assembled sixteen hundred men. The remaining units of his army were encamped at the most vulnerable points of the frontier.

After a patriot squad surprised and captured a royalist detachment stationed at Los Corrales de Bonza, Barreiro made a movement in that direction, and the patriots advanced to meet him. Upon catching sight of Santander's division, he withdrew to La Peña de Tópaga, an almost inaccessible height facing the Gámeza River. After he recrossed the river on the following morning, he again started to withdraw to his encampment as soon as he came upon the patriot columns that had camped at Tasco the preceding night. Bolívar gave orders to attack him in the formidable position he occupied, for he calculated that Barreiro would be receiving new reinforcements from day to day. The latter took a firm stand at the Gámeza bridge to defend it, but he was dislodged with losses. On falling back toward Los Molinos de Tópaga, he showed little willingness to accept a battle on equal terms, which obliged his opponent to withdraw his forces. The action at Gámeza started at ten in the morning and ended at nightfall, and the royalist and patriot losses were about equal.

It was clear that the royalist leader was determined not to offer or accept battle until all available troops had joined him, since the nature of the terrain was favorable for defensive warfare. Bolívar therefore decided to organize his small force and promote a general uprising among the inhabitants. His efforts were not in vain, for the fugitive patriots who had hidden in remote sections of the country now began to emerge and offer their services to the liberating army. Since it was well nigh impossible for Bolívar, with the few forces at his disposal, to force the position occupied by Barreiro, he had to pull back and try a flank movement. As a result, the patriots gained possession of the fertile and populous territory of Santa Rosa and established communications with the provinces of El Socorro and Pamplona.

After obtaining horses and provisions in the pleasant valley of Cerinza, which reminded the English officers of home, Bolívar advanced with the army on July 20 over the spacious plains of Bonza, where the royalists had already concentrated nearly all their forces in positions almost as inaccessible as those of Peña de Tópaga. The whole day was spent in skirmishes and maneuvers, with no real loss on either side, but the royalists were not willing to accept the battle offered them. The patriots, however, gained advantages from the apparent timidity of the enemy, for they had time to bring up the column left in Paya and to win the support of the native inhabitants.

The unit from Paya, commanded by Colonel Rooke, joined the army on July 22. He gave the most satisfactory answers to all the questions asked him by General Bolívar and assured him that his unit had not suffered at all on the paramo. When it later developed that one fourth of the English soldiers and two officers had perished during the march, Rooke did not deny it. "But it is also true," he exclaimed, "that they deserved their fate, for those men were the most poorly behaved in my corps, and the corps has profited by their death." The philosophical attitude of the English leader made the general smile.

After vain efforts to force the enemy to fight, Bolívar executed an encircling movement against their right flank. At dawn on July 25, the anniversary of the patron saint of Spain and Bolívar's birthday, the army began to cross the Sogamoso River, which runs through the plains of Bonza. At midday, when the army was passing by Pantano de Vargas, the enemy appeared on the heights ahead. Barreiro started the battle by sending the First Del Rey Battalion against the left wing of the patriot army. On seeing that this unit had taken possession of the heights occupied by Santander and his division, he attacked the center of the position with such daring that the Rifles and Barcelona battalions gave way and let him through. Everything seemed lost, but Bolívar flew to rally the routed units and ordered Colonel Rooke to take the British Legion and dislodge the enemy from the heights, which the gallant Englishman did in the most brilliant fashion. In the meantime, the royalist general repaired the damage done with another vigorous attack on the front lines of the patriot army. When everything seemed to favor the Spaniards and everyone except Bolívar despaired of victory, Rondón appeared at the head of a squadron of *llaneros*. Bolívar spoke words of encouragement to them and said to their leader, "Colonel, save the country." The latter, followed by his intrepid soldiers, hurled himself against the advancing enemy squadrons and routed them with heavy losses. The infantry followed the example of Rondón, and it was no longer possible for the royalists to resist the impetus of the combined attack. Night brought an end to the bloody combat.

The gallant conduct of Rondón and the cool bravery of the few British troops were very effective in winning the victory, that is to say, in saving the liberating army of New Granada from complete destruction. In the general order published the following day Bolívar conferred upon these brave foreigners the Cross of Liberators, a distinction they well deserved. On the following morning the patriots returned to the bloody scene of the fighting, once more prepared to battle the enemy, but the latter refused to fight. That same day both armies returned to their former positions in Bonza. The losses were really immense, considering the small number of combatants. Fortunately for America, the enemy was so disheartened by the result of the battle of Pantano de Vargas that there was no reason to fear him until he received reinforcements.

The activity and energy of the republican chief seemed to increase in proportion to the mounting difficulties. Since General Páez had failed to abide by the combined plan of operations calling for the invasion of New Granada through Cúcuta, the army could only rely on Bolívar's talents and the resources suggested by his genius. After the promulgation of martial law on July 27, recruits began to appear at headquarters, but much remained to be done to transform these hapless, though patriotic, peasants into soldiers and give them a warlike appearance. Nothing could be less military than the clothes they wore. Despite everything, within a very few days eight hundred of these recruits, divided into companies, made a very imposing appearance at a distance. At the battle of Boyacá, as in all the battles fought thereafter, the native rustics proved that South America has no better infantry soldiers than they.

The march on the enemy was undertaken on August 3, whereupon Barreiro was forced to evacuate the town of Paipa and to withdraw his outposts to the heights overlooking the road to Tunja. The following day, after the army recrossed the Sogamoso River at sunset, Bolívar issued a countermand and started a night march on Tunja by the road through Toca, leaving the enemy to the rear. At eleven o'clock in the morning he occupied the city and captured the few soldiers of the garrison. The patriot army was given the same joyous welcome in Tunja that it had received everywhere.

Bolívar's daring maneuver frightened the royalists and decided the fate of the campaign. The maneuver was not known in the enemy camp until the following morning. Barreiro started toward Tunja along the main road, veered a little to the right during the night, and entered Motavita, a small village close to the city, on the following morning. When he resumed his march on August 7, 1819, Bolívar, having found out the direction being taken, ordered his army to march toward the point where the enemy was bound, with the intention of getting between Barreiro and Santa Fe. At two o'clock in the afternoon the patriot advance guard attacked the first royalist column as it was passing over the bridge of Boyacá. At the same time Santander's division was occupying the heights overlooking the spot where Barreiro had deployed his army. The battle started with skirmishes between light horsemen, during which a column of royalist chasseurs under Colonel Francisco Jiménez crossed the bridge and formed in battle line. Barreiro ordered the main body of his army to withdraw about three-quarters of a mile from the bridge, thus giving the patriots time to cut his communications with Santa Fe. Orders were immediately issued for Santander to storm the bridge and for Anzoátegui simultaneously to attack the right wing and center of the royalist position. The fighting then became general. Anzoátegui and his lancers encircled the right flank of the Spanish infantry and captured their artillery, which the Rifles Battalion had attacked from the front. When the fleeing cavalry were slashed to pieces, the infantry surrendered. A bayonet charge decided the day. Jiménez, who was defending the bridge and holding Santander's division in check, fell back when he witnessed Barreiro's confusion, and the defeat became general. Sixteen hundred men laid down their arms. Barreiro, Jiménez, and most of the leaders and officers were taken prisoner, and a large amount of war matériel fell into the hands of the victor. Bolívar personally pursued the fugitives as far as Venta Quemada, where he spent the night. Thus ended this glorious battle in which two thousand republicans defeated three thousand royalists.

The victory of Boyacá left the road to the capital open to Bolívar. After leaving orders concerning the movements of the army, part of which had already been sent to occupy the provinces of El Socorro and Pamplona, he marched toward the capital on August 8 with the Llano-arriba Squadron. Viceroy Sámano departed in haste for Honda with an escort and the principal authorities on the morning of August 9, ten hours after receiving the news of the defeat of the royalist army. On the afternoon of the tenth, Bolívar entered Santa Fe amidst the acclamations of the people, whose delight could be compared only to their surprise at the sudden, as well as unexpected, transition from the most oppressive tyranny to the enjoyment of liberty. And the surprise of the inhabitants was really not so strange, for Sámano had kept them in the most complete ignorance of everything pertaining to the opposing armies, except for vainglorious bulletins proclaiming the defeats of the patriots and the repeated victories of the royalist arms. It was not until the morning of the ninth that they learned the truth of what had happened at Boyacá on the seventh.

Bolívar found 500,000 pesos in cash in the coffers of the public treasury and about 100,000 pesos in gold bars. These resources provided for the most urgent needs, and measures were taken to ensure the strictest economy. In addition, a decree was issued for the confiscation of the properties of the Spaniards and the Americans who had emigrated. Unfortunately the intendant appointed was not worthy of the trust required by his task, and the proceeds from the confiscations were shamefully dissipated.

Soon after Bolívar had re-established order, he devoted himself exclusively to war matters. Though Barreiro's army had been destroyed, it was to be feared that once news of the invasion of New Granada reached Morillo's ears he would use every means to send forces to the country to rescue it from the hands of the patriots. Bolívar, on his part, was determined to hold on to his conquest, and he acted with the greatest skill and prudence in furthering this end. In order to build up the army quickly, he incorporated in it the American soldiers taken prisoner at Boyacá. He hurriedly sent a strong division commanded by Soublette to occupy the valleys of Cúcuta and to defend the frontier in that area. He dispatched a unit to pursue Calzada, who had withdrawn toward Popayán with the Aragón Regiment and the remnants saved at Boyacá, with orders to occupy that city and watch the royalists in Quito. Lieutenant Colonel José María Córdova left Honda with 150 men and instructions to provoke rebellion in the towns of Antioquia and to drive the Spaniards out of the province.

Meanwhile, the liberated provinces naturally served as a base of operations for raising new bodies of troops, furthering the cause of independence, and maintaining the liberty of the country, for no one knew better than Bolívar how to take advantage of a burst of enthusiasm and keep it alive. Amidst the din of warfare he did not neglect the needs of the political administration or public education. The military leaders entrusted with the command of the provinces were granted civil authority, because people accustomed to such a system would have paid little attention to the latter authority if it had not been backed by military authority. Then Bolívar formed a provisional government for New Granada and placed General Santander at its head with the title of vice-president. His talents, services, and knowledge of the country made him worthy of this signal demonstration of confidence. The duties of this magistrate were the same as those assigned by the Congress of Venezuela to the executive power in that state.

Among the deeds that brought the greatest honor to Bolívar in this fruitful and glorious period of his public life, one should mention his generous treatment of the prisoners taken at Boyacá. All the Americans who showed regret for their part in the struggle or who proved that they could not have done otherwise were pardoned and either admitted into service at their same ranks or sent home without any restrictions. Barreiro and the principal Spanish leaders and officers were kept in prison, but without being subjected to any annoying restrictions other than those necessarily required to guard against an escape. When Bolívar reached Bogotá, he took advantage of the first opportunity to inform the viceroy that he preferred an exchange of prisoners "individual for individual, rank for rank, position for position." This communication was entrusted to three Capuchin monks who had been detained in Honda while fleeing from Santa Fe.

Unfortunately, the charitable intentions motivating this noble and generous action were frustrated by a bloody deed that had its origins in sentiments diametrically opposed to those of Bolívar. It so happened that Bolívar had to absent himself from the capital to attend to matters concerning the war. Scarcely had he left when General Santander, assuming the loathsome responsibility for an unnecessary and cowardly crime, had Barreiro and thirty-eight of his unfortunate comrades shot in the public square within sight of the government palace where

Sámano had signed his unjust orders a short time before. The brutal manner of the execution made this infamous act seem even more shameful and more unworthy of the noble cause in whose name it was perpetrated.

Shortly before noon on October 11 the prisoners were led four abreast across the square, having to traverse the entire distance on foot, despite the heavy shackles that they were dragging along. A few moments later Barreiro was ordered to kneel down and was shot in the back! This despicable death was not worthy of the gallant soldier who had always exposed himself to enemy bullets on the battlefield. The other prisoners met the same fate. After witnessing the bloody scene from the entrance to the palace, General Santander addressed a few words, not at all appropriate for the occasion, to the populace. Then, preceded by a few musicians, he paraded through the principal streets of the capital, singing the chorus of a song having to do with the act just carried out. The celebration ended with a ball at the palace. Ever so many circumstances point toward Santander's conduct as being unworthy of a gentleman, of a soldier, and of a man. Furthermore, it was all the more odious because of the way it contrasted with that which Bolívar observed.

In the interest of the country's good name I should make it clear that this action of Santander was condemned everywhere. In Venezuela they did not want to record it in the archives of public acts. Señor Zea, the vice-president of Colombia, who was in St. Thomas at the time on the way to England, was a witness of the indignation that it caused there, and he wrote officially to the president reproaching Santander for the crime he had perpetrated and asking for an explanation of the event. In his official letter of October 17, Santander gave as the principal reason for the execution the dangerous situation created by the subversive statements spread by the imprisoned officers, whom he considered to be the executioners and murderers of peaceful compatriots. In a private letter of the same date, he told Bolívar that it was necessary to get rid of Barreiro and his thirty-eight companions because the rumors had driven him crazy, the people were indifferent, and he saw nothing favorable to be gained from keeping them imprisoned. He added that the judicial proceedings were well disguised, but that it was necessary for Bolívar's reply to cover him permanently.

I have gone a little ahead of myself so as not to interrupt the narration farther on with the details of this unfortunate occurrence. Now that I have completed this task, I shall turn to a more pleasant subject in the following chapter.

CHAPTER THIRTEEN

AT A CEREMONY held in the main square of Santa Fe on September 18, 1819, a vote of thanks was given to the victors at Boyacá, and a crown of laurel was presented to Bolívar as an emblem of his triumphs. He refused to accept it, however, saying with becoming modesty that those who really deserved it were the leaders and soldiers who had accompanied him. A few days later he bade farewell to the Granadines in a proclamation recalling how he had returned to New Granada with a liberating army for the third time and expressing the hope that New Granada and Venezuela might become one republic.

Bolívar's trip to Pamplona was like a march of triumph. All along the road there were arches erected in his honor, and huge throngs appeared to express their gratitude to him. On the way he gathered facts on the conditions in the towns, investigated the evils that beset them, and either endeavored to remedy these evils himself or brought them to the attention of the vice-president. He exempted many of the towns from the payment of the most burdensome taxes, and in others he distributed honorary rewards that in no way affected the public treasury. But he did not distribute gifts from his own funds with such strict economy. Before leaving the capital, he had set up pensions from his private fortune for some of the widows of the patriots sacrificed to Spanish vengeance. While thus attending to the needs or comforts of others with regal liberality, he neglected his own comfort almost completely. There was no bed in his campaign equipment, and his clothing was more simple and his table more frugal at this time than that of many of the generals in his army.

About the same time that Bolívar and the division that was to replace Soublette's were entering Pamplona, La Torre, at the head of an excellent division, was entering Cúcuta, which Soublette and his units had just left with orders to join the Apure army. This was the tardy reinforcement sent by Morillo to the aid of Barreiro. When the Spanish leader heard of Bolívar's presence in Pamplona, he stopped where he was, apparently not at all anxious to come to grips with the redoubtable republican chief. Anzoátegui, who had been assigned to command the Army of the North, reached headquarters in Pamplona on October 25.

At this point Bolívar received extremely unpleasant news from Angostura, which obliged him to start out immediately for the capital. Before his departure he had left instructions for Anzoátegui, urging him above all to stay on the defensive. He had not gone far from Pamplona when he received word of General Anzoátegui's death there on November 15. This news surprised him greatly, for he had just said good-bye to his valiant lieutenant, who had appeared to be in the best of health. The loss of this brave and skilled soldier was a tremendous one for the army, a loss as untimely as it was sad. The day before receiving the tragic news, Bolívar had written Anzoátegui a long letter, concluding with these words: "It may happen that Cuzco will receive the benefit of our arms and that our conquests will extend as far as the silver mines of Potosí." Perhaps, when putting these prophetic words on paper, Bolívar was only endeavoring to arouse the noble aspirations of Anzoátegui, but the ensuing events resulted in the fulfillment of his prediction, the very one he had made to the army two months previously in his proclamation: "And the flags of Venezuela, New Granada, Argentina, and Chile will fly at one and the same time over rich Peru."

Notwithstanding the evident proofs of patriotism and unselfishness manifested by Bolívar, the despicable jealousy of some of his compatriots was not appeased. Soon after it was known in Angostura that he had actually invaded New Granada in the dead of winter with fewer than two thousand men, his personal enemies called the undertaking an abandonment of the interests of Venezuela. Some conspirators, even more daring than the rest, tried to force Congress to declare him a deserter and outlaw. The plots began to take definite form after the arrival of General Arismendi in the capital, where he had been sent after the government ordered General Urdaneta to arrest him for having provoked insubordination on the island of Margarita in connection with the recruitment of a battalion for service on the mainland. Arismendi's character inspired confidence in the agitators who flocked to his prison as the center of the clique. To discredit the government they spread false rumors about the approach of the royalists and the apathy of the vice-president. These fabrications gained ground, and Zea, already disgusted, was forced to offer his resignation to Congress, which immediately accepted it. Arismendi emerged from prison and took over the reins of the government on September 14, 1819.

Elevated to the highest office,[1] Arismendi took what he called vigorous measures, some of which were in complete contradiction to Bolívar's provisions. In justice, however, I must admit that during the time that he remained at the head of the government he displayed his characteristic energy in procuring troops and supplies for the continuation of the war. When the news of Bolívar's first victories reached Angostura, great importance was not attached to them, but all doubt disappeared upon the arrival of the bulletin printed in Bogotá about the battle of Boyacá. Bolívar's friends received the news with the greatest rejoicing, while his enemies, though not displeased, would have given

[1] As vice-president, he was in charge of the government during Bolívar's absence. —Ed.

a great deal to have had the news arrive some time previously. Arismendi, who had instigated the plots and had profited from them, was by no means the least astonished, since he was the most guilty. Under the pretense of carrying out certain measures of public interest, he started out for Maturín on September 21.

On December 10, after he had announced his return, Arismendi reached Soledad, opposite Angostura. The ringing of the bells and the artillery salvos, along with the skyrockets and bonfires, delighted him, for he thought that these demonstrations were in celebration of his return. When no *flechera* appeared for the trip across the Orinoco, even though he had dispatched an aide and several messengers, he finally crossed the river in a small canoe, accompanied only by his secretary. Once he was ashore, people passed directly by him without showing the slightest sign of respect. The shouts of "Viva Bolívar" and a "Good-bye, General," from his secretary confirmed an idea that had just assailed him—that his friends had abandoned him.

That morning the Liberator had unexpectedly arrived at the capital. His presence had the twofold effect of restoring public confidence and of slaying at birth the hydra of discord. Magnanimously overlooking the warped designs of his enemies, he made no attempt to investigate their guilty conduct. Thus it was that a few days later he conferred the supreme command of the Army of the East upon General Arismendi. This policy won for him as many friends as his deeds of valor had won admirers for him. Arismendi's faction became a nonentity, and for the first time since Venezuela was raised to the rank of a nation there was but one party—that of the defenders of independence.

Congress sent a deputation to congratulate Bolívar on his victories and to accompany him to the hall where Congress met. He gave a detailed account of everything he had done during his absence. After describing the hardships endured with unexampled perseverance by the liberating army, he pointed out that in less than three months it had freed twelve provinces of New Granada. In his conclusion he emphasized the desire of the Granadines for union with Venezuela, a union that had been his sole aim since he first took up arms. In the name of the Congress, President Zea thanked Bolívar for the marvelous feats of valor accomplished by him and the army in having raised the banner of liberty over the eastern and western Andes. He proposed the union of Quito, Santa Fe, and Venezuela as of infinite value to the cause of independence. Addressing the assembly again, Bolívar repeated to them: "Decree the political union of the two states and you will have fulfilled my most cherished desire and amply rewarded the army for its services."

This vast project was the favorite subject of Bolívar's conversations, in which he delighted in pointing out the advantages that would be brought by this union to all America. To his intimate friends he said: "It gives us the opportunity of remedying in part the injustice that has been done to a great man, to whom, in this way, we shall erect a monument that will attest our gratitude. Calling our republic Colombia and naming the capital Las Casas, we shall demonstrate to the world that we not only have a right to our freedom but that we are also considerate enough to pay honor to the friends and benefactors of humanity. Columbus and Las Casas belong to America.[2] Let us do honor to ourselves by perpetuating their glorious memories."

Bolívar had the good fortune to see his noble efforts triumph. The fundamental law establishing the Republic of Colombia was ratified in Angostura on December 17, a memorable date in the annals of the country for two reasons: it was the birthday of the great republic and the anniversary of the death of its founder. In the eleven-year period that elapsed between 1819 and 1830, the first date marked his triumph, the second, his death. On both days the friends who surrounded him heard these patriotic words from his lips: "Union, union, or anarchy will devour you."

The new law abolished the name of New Granada in providing that the Republic of Colombia should be divided into three large departments—Venezuela, Quito, and Cundinamarca—each to be governed by a vice-president. The capitals of these departments were to be the cities of Caracas, Quito, and Bogotá, without the addition of Santa Fe. A new city bearing the name of Bolívar was to be the capital of the

[2] Bartolomé de las Casas (1475–1566) was a Spanish Dominican missionary in the New World who became known as the "Apostle of the Indians" because of his unceasing efforts to secure the passage of laws protecting the Indians from unjust treatment and slavery. —Ed.

Daniel Florencio O'Leary. Oil painting by Martín Tovar y Tovar, in the Federal
Palace of Caracas.

Boletín de la Academia Nacional de la Historia, Caracas

Proclamation of war to the death.

Cruz Herrera, *Bolívar*

Francisco de Paula Santander.

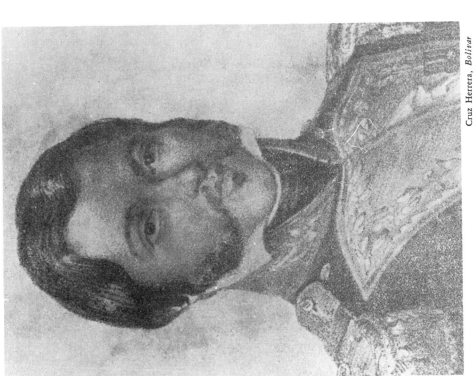

Cruz Herrera, *Bolívar*

José Francisco Bermúdez.

Cruz Herrera, *Bolívar*

José Antonio Páez.

Cruz Herrera, *Bolívar*

Rafael Urdaneta.

Cruz Herrera, *Bolívar*

Pedro Luis Brión.

Revista de la Sociedad Bolivariana de Venezuela

Santiago Mariño.

Crossing of the Andes, 1819. By Tito Salas.

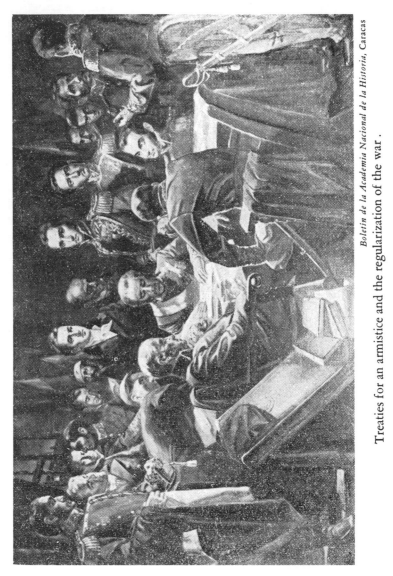

Boletín de la Academia Nacional de la Historia, Caracas

Treaties for an armistice and the regularization of the war .

Revista de la Sociedad Bolivariana de Venezuela

Antonio José de Sucre. By Martín Tovar y Tovar, after an original portrait of the period.

Cruz Herrera, Bolívar

Carlos Soublette.

Meeting between Morillo and Bolívar.

Republic. Since New Granada was represented in Congress by only one of her provinces, Casanare, a constituent assembly was to convene in El Rosario de Cúcuta to discuss the great national law and to confirm it or to modify it in the presence of the representatives of the liberated provinces. The Congress of Angostura proceeded to appoint the principal magistrates on the same day on which it decreed the Republic of Colombia. Bolívar was elected president, and Dr. Juan Germán Roscio and General Santander were appointed vice-presidents of Venezuela and Cundinamarca respectively. Bolívar's services were also rewarded with the most exalted title that a free people can possibly confer, that of Liberator of his country.

These decrees occasioned general rejoicing in the entire country. With this great act Bolívar ceased to be the favored leader and assumed the high rank of chief magistrate in a far-flung and powerful state. Even the royalists semed to respect this change in fortune, but the greatest of all the benefits that it produced was the standing that the nation acquired in foreign countries.

Despite the many affairs of state, Bolívar did not interrupt his military activities. The legion that General John D'Evereux had recruited in Ireland was now beginning to arrive on the island of Margarita. This fine auxiliary unit would have been of great service to the country if various incidents had not occurred to prevent the utilization of its services. The Liberator appointed Colonel Mariano Montilla, pending D'Evereux's arrival, to the command of this unit, with orders to harass the coast from La Guaira to Portobelo once the available strength numbered a thousand men. If the legion reached two thousand, it was to occupy Caracas and then take La Guaira. Thereafter it was to make its way to Río Hacha and Santa Marta, jointly with General Urdaneta. Admiral Brión was ordered to convoy this expedition, which was to begin its operations in January.

In the short space of two weeks of incessant labor and diligence Bolívar laid the foundations of a great republic and dictated measures calculated to ensure its successful progress in the interior and to establish its credit abroad. For the latter purpose he appointed Don Francisco Antonio Zea as special commissioner. The chaotic state of the public treasury was a great threat to the Republic's credit. The agents

who had hitherto been sent to Europe had contracted debts of which
the government had no knowledge, and every day claims were being
presented that could not be satisfied. Zea was under instruction to examine all the pending claims, to consolidate the debt, and to contract
a loan. He also was to seek recognition of the Republic of Colombia
and to arrange treaties with the nations that wanted them. Then Bolívar proceeded to send arms and ammunition to the army of New
Granada. Having done all this, he left Angostura for Bogotá on the
night of December 24.

The Liberator's main purpose in going to Bogotá was to promote
the speedy acceptance of the fundamental law decreed by the Congress
of Angostura. In El Socorro he had the satisfaction of learning that
Santander had obtained a vote of approval from the officials and prominent people of the vicinity, who had great confidence in Bolívar and
recognized, as did everyone, the desirability of the union. On his way
through Apure, Bolívar reviewed the various units quartered there, and
he sent General Antonio José de Sucre from San Juan de Payara to
buy arms in the West Indies with funds raised by General Santander
in Cundinamarca. He neglected nothing and foresaw everything. In
his letters to the vice-president of Venezuela and General Páez, he
emphasized the importance of having Páez take the province of Caracas
if the enemy should move westward or eastward and of having him
then liberate the rest of Venezuela.

Upon learning of the defeat of Colonel Antonio Obando in the
South and of the occupation of Popayán by Calzada, the Liberator
ordered General Valdés and Colonel Mires to march to Obando's aid
with the division that had come into New Granada by way of the salt
mines of Chita. For the troops' march and to facilitate the transportation of the armament that Urdaneta was to bring by way of the Orinoco
and the Meta, he assembled boats and beasts of burden and collected
provisions at designated stopping places. But where he displayed particular zeal was in recommending to Vice-President Roscio the prompt
shipment of the arms so urgently needed by the army. "With two
thousand rifles," he said, "the South can be taken as far as Lima, due
to the favorable state of affairs in that section. What a huge force we

shall be able to mass against Spain through this operation! All America will be freed by this master stroke."

On March 3, 1820, Bolívar entered Bogotá and immediately busied himself with his cherished project, the union of the two republics. On the eighth of the same month he delivered to the Colombians a proclamation in which he pictured the day of peace when the Republic of Colombia, completely free of Spanish domination, would assume its rightful place among the nations. By a remarkable coincidence this proclamation was published on the very day that Ferdinand VII accepted the Constitution of Cádiz, proclaimed by the leader of the rebellion on the island of León. The revolution in Spain had tremendous influence on the fate of America, for it not only freed her from the peril of invasion but also weakened the prestige that Spain still maintained in her far-flung dominions.[3] The state of affairs was really promising for the patriots: the bond uniting the people of Colombia to the Spanish nation was at last broken, and the love of independence, limited previously to certain individuals, now became general. But be it said in honor of the Spaniards that they did not retreat before the peril of their present isolation.

During the Liberator's absence nothing unusual had occurred in Cundinamarca except for the triumph of the royalists in Popayán. This city and the entire vicinity fell into their hands because of the lack of valor and skill on the part of Colonel Antonio Obando. The task of redeeming this loss was given to the Albión Battalion under Colonel Mackintosh, and a column led by Colonel Mires set out to reinforce this battalion. After joining forces, they were to open operations to the south of the Republic, under the command of General Valdés.

On March 20 the Liberator left for El Rosario de Cúcuta, from where he dispatched Colonel Lara with a column composed of the Rifles Battalion and a cavalry squadron to occupy the Valle de Upar in order to create a diversion for Colonel Montilla's expedition, which had occupied Río Hacha on March 12. With no news from General

[3] On January 1, 1820, the troops intended to pacify America rose in revolt against the absolute monarchy and proclaimed the Constitution of Cádiz (1812). When the revolution spread, Ferdinand was compelled to accept the constitution. —Ed.

Urdaneta, who was to have attacked Maracaibo, Montilla marched to the interior, where he soundly defeated a superior royalist force under Colonel Sánchez Lima at Laguna Salada on May 25. The insubordination of an element in the Irish Legion prevented his union with Lara's column, which had succeeded in penetrating into the Valle de Upar. As a result, Montilla was forced to evacuate Río Hacha on June 5, after discharging the insubordinate Irish. In the meantime, Colonel Córdova occupied Mompox on the Upper Magdalena, and subsequently the important positions of Tenerife and Barranca. Montilla headed toward the mouth of the Magdalena, landed in Sabinilla, and followed the river as far as Soledad, where Colonel Córdova joined him. Then he advanced into the interior of the province of Cartagena, where he forced the enemy to take shelter within the walls of the capital.

While this was going on, the Liberator was in Cúcuta, not really idle but enjoying a rest, the first one he had allowed himself for many years. Some details concerning his life there may well be of interest to the reader. After arising at six and dressing, he went to the stables to see the horses, for which he provided excellent care. Upon returning to his room, he read until nine and then ate breakfast, following which he received the reports of the minister of war, his private secretary, and the chief of staff. He listened to them while striding up and down the room or seated in his hammock. Then he had them read to him the dispatches and petitions addressed to him, and proceeded at once to dictate his answers, which were generally very concise and always pertinent. Since he knew all the officers of the army and the civilians, their faults and failings as well as their services, it was an easy matter for him to handle their petitions without any loss of time. The secretary generally began by identifying the petitioner, and if the Liberator was in any doubt at all, he asked if the person applying to him was so and so. Then he would say, "Oh, now I know, he wants a promotion, but read on." After hearing the request, he often added, "Well, half of what he says is not true, but he's a good officer; give it to him." Or else, "No, that fellow is worthless." The secretary then went on to another petition, and with a yes or a no the matter was decided. His decisions were odd at times, and I shall mention one of those that he dictated to me. A doctor, who had availed himself of the anarchy that prevailed in Bogotá between Sámano's flight and Bolívar's arrival to plunder some warehouses, asked for an appointment as staff doctor with the rank of lieutenant colonel. "Be satisfied with what you have stolen," was written on the margin of his petition.

The handling of official matters generally took three hours, at the end of which he gave instructions to his private secretary concerning answers to be written by the latter to the less important letters. He then summoned a trusted aide-de-camp and dictated to him the more important letters, always either walking back and forth or reclining in his hammock, a book in his hand, which he read while the amanuensis was writing a sentence. He expressed his thoughts with great rapidity, and any mistake or hesitation on the part of the writer annoyed him. Once this work was finished, he read until five o'clock in the afternoon, the dinner hour. His fare at the time was very frugal, but this frugality was more a matter of necessity than of preference. When the market afforded them, there was no lack of choice viands and fine wines on his table.

Immediately after dinner he took a horseback ride in the company of his aide and sometimes of his secretary. At night he talked for a while with his friends or with the officers visiting him, and he retired to his bedroom at nine o'clock. There, lying down in a hammock in which he regularly slept, he read until eleven o'clock. His favorite authors at that time were Montesquieu and Rousseau, but he read everything. In his leisure hours he preferred history, and he had a remarkable memory for dates, names, and events. In addition to these activities he frequently wrote articles for the newspapers published in Angostura or Bogotá. His articles were characterized by a certain nervous and forceful style when he was discussing political affairs, but when it came to personal matters, his style was terse and very sarcastic. He enjoyed writing poetry in his free moments, and no less a judge than Olmedo frequently said and even wrote that if Bolívar had devoted himself to poetry he would have been superior to Pindar.[4]

Colonel Briceño Méndez, who was then minister of war, Colonel Salom, and Lieutenant Colonel J. Gabriel Pérez were very close to

[4] José Joaquín Olmedo, the famous Ecuadoran poet, who played an active role in the revolutionary activities of Ecuador and Peru. —Ed.

Bolívar in Cúcuta. A native of Barinas, Briceño was a highly intelligent, well-bred, and good-natured man. Bolívar became acquainted with him in 1813, when he appointed him his secretary. Honored with the general's friendship, Briceño followed him in good times and bad with unselfish loyalty, constantly refusing the military ranks offered him until 1818, when he finally did accept the rank of colonel. As minister of war he displayed talent and diligence and found favor with everyone. His calm and modest manner contrasted greatly with the changeable and fiery disposition of the Liberator. Colonel Bartolomé Salom, the chief of staff, was the opposite of Briceño in temperament, but he was the right man for the role he played at the Liberator's side. However extravagant the orders given him by Bolívar, he had to be convinced that it was absolutely impossible to carry them out before he would offer the slightest objection. His energy was limitless, and he worked night and day, considering himself obliged to perform any kind of task. He was never known to ask a favor.

A few days after the arrival of the Liberator in Cúcuta, the tenth anniversary of the revolution was celebrated, and on the occasion of this happy event he delivered an address recalling how the patriot soldiers had redeemed the American people from death and oblivion over the ten-year period. Aside from his eloquence, the Liberator had very little to give the army. A few pesos to the leaders and officers and a few cents to each soldier were all he could offer them as compensation. Although the resources of New Granada were relatively plentiful, they were not sufficient to supply the needs and requirements of the government, and the money collected was necessarily used for the purchase of arms, for which there was a dire need.

About the middle of April, Morillo received instructions to enforce recognition on the Spanish Main of the constitution that the King of Spain had accepted and to begin negotiations with the dissidents. He wrote to the various leaders of the patriot army and to the Congress in Angostura at the time that he wrote to the Liberator, proposing a brief armistice for the purpose of discussing peace. The Liberator went to San Cristóbal to receive Lieutenant Colonel Don José María Herrera, field adjutant of General La Torre. This was the first time in the course of the war that an envoy bearing a flag of truce, in accordance with the rules of warfare, was sent or received by the belligerents.

The Liberator gladly assented to La Torre's proposal for the suspension of hostilities for a month in order to allow time for General Morillo's commissioners to reach Cúcuta, but he replied to La Torre that he was determined not to receive the commissioners nor to listen to their proposals except on the basis of the recognition of the independence of Colombia. In his answer to Morillo on July 21, Bolívar made it very clear that the people of Colombia had decided for complete independence and that recognition of this independence was a necessary basis for any negotiations. The answers received by Morillo from the patriot leaders showed the unanimity that existed among them with respect to independence. The commissioners sent to negotiate with Congress were not permitted to land in Angostura. Once the Liberator was certain of the loyalty of his subordinates, he resolved to test the good faith of the royalists by employing against Morillo the artifice that the latter himself had used with so little success. He left for Cartagena to inspect in person the state of the troops in that province, to encourage the operations against Santa Marta, and to listen to whatever proposals the royalist commander of the stronghold of Cartagena might want to make to him. On July 1 he had addressed a proclamation to the Spaniards reminding them that liberty had returned to the Peninsula and offering to restore them to the bosom of their families.

At his departure from Cúcuta the Liberator authorized General Urdaneta and Colonel Briceño Méndez to receive Morillo's commissioners and to enter into negotiations with them on the basis of the recognition of independence. Although these negotiations did not bring any satisfactory results, they at least proved useful to the patriots in some respects, especially in the matter of convincing the royalists, if they really needed any further convincing, that the more recent years of the very long war had served to strengthen the determination of the people and government of Colombia to be independent or to die.

After reviewing the various units of the Magdalena Division, the Liberator proceeded to Turbaco, where he arrived on August 26,

1820. The headquarters of the division besieging Cartagena was located there. In an exchange of correspondence with Brigadier Torres, the governor of Cartagena, regarding a suspension of hostilities, Bolívar assured him that nothing was more in conformity with his wishes. Torres was under the impression that the Liberator would sacrifice the independence of his country. His second letter, written in a fit of temper caused by wounded vanity, insulted Bolívar, who, indignant at the discourteous tone of the Spaniard, dictated a characteristic answer in which he pointed out how absurd it was to propose submission to Spain, a detestably governed nation that was the laughingstock of Europe and that was cursed by America for her atrocities. He added that the Colombians were determined to fight for centuries rather than suffer the humiliation of being Spanish. Indignant in his turn and hopeful of being able to take Bolívar prisoner, the governor of Cartagena ordered the León Regiment to make a sally from the stronghold. It obtained no advantage other than that of temporarily putting the besieging troops to flight. Bolívar had already left Turbaco to return to the army, which he had left in Cúcuta.

Aware that the communications established with the Spaniards had provoked the desertion of Americans serving in the royalist ranks, the Liberator decided to renew his correspondence with General Morillo. Although he was not willing to yield an inch of territory, he was ready to sacrifice any protocol, provided any benefit, however small, were obtained. On his arrival in San Cristóbal on September 21, he wrote to the royalist general in chief, designating San Fernando de Apure as the most appropriate site for the conferences, since, he said, he intended to establish his headquarters there about the end of October. Morillo, who was very eager to end hostilities, lost no time in giving his consent and in appointing commissioners with instructions to proceed to San Fernando.

The Liberator, in the meantime, continued his march in order to assume command of the army, which had moved toward Mérida when it received his orders. After overtaking it at the Chama bridge, a strong position that the enemy had abandoned, he himself led the pursuit of the enemy at the head of two battalions of light infantry. On October 1 he entered Mérida, accompanied only by his staff, the enemy having evacuated the city the previous day. The pursuit was vigorously continued, and the royalists suffered greatly in their rapid retreat. They did not stop until they were beyond the confines of the provinces of Mérida and Trujillo. The patriots continued their advance after a brief rest in the capital and went on to Trujillo.

Morillo's answer to the letter that the Liberator sent him from San Cristóbal was considerably delayed because of the destination to which it was sent. The explanation of the delay is that one of the Liberator's motives in writing his letter was to conceal his movements. Now, in order to explain the different route that had been assigned to the army and to hasten the negotiations, he wrote again to Morillo on October 26. In his letter, after explaining that the illness of General Urdaneta had prevented him from going to San Fernando, Bolívar proposed an armistice for a period of four to six months during which the Colombian army would occupy the positions it held at the time of the ratification of the treaty. If any part of the proposal were considered contrary to the interests of Spain, stated areas could be left open to hostilities. In his reply of the twenty-ninth, Morillo stated that he was not authorized to accept the proposals, but he went on to say that his commissioners were prepared to discuss the articles and to open negotiations. Several other letters passed between Bolívar and Morillo on the same subject before the arrival of the commissioners.

In the meantime, military operations continued, and the losses to which Morillo had alluded in one of his letters were not exaggerated. Among other American officers, Colonel Reyes Vargas, whose name I have mentioned in the early pages of these memoirs, deserted from the Spanish ranks and, as on the previous occasion, brought to the side that he joined something more positive than the doubtful faith of a deserter. His influence was great in the western sector of Venezuela, and his natural sagacity and knowledge of the country made him a very valuable acquisition. When Morillo moved from Barquisimeto with 2,500 of his best troops, Reyes, with his guerrilla band, harassed his flanks and rearguard, keeping him in a constant state of alarm, and not even in Carache, where the royalist general established his headquarters, was he free from the attacks.

Neither Bolívar nor Morillo was in a hurry to engage in combat.

The republican leader, despite the haughty tone he had employed in his communications with the royalist general, was scarcely in a position to take the offensive, as much because of the weakness of his forces as because of a lack of ammunition. To this must be added the fact that Morillo was making his stand in the mountainous country, where the badly crippled patriot cavalry could not operate. No one, however, could match Bolívar in the art of commanding respect from the enemy. By spreading reports that, though extremely exaggerated, seemed quite authentic, he frequently managed to convince the enemy that he commanded superior forces. On this occasion he resorted to the same stratagem and succeeded in deceiving his opponent, who, had he advanced a few leagues beyond Carache, would have seen for himself that Bolívar was in no position to oppose him.

The commissioners finally reached Trujillo, where they were received by General A. J. de Sucre, Colonel Pedro Briceño Méndez, and Colonel José Gabriel Pérez, appointed by Bolívar to negotiate with them. The patriot army had withdrawn to Sabana Larga, a plain located seven leagues to the south of Carache. During the negotiations the two chiefs suspended hostilities by tacit agreement, but in the rest of the Republic the war continued unabated. The Liberator gave instructions to the various units to advance with as much speed as prudence dictated so as to occupy the widest expanse of territory and the most advantageous positions at the time when the armistice would be announced. These orders were carried out at most of the military posts, and advantages of great importance were thus gained, except in the Maracaibo area.

Since both sides were equally anxious to obtain the same result, the conferences were not prolonged with useless debate. On November 25, 1820, two treaties were concluded, both of which were favorable to the cause of humanity, but particularly to the cause of America's independence. In the first of these an armistice of six months' duration, with each article favorable to the Colombians, was agreed upon. The second, a treaty for the regularization of the war, does honor to Bolívar and his humanitarian views, since it was he who proposed and worded it, as well as to Morillo, who accepted and ratified it. According to this treaty, all captured personnel were to be kept as prisoners of war within the territory of Colombia until an exchange could be effected. The wounded and the sick would be free to rejoin their units after they had recovered. The chiefs of both armies would have the right to appoint commissioners to examine the condition of the prisoners. The inhabitants of towns alternately occupied by the opposing armies would enjoy complete liberty no matter what their previous services or opinions had been.

It should be observed that in this treaty the royalist general expressly recognized the Republic of Colombia and Bolívar as its president. Everyone attributed great significance to this recognition, but for the Liberator it was of little moment compared with the solid advantages he had cleverly and skillfully obtained. Every article of the treaties contained something favorable to the Colombians, and, as the facts proved, this negotiation decided the independence of the country.

At the conclusion of this important negotiation General Morillo expressed a keen desire to meet Bolívar, and a meeting was arranged in the wretched village of Santa Ana, halfway between the two camps. On the morning of November 27, General Morillo appeared with fifty ranking officers and an escort of a squadron of hussars, which latter he ordered to retire when I told him that Bolívar would soon arrive with only ten or twelve officers and the royalist commissioners. When the Liberator's party came into sight, the Spanish general, who was wearing his dress uniform with many decorations, wanted to know which one was Bolívar. When Bolívar was pointed out to him, he exclaimed, "What, that little man with the blue coat and the campaign cap, riding a mule?" No sooner had he finished speaking than the little man was at his side, and they both leaped to the ground and embraced each other warmly and cordially. Then they proceeded to a house where General Morillo had arranged a simple banquet in honor of his illustrious guest.

During the meal and throughout the day they talked cheerfully about the events of the war, showing a great deal of mutual tolerance. Each admired the perseverance of his adversary in overcoming the obstacles with which he was confronted, and both expressed the hope that no unfortunate incident would force them to renew hostilities. General Morillo proposed the erection of a monument on the spot where he had embraced his opponent, in order to remind future generations of the sincerity with which the belligerents had cast aside their personal rancor and their national enmity. This noble proposal was gladly seconded by Bolívar, and all the officers present set to work and dragged a huge square stone to the selected site, to be used as a base for the proposed column. Standing upon this stone, the chiefs who had fought each other so furiously for so many long years reiterated their ardent wishes for peace and mutual understanding. Night put an end to the day's rejoicings, but it did not separate the rival generals. Under the same roof and in the same room Bolívar and Morillo slept soundly, making up, perhaps, for the many wakeful nights they had caused each other. On the following day Morillo accompanied the Liberator to the place where they had met for the first time as friends. There they said good-bye and separated forever. The rough stone that they and their officers moved to that spot is still to be found there, commemorating this interesting meeting.

It was Bolívar's destiny to have no respite, not even after triumphing on the field of battle or in the political arena. By every post he now received letters from some of his friends and from various military leaders who were especially opposed to an armistice that would not ensure the end of the war and the immediate recognition of independence. It required all the force of his character to weather the struggle between his own convictions and the mistaken conclusions of those who were opposed to the treaty. Happily for America, his good judgment did not desert him in such momentous circumstances. There were, however, those who accused him of ulterior motives and the most selfish of aspirations, but in the face of such calumny he maintained a dignified silence.

The Liberator left Trujillo by way of Niquitao, because he wanted to inspect in person the line of demarcation between the two sides in the province of Barinas, as well as to visit the army encampments during the armistice. On December 7, 1820, from Barinas, he made an announcement to the army about the treaty he had signed, in a proclamation characterizing the truce period of six months as the first step toward peace and as a prelude to their future tranquillity.

CHAPTER FOURTEEN

I T WAS IN BARINAS that the Liberator received the news of the political upheaval in Guayaquil on October 9, 1820, which resulted in the separation of that province from the Spanish government. Although he was not satisfied with the course taken by the revolution there, since the province had declared itself an independent state, he realized the advantages that step would bring to the general cause, comforting himself with the hope that experience would convince the inhabitants of Guayaquil of the necessity of uniting themselves politically with Colombia.

The political and military events of the year 1820 resulted in very important advantages for the Republic. Public opinion, previously unfriendly to the patriots, was now, even more than arms, their principal support, and this can be considered the greatest triumph won by Colombia during the year. Along with this improvement in morale, the territory of the Republic had been extended to a considerable degree. In addition, the army swelled its ranks with the great number of Americans who were abandoning the Spanish standards.

It was during this trying period for the royalist cause that General Morillo, called to Spain by the government, announced his departure to the army and to those inhabitants of Venezuela who still remained faithful to the King. General Don Miguel de la Torre succeeded Morillo as commander in chief of the army. Great changes had taken place on the mainland during the five years that had elapsed since Morillo's arrival in Venezuela, which he had found subjugated by the cruel Boves. The mere show of arms was sufficient to overcome the timid defenders of independence in New Granada, with the exception of Cartagena and a few places where the defenders of liberty stood their ground. Such was the state of the country in 1816 when an exile, and *insurgent*, relying on the inexhaustible resources of his genius, landed in Venezuela and, unfurling the standard of revolt, established the foundations of a great republic in the midst of the solitude of the Orinoco. Scorning perils and reverses, he fought steadily and courageously until he overcame the adverse blows of fate. Morillo's unwise administration was, no doubt, the most powerful ally of the patriots, for if he had governed with the forbearance called for by his title of peacemaker, it would have been more difficult afterward to awaken the people from their apathy.

However great the political errors of Morillo may have been, there can be no denial of his unusual talents as a soldier. He had been born to be a soldier in the literal sense of the word, and he felt at home only in army camps. Nor can one overlook the fact that his personal courage showed evidence of the intermingling of Iberian blood with that of the Goth and the Carthaginian. The *llaneros*, who are not free with their praise, remarked that "it was a pity that he had been born in Spain and a shame that he was not a patriot." There is, however, no parallel between Morillo and Bolívar. I might say of them what Voltaire said of Charles XII and Alexander the Great, that the former would have been the outstanding soldier in the army of the latter.

It is likely that history will pass judgment on Morillo's conduct with more harshness than justice. His noble efforts in support of the independence of his native country will remain obscure in the face of his futile solicitude in enslaving America, and the many lives that his valor saved in Spain will be forgotten. On the other hand, the blood of Caldas, Torres, and Camacho will be an everlasting stain on the pages of his history, and Zea's immortal eloquence will stand as a terrible indictment against him. I must also emphasize the fact that from the memorable day when Morillo met Bolívar he forgot his old animosity and lost no occasion—and I was a witness of this years afterward—to speak most highly, with a friend's devotion, of his opponent and his noble deeds.

On January 5, 1821, the Liberator reached Bogotá, where he was greeted, as always, with the greatest enthusiasm. Matters in the southern sector of the Republic were now demanding the government's entire attention. The division under the command of General Valdés had routed an enemy unit in La Plata on April 26, 1820, thus opening a line of communication to the Cauca Valley, which was occupied after a decisive victory in Pitayó on June 6 over a column of nine hundred royalists. Although the Spaniards evacuated Popayán after this defeat, the success of the Colombian forces was not commensurate with the hopes thus aroused. Valdés had military talent, but his gruff, domineering manner offended the inhabitants of Cali and provoked a disagreement that deprived the division of the resources being supplied for the sustenance of the troops. Provided with reinforcements, he was able to proceed to Popayán, where he remained for some time before invading enemy territory in November, after he had received orders from the Liberator to attack Pasto "even if he had no troops other than his aides." By the time of the arrival of the commissioners sent from Trujillo with orders to suspend hostilities, an encounter had already taken place in Genoy, south of the Juanambú River, with calamitous results for the Colombian troops. Learning of these events upon his arrival in Bogotá, the Liberator decided to relieve Valdés of the command of the army and the management of affairs in the South. Seeking a replacement, he decided upon Sucre, a young man who was worthy of being chosen for this honor.

A native of Cumaná, where he was born in the year 1793,[1] General Antonio José de Sucre ardently embraced the cause of the revolution while still quite young. After Miranda's capitulation, he found asylum outside his native land and then returned under Mariño's command to help free it. After witnessing the subjugation of his country for a second time, he served with distinction in the Army of the East during the third period of independence until his appointment to Bolívar's staff. In the year 1819, Bolívar had been quite displeased when Zea promoted Sucre to the rank of brigadier general. A chance encounter on the Orinoco after the battle of Boyacá marked the beginning of the friendship between these two men who contributed the greatest share in bringing liberty to South America. On that occasion Sucre explained that he had not thought for a moment of accepting the promotion without General Bolívar's approval. Some months before Sucre was appointed to the command of the Army of the South, he went out to meet the Liberator as the latter was entering Cúcuta on his way back from Cartagena. On seeing him, I, who did not know him, asked the Liberator who the poor horseman approaching us was. "He is one of the best officers in the army," he replied. "Strange as it may seem, he is not well known, nor does anyone suspect his capabilities. I am determined to bring him out of obscurity, for I am convinced that some day he will rival me."

Sucre immediately left Bogotá and met Valdés as he was withdrawing, surrounded by trouble on all sides. Sucre's arrival and the notice given the royalists about the armistice greatly improved the army's morale. His conciliatory conduct and affable manner, coupled with his energy and strength of character, were productive of a salutary reaction in public opinion, resulting in an improvement in the state of affairs within a short time.

The Liberator himself had already left Bogotá to go to the provinces in the South, but he found it necessary to return to the capital in order to expedite the departure of J. Rafael Revenga and Tiburcio Echeverría, whom he had delegated to go to Spain in order to seek recog-

[1] Sucre was born on February 3, 1795. See Villanueva, *Vida de D. Antonio José de Sucre* (Caracas, 1945), pp. 5–6; the baptismal certificate is published in a note. —Pedro Grases.

nition by the King of the independence of Colombia. In the letter he addressed to the King he praised the role of the King as peacemaker and pointed out to him that Colombia's existence was necessary for his peace of mind and for the welfare of the Colombians, who would offer a second homeland to the Spanish people.

After making these arrangements, the Liberator set out for the North at the beginning of February. Before reaching Cúcuta, he was informed that the inhabitants of Maracaibo had thrown off the Spanish yoke and sought the aid of Colombian troops to support their insurrection. This incident gave rise to a lengthy correspondence between General Urdaneta and General La Torre, as well as between La Torre and the Liberator. Since the facts were not set forth in this correspondence with the preciseness and truth that history demands, and since later writers may fall into error if they accept the story of that event as it has been published, I am going to give an exact account of what happened.

When the Liberator granted the armistice, he was convinced that Spain would not consent to recognize the independence of Colombia. He was of the opinion, however, that at the moment there were greater advantages to be gained in adopting a policy of negotiation than in continuing military occupations. The suspension of hostilities would permit communication, interrupted for so long, between people of the same social background and would afford new opportunities in the broad field of intrigue.

General Urdaneta, a native of Maracaibo himself, began to use his influence with the prominent people there to bring about a change. The military authority was in the hands of Lieutenant Colonel Francisco Delgado, who had feelings of personal resentment against the very people he was serving. Once arrangements were made, Urdaneta sent Lieutenant Colonel José Rafael las Heras with the Tiradores Battalion to occupy a point in the vicinity of Lake Maracaibo and then the island of Gibraltar. After a decision had been made to start a revolt, Las Heras received a deputation from the conspirators who implored him to take the city under his protection. On January 28, 1821, the civil and military authorities met with the prominent citizens and drew up a proclamation in which they declared their separation from Spain and their submission to the government of Colombia. Las Heras arrived with his troops on the following day. This important acquisition was of inestimable value to Colombia, inasmuch as Maracaibo was of supreme importance as a base of operations. The royalists were reduced, as a result, to the city of Cumaná and the provinces of Coro and Caracas, the first of which remained isolated after the occupation of Maracaibo.

General La Torre protested, as was natural, against the conduct of Las Heras. Urdaneta maintained that, since it was lawful to accept a deserter, Maracaibo, as a deserter in a larger sense, had the same right to protection. In his note to General La Torre, the Liberator stated that he could find no evidence of a violation on the part of the Colombian government in the occupation of Maracaibo at the invitation of its people. Since the people of Maracaibo had proclaimed their independence, they were free to join any nation. Furthermore, there was nothing in the Trujillo armistice that guaranteed the integrity of territories or denied the right to assist persons seeking protection. If arbitration were necessary, Colombia's choice would be Brigadier Correa. Bolívar ended this note with an inquiry concerning the possible outbreak of hostilities before the expiration of the armistice.

The royalist general maintained silence concerning the suggested arbitration, but he notified Bolívar that he would respect the armistice. La Torre was forced to content himself with futile complaints and to witness helplessly the loss of one of the most important provinces under his command. Since his army was visibly being weakened by numerous desertions, his position became more precarious as the days went by. His opponent, having gained even more advantage than he had in mind when he signed the Trujillo treaty, wrote to him on March 10, 1821, to inform him that he regretted to announce that the circumstance covered by Article 12 of the Trujillo treaty had arisen and that consequently hostilities would be resumed forty days from that date.[2] "Between the doubtful outcome of a campaign," he added, "and

---

[2] When La Torre refused to accede to Bolívar's request that certain Venezuelan territory be turned over to the patriots, Bolívar informed him that hostilities would be resumed in accordance with the provision in Article 12 that either side might decide to end the armistice if dissatisfied with the existing conditions. —Ed.

the certain sacrifice of our army to pestilence and hunger, there can be no choice. My duty, then, is to make peace or to fight. Necessity is the first law, the most inexorable of all laws—to it I must submit." La Torre replied that the truce would terminate on April 28, because neither he nor the commissioners were authorized to recognize independence. He then appealed to the world in a manifesto that the world perhaps read indifferently, if, indeed, it read it at all. In a proclamation addressed to his soldiers, Bolívar called upon them to complete the emancipation of Colombia and to be ever mindful of their obligation to be compassionate toward those who surrendered to their victorious arms.

In the meantime, the Liberator visited the Apure llanos to confer with Páez about the next campaign. He entrusted General Soublette, whom he had appointed vice-president of Venezuela the previous year, with the direction of the campaign in the East, and ordered him to try to capture Caracas by the middle of May. He instructed General Urdaneta to subdue Coro and then to proceed through Barquisimeto as far as the mountain of El Altar, where the main body of the army, coming from San Carlos, would join him. Páez was to cross the Apure at the Nutrias crossing and, following the route taken by the La Guardia division under Colonel Ambrosio Plaza, to join Urdaneta's division at the appointed spot. Upon his return to Barinas and before undertaking operations, the Liberator issued a proclamation to the army and another to the Spaniards, outlining the reasons that impelled him to renew hostilities. He told the soldiers that hostilities would be resumed within three days and warned them of the strict obligation, under pain of death, of complying with the articles for the regularization of the war. In his proclamation to the Spaniards he declared that it was the Spanish government that wanted war, for it had absolutely refused the offer of peace made through the Colombian emissary in London. He informed them that the government of Colombia had not violated the armistice except in that its troops had taken up quarters inside Barinas rather than in the environs. Finally, he assured them that the Colombians would observe, with utter strictness, the treaty for the regularization of the war.

The campaign of 1821 began on the morning of April 28 when a

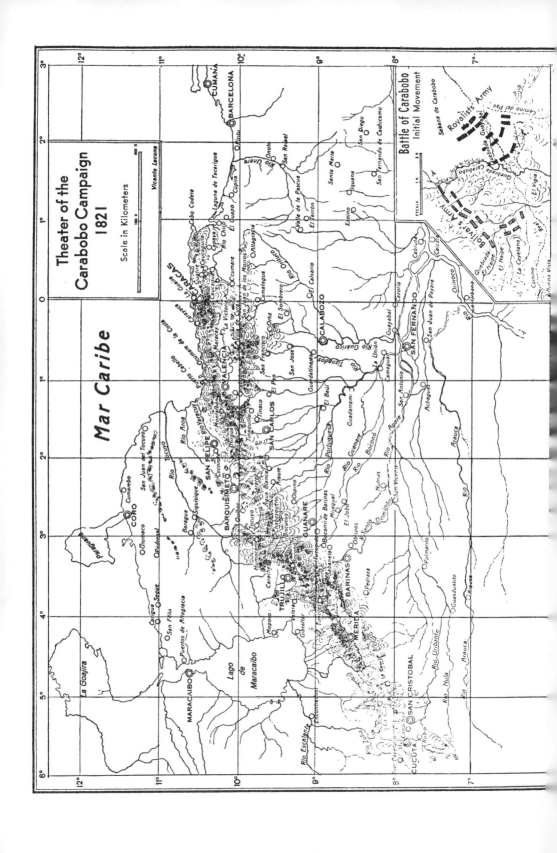

Theater of the
Carabobo Campaign
1821

Scale in Kilometers

Vicente Lacuna

Mar Caribe

Battle of Carabobo
Initial Movement

detachment of Colombian cavalry crossed the Santo Domingo River and routed the royalist outposts in Boconó. Immediately thereafter, Colonel Plaza's division, at the Liberator's orders, invaded the territory occupied by the Spaniards, entered Guanare, and then marched upon San Carlos, which was evacuated by the royalists. Bolívar established his headquarters there in order to allow time for the incorporation of the divisions of Páez and Urdaneta before moving against La Torre, who had concentrated his troops in the vicinity of Valencia.

There is, perhaps, no country in the world where military operations are more difficult than in South America, a land where distances are considerable, the population small, and the roads generally very poor. The nature of the terrain and all kinds of privations combined to delay the arrival of the various army units. General Urdaneta, with the first La Guardia division, occupied Coro on May 11. After taking all necessary precautions, he started out for the Liberator's headquarters, but traveling difficulties and illness prevented him from arriving on time. General Páez also had obstacles to overcome, and he was unable to reach San Carlos until the middle of June. There the army was organized into three divisions, commanded respectively by General Páez, General Cedeño, and Colonel Plaza. General Mariño was the adjutant general. The entire force contained 6,500 men when it passed in review in Tinaquillo on June 23.

The division in the East was able to carry out its assignment with more punctuality. General Bermúdez marched along the coast, defeated a royalist force of seven hundred men in Guatire on May 13, and occupied the capital of Venezuela on the following day. Naturally alarmed by this movement to his rear, La Torre detached a unit commanded by General Morales to protect Caracas. When Bermúdez was attacked by superior forces, he had to give way, with the result that Caracas was once more occupied by the royalists. Morales, with the majority of his troops, had time to rejoin La Torre before the Liberator could attack him. The small column of Colonel Cruz Carrillo was more fortunate in the diversion that it created near San Felipe. Unaware of the size of Carrillo's forces, the royalist general assigned two infantry units headed by Colonel Juan Tello to halt them, just at the moment when the Liberator was a few leagues from his headquarters.

At dawn on March 24, 1821, the liberating army began its march. When it reached the heights of Buenavista, the royalists were already drawn up in battle formation on the Carabobo plain below and the surrounding hills, ready to block the entrance of the Colombians on to the plain, whether by the road from San Carlos or by the one from El Pao. Both entrances were well defended, especially the one on the San Carlos road, where La Torre had placed his artillery.

The Liberator, convinced that La Torre expected only a frontal attack, ordered General Páez to make his way along a narrow and rough trail, which led off to the left from the San Carlos road, and to fall upon the right flank of the royalist army. Despite having to pass through a narrow defile two by two and to form under a deadly fire from a large number of enemy skirmishers deployed on top of a very steep high hill that had to be climbed, the Colombian infantry advanced and gained possession of the heights, thanks to the bravery of the leading Apure Battalion, a brilliant bayonet charge by the Británico Battalion, and the prompt aid of several companies of the Tiradores Battalion of the Second Division. This position was won at the cost of much bloodshed; in less than a quarter of an hour one-third of the effective force of these battalions was out of action. The royalists rallied, but the Colombian divisions had already passed through the defile and were debouching on to the plain at two points. The cavalry attacked furiously and put the royalist cavalry to flight. The royalist infantry also gave ground, and whole battalions surrendered. Abandoning his artillery, La Torre retreated with his reserves and a part of his cavalry. The Liberator pursued him with the Granaderos and Rifles battalions and the cavalry of Páez; but such was the discipline of the Spanish infantry and the skill with which the royalist general led them that he was able to cover in good order a distance of six leagues in open country, despite the repeated attacks of the Colombian cavalry. Nonetheless, the Valancey Battalion was the only unit that succeeded in reaching Valencia.

The Spanish field forces at Carabobo were somewhat inferior in number to those of the republicans, but scarcely half of the latter were in combat. The losses in dead and wounded were considerable on both sides, but the patriot losses in leaders and officers were much greater.

Cedeño and Colonel Plaza, the commanders of the second and third divisions, fell victims of their own fearlessness after displaying the heroic courage characteristic of their respective units. The prisoners taken on the battlefield were treated with every consideration and courtesy, and the wounded were given the best of possible care. As soon as they had recovered their health, they were returned to their own units, in conformity with the treaty of Santa Ana.

On the day after the battle of Carabobo the Liberator wrote an account of the victory in a letter to the vice-president of Colombia.[3] As he expressed it, "Yesterday a splendid victory confirmed the political birth of the Republic of Colombia." Singling out General Páez for special mention, he said that in the name of the Congress he offered him on the battlefield the rank of general in chief of the army. A glowing tribute paid to the outstanding heroism of General Cedeño and Colonel Plaza is followed by an expression of grief over their loss to the Republic. His final words describe the army as "the greatest and finest ever to bear arms on any battlefield in Colombia."

After the necessary instructions had been given to Colonel Rangel regarding his assignment to blockade Puerto Cabello, and a unit commanded by Colonel Las Heras had been sent out against Tello, and another unit had been dispatched in pursuit of the scattered enemy who had gone off in the direction of El Pao and Calabozo, the Liberator, at the head of three of the La Guardia battalions and a squadron of lancers, set out to occupy Caracas and to make a demand for surrender to the column headed by Colonel José Pereira, which was pursuing Bermúdez. After an attempt to proceed to Puerto Cabello along the coast when he heard of La Torre's defeat, Pereira had returned to La Guaira. The Liberator reached Caracas on the night of May 29, accompanied only by General Páez and his staff. On the thirtieth he learned of Pereira's move and sent Lieutenant Colonel Ibarra, his aide, with a picket of dragoons to occupy La Guaira. This he did, but Pereira's countermarch forced him to withdraw. When the Liberator was informed of what had happened, he went to the port with the troops that had arrived from Valencia. Pereira, all hope of aid lost, accepted

---

[3] In Bolívar's *Obras completas* (1947), I, 566–567, this document appears as one addressed to the president of the General Congress of Colombia. —Pedro Grases.

the terms of the most honorable surrender, which Ibarra offered him and which met with the Liberator's approval. Colonel Tello's unit was more fortunate and succeeded in getting into Puerto Cabello before the blockade of the stronghold was established. The entire country, with the exception of this fortress and Cumaná, was now under the control of the republican government. After an absence of seven years, during which he experienced trials, reverses, and victories, Bolívar had the good fortune to return in triumph to the city of his birth.

The enthusiasm of the inhabitants of Caracas almost reached the point of delirium when they witnessed the arrival in their midst of the vigorous champion of American independence. A great throng of people from every walk of life flocked to his home, eager to see him. Notwithstanding his long absence and the deep affection he had for the city, he stayed there for only a few days. After he had organized the government of the province and left instructions with Soublette for the efficient handling of the administration, he returned to Valencia. On the main highway from Caracas was his San Mateo estate, which held many fond memories for him from the time of his childhood. Here he spent several days, devoting his time to the pleasant activities of the country life he enjoyed so much. Of the thousand slaves he owned before the revolution, he found only three, and he immediately gave these their liberty. Then he went back to Caracas for a very short visit before departing finally for Bogotá on August 1 to complete the glorious project that was then his chief concern—the liberation of the southern sector of the Republic.

While the military events that I have recounted were taking place, the general government of the Republic had moved, early in 1821, to El Rosario de Cúcuta, the city designated by the Congress of Angostura as the seat of the capital of Colombia. Shortly thereafter Vice-President Roscio died, and the worthy citizen named by the Liberator to succeed him, General Luis Eduardo Azuola, survived his predecessor only a short time. Chosen to replace him was the distinguished General Nariño, a man of unusual gifts who had long been active in the cause of the revolution. On May 6 the first Constitutional Congress of the nineteen free provinces of Colombia was installed.[4] After a lengthy dis-

---

[4] The representatives of only nineteen provinces attended this meeting.

cussion and a considerable amount of sustained opposition, it was agreed to adopt the central system of government. The union was unanimously voted, and on June 6 this was announced to the people in a proclamation.

At the same time that the president of the Congress notified Bolívar of its installation, the latter learned that his enemies were busy spreading spiteful calumnies in order to ruin his reputation. No one was more sensitive to such attacks than Bolívar. Many times did I see him provoked to anger or rather suffering indescribable torment as the result of reading an article written against him in some contemptible scandal sheet. This reaction may not be a mark of a great mind, but it does, indeed, indicate high regard for public opinion. His congratulatory letter to the Congress shows clearly the emotions he felt when writing it. Rejoicing over the installation, he declares that he is not the president of this republic because he was not elected by this body. He adds that he is weary of hearing himself called a tyrant by his enemies. His final comment is that if the Congress persists in continuing him in the presidency, he will renounce everything and leave his native land. Despite this forceful letter and other efforts, Congress did not see fit to accept his resignation. This body of talented and respectable men did not wish to endanger the country's welfare by entrusting the direction of affairs of state to inexpert hands. They made an appeal to Bolívar's spirit of patriotism, an appeal that was never made to him in vain, and both continued their useful labors—Congress establishing the Republic and Bolívar crowning it with the laurels of victory.

The triumph of the Colombian army on the field of Carabobo filled Congress with jubilation, as was to be expected. It voted honors for the triumph to the Liberator and to all the other heroes of the battle, and it ordered an Attic column to be erected on the field of Carabobo to record for posterity the glory of the day. More than once did the grateful Congress honor Bolívar's deeds of valor with similar decrees. However, throughout the length and breadth of Colombia there is no column, no statue, no bust that "records for posterity his name" or his deeds.[5] The Liberator, though not unresponsive to just praise, was indifferent to this type of monument, perhaps because he was aware that

[5] This was written in 1832.—Simón Bolívar O'Leary.

monuments erected in his honor would some time be destroyed, since partisan hatred is, unfortunately, more violent in South America than in any other part of the world.

On the way to Bogotá the Liberator passed through Valencia, San Carlos, Barquisimeto, and Trujillo, receiving in all the cities along the way the respectful tribute of a grateful people. After crossing Lake Maracaibo in a small schooner, he landed at the port of the same name on August 28, 1821. Preparations for the campaign were continued with unceasing activity. The Liberator, as usual, was constantly busy supervising all the work and rushing it to completion. He ordered the units he had selected to be sent first to Santa Marta, where he himself was planning to go as soon as he had taken care of the affairs of state that had accumulated during his last journey.

It was at this stage that he received a communication from the president of Congress announcing his unanimous re-election to the presidency and urgently summoning him to take over his office. In compliance with this mandate, he set out for Cúcuta, where he arrived during the night of September 22. He found that the constitution had already been ratified, and although the defects that it contained did not escape his sharp eye, he believed any objection to be futile. An omnipotent legislative power and an executive who was without power except in unusual circumstances were the outstanding features of this document. The legislators in Cúcuta were undoubtedly motivated by highly patriotic and honorable principles, but they seemed to forget that they were making laws for a people who were totally unprepared for the enjoyment of a democratic system. A small and heterogeneous population, made up of whites, Negroes, Indians, and individuals with mixed blood, scattered over an extensive territory of varying climates, and with no bond other than religion and language, the former corrupted, the latter degenerate, could certainly not be considered ready to make good use of its sovereignty. But the evil genius of the Republic, the genius of demagogy, triumphed over the dictates of reason and the counsels of experience. When the bells of El Rosario were rung to celebrate the constitution, the Liberator exclaimed: "They are tolling for Colombia."

The Congress of Cúcuta established a central government and

divided the territory into departments, provinces, and cantons, abolishing the former vice-presidencies. At the head of the departments were placed magistrates called intendants, who were the immediate agents of the executive. The legislative power was exercised by the Senate and the House of Representatives, whose members were chosen by electoral colleges that received their powers from the vote of the citizens who had the franchise. The president's term of office was four years, and he could be re-elected for a second term, as could the vice-president, who assumed the executive power in his absence. The president was commander in chief of the armed forces. He was responsible for the acts of his government, but his authority was extremely limited except in case of a foreign invasion or a domestic disturbance, at which time he would assume complete control of the nation. According to Bolívar, "the government of Colombia was a limpid stream or a devastating torrent." The ministers of state, as mere subordinates, were responsible for their acts only to the head of the nation. The judiciary was absolutely independent of the executive power, though the latter was responsible for the enforcement of the laws. In this respect the administration of justice in Colombia was radically defective, with the result that the judges often were protectors of criminals.

Congress partially confirmed Bolívar's decrees abolishing slavery. From the date of the promulgation of the new law, the children of slaves were born free, and the owners of mothers were obliged to support them until their eighteenth birthday. A tax of from 3 to 10 percent was established on property inherited in Colombia, in order to provide a fund for the manumission of the slaves. Although this law was humanitarian and equitable in part, it did not satisfy Bolívar, who always pleaded for the absolute and unconditional abolition of slavery. He had sought to have the Congress "decree the absolute freedom of all Colombians by the fact of their birth in the territory of the Republic." No selfish designs or petty ideas born of expedience could reconcile him to a system so palpably unjust. Not even his most ardent political enemies can question the motives governing his conduct, for from the beginning of the revolution he gave manifest proof of a generous love for mankind that has seldom, if ever, been surpassed. When he freed the many slaves he had inherited, he sacrificed a respectable fortune and became worthy to plead for complete emancipation. In the period of his greatest popularity there were people who, in their anxiety to win his good will, destroyed with their own hands the infamous titles that gave them property rights over their unhappy fellow men.

Among the measures of doubtful value adopted by the Congress, the most important was the removal of the capital from El Rosario de Cúcuta to Bogotá. Even though Cúcuta was farther away from the theater of the war in the South than Bogotá, its location was undoubtedly preferable for the capital of Colombia. One special advantage was that the trip to it from any point in the Republic could be made by water most of the way. But the principal advantage came from its nearness to the important departments of Venezuela. Unfortunately, all this was completely disregarded in order to satisfy the whims of Santander, who had been raised to the vice-presidency through the influence of the Liberator. This decision was fatal to the peace and harmony of the two sections of the Republic in later years.

The Cúcuta legislators did not limit themselves to proclaiming a constitution. Usurping the powers of a constituent congress, they repealed several of the old laws and passed others to take their place. Their financial measures bear the seal of liberality, but they were not at all consistent with the backward state of the country. Excise taxes were abolished, being replaced by the direct territorial tax. Some convents were taken over, and, although they were transformed into educational institutions, the religious feelings of the people were thereby offended. The previous censorship that had shackled the freedom of the press was abolished. But the country was not ready for such advanced steps. The Congress of Cúcuta made many blunders, which originated in a lack of experience and an exaggerated devotion to liberty; but the search for perfection is always praiseworthy, even when it does not attain the desired goal. How happy Colombia would have been if less noble sentiments had not influenced the deliberations of her future congresses!

The day appointed for the installation of the eminent public officials was drawing near, and Bolívar, who was especially anxious to carry on the war, once again refused the honor offered him, in a letter addressed to the president of the Congress. He declared that he was a soldier by necessity and by choice, and that a government office was a torture chamber for him. If the Congress persisted, he would accept only as an act of obedience, and he would take the title of president only for the duration of the war and on condition that he might continue the campaign at the head of the army, leaving the government in the capable hands of General Santander. The frankness and sincerity of this letter are characteristic of the nature of its author. He never could endure the ceremonies and the tedious routine of official life. So great was his distaste for them that only very rarely did he occupy the residence of the chief magistrate in the capitals where he exercised command. Nor was he the man, as he said so frequently, to govern in times of peace and tranquillity. Although there were few who could endure hardships as well as he and dispatch public business with such tireless energy, his military habits, which he called his natural inclinations, rendered him unfit for the performance of the duties of a chief magistrate in an established government.

The Congress did not accept his renunciation, and the date of October 3 was finally chosen for the inauguration. At the appointed hour the Liberator appeared before the Congress and, after taking the oath, addressed its president, saying that he would continue to defend the Constitution of Colombia and would march in its name to break the chains of the people of Ecuador and invite them to be part of Colombia. After this union had been completed, he would want to be only a simple citizen, preferring this title to that of Liberator. Through a special decree he was authorized to assume personal command of the army and to exercise complete authority in the departments where he would be carrying on the war.

Before the Liberator's departure from Cúcuta, he formed the cabinet and delegated the supreme authority to the vice-president, General Santander. The aptitudes shown by the latter official during his administration of Cundinamarca, his assiduous attention to affairs of state, and the experience he had acquired during the last two years aroused great hopes that his government would redound to the benefit of the country and to his own honor. Nevertheless, the haughty and even despotic conduct of Santander—and I shall not be accused of exaggeration in thus characterizing it—was not in accord with his protestations of staunch republicanism. These defects, however, were looked upon indulgently by everyone, with the exception of his comrades-in-arms, who were unable to tolerate the promotion of a man whose military abilities, according to them, were inferior to their own.

The cabinet secretaries were chosen from among the members of Congress, with the exception of Colonel Briceño Méndez, who stayed at the head of the War Department, which he had directed so ably. The Department of the Interior was entrusted to Dr. José Manuel Restrepo, who had already filled some of the most important posts in the Republic of New Granada, whose history he has written. The talented Dr. Pedro Gual was appointed to head the Department of Foreign Affairs. The Department of the Treasury was placed in the charge of Dr. José María Castillo, a loyal patriot and gifted scholar who had just stepped down from the vice-presidency of the Republic out of pure deference to the Liberator.

In a proclamation dated October 8, Bolívar announced to the people the result of the labors of Congress. He told them that the General Congress had given the nation a law of union, of equality, of liberty, making one family out of many peoples. It had established the seat of the government in Bogotá. Addressing the people of Quito, he said that the liberating army was marching to Ecuador. Finally, he announced that the vice-president would be chief of state while he was serving as a soldier.

CHAPTER FIFTEEN

W HILE THE EVENTS that I have just related were taking place, there were others of great importance happening in Cartagena. Colonel Mariano Montilla, the leader of the republican forces besieging that stronghold, launched an attack on the night of June 24 in conjunction with José Padilla, the valiant naval commander, who had succeeded in getting into the bay after the garrison of the Bocachica forts retreated to the city. Thoroughly deceived, the besieged committed all their forces on the landward side to oppose a false attack directed by Colonel Friedrich de Adlercreutz, a Swedish count in the service of the Republic. In the meantime, Padilla was taking eleven ships from them; as a result, they were completely cut off from the Bocachica forts and the bay was now in the control of the patriot flotilla. Not wishing to take advantage of the sad state of the defenders of the city, Colonel Montilla, a true gentleman as well as a good soldier, offered an honorable surrender to the gallant Brigadier Gabriel Torres, which he finally accepted. The surrender on October 1, 1821, of the strongest fortified city in South America, in addition to placing quantities of war matériel in the hands of the patriots, produced a favorable impression abroad. Not long thereafter, on October 16, the city of Cumaná formally surrendered to General Bermúdez, and the Spanish garrison of eight hundred men set sail for Puerto Rico in Colombian ships.

Coming back to Bolívar, whom we left on his way to Bogotá, I shall first relate two examples of his unselfishness and generosity that, although they occurred in previous months, are concerned with the Congress. In a memorandum addressed to the Congress of Cúcuta he waived all rights to the credits and salary due him as general in chief of the army and president of the Republic. He explained that he had received adequate recompense for everything from the loan of about fourteen thousand duros that he had taken from the treasury in Bogotá in 1819 to take care of the needs of friends and members of his family who sought asylum in the West Indies. The Congress hastened to accept this splendid donation in the name of the nation. The second example shows more clearly the generous sentiments of a great and noble soul. When independence was won, the government confiscated the property of Don Francisco de Iturbe, the Spaniard through whose kind intervention Bolívar had been granted a passport to leave the country after being placed at the mercy of Monteverde. Pausing briefly in the course of his victorious career, Bolívar requested a favor for his friend. "For the first time I appeal to the generosity of the government of Colombia regarding a matter that concerns me personally," he said in his petition to the Congress, seeking only the return of the property confiscated from his generous protector. Since the Congress felt flattered by this manifestation of respect and duly admired his conduct, it ordered Iturbe's property to be restored to him.

The southern department, which was to be the scene of the operations of the liberating army, is one of the most interesting parts of Colombia's territory, not only because of its geographical position and its beautiful, varied scenery, but also because of its history, which goes back to legendary times. The provinces of Quito, up to the border of the province of Pasto, were added to the empire of Peru during the reign of Huaina Cápac, the most powerful of the Incas; but while his sons, Huáscar and Atahuallpa, were fighting over possession of the territory, the bloodthirsty Pizarro invaded the land of the sun worshipers. The Peruvian Polynices and Eteocles fell into the clutches of the clever and cruel conquistador, and their hapless subjects were enslaved or put to death.

Quito, as well as the other provinces of Peru, was subjected to servitude for three long centuries; but to it fell the honor of being the first part of Colombia to attempt the patriotic task of throwing off the yoke of oppression. On August 10, 1809, the Spanish authorities were deposed, and a junta was set up in their place to represent Ferdinand VII. When Cuenca, Guayaquil, and Pasto joined forces to overthrow this mere shadow of a government, the members of the junta restored to office Count Ruiz de Castilla, the magistrate whom they had deposed. The arrival of troops from Lima brought imprisonment, plundering, and a general slaughter, which the people bravely resisted. Shortly afterward, Fuertes, the principal instigator of this great crime, was a victim of the fury of the populace, as was the unfortunate Ruiz de Castilla, a weak eighty-year-old man, who was cruelly put to death in 1811, just at the time when the city was declaring its independence from Spain.

This period of independence was of very short duration, for Quito was forced to surrender in November of the following year. When the fires of revolt blazed in Guayaquil in 1820, it was the very sons of heroic Quito who came to the aid of their own rulers. Guachi was the scene of the bloody conflict in which the free men of Guayaquil succumbed while fighting the royalist troops on uneven terms, thus exposing Guayaquil itself to an invasion. At this critical stage Colombia extended her friendly hand, asking in return only that the province become part of the Republic. Guayaquil, whose interests predisposed her to re-establish her former union with Peru, refused to sacrifice her independence, but she did accept the protection offered her, thereby tacitly acknowledging submission. General Sucre was selected by the

Liberator to go as an envoy to present to the junta of Guayaquil the fundamental law of Colombia. He negotiated a treaty guaranteeing the friendship of this region and the maintenance of the Colombian troops; he left for later the question of the incorporation of Guayaquil's territory into Colombia.

Her independence was once more endangered when the president of Quito sent three thousand men in two divisions against Guayaquil. Though his force was less than half the size of his opponent's, General Sucre, by means of clever tactics, prevented the meeting of the two columns, routing the first one and forcing the second to withdraw. Confident of success, he advanced toward Quito, but the rash valor of General Mires, second in command to Sucre, cut short the triumphant march of the conquering hero of Yaguachi and shattered Quito's hopes on the very battlefield where the patriot forces had met with disaster the previous year. Then Sucre, imitating the Liberator, negotiated on November 21, 1821, a favorable treaty that saved the honor of the Colombian forces and removed the threat of invasion.[1] The victory of the Spaniards, however, gave them time to prepare their defenses and increase the size of their army. North of Quito the tenacity of the people of Pasto, the inaccessible cliffs of the Juanambú River, and the deadly climate of Patía were formidable obstacles, enough to discourage the most determined efforts to free Quito. The many obstacles hindering Bolívar's plan to liberate Quito were increased when General Juan de la Cruz Mourgeon, a talented soldier, arrived with six hundred veterans led by experienced officers.

Such was the state of that region when the Liberator started out on December 13, 1821, for the Cauca Valley and Popayán, after ordering the columns of the La Guardia Division to march by different routes toward Popayán, the assembly point. Busy as he was all along the way to Cali, which he reached on January 1, 1822, he was turning over in his fertile mind a vast project of his own design that was most dear to his heart. For a long time he had cherished the hope of effecting a union of the various states of South America based on bonds of mutual interest. The victories of the patriot forces in recent years and

---

[1] The treaty of Babahoyo. —Ed.

Colombia's present state of prosperity now facilitated his plans. After consulting the executive power and many influential members of Congress and of the government, he decided to dispatch special envoys to invite the other governments of South America, as he had already done in the case of Mexico, to send plenipotentiaries to the Isthmus of Panama for the purpose of forming a confederation and establishing an assembly modeled after the amphictyonic league. Don Joaquín Mosquera, who accompanied the Liberator from Bogotá, was entrusted with the mission to the republican government of Lima; he left for that capital as soon as the headquarters of the liberating army was established in Cali.

The Liberator's first intention was to embark at the Pacific port of Buenaventura with two thousand of the best troops from the La Guardia Division in the transports that he had ordered General Sucre to send to this port, and to direct the campaign personally. This plan for a campaign from that side of Ecuador had obvious advantages, but it was rumored that two Spanish frigates were cruising in those waters. Since the Republic had no warships in the Pacific to act as an escort for the transports, Bolívar had no choice but to march by way of Patía and Pasto. He informed the junta of Guayaquil in no uncertain terms of his plans with respect to that territory. Addressing his remarks to José Joaquín de Olmedo, the president of the junta, he added: "I am pleased to believe, Most Excellent Sir, that the Republic of Colombia shall be proclaimed in that capital before my entrance therein. Your Excellency must know that Guayaquil is a part of Colombian territory."

After visiting the various towns of the district in order to expedite the execution of his orders concerning recruiting and the maintenance of the army, Bolívar returned to Popayán to plan operations and to organize the army units already assembling in that city. In order to appreciate fully the Liberator's efforts and his military talents, it is necessary to study the marches made at that time and to keep in mind the meager resources of the territory. Some battalions, starting from Valencia, had had to travel more than seven hundred leagues by land, by sea, by river, across paramos and burning plains, and over the lofty cordillera of the Andes before reaching Popayán. It is not surprising that some units lost a third of their men, nor that the majority of the men had to be hospitalized. Popayán became infected with the germs of all kinds of diseases, and a great number of veterans of the victorious battles of Boyacá and Carabobo came to an untimely end there. The recruits assembled to replace them were, as a rule, forlorn creatures who had no interest in the cause they had to defend. We should not be surprised to learn that they deserted at the first opportunity. New Granada alone had supplied 20,000 recruits to form the army of 6,000 men that won the victory at Carabobo. An examination of the registers of the various units will, however, give one a more complete picture of the destructive nature of the war. Over a period of four years the Rifles Battalion received 22,000 recruits into its ranks, and it barely had a total of 600 men when it reached Quito in June, 1822. Led by the gallant Colonel Arthur Sandes, it was the best disciplined and the most orderly unit in the Republic.

The Patía district, which the army would have to cross, is cursed with one of the deadliest climates in the world, and its barren wastes are the abode of all that is pernicious and destructive in nature. The ferocious people of Patía, who are descendants of fugitive slaves or freedmen, had joined the royalist side mostly out of love for plunder and crime. The guerrilla bands, which sprang up everywhere, did not venture to attack the troops unless they had a great superiority in numbers. They did, however, frequently swoop down upon the baggage trains and the stragglers and cut communications between the army and Popayán.

Upon leaving Patía behind, one comes to the Juanambú River, a mountain torrent whose rugged cliffs are a most formidable barrier. Beyond this and extending to the Guáitara River, the impenetrable thickets of a fog-covered area provided any number of hiding places where the savage people of Pasto could seek refuge or take up impregnable positions. They really did not know their own rights, but they had definite fanatical prejudices. The bishop of Popayán, a real rascal of Spanish birth, had abandoned his flock and established his residence in Pasto, from where he denounced the government of Colombia, thus arousing the passions of the people. Everyone there, without exception, was hostile to the Colombian cause and was ready to sacrifice his life and possessions in defense of the King and religion. Pasto also had the protection of a Spanish garrison. What has been said above is hardly more than a bare outline of the obstacles that awaited the Colombian La Guardia Division in the approaching campaign of 1822.

The news of the revolution that made the province of Panama a part of Colombia consoled the Liberator for the failure of negotiations with the royalists in Quito, since the revolution facilitated the subjugation of the latter part of the Republic by opening up communications between the northern and southern extremities of Colombia. No sooner had he been informed of this happy event than he sent me to Panama to bring a column of troops that he had ordered to proceed to the Isthmus before continuing on from there to reinforce Sucre's division in Guayaquil. Eight hundred embarked for that point and joined the Colombian forces in the South toward the end of March.

Despite the noise and confusion of camp life and the work involved in preparing for the campaign, the Liberator did not forget his duties as a magistrate. Since the beginning of the revolution the people of the province of Cauca, and especially those in Popayán, had suffered all the horrors resulting from the abnormal state of affairs without gaining a single benefit. The magistrates appointed by the new government appeared to be competing with one another in a dishonorable career of plunder, murder, and all kinds of excesses and vice. The government was aware of these serious crimes, but the unfortunate people of Cauca had to suffer not only the oppression of the local authorities but also the indifference with which the government of Cundinamarca greeted their outcries. These people had heard that the Liberator was a just man, and they decided to appeal to him for help. When he learned of the violence and crime, he exploded in anger against the criminals and against the magistrates who had condoned or tolerated such great infamy. He presented the complaints to the general government, even though it was headed by the same individual who governed Cundinamarca when those crimes were committed. In a note to the secretary of justice he mentioned the bitter complaints made about almost all the officials, and he observed that there was no evidence of any prosecution or punishment. He insisted that the inhabitants of Cauca must be made aware of the fact that the government did not tolerate crime, but punished it severely.

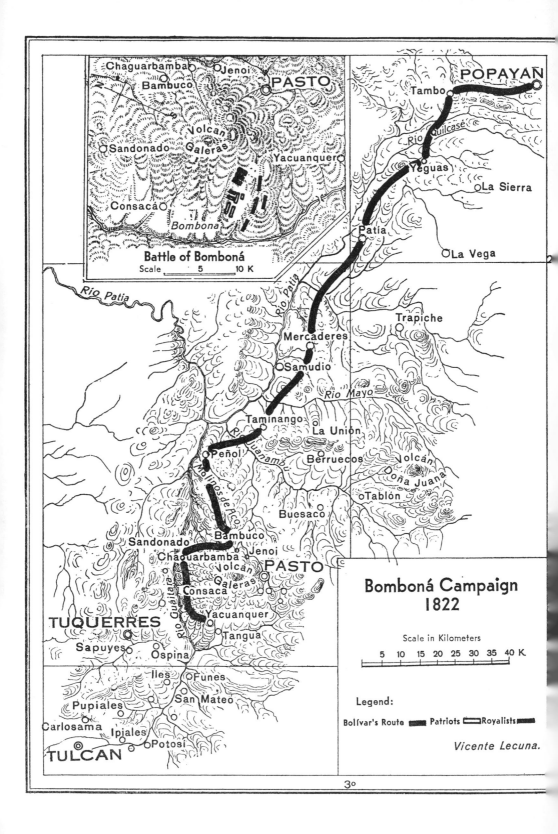

Inset map — Battle of Bomboná:

Chaguarbamba · Jenoi · Bambuco · PASTO · Volcan Galeras · Sandonado · Yacuanquer · Consacá · Bombona

Battle of Bomboná
Scale   5   10 K

Main map:

POPAYAN · Tambo · Rio Quilcasé · Yeguas · La Sierra · Patía · La Vega · Rio Patia · Trapiche · Mercaderes · Samudio · Rio Mayo · Taminango · La Unión · Rio Juanambú · Peñol · Berruecos · Volcán Doña Juana · Molinos de Rio · Tablón · Buesaco · Bambuco · Sandonado · Chaguarbamba · Jenoi · Volcán Galeras · PASTO · Consaca · Rio Guáitara · Yacuanquer · TUQUERRES · Tangua · Sapuyes · Ospina · Iles · Funes · Pupiales · San Mateo · Carlosama · Ipiales · Potosí · TULCAN

**Bomboná Campaign
1822**

Scale in Kilometers
5   10   15   20   25   30   35   40 K.

Legend:
Bolívar's Route ▬▬ Patriots ▭▭ Royalists ▬▬

Vicente Lecuna.

3º

Bolívar was a protector not only of innocence and human rights but also of the sciences and every useful public project. One proof of this is that after his arrival in Cauca he sent commissioners to explore the territory situated between the San Juan River, which empties into Buenaventura Bay on the Pacific Ocean, and the Atrato River, whose waters are carried to the Atlantic Ocean. He ordered a careful examination to be made of the route discovered by the parish priest of Navilla. In a communication addressed to Colonel Cancino, governor of Chocó, he instructed him to have a route laid out for a canal, because he was determined to carry out this useful project of connecting the two oceans. But this official did not give sufficient attention to this important matter, and, as a result, the Liberator's useful plan was not carried out. He was unable to give it any further consideration because of the most pressing affairs of the campaign.

Upon reaching Cauca, he had addressed the inhabitants to assure them that the liberating army was coming to bring them peace and liberty. He had urged the people of Pasto to have no fear, for the weapons of Colombia were for protection, not for fratricide. Before joining the army, which had marched toward the Juanambú River, he addressed a proclamation to the people of Patía and Pasto and to the Spaniards. He explained to them that the Colombian army sought to end the war, that it would treat them as sincere friends, and that it would not appropriate anything without paying for it. He urged the Spaniards to come to the realization that the war they were continuing was a hopeless war and that they could expect nothing from Spain. The Colombian government would either send them to their country with their families or would gladly welcome them as Colombians. But if they were obstinate, they might well beware of the severity of the laws of war.

The campaign of 1822 was started early in March. Despite the untiring efforts of the Liberator and his lieutenants, only three thousand men marched from Popayán. After crossing the weakly defended Juanambú River, they advanced on the royalist position atop the formidable rocky heights of Cariaco, where a division of two thousand men commanded by Colonel Don Basilio García was stationed. Despite the great strength of the position, the Liberator did not hesitate to attack it on April 7. The vanguard division, composed of the Vargas and Bogotá battalions, attacked the center and left; but it was repulsed and its leader, General Pedro León Torres, was mortally wounded. A renewed attack by Colonel Carvajal met with no greater success, and he also fell wounded. The slaughter was frightful, but the Liberator remained calm, awaiting the result of the attack led by General Valdés, who had climbed the heights of El Yusepe with the Rifles Battalion in order to fall on the enemy's right flank. When the Liberator saw that Valdés had reached the summit overlooking the Spaniards' position, he ordered the Vencedor Battalion to attack vigorously. Despite the same resistance as before, this unit succeeded, though with great losses, in dislodging the royalists just when they were being thrown into confusion on their right flank by the advance of the Rifles Battalion. The flight then became general. The Liberator occupied the battlefield, not to celebrate the victory of Bomboná, but to lament the precious blood it had cost. Although the royalists had few casualties in the battle, the units scattered when the retreat started, and Colonel García entered Pasto almost alone.

Since the Liberator did not want to leave his wounded men at the mercy of the swarming guerrilla bands, he was not able to pursue García or to make the most of the victory. After a few days the Liberator decided to recross the Juanambú River and await the reinforcements he had requested from Popayán. The deadly climate and the absolute scarcity of provisions threatened the troops with complete destruction, but they did not become discouraged, so great was the confidence they had in their leader. Bolívar's own health had been so affected that he had had to be carried on a litter to El Peñol after the battle of Bomboná. On May 26, after receiving the expected reinforcements in the town of Trapiche, and encouraged by the recent victory, the Colombian army once more went on the offensive.

The Liberator had previously written to the royalist leader, offering him an honorable capitulation, which the latter said that he was ready to accept, provided he could first obtain the consent of the president of Quito. The Liberator refused to assent to this, for he knew that García only wanted to gain time to reorganize his army and obtain news from Quito. It soon became apparent that there was no need to accept any condition, for the fate of Quito had been decided and President Don Melchor Aymerich was a prisoner. It cost Colonel García no little effort to persuade the tenacious natives of Pasto to enter into negotiations with the patriots, and all the influence of the bishop was necessary to overcome the obstinacy of the people. The Spanish commissioners appointed to arrange the capitulation left Pasto on May 30 and met the Liberator in Berruecos as he was marching on the city with the army. After appointing Colonels José Gabriel Pérez and Vicente González to negotiate with them, Bolívar continued toward the city, escorted only by his aides. He cherished the hope of removing every vestige of suspicion by thus entrusting himself to the honor of the most obstinate enemies of the Republic.

The capitulation that he so generously granted to the inhabitants of that region was well calculated to appease them, because it exempted them from taxes and military service and allowed the officials to retain their posts. When the Indians of Pasto congratulated Bolívar on his arrival, he pointed out to them the great benefits that the constitution of the Republic would bring to them and offered to grant them any favor they wanted. They replied that they only wanted to continue paying tribute. They understood their social position better than did the representatives of Cúcuta. The payment of six to nine pesos by the males from eighteen to fifty years of age freed them from all other taxes. The Liberator left Pasto under the protection of the good faith of its inhabitants and continued his march toward Quito.

After the treaty of Babahoyo, General Sucre had concentrated on the organization of another army in the province of Guayaquil. Forced to look elsewhere for auxiliaries, he claimed the Numancia Battalion, composed of natives of Colombia led by Commander Tomás de Heres, which had gone over to the ranks of the republicans when General José Francisco de San Martín landed on the coast to the north of Lima.[2] But San Martín, guided by expediency, chose to send the division of eleven hundred men situated in Piura under the orders of Colonel Andrés de Santa Cruz. After joining forces in Saraguro, in the province of

[2] In September, 1820, San Martín had landed with some four thousand Argentines and Chileans on the Peruvian coast at Pisco. In less than a year he had entered Lima and had proclaimed the independence of Peru.—Ed.

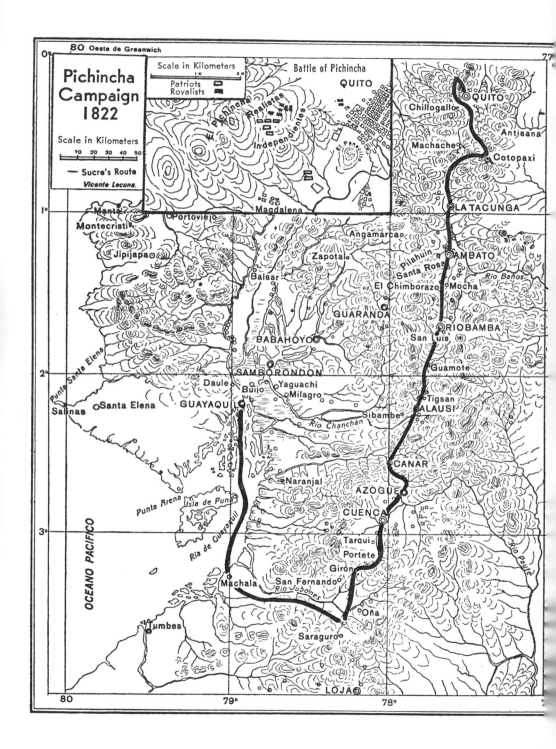

**Pichincha
Campaign
1822**

Scale in Kilometers

— Sucre's Route

Vicente Lecuna.

Scale in Kilometers
10 20 30 40 50

Battle of Pichincha

Patriots
Royalists

QUITO

Realietas

Independientes

El Panecillo

Magdalena

OCEANO PACIFICO

Loja, they marched together against Cuenca and occupied it without resistance on February 21, 1822. Complying with instructions received from the Liberator, Sucre marched on Quito at the beginning of April. After crossing the cordillera of El Azuay, his forces occupied Riobamba after a brilliant cavalry charge at the foot of stupendous Mount Chimborazo. In La Tacunga, Sucre was joined by the remnants of a unit that had contained eight hundred men when it left Panama in the month of March but had lost two-thirds of its force in the march from Guayaquil to headquarters.

After forcing the enemy to abandon the formidable position of Jalupana, Sucre appeared on the plain of Jurubamba in front of Quito on May 21. By another skillful maneuver he skirted the royalists' right flank and climbed the steep heights of the volcano of Pichincha before dawn on the twenty-fourth, in order to take a position between Quito and Pasto. This daring movement led to another very imprudent one by the Spanish leader, who rushed forward to meet the Colombian general when he realized his intentions. The result of the battle was the complete rout of the Spaniards and the subsequent occupation of the second city of the old empire of the Incas. The inhabitants of Quito hated the royalists as much as those of Pasto hated the Colombians, and they had been in constant communication with Sucre during his march, furnishing him everything needed to maintain the army and assure victory.

Before his departure from Pasto, the Liberator had announced the happy outcome of the campaign to the Republic. In this proclamation he noted that the victories of Bombóná and Pichincha had left the entire country free except for one stronghold and that the Colombians of the South would soon be able to enjoy the sacred rights of liberty and equality. A true lover of nature, he was delighted with his trip to Quito and the view of the snow-covered volcanoes and the picturesque valley of Ibarra and Otavalo. In this beautiful part of Colombia one can enjoy every kind of climate, and in a space of a few leagues the most highly prized products of various zones are raised in abundance. On June 16 the Liberator entered the city of Quito, and he was received there in the manner one would expect, in view of the enthusiasm of its inhabitants for the cause of independence. Their delirious joy was equalled only by their gratitude to the hero whom they were seeing for the first time and to whom Colombia owed her political existence and Quito her liberty.

When General Sucre occupied the city after the capitulation, he invited the various corporations and the principal citizens to declare solemnly that the provinces which constituted the former presidency of Quito desired to join the Republic of Colombia. On May 29 they definitely sealed their political fate, perhaps with more enthusiasm than reflection and prudence, by declaring their provinces to be part of the territory of the Republic. The usefulness of this measure was questionable, for the natives of Quito had nothing in common with the people of the northern sections. Nature itself seemed to have designated the Guáitara and Juanambú rivers as appropriate boundary lines. There is reason to believe that the Liberator's reputation greatly influenced the deliberations of the people of Quito, and it is certain that only loyalty to his person could induce them to maintain the union with Colombia once they became fully aware of the incompatibility of interests. In addition to this notable proof of regard for the founder of the Republic, the popular assembly accorded honors to him and his comrades-in-arms.

Even though the Spaniards had been defeated and the southern provinces were free of royalists, Guayaquil continued to refuse to recognize the government of the Republic. The possession of power and the desire to retain it led the governing junta to decide in favor of independence. Olmedo, its president, was an excellent man, but he was also the person least suited for that position in such circumstances. As a poet, he was less desirous of governing his country than of singing its praises in his verses. The idea of independence appealed, perhaps, to his sense of patriotism as a native of Guayaquil. Although Bolívar's genius won his respect and admiration, he would have preferred to see his own country annexed to Peru, should it fail to establish its independence. Francisco Roca, another member of the junta, hated Colombia. Rafael Jimena, the third and least influential member, better known for his elegant manners than for his ability, was very much in favor of independence, though he did feel favorably disposed toward Peru.

The Republic of Peru undoubtedly had some right to the province under dispute, since it had formerly belonged to the viceroyalty of Peru. Even after it had been ceded to New Granada,[3] it was always subordinate to Peru in ecclesiastical and military affairs. On the other hand, since the states of South America recognized by tacit agreement the territorial divisions of the Spanish government in 1809, Colombia claimed jurisdiction over Guayaquil. Although the Protector of Peru was not in a position to enter into a dispute with Colombia over her fundamental law, he tried to obtain through intrigue what he did not dare to attempt by force of arms. Under various pretexts he sent officers of his army to Guayaquil, and he always tried to keep active agents there to further his designs. The most outstanding among them was General Francisco Salazar, who lived as ostentatiously as an ambassador. The young men of Guayaquil became devoted followers of San Martín. General José de la Mar, a Colombian by birth, who recently, as he expressed it himself, "had left the royalist forces in order to join the Peruvian army with a higher rank," supported the Protector's claims out of a desire to show his gratitude to San Martín. The Colombian faction was perhaps weaker numerically, but the determination and activity of the members made up for the lack of numbers.

After news of the victory of Pichincha was received in Guayaquil, the situation became really dangerous, but the junta hesitated to take any action. Those who stood for independence still had one hope: the unit that Santa Cruz had led into the campaign had orders to return to Guayaquil in order to embark for Peru in the ships of Admiral Manuel Blanco Encalada's squadron, which had arrived in port for this purpose. The Liberator, who had foreseen this possibility, detained Santa Cruz for a few days and sent General Salom with part of Sucre's division to occupy Guayaquil. This step disconcerted Colombia's enemies.

Bolívar's captivating charm endeared him to all the inhabitants of

[3] By a royal order of July, 1803, the viceroy of Peru took over the defense of the port of Guayaquil, and after the Quito revolution of 1809 he assumed complete control of the province. In 1819, at the request of the city of Guayaquil, the province was returned to the jurisdiction of the presidency of Quito, which had been part of the viceroyalty of New Granada for almost a century. —Ed.

Quito. Quite unlike the Spanish rulers, he was hospitable and welcomed all those who called on him. His departure caused general regret in the capital. In all the towns of the populous province through which he passed, he was greated with enthusiastic acclaim. The greatest confusion reigned in Guayaquil when he arrived on July 11, at almost the same time as the troops led by General Salom were coming ashore. So many people crowded the streets that he made his way with great difficulty to the house that had been prepared for him. The head of the municipal council, José Leocadio Llona, welcomed him, in the name of his fellow citizens, with a speech that greatly offended the junta and the supporters of independence, who were expecting to hear the speech he had read to the junta the day before. Much to their disappointment and surprise they heard this same Llona address the Liberator in their presence and say that "the people were eager to raise up in triumph the beautiful statue of liberty, which had been scornfully thrust aside by those (pointing to the members of the junta) who, laboring under a spell, had tolerated the cries and cheers of 'Hurrah for free Guayaquil' on the day of greatest glory for the people."

The Liberator's reply to this speech showed even less agreement with the sentiments of the junta and its faction, and the members of the junta felt ashamed and humiliated when they left. On the following day a memorial signed by many prominent people was presented to the Liberator. It stated very clearly that a definite majority of the people of the province were in favor of annexation to Colombia, that the people were eagerly looking toward Colombia for the peace and happiness they could never obtain through their own efforts, and that formal action should be taken to recognize the Republic. The Liberator stopped the attempts made that day by the faction to proclaim the Republic, because he wanted to make the annexation look like a mandate from the people. His proclamation to the inhabitants of Guayaquil was a mortal blow to the junta and its supporters. He spoke of how the people had been placed in a completely false situation, exposed to the threat of anarchy. Colombia offered them justice and order, peace and glory. He considered them to be Colombians at heart because all their clamors had been for Colombia and because they had belonged to its territory. He wanted, however, to discuss the matter with them.

The junta consequently convoked the electoral college in order to observe the formalities. There were, in the meantime, frequent clashes between the factions in the city. On July 13 a mob lowered the flag of Guayaquil from the pole in front of the Liberator's house and raised in its place the tricolor of the Republic, which was cheered by the populace and given a salute by the ships in the river. Just at that moment the members of the junta were leaving the Liberator's house after a conference with him. Fearing the worst consequences, they fled and took refuge in a neighboring house. As soon as the Liberator learned what was going on, he ordered the flag of Guayaquil to be restored and assured Olmedo that he completely disapproved of the incident that had alarmed him so much. This was, however, the last time that the flag of Guayaquil was raised.

Wishing to put an end to this state of anarchy and scandalous confusion, the Liberator immediately took charge of the civil and military government of the province. He informed the junta of his action and added that this measure in no way limited the freedom of the people to express through their representatives their opinions concerning their future welfare. The disturbances in Guayaquil therefore ended for the moment.

CHAPTER SIXTEEN

THE UNEXPECTED ARRIVAL OF SAN MARTÍN at the Guayaquil estuary on July 25, 1822, not only occasioned surprise but also made everybody forget for the moment the excitement of recent days. When the Liberator learned of his arrival, he sent his aides to welcome him and commissioned Colonel Ignacio Torres to deliver to him a letter in which he expressed his pleasure over the surprising news and deplored the fact that there was not enough time to prepare an adequate welcome. He added that he was extremely anxious to meet the father of Chile and Peru. When San Martín's ship, the schooner *Macedonia*, approached the harbor on the morning of the twenty-sixth, Bolívar went on board and had the pleasure of embracing his most distinguished collaborator in the fight for South American independence.

General San Martín was received by the people of Guayaquil in a manner befitting his high rank and his great contribution to the American cause. During his two days' stay in the city he divided his time between important official business and the festivities improvised by the hospitable people to celebrate the happy occasion. He spent the morning in conferences with the Liberator; after dinner in Bolívar's house, they both attended the balls given in San Martín's honor. The subjects of his conversations with the Liberator were the state of America and the best way to bring the war to a successful conclusion. A short time previously, plenipotentiaries from Colombia and Peru had agreed upon a treaty that bound both republics to render each other mutual assistance until the end of the war with Spain. Since the war in Colombia had already ended, San Martín had come to ask the Liberator for aid in order to bring the war in Peru to a close.

This was the apparent object of his visit, but the current rumor was that the Protector's motives were not as friendly and sincere as they appeared to be. It was said that his aim was to reach Guayaquil at the time of the arrival of the division of Santa Cruz, while the Liberator was still occupied in Quito, in order to encourage the Peruvian party with his presence and obtain, perhaps, the annexation of the province to Peru. San Martín's character might have given grounds for this suspicion, which became stronger during his short stay in Guayaquil when it was noticed that he looked rather displeased and preoccupied.[1]

It would be difficult to find two individuals less alike in character than Bolívar and San Martín. Bolívar was frank, candid, passionately devoted to his friends, and generous to his enemies; San Martín was cold, reserved, and incapable of pardoning offenses or of bestowing

---

[1] Though we have no written account by San Martín about the much-discussed meeting between these two great leaders, most historians agree that San Martín was deeply disappointed to find that Bolívar had assumed control of Guayaquil. The definite information we do have consists of three letters dictated by Bolívar the day after San Martín's departure. According to Bolívar, San Martín stated that he did not wish to become involved in Guayaquil's affairs, that his forces in Peru were stronger than those of the Spaniards, that he intended to retire to Mendoza, Argentina, after strengthening the government of Peru but without waiting until the end of the war, and that he favored a constitutional monarchy for Peru. In other letters written shortly thereafter, Bolívar spoke favorably of San Martín. —Ed.

favors that did not work to his own advantage. Both of them achieved the goals they had in mind, but by means as different as the routes they followed to their meeting place in Ecuador. The Argentine, after being rewarded for his services to Peru, abandoned her cause; the Venezuelan, after being banished by his compatriots, returned to Colombia and gave them liberty. The former was born and grew up in poverty and acquired a fortune. The latter inherited a large fortune and died almost in poverty. San Martín accepted the title of Protector of Peru; Bolívar rejected the crown offered to him in Colombia. Both were benefactors of their countries, and both were victims of the ingratitude and the persecution of the peoples whom their genius and their courage had redeemed. My references to San Martín are based solely on what I have heard about him from people who knew him. On the other hand, I speak of Bolívar from my intimate knowledge of his character. But I should be committing an injustice if I did not mention the glories of Chacabuco and Maipú.

San Martín spent the greater part of his youth in Spain and served with distinction in the Spanish army as a cavalry officer. Having returned to Buenos Aires in 1812, he achieved renown in the battle of San Lorenzo and was given command of the Army of the Andes. He skillfully executed the crossing of the cordillera that separates Mendoza from Chile, and the battle of Chacabuco was the reward for his daring. On the glorious battlefield of Maipú he gave manifest proof of his genius by gaining independence for Chile. Inasmuch as he was convinced that Chile would never be able to enjoy the blessings of peace while Peru had sufficient means to cause trouble, he made plans to rescue Peru from Spanish domination. His undertaking was crowned with the most surprising success in the beginning. The best veteran unit of the royalist army transferred its allegiance to his forces. José de la Mar, Andrés Santa Cruz, Antonio Gutiérrez de la Fuente, and other leaders also joined his army. The gates of the capital were opened to him, and Callao delivered itself into his hands.

In Lima, San Martín encountered what Hannibal had encountered in Capua: the luxury that begets soft living and the seduction that produces the vices that soon demoralize an army. But the Argentine was very inferior to the African and was not able to conquer these great evils. The soldiers from Chile succumbed to the effects of the climate, and the veterans who had followed him from the banks of the Río de la Plata were seeking an opportunity to throw off the weight of an authority that they could not tolerate, either because of envy or because they resented his arrogance as Protector of Peru. Plots and conspiracies followed each other in rapid succession and threatened to destroy San Martín's authority. The defeat at Ica broke the magic spell that seemed to bring him success.

His enemies took advantage of his absence in Guayaquil to punish the insolent haughtiness of his prime minister, Don Bernardo Monteagudo. After causing a popular uprising, they deposed him and drove him into exile. This was the welcome they gave San Martín upon his return. Although he assumed the supreme command again, he remained in power for only a month. After installing the Congress he had convoked, he presented his resignation, which was accepted immediately. Then he embarked secretly, leaving Peru in a state of anarchy and subject to the selfish desires of a few impudent demagogues. The country was, in addition, threatened by the royalist army, which had regained its superiority.

The Liberator, who was accustomed to solving almost impossible problems, overcame the few difficulties that arose in Guayaquil. When the electoral college met on July 31, a heated debate took place, and anger was beginning to rise to a high pitch when the Liberator made known his desire to have the meeting ended, since its only object was to proclaim the annexation of the province to the territory of Colombia. The electoral college thereupon declared that thereafter the province was forever to be a part of the Republic of Colombia. The few dissatisfied members made a protest, which they later published in Peru. The members of the junta made it a point of honor to leave the country. The local troops were either discharged or redistributed among the units of the Republic, but the Liberator gave the officers complete freedom to do as they pleased. All the officers and officials who left the country were well received in Peru, where they obtained posts. Before long they forgot their pretended wrongs. Olmedo sang the praises of Bolívar, Jimena served him faithfully, and Roca became one of his admirers.

The annexation of Guayaquil to Colombia awakened the jealousy of the southern republics, which claimed that it was an act of usurpation and viewed as despotic the measures adopted by the Liberator to effect the union. In reality, the Liberator was only performing his duty in obedience to the sovereign will of the people of Colombia, whose fundamental law included Guayaquil in Colombia's territory. If the uti possidetis was the rule observed by Mexico and Chile, Colombia had a right to act in the same way. If each province were permitted to establish its sovereignty, South America would soon fall into a most frightful state of anarchy. The Liberator established the framework of society on a firm foundation by getting rid of this source of trouble.

Only a captious critic would condemn the means employed to effect the annexation. The Liberator could not, without failing to do his duty, recognize the Guayaquil junta as anything other than a de facto government. Congress had given him authority to subjugate the southern provinces. The separation of Guayaquil from the rest of the Republic would have established a dangerous precedent. Any other province had the same right to seek independence and constitute itself into a sovereign state. If Guayaquil had opposed annexation, the Liberator would have been justified in having used coercive measures. His conduct on the occasion was extremely considerate. He had made his plans known well in advance, and he carried them out without cruelty or bloodshed. The factions disappeared quickly, and there was more peace and quiet in the city than had been known since the year 1820. Guayaquil was declared a department of Colombia, and a school and a court of commerce were established in the capital. These and other benefits conferred upon it by the Liberator won for him the affection and the blessings of a grateful people.

The division commanded by Santa Cruz returned to Peru after receiving replacements for the casualties it had suffered in the campaign. Two thousand Colombian soldiers requested by General San Martín also embarked for Peru. The Liberator offered him a larger number, but he did not believe that more were needed or that the country could maintain a larger force than the one it had under arms. In his interview with San Martín, the Liberator asked him insistently if it would not be better to march to the interior of Peru with all available forces rather than to divide them and thus expose the army to the risk of being defeated in piecemeal fashion. The Protector answered with the objection that the independent provinces of Peru did not have sufficient resources to move a large force across the Andes. The governments that succeeded San Martín in power made the same mistake, with unfortunate consequences for the country. Finally, the Liberator, although without control of the vast territory they had possessed, other than the department of Trujillo, and although the royalists occupied the rest of the country, convinced the Peruvians of the serious mistake they had made and showed them the superiority of his genius in the brilliant campaign that he directed in Peru.

On September 1, 1822, the Liberator departed from Guayaquil to visit the provinces of Cuenca and Loja, leaving General Salom in charge of the administration of the new department, a happy choice that satisfied everybody and resulted in many useful improvements. The fact that he had established the independence of his country did not satisfy the Liberator, for the task would not be complete until he had made that independence permanently secure. The picture of the state of Peru given him by San Martín was not really satisfactory. Bolívar did not find San Martín very sincere, but neither his own frankness nor the offers he made enabled him to break down the Protector's reserve. A mistaken sense of pride, Bolívar thought, had prevented him from describing the real state of the country he had planned to liberate. When Bolívar later consulted men who had an intimate knowledge of Peru's resources and the ability of the royalist generals who commanded the army there, his suspicions regarding San Martín were confirmed, and he immediately decided to renew the offers he had made to him. The opinions of the members of the new political government of Peru are apparent in the imprudent and discourteous answer made to his proposals by the governing junta.

After having accepted San Martín's resignation, the Congress entrusted the executive power to a three-man junta made up of General José de la Mar, Don Felipe Antonio Alvarado, and the Count of Vista Florida, the first two of whom were foreigners. Olmedo and others of the group who had left Guayaquil managed to obtain seats in Congress, where they showed evidence of their injured pride and their desire for vengeance. The machinations did real harm to the reputation of the Liberator. La Mar himself, the president of the junta, was not above the petty jealousy that dishonored some of his colleagues. Herein must lie the explanation of the resolution of Congress with respect to the Liberator's generous offer and the rude manner in which the governing junta transmitted it to him. Everything indicated a need for the help offered them in support of the wavering state of independence, which was threatened by civil strife and by a foreign enemy who was energetic and daring.

The imprudent conduct of the government and its supporters did not stop there. The auxiliaries from Colombia were also slandered for no good reason in the libels that appeared daily, being singled out as false friends and dangerous allies despite their irreproachable conduct. The junta regarded with indifference the frequent protests submitted by the Colombian general. It soon became apparent that there was need for a treaty that would guarantee the subsistence, clothing, and pay of the Colombian troops. Colonel Juan Paz del Castillo was consequently given instructions to propose such a treaty, but the governing junta of Lima rejected it. The Colombian troops thereupon withdrew and returned to their country with the consent of the junta, whose conduct on this occasion gave rise to dishonorable charges that I believe to be unfounded.

The decision of the Colombian general was a fatal blow for the junta. The moment could not have been more inopportune, because everything seemed to conspire to multiply the misfortunes of the country. The fiscal measures adopted by Congress increased rather than relieved the general uneasiness. The issuance of paper money brought an end to credit and paralyzed commerce. The government consoled itself with the hope that victory by the republican forces in the South would re-establish confidence and produce a favorable reaction; but near Moquegua in January, 1823, the Spanish General Jerónimo Valdés finally routed the large, well-organized division comprising the troops brought by San Martín from Chile and the Río de la Plata. General Rudecindo Alvarado, a brother of the member of the junta with the same name, was barely able to save five hundred of the four thousand men with whom he had landed at Iquique two months previously.

While preparations were being made for the proposed expedition to Peru before news came of the rejection of his offer, the Liberator busied himself with the organization of the civil government of the departments. He visited the provinces and the capital of Cuenca, and then the capital of Loja, which borders on Peru. In all the municipalities and villages along his route he made as many improvements as he could. But he was able to devote only a short space of time to this peaceful work in the South, for it was interrupted by the Pasto rebellion in the North.

The stupid inhabitants of these provinces allowed themselves to be seduced by a Spanish officer who had escaped from among the group that had surrendered in Quito. A nephew on his mother's side of the devastator of Venezuela, he took the name of Boves rather than his father's name. Though he lacked talent and courage, that terrible name was sufficient recommendation for the people of Pasto. The area between the Guáitara and Juanambú rivers quickly became a vast center of rebellion and disorder. The Liberator immediately ordered General Sucre to march there with troops from the garrison in Quito and the surrounding towns. Sucre was repulsed on November 24 when he attacked the natives of Pasto on the almost inaccessible ridge of Taindala, overlooking the Guáitara River, but after he received reinforcements, he made a strategic move that fooled the rebel leader and completely upset his defense. The capture of the Taindala position marked the completion of the major part of the campaign.

Sucre advanced immediately and overtook Boves at Yacuanquer. The valor of Colonels Córdova and Sandes and the aggressiveness of their troops decided the battle, and the rebels were completely routed. On the following day Sucre demanded the surrender of the city, but his demand was ignored. Though twice defeated, the natives of Pasto regrouped in the outskirts of the city. There, for more than an hour, they stood their ground with characteristic courage before finally giving way. In the horrible slaughter that followed, soldiers and civilians, men and women were indiscriminately sacrificed. Boves, seeking safety in flight, went through the mountains leading to the headwaters of the Marañón River, descended the river, and reached the coast of Brazil. The people of Pasto received the punishment that their crimes and stupidity merited.

During the course of these events the Liberator retired to a country house near Ibarra, a city between Quito and Pasto, where he seemed to forget the cares of the war and of government, dividing his time between study and hunting. Ever since the year 1820 his varied and constant activity had left him almost no time for rest. During this period of seclusion he was visited by Colonel Don Bernardo Monteagudo, who had been deposed and exiled from Peru in the absence of the Protector. Bolívar received him with courteous hospitality, even though Monteagudo had stood out as a vehement critic of his administration. Monteagudo was a talented man of great learning and experience whose political ideas went from one extreme to another when he finally occupied positions of great responsibility. After San Martín appointed him secretary of state, he incurred the hatred of the inhabitants of the capital with his decree of proscription. Nonetheless, the short period of his administration revealed his great gifts as a statesman and the vigor of his resolute character, as seen in the impetus he gave not only to military affairs but also to the whole complex mechanism of government. His policy may have been unwise, but it shows him to be a man who was superior to his contemporaries. After his fall he was charged with having accumulated great wealth during his administration. I take pleasure in stating that these charges are not only unjust but also slanderous. The best proof of his integrity is that he died poor. During his visit with the Liberator he delighted the group gathered there with his pleasant conversation and his vast store of knowledge. Bolívar, who knew how to profit from the experience of others, obtained from him a complete knowledge of the character of the Argentines.

Near the end of December the Liberator left Ibarra for Pasto, where he arrived January 2, 1823. Convinced that generosity was wasted on a people who were incapable of appreciating it, he decided to punish them severely. Since, however, he always adhered to the principles of justice, he first tried to find out what reasons they had to offer in justification of their crime, but they maintained an obstinate silence. He thereupon ordered General Salom to enroll in the army all the citizens of Pasto who had taken up arms against the Republic. After making other provisions and appointing Colonel Juan José Flores governor of the province of Pasto, he returned to Quito.

Salom carried out his assignment in a manner that did little honor to him or to the government. The inhabitants assembled in the public square of the city in answer to a summons from Salom, and they had read to them the law stating the duties of the magistrate and the rights of the citizens. Then, however, a picket of soldiers entered the square and seized about a thousand of the men, who were immediately sent to Quito. Many of them perished on the way or at a later date after declaring in unmistakable terms their hatred for the laws and the name of Colombia. None of the men taken from Pasto proved useful to the Republic, for nothing could ever reconcile them to military service in the cause of independence.

While on the way from Ibarra to Pasto, the Liberator had received alarming dispatches from the government in Bogotá informing him that the municipal government of Caracas had accompanied its oath to observe the constitution with a formal protest against it. The government unwisely ordered the prosecution of those who had protested, but the courts declared that there was no ground for action. This incident did implant the seed of discord, and during this period there was born an opposition party that bitterly attacked the executive power in the press. The vice-president reported all these events to the Liberator with the exaggeration that comes from injured pride. He also conveyed the suspicion that all the members of Congress were imbued with the ideas that prevailed in the Caracas faction, as he called the opposition. The Liberator, whose own painful experience had made him more hostile toward the federal system than was perhaps wise, obeyed on this occasion, as on others, the dictates of sincere patriotism. In a communication to the vice-president he categorically expressed his disapproval of the innovators and urged the executive power to do its utmost to prevent the legislators from making any changes in Colombia's fundamental code of laws, which he had sworn to uphold.

In a communication addressed to the Congress on the same subject, he offered the representatives the brilliant victories won by the liberating army. Then he declared: "The Constitution of Colombia is sacred for ten years and shall not be violated with impunity while I have any blood running through my veins and the liberators are under my orders." Contrary to the expectations of many people, who did not consider proper the use of such plain and unambiguous language, Congress gave him a most sincere vote of thanks for the sentiments he had expressed. This frank declaration produced the effect desired. All thoughts of innovation were abandoned, and the government, with the Liberator's support, won a victory. Bolívar's influence in Colombia was so great during that period that it was limited only by his moderation. He could have had anything he wanted then.

Upon his return to Quito near the end of January, after the pacification of Pasto, the Liberator learned that the Peruvian government had discharged the Colombian auxiliary troops and that the troops had arrived on the coast during the season when its climate is most unhealthy. Despite the torrential rains, he started for Guayaquil immediately, and on his arrival he found the troops dreadfully ravaged by disease. His presence helped to encourage the subordinate authorities to do everything possible for the sick, who, thanks to their care, soon regained their health. A few days after his arrival, when he was hoping for a rest, he received news of a disaster in the northern part of the Republic and an appeal for help from the Colombian government. In all its conflicts it confidently turned to the Liberator, for it felt sure that his advice would bring a solution.

After the battle of Carabobo the general staff and the remnants of the royalist army took refuge in Puerto Cabello, from where, with a superior naval force, they could easily move their troops along the coast. The province of Coro, like Pasto loyal to the King, served them as a base of operations. La Torre met with stiff resistance in his efforts to regain territory, but his successor, General Morales, succeeded in occupying the city and province of Maracaibo and then invaded the provinces of Trujillo and Mérida. The government of Colombia proclaimed martial law and had it enforced with excessive rigor. When informed of this alarming state of affairs, the Liberator immediately left Guayaquil for Bogotá, but he decided to turn back after five days' travel when two messengers brought news of Morales' withdrawal and the government's energetic action. The defeat of Alvarado's army at Moquegua made his presence in the South indispensable.

Once aware of the extent of the danger, the Liberator promptly ordered the various units stationed in the South to make ready to march. The terrible disaster of Moquegua filled the inhabitants of the free provinces of Peru with sorrow and consternation, but the governing junta appeared to be more apathetic than ever. Though La Mar, its president, was a brave soldier, he was hesitant about making decisions. The army units quartered in the environs of Lima demanded that Congress appoint Don José de la Riva-Agüero chief executive of the nation, and he was so appointed on February 27, 1823, after a second demand from the army. The first act of the new president was to send General Mariano Portocarrero to Guayaquil to apologize to the Liberator for the conduct of the junta and to request the aid he had offered.

The Liberator assured General Portocarrero that Colombia would do her duty in Peru, sending her soldiers as far as Potosí. He told him to tell the Peruvian government that Colombian soldiers were already hurrying toward Peru on board the ships of the Republic. Bolívar was not exaggerating matters when he said this, for the ships carrying two thousand men were already on their way down the river. Furthermore, two thousand more men set out for the same destination two days later. The Peruvian general, who was accustomed to the listless manner in which all governmental action was taken in his country, was filled with admiration and astonishment when he saw the ease with which the Liberator handled the large number of affairs under his charge and supervised everything of any consequence. While busy with these preparations, the Liberator decided that it would be wiser to protect the Colombian troops in Peru by compelling that government, through a treaty, to fulfill its promises. On March 18 the plenipotentiaries of the two nations subscribed to a formal pact, according to which Colombia was to send six thousand men to the aid of Peru. In return, Peru was to pay all expenses and adequate compensation to officers and men, as well as supply necessary ammunition and mounts and replace the army losses numerically with men from her own territory. This pact gave rise in later years to disputes between the two negotiating parties.

After the Peruvian envoy expressed his gratitude to Bolívar for taking such prompt and generous action, he went on to say that his mission would not be complete unless he obtained the Liberator's promise to go to Peru to direct the campaign. The Liberator replied that he was ready to go provided the General Congress of Colombia was not opposed to his absence. When General Portocarrero returned to Peru with the most promising news, the joy of the Lima patriots exceeded all bounds, for they had feared that the Liberator would treat them with the scorn they deserved in view of the insults hurled at him by the Lima newspapers and the government suspicion of his motives.

The Liberator thought that it would be better to carry the war to Peru and use the resources of her free provinces against the royalists rather than to maintain a defensive position and eventually endanger the entire Republic of Colombia. It was, however, only after serious and mature deliberation that he decided to risk his reputation on what was then believed, with reason, to be a reckless undertaking—that of rescuing Peru from the domination of Spain, thus wresting from Spain the last of her richest possessions. The undertaking was, indeed, to be even more daring than Bolívar with his keen insight judged it would be.

While awaiting a reply from the Congress of Colombia to his request for permission to go to Peru, he devoted himself more earnestly than ever to making the necessary preparations. He had conferred the command of the troops sent to Lima upon General Manuel Valdés, but he appointed General Sucre to the post of minister plenipotentiary to the Lima government, with sufficient authority to intervene whenever necessary. General Salom succeeded Sucre in the civil and military command of the southern department. The second division of the expeditionary army embarked at Guayaquil during the course of the following month, and it was necessary to make really extraordinary efforts to complete the complement of six thousand men.

The president of Peru sent a second deputation to urge the Liberator to come to Peru to direct operations. They believed that without his presence there all efforts to destroy the Spanish army would be of no avail. The Peruvian Congress, grateful for the timely assistance he had sent them, gave him a solemn vote of thanks. Despite Bolívar's ardent desire to satisfy the eager wishes of the Peruvians, his respect for the fundamental institutions of his country hindered him from doing so. He decided to wait in Guayaquil for the permission he had requested from Congress. Aside from this consideration, new disturbances in Pasto required his presence in that area.

When the inhabitants of that turbulent province observed that most of the troops had gone to Peru, they conceived the idea of re-establishing the authority of the King in the provinces of Quito. A large number of those who had hidden in the woods banded together with other malcontents and marched on the city of Pasto on June 12. The attack was so violent that the veteran troops under Colonel Flores could not resist it. Flores was defeated and barely managed to retreat to Popayán with a few officers and a small cavalry unit. The leader of this revolt was Agustín Agualongo, an astute Indian of exceptional courage. Informed of the defenseless state of Quito, he marched on the capital after organizing his increased forces. When Salom received news of Flores' fate, he sent a courier to inform the Liberator and left with the few troops in the city to check the advance of the rebels. He had to withdraw before Agualongo's superior forces, leaving the road to Ibarra open to him.

It did not take Bolívar long to come to a decision. He immediately ordered all the convalescents in the hospitals to march to Quito, and he himself hurried to that city and called the militia into active service. Convinced that deception was the only means of compensating for the lack of adequate forces, the Liberator feigned a withdrawal, thus leading the rebels to believe that they could take possession of Quito. At noon on July 17, while the rebels were making merry in the streets of Ibarra, the Liberator himself, accompanied by his staff and an escort of lancers, surprised their outposts and put them to the sword. When advised of this unexpected attack, Agualongo made a hurried departure from the city with his troops and proceeded to take up a position on the Pasto road. Before he was able to arrange his men on the height overlooking this road, he was attacked again and completely routed. Some six hundred of his fifteen hundred men perished within half a mile of the city, and the rest scattered in all directions. Agualongo himself succeeded in escaping with about fifty cavalrymen to the mountains, where some of his scattered men joined him later. Not even in the midst of defeat did the rebels lose their indomitable courage, and they rejected the pardon offered to them if they would lay down their arms. The Liberator personally pursued the fugitives until very late at night. On the following day he had Colonel Salom advance to occupy Pasto, which he did without opposition. The night before the engagement at Ibarra the Liberator had dictated to an amanuensis one of the best and most eloquent articles he ever composed, on the American confederation. This was the way he used his time to help the common cause, despite the most distressing circumstances.

Upon his return to Quito, the Liberator found the third deputation from Peru waiting for him, this time from the representatives of the people, which must have made it more pleasing to him. Olmedo, who had a seat in the Peruvian Congress, was the principal member of the commission. This circumstance was very gratifying to the Liberator, who gave him a hearty welcome that did honor to both of them. When Olmedo informed the Liberator of the object of his mission, the latter replied that permission had not reached him yet, but that he was eagerly awaiting the opportunity to go to Peru. Olmedo was accompanied by Don José Sánchez Carrión, also a representative and a very talented and scholarly patriot.

The Liberator left for Guayaquil as soon as he had restored peace and quiet to Quito. Upon his arrival on August 2 he found waiting for him an aide of the Marqués de Torre Tagle, who had replaced Riva-Agüero in the government of Peru and was requesting the immediate presence of the Liberator in Lima, where recent events made it more necessary. At six o'clock on the morning of the seventh, the Liberator received the decree in which Congress granted him the permission he had so urgently requested. This decree arrived just after he had signed and sealed a letter to General Santander telling him that he had decided to go to Peru without awaiting the decision of Congress, because the safety of Colombia depended on his presence in that country.[2] He

[2] Even though O'Leary was an eyewitness, he is wrong when he says that the Liberator had decided to embark for Peru without receiving the permission of the Congress of Colombia. See the truth of the matter in Vicente Lecuna, *Crónica razonada de las*

tore up the letter and embarked an hour later for Callao in the government brig *Chimborazo*. "Today is the anniversary of Boyacá," said a member of his staff upon embarking, "a good omen for the future campaign."[3]

---

guerras de Bolívar, III, 302–303. The antecedents are on pages 272–273. —Vicente Lecuna.

Lecuna states that a communication from Bolívar's secretary, José Gabriel Pérez, to the secretary of foreign affairs of Colombia, dated August 3, 1823, proves conclusively that the permission from Congress had arrived in Guayaquil by August 3. —Ed.

[3] The date for the Liberator's departure does not agree with what is said in the communication found in *Memorias*, XX, 265. But we do not believe that O'Leary was mistaken, for he was one of the group that accompanied Bolívar. —Simón Bolívar O'Leary.

In the communication referred to above, dated August 6, 1823, Bolívar's secretary stated that Bolívar was embarking right away. But in a letter to General Salom dated August 7, 1823, Bolívar said: "I am embarking right now." —Ed.

CHAPTER SEVENTEEN

A T THIS POINT I SHALL OUTLINE briefly the situation of Colombia about the middle of the year 1823. Thanks to the Liberator's genius, all that vast territory was under the control of the republican government with the exception of the single stronghold of Puerto Cabello. The political constitution was firmly established, a valiant army was defending it, and the country's revenues were ample, providing they were ably administered. Although the Europeon governments did not recognize Colombia, they were by no means hostile to it. Great Britain had helped it and protected it, and the United States, though it had done neither of these things, had been the first country to recognize its independence. Federalists, centralists, royalists or *godos,* Venezuelans, and Granadines forswore their enmities in the interest of union and adopted the beloved national name of Colombian. Such was the heritage that the Liberator bequeathed to Vice-President Santander when he left his country, after having given it a political structure, in order to go to distant shores to risk amidst the chaos of Peruvian anarchy the glory he had acquired in twelve years of fighting and arduous labor.

Riva-Agüero displayed great energy and achieved satisfactory results after his elevation to the presidency of Peru. What most pleased the people was the creation of a national army commanded by Peruvian officers. He did not, however, have any experience as an executive, and he quickly revealed his weak character, especially his excessive vanity. The dissension between him and Congress eventually reduced the country to a state of misery and led to civil war. The Spaniards, meanwhile, assembled their fighting forces in Jauja and marched on Lima with 7,500 combatants. They were in complete ignorance of the size of the expedition, some 5,500 men, that General Santa Cruz had led to Intermedios near the end of May, after the Colombian auxiliaries had reached Callao. The news of this royalist movement disconcerted Riva-Agüero and made Congress realize the imminence of the danger, but it was impossible to unite the factions. When the enemy approached, General Sucre finally accepted, though reluctantly, the supreme command of the army.

Sucre decided to abandon Lima and defend the port of Callao, whereupon the government and many civilians moved there. It then became exactly like the legendary camp of King Agramante. The dissension that started in Lima between the executive power and the houses of Congress assumed greater proportions in Callao, and Congress finally voted, on June 22, 1823, to depose the president. Then it decided to transfer its sessions to Trujillo, leaving General Sucre with complete authority in Callao and in any provinces he should occupy with the army under his command.

General Canterac set up camp between Lima and Callao on June 18. After threatening to burn the city, he exacted large sums of money from the inhabitants of Lima. Although he pretended to despise Santa Cruz, he realized, after learning the exact size of the latter's forces, that he had to abandon for the time being the hope of subjugating the northern provinces of Peru and hurry down to the southern provinces to rescue them from the hands of the patriots. After plundering Lima, this proud Spaniard decided to evacuate the city on July 17. He had already dispatched General Jerónimo Valdés to oppose Santa Cruz and to reinforce the royalists of the interior.

When Sucre saw that Canterac would have to rush to the defense of Upper Peru, he conceived the plan of having a second expedition either sail from Callao to reinforce Santa Cruz or go inland to Cuzco and defend the right bank of the Apurímac River. This expedition of three thousand men left for Chala about the middle of July, and Sucre sailed to direct operations after delegating to Torre Tagle the authority conferred upon him by Congress. On August 30 he occupied Arequipa, which had been abandoned by the royalist garrison. There he received communications from Santa Cruz in which the latter indicated his refusal to accept the reinforcements Sucre had offered to him. This unfortunate refusal decided the fate of the campaign and proved disastrous to his army, which was ignominiously routed, almost without a fight.

Santa Cruz had landed at Ilo, crossed the cordillera, and occupied the city of La Paz on July 8, sending another column under General Gamarra to occupy Oruro. This was the situation when the energetic royalist General Valdés joined Viceroy José de la Serna after a march at top speed from Lima. Taking fresh troops, he advanced against Santa Cruz, who repulsed him at Zepita but then withdrew to the other side of the Desaguadero River when informed of the arrival of reinforcements for Valdés. After adding Gamarra's column to his army, Santa Cruz hesitated to act and lost an opportunity to defeat Valdés at Sepulturas before the arrival of Pedro Antonio de Olañeta from Potosí. He started to withdraw, now closely pursued by Valdés and Olañeta, who had joined forces. Before long the withdrawal turned into a headlong flight; all discipline disappeared and the general cry was "Save yourself if you can." Barely fourteen hundred men reached Ilo after this disastrous campaign. The division from Colombia would have been endangered had it not been for the great skill with which Sucre directed it. The failure of this expedition did not surprise the Liberator, for General Sucre had kept him informed of everything relative to it and of his fears of disaster.

In the meantime the flames of civil strife were threatening to spread with greater intensity throughout the North. In Trujillo on July 19, Riva-Agüero, despite the decree that had deposed him, issued a decree dissolving Congress and put it into effect on the same day with the use of armed force. He exiled the members who were hostile toward him and appointed ten members to serve as a senate, so that they might ratify any measures he proposed. Most of the representatives made their way back to Lima and sought the protection of Torre Tagle, who reconvened Congress and brought it under his control by paying the members huge sums of money taken from the public treasury. It is not surprising, therefore, that they declared Riva-Agüero a traitor and an outlaw and elevated Torre Tagle to the presidency.

This was the desperate situation of Peru when the Liberator arrived to assume the burden of saving it from anarchy and despotism. But the worst was yet to come, for the eruption of all the elements of discord would make the situation even more frightful. On September 1, 1823, after landing at Callao, the Liberator entered Lima amidst the very enthusiastic applause of the entire populace. A committee from Congress assured him that Congress welcomed his arrival as a most propitious event. After thanking them, the Liberator assured them in turn that Congress could count on his efforts, "provided abuses were removed and radical reforms were introduced in all branches of the administration, which had previously been vicious and corrupt." Torre Tagle and his ministers, who were present, doubtlessly judged these words to be ominous for everyone in their group, for they had every reason to fear an investigation of their conduct.

The political situation in Trujillo became more serious every day. Riva-Agüero, believing a reconciliation with Congress impossible, already had three thousand men under arms in the provinces that recognized him. Since he blamed General Sucre, without reason, for the dissension between him and Congress, he came to the conclusion that the Liberator must be hostile toward him. This supposition was strengthened by the fact that the Liberator had not answered the notes in which Riva-Agüero had informed him of the forceful dissolution of Congress in Trujillo. This idea led him from error to error and impaired his position. But Sucre was innocent of the charge, as can be seen in his correspondence with the Liberator, in notes from the Peruvian government, and in private letters written to him by prominent men of that country during the period.

Since Congress was convinced that it could not find a better mediator than the Liberator, it was prompted by the above considerations to issue a decree on September 2, authorizing him to seek a solution to the problem. It was not doubted for a moment that Riva-Agüero would accept this distinguished personage as arbitrator. Bolívar had accepted the task because Riva-Agüero had not completely overstepped the bounds. Acting in accordance with his own patriotic ideas, the Liberator wrote to him an admirable letter in which he pointed out that Riva-Agüero was engaged in an open war with the national assembly, to which he owed his appointment to the presidency and to which he had sworn a solemn oath of obedience. He urged Riva-Agüero to accept his offer of friendship and protection rather than pursue an impossible goal that might cause the downfall of Peru and would have a harmful effect on America. This letter was entrusted to Señor José María Galdiano and Colonel Luis Urdaneta, who were authorized to grant an amnesty and to offer Riva-Agüero the command of the Peruvian army or a diplomatic mission in Europe. This was the only step the Liberator took, because he doubted whether it was proper for him to intervene in the domestic quarrels of Peru.

It was the general belief of all those who knew the state of the country that the best way to assure its future was to entrust the reins of government to the Liberator, but he opposed the idea with all his ardor and eloquence. When Congress informed him that all its deliberations would be submitted to him before final action was taken, he declared in his reply that his offer of active cooperation included only his military services, but that the Colombian army would protect the national assembly, and he would assist the executive power to the full extent of his ability. On September 10, however, Congress conferred upon the Liberator the supreme military command of the territory of the Republic, together with the ordinary and extraordinary powers needed in the existing situation. He became, in fact, a real dictator, because Torre Tagle, as nominal president of the Republic, had but a sem-balance of power. This was enough for him, for he was incapable of exercising power.

On September 13, the Liberator, in conformity with the status given him by the decree of the tenth, appeared before the sovereign Congress to assure it of independence and to offer it his services. When he entered the chamber, the entire audience burst into wild applause, and all the members of Congress stood up to show their respect. The Liberator expressed his gratitude for the unlimited confidence shown in him and promised that the soldiers of the liberating army would not return to their countries until they had left Peru free. He went on to say that he offered victory, relying on the valor of the united army, the good faith of the Congress, the executive power, and the Peruvian people. When he returned to his house, he was accompanied by Torre Tagle, who undoubtedly must have realized during this ceremony what little support he had.

The costly manner in which war had been waged during San Martín's administration and those that followed his, the extraction of large sums by Canterac during his occupation of the city, and Torre Tagle's shameful embezzlements had reduced the once wealthy capital almost to a state of poverty. Finding the treasury empty, the Liberator requested and obtained a loan of 300,000 pesos in his own name from the principal capitalists in order to take care of the most urgent needs. The four thousand men stationed in the capital were poorly equipped, and there were not enough stores to outfit the forces expected daily from Colombia. The Liberator provided these needs and placed the army in a position to undertake the campaign within a few weeks. He pointed out to the government the desirability of sending a special mission to Chile to ask for reinforcements, and he repeated to the vicepresident of Colombia the request he had made for this purpose.

While he was busy with this and other important affairs, it had been discovered through intercepted letters that Riva-Agüero was maintaining correspondence with the royalists. Although the first letters did not reveal his complicity with them, they did, indeed, throw abundant light on the peril threatening the country. Neither the Liberator's letter nor the mission he had sent to Riva-Agüero produced the result expected. When Colonel Antonio Gutiérrez de la Fuente, who commanded a unit of the former president's troops, arrived in Lima with communications for the Liberator, Bolívar asked him how the negotiations with the royalists were progressing. La Fuente, who was surprised to hear such questions, declared his ignorance of the existence of any treasonable correspondence. When the Liberator placed the intercepted letters in his hands and spoke to him at length about the disrepute that such conduct would bring upon Peru, he did not hide the indignation he felt over the suspicious dealings of the former president.

Acting with laudable zeal, La Fuente exceeded his instructions and proposed to the Liberator terms of capitulation that were advantageous to Riva-Agüero and honorable for the Peruvian government. The Liberator, who shared the same sentiments, accepted the terms with slight modifications. La Fuente returned to Trujillo with this agreement and with the firm resolution to watch carefully the steps of the dissident group. When Congress heard that Riva-Agüero was indifferent about the conciliatory measures proposed and that he was corresponding with La Serna, it ordered the Liberator to start in pursuit of this proscribed leader and to use force and any other means needed to put an end to the anarchy. In compliance with this decree, the Liberator sent four thousand men toward the headquarters of the dissidents. He himself moved to the theater of operations about the middle of November, after the promulgation of the provisional constitution of the Republic, which Congress had ratified.

In the final moments of his uncertain rule, Riva-Agüero displayed a vigor that would have been of great value had it been displayed in support of an honorable cause. In addition to the negotiations he had opened with the royalists, he wrote for assistance to Santa Cruz, who was still in the southern provinces with the remnants of his army, and sent an agent to Chile and Buenos Aires to defend his cause and to point out to them the danger involved in giving approval to Bolívar's conduct, which he called arbitrary and despotic. This messenger had also been commissioned to deliver a letter to General San Martín, then in Mendoza, urging him to return to Peru in order to place himself at the head of the army. The former Protector rejected the proposal with the scorn that it deserved, and he also refused the invitation extended to him by Santa Cruz, Portocarrero, and Vice-Admiral Martin George Guise, an English officer commanding the Peruvian fleet who supported Riva-Agüero out of gratitude.

These and other adverse circumstances made the Liberator's situation very alarming. In the belief that the only way to extricate himself from this difficult position was to take very prompt and resolute action, he placed himself at the head of the forces that were marching to subjugate the dissidents and took up a position between the latter and the royalists, thus cutting their lines of communication. An unexpected event happily prevented the shame and horrors of civil war on this occasion. La Fuente intercepted some correspondence that removed all his doubts about the extent of the crime. Accompanied by the officers of his unit, who agreed to help him, he entered Trujillo at dawn on November 25 and arrested Riva-Agüero and his accomplices. The blow was decisive, and although many of those who were most involved remained free, they had no alternative, upon learning of the Liberator's approach, but to recognize the government established by Congress. Colonel La Fuente sent the official report of the happenings to Lima, but he did not carry out Torre Tagle's order for the secret execution of the former president. He took upon himself the responsibility of sending Riva-Agüero by ship to Guayaquil, from where, by order of the Liberator, he was allowed to proceed to Europe.

The consequences of the former president's resistance were felt for some time, since he had succeeded in instilling in the troops under his command a great aversion toward the Colombians. This feeling never disappeared completely. Now that he was able to give his entire attention to military affairs, the Liberator visited the northern provinces and ordered general recruiting in order to increase the size of the army. He had already become convinced that, apart from Colombia's aid, Peru could expect nothing from her allies. Buenos Aires had tacitly withdrawn from the struggle, after having concluded early in July a preliminary convention with Spanish commissioners and having recommended that the other South American governments accept it. This convention stipulated that sixty days after ratification hostilities would cease for eighteen months. During this period the Spanish forces in Peru would hold the positions they were occupying, and trade would be fully restored. Another article obligated the government of Buenos Aires to negotiate a definitive treaty of peace between His Catholic Majesty and the states of the American continent.

This was the great plan of the minister from Buenos Aires, Don Bernardino Rivadavia, an exceedingly vain man who had the absurd notion that he could emulate the Liberator by opposing him in every way he could. He liked to believe that the preliminary convention would establish peace in South America and that he, not Bolívar, would deserve the title of Liberator. His ill-conceived designs were frustrated, but they did do some harm to Peru, because this policy paralyzed the efforts of the Salta authorities, who were ready to create a diversion in the provinces of Upper Peru.[1]

Chile had offered at the beginning of the year to help Peru, provided that the Liberator took charge of the direction of the war. According to the campaign plan drawn up on this basis, the Chilean contingent was to land at Intermedios and threaten the enemy in that section, while the Liberator would make a frontal attack, marching on Jauja. The Chilean division sailed from Valparaíso on October 15 and reached Arica on the twenty-sixth. Colonel José María Benavente refused to cooperate with General Santa Cruz, who was still there. Since political events forced the Liberator to change his campaign plan, the Chilean contingent was ordered to proceed to Callao, but the commander in charge ignored the Liberator's order and returned to Coquimbo and Valparaíso, abandoning Peru to her fate at the very moment when the common enemy was marching on the capital.

This ignoble conduct was approved by the Santiago government but roundly censured by the people. Since I was then in Santiago as a commissioner from the Liberator to that government, I immediately addressed a letter to the director of Chile, Don Ramón Freyre, reminding him of Chile's offer of aid and requesting him to order the immediate return of the expedition to any point on the Peruvian coast considered

---

[1] From the beginning of the revolution in 1810, the Argentines had promoted rebellion in Upper Peru. The government of Salta, a province in the northwest part of Argentina, was now ready to launch an attack on the royalist forces in Upper Peru. —Ed.

appropriate. He repeated to me his offer of assistance and his protestations of sympathy for Peru, but his disloyal conduct was more harmful to the Liberator's plans than an open and frank refusal would have been. Shortly afterward he was shamefully routed when he attacked Chiloé with the same division that had returned from Peru.

Colombia alone remained faithful to Peru in misfortune. Approving the Liberator's noble sentiments and vast designs, she generously supported his glorious efforts. The people and the army were more devoted to the cause than the government, whose actions at times concealed petty jealousy under the cloak of national interest. Even though a great part of the burden of the Peruvian war fell upon Colombia, her government could have taken more resolute and energetic action in the dispatch of auxiliary units.

The state of affairs in Peru and the great obstacles that surrounded the Liberator at the end of the year 1823 are faithfully described in the official communication that he addressed to the secretary of war. This communication shows, besides, the very careful attention he gave to everything connected with the army. He sees a need for stern measures to be applied against all conspirators, and he states that Colonel Cordero should set out from Callao for Canta with the Vargas Battalion in order to destroy the enemy and rebel guerrilla bands. One of his final remarks is that it is urgently necessary to send the entire army to the mountains for acclimatization in the region where the war must be waged.

While prescribing measures to help augment and supply the Peruvian units stationed in the northern provinces, the Liberator learned of Admiral Guise's arrival at Huanchaco and of his arbitrary actions. Leaving Cajamarca, he arrived in Trujillo on December 20, and he did not take long to settle the disputes with Santa Cruz and Guise, managing to have them, and others who had previously refused, recognize the government. Nevertheless, new forces of destruction, ever more threatening, were mounting in opposition to the independence of Peru. It is therefore not at all strange that the Liberator was saddened when he looked ahead to the obstacles that he still had to overcome. In the belief that his presence would soon be needed in the capital, he left Trujillo on December 25, but he was unable to continue his trip beyond Pativilca, where he arrived on January 1, 1824, because he became so seriously ill that it was feared he would not live.

At about this time Don Félix Alzaga, with the title of minister plenipotentiary for Buenos Aires, arrived in the capital to request the Peruvian government to agree to the famous preliminary convention, and the government did not hesitate to give its assent. Since, however, the chief executive's approval would not suffice, Torre Tagle's faction employed intrigue and deceit to win followers in Congress who would support it. When the Liberator was officially informed of Alzaga's mission, he replied that he hoped any negotiation would be based on independence but that he had no intention of becoming involved. He did, nevertheless, write to his confidential agents in Lima that he had no objection to the government's sending a commission to Viceroy La Serna in order to sound him out and to give time for the troops expected from Colombia to arrive.

Since both the Congress and the government of Peru were weary of the war and of the sacrifices they had made, they conceived the idea that the preliminary convention might perhaps serve to bring the prolonged struggle to an end. Nevertheless, the majority of the representatives had the good sense to consult the Liberator before making a final decision. Despite their protestation that they would respect his opinion, he sorrowfully realized that the representatives of the people had been affected by the widespread dismay. In his reply to Congress he refused the responsibility of deciding what was best for Peru, limiting himself to expressing his personal feelings. "A life of sacrifice and death," he said, "seems to me to be the height of supreme happiness in comparison with tyranny, and war and bloodshed seem to me preferable to submission and peace with the oppressors." This note made a favorable impression on the real patriots, of whom there were many in Congress, and brought renewed hope to them.

The chief executive had meanwhile sent General Juan Berindoaga, the secretary of war, to Jauja to invite the viceroy to accept the preliminary convention and to obtain an armistice for Peru. The envoy was unable to meet with La Serna or Canterac, but he did have some conferences with General Juan Antonio Monet and General Juan Loriga. This was the entire result of his mission. Torre Tagle and

Berindoaga have been accused of having availed themselves of the latter's mission to start the vile betrayal that they completed later. Despite some attendant circumstances and impressive proof, I am inclined to absolve them of the crime, after a careful examination of the documents I have before me. If, when I acquit them of a single crime, the curses of posterity weigh less heavily on their memory, I shall be satisfied.

On February 5, 1824, four days after Berindoaga's return to Lima, the Callao garrison revolted, deposed General Alvarado, and seized both him and all the officers of the fortress. The leader of this revolt was soon identified as Dámaso Moyano, a colored sergeant in the Río de la Plata Regiment, which, with other troops from Buenos Aires and Peruvian artillery, constituted the garrison. Though this atrocious crime cannot be excused, the treatment they had received from the government should be taken into consideration. Not only did they receive insufficient rations, but their pay was held back, and so great was the apathy of the government that no steps were taken to relieve the misery, despite the frequent demands made by General Enrique Martínez.[2] The truth is that the entire army suffered privations in like manner because of the government's neglect.

Moyano hesitated before becoming more and more involved. When the conspirators gave their word that they would return the fortress if the government gave them their back pay and returned them to their country, Torre Tagle claimed that these conditions were dishonorable and avoided all the courses of action suggested to him for the recovery of the fortress. The tragic news of the revolt reached Pativilca on February 7, and the Liberator, comprehending at once the complete significance of the catastrophe, acted without delay. He ordered General Martínez to evacuate the capital after removing all useful military equipment and to impose a tax on the people of means. He also ordered Admiral Guise to destroy all the ships in Callao Bay that he could not remove from the port.

The Liberator's fears were realized before long. On February 10 the rebellious troops freed the imprisoned royalists, raised the Spanish

[2] An Argentine general in charge of the defense of Lima.—Ed.

flag, named Colonel Casariego as their leader, and sent a commission to seek assistance from Canterac. Their demand on the same day for the surrender of the capital caused the greatest consternation. Congress, in the midst of this terrible crisis, took a giant step toward the salvation of the country. After a short debate it appointed Bolívar dictator and suspended the code of laws and constitutional authority.

The situation of Peru when this decree was issued was very different from what it was at the time when San Martín had disembarked four years earlier. San Martín had only to come, see, and conquer; he came, he saw, and he could have conquered. The undertaking was, perhaps, too much for him, or at least he thought so; he approached it hesitantly and finally abandoned it. When Congress entrusted to Bolívar the salvation of the Republic, it turned a corpse over to him. On the other hand, the enemy, with a large, well-supplied army, was occupying excellent positions. All thoughtful men considered Peru lost, and the few with whom Bolívar was on intimate terms urgently advised him not to accept a post that would inevitably jeopardize his reputation. Even Sucre, the illustrious Sucre, unaware of his brilliant future and heedless for the moment of the call of glory, also advised him to withdraw to Colombia. But Bolívar did not listen to them, because it was in crises like the present one that he proved to be superior to himself. Calling upon the vast resources of his genius, which seemed to grow as the number of obstacles increased, he surveyed the forces at his command and decided that he could overcome the difficulties confronting him.

The instructions given Martínez were not carried out, because of the intrigues of Torre Tagle and Berindoaga, and at a council of war it was unanimously agreed that Lima should be defended at any cost. General Martínez was replaced by the brave General Mariano Necochea, whom the Liberator named civil and military commander of the capital. While Necochea was busy sending the war equipment to headquarters, there fell into his hands a letter from Canterac to Torre Tagle's agent, which revealed the nature and extent of the president's treasonable acts. Yielding to the generous impulses of his nature, he decided to consult the Liberator before taking any action. When the order arrived for the arrest and transfer of the criminals to Pativilca, he warned the president and tried to induce him to appear voluntarily at the Liberator's headquarters. Torre Tagle protested his innocence and pretended that he was leaving soon for Pativilca, but he deceived Necochea by taking refuge instead in the fortress of Callao, which was destined to be the scene of his tragic end. No one had been more devoted to the cause of Peruvian independence, but the unfortunate Marqués de Torre Tagle was vain and a victim of weakness, even in his home, where he was blindly submissive to his wife. According to some people, his wife's anger over an insulting remark led her to prompt him to take part in the shameful treason. Putting aside these petty matters, which do not excuse his treason, I am going to narrate the fateful consequences of his crime.

General Necochea evacuated Lima on February 28, 1824, and the royalists took possession of it on the following day. In addition to Torre Tagle, the principal officials of the state and 337 officers of the Peruvian army ignominiously abandoned their country's banners and humbled themselves before its oppressors. Furthermore, Torre Tagle published a manifesto and a proclamation in which he accused the Liberator of crimes that could make him more hateful to the Peruvians. Bolívar scorned to answer him, entrusting his defense to the success of the undertaking.

It gives me pleasure to leave these scenes of villainy in order to view the interesting picture of a great soul struggling with adversity and courageously rising up to fight for the cause of humanity. When Torre Tagle delivered Lima to the Spaniards, Bolívar was still in Pativilca, his constitution weakened by the recent afflictions that he had suffered. Setting his mind to the task before him, he surveyed with surprise, but not with despair, all the perils that surrounded him. The united army was composed of seven thousand not-very-well-equipped combatants quartered between Cajamarca, Trujillo, and Huaraz. The available public revenues were woefully insufficient for the maintenance of this force. In order to suppress the abuses in Peru, it was essential to employ stern measures. Even more alarming was the fact that in order to obtain money it was necessary to struggle with the prejudices and the fanaticism of the people.

Despite everything, Bolívar resolutely set to work. Eliminating all unnecessary positions, he concentrated the management of all civil and political affairs in the hands of a single secretary-general. Don José Sánchez Carrión, a very able Peruvian, received this post and proved with his talent and industry that he deserved the confidence placed in him. Besides reducing the salaries of the civil employees, the Liberator reduced the soldiers' pay to a quarter of the amount fixed by law, but he took steps to make it a reality. Although the governments of Colombia, Chile, Mexico, and Guatemala were invited to assist him, only Colombia complied with his wishes. The troops he sought were not sent as promptly as the danger required, but the promises made to him encouraged him in his undertaking. He added recruits from the provinces that recognized his authority and placed them under the command of General La Mar. As commander of the united army he chose General Sucre. He quartered the Peruvian units in the North and the Colombians over toward the sierra, thus managing to prevent the former from going over to the enemy and the latter from deserting.

Military affairs were not his only concern. It was necessary to create revenues in order to maintain the army. He persuaded the ecclesiastical authorities to contribute silver church vessels; he assigned to the state the income from the holdings of those who had deserted to serve the enemy; and he established taxes and had them collected—in a word, he sought resources and obtained them from out of nowhere. The navy also benefited from his energetic action, for he increased it considerably. On February 24, under the orders of Admiral Guise and Captain Addison, it was able to destroy some ships in Callao Bay.

The situation of the royalists at this time contrasted notably with that of the patriot army. They occupied all Peruvian territory except for the department of Trujillo and part of Huanuco. Eighteen thousand men, from Jauja to Potosí, were defending the King's cause. Possession of Callao gave Spain immense military stores as well as some ships, which were armed later for privateering. With the restoration of Ferdinand VII to absolute power in 1823, the viceroy had hopes of reinforcements, and he received them in fact when the *Asia,* a battleship of the line, and the brig *Aquiles* arrived in the Pacific. Together with the armed vessels at Callao, they gave the royalists control of the sea, which had been the only advantage previously enjoyed by the patriots.

At the beginning of March the Liberator established his head-quarters in Trujillo. The work of treason was still not complete, and new desertions were to increase doubts concerning the Peruvian army. The calumnies spread by Torre Tagle, Berindoaga, and other traitors did not fail to influence the inhabitants of the provinces that recognized the authority of the dictator. Nor did the officers of the Peruvian army remain unaffected by the suspicions aroused in them by the calumnies. In order to remove these suspicions and to repudiate the designs imputed to him, the Liberator issued a proclamation stating that the Congress had entrusted to him the hateful authority of a dictator in order to save Peru. Refuting all the slanderous remarks made about him and the Colombians, he declared that once liberty had triumphed he would throw off the mantle of dictatorship and return home to Colombia with his brothers-in-arms without taking a grain of sand from Peru. This proclamation partially checked the sinister intrigues, re-established confidence, and aroused the enthusiasm of many people.

Some of the measures the Liberator had to take were extremely harsh, but the circumstances required such action. Trujillo was declared the provisional capital of the Republic, and a decree was issued for the establishment of a court of justice. Court costs were reduced, and the military courts were abolished. Even in those moments of terror and despair the Liberator showed more solicitude for the younger generation than had all the previous administrations of Peru. A university was founded in Trujillo, and he established schools in all the places he visited. During the month he spent in Trujillo the city took on the appearance of an immense arsenal where no one was idle. Under his immediate supervision everything needed by the army was made, including a large quantity of uniforms, leather belts, arms, and ammunition. He himself taught people how to make horseshoes and nails and how to mix the various kinds of iron. In order to economize on cloth, he furnished the patterns for the shape of the jackets.

No one has ever been known to display such great energy, and never have results corresponded more closely to the efforts expended. A month before, everything was needed, and now everything was ready. It seemed as though a magic wand had been waved or as though from the head of a new Jupiter there had issued forth, not a new Pallas armed from head to foot, but eight thousand warriors ready for combat.

CHAPTER EIGHTEEN

A FTER HAVING MADE PREPARATIONS to defend the territory occupied by his army, the Liberator established his headquarters in
Huamachuco on April 22, 1824. Now he devoted himself to the task of
expanding and training the army, rounding up cattle, and storing food
at various points in the cordillera. In all this work he was greatly aided
by the unceasing efforts of all his subordinates, but the one who did
the most was Sucre, who was the Liberator's right arm and the main-
stay of the army. An indefatigable worker, he crossed the Andes three
times, in spite of the inclement weather and the hardships of the
journey, and obtained supplies from the most remote points. Even the
harmful effects of the climate of those inhospitable regions were
warded off through the foresight and diligence of this eminent man.

Unlike the civil and military authorities, the naval commander,

Martin George Guise, placed all kinds of obstacles in the Liberator's path. The crews of the warships had not been paid for a full year, and the ships themselves were in deplorable condition. The Liberator immediately set about remedying these deficiencies. The contagion of civil strife had extended its pernicious influence to the naval officers, and many concessions had to be made in order to persuade the fleet to obey the government. Admiral Guise was brave, as befitted an English naval officer, but he was capricious and stubborn. All the ephemeral governments of Peru had flattered his vanity and overlooked his weaknesses, but the Liberator, who was exceedingly proud and incapable of such servility, lost his friendship. Guise continually made exorbitant demands, and the great sacrifices being made did not suffice to satisfy them. More than once he threatened to abandon the service and take his ships to Chile. Be it said in justice, however, that when danger arose, no one was quicker to face it than the courageous Guise.

The transport service also gave the Liberator great trouble. The lack of necessary articles made the sea voyage from Guayaquil and Panama very uncomfortable for the troops, and the privateers presented a constant threat. Many times the transports separated from the convoy and entered the nearest Peruvian port, where the troops soon fell victims of disease when delayed there for days or weeks because their arms and stores had, through carelessness, been shipped on other vessels. On other occasions they had to cross waterless deserts, and many soldiers perished from fatigue and thirst. If the royalists had advanced in the months of March and April, the patriot army would have had to fall back toward the northern frontiers. Fortunately for America, however, discord prevented them from attacking the liberators of the country before the latter could offer effective resistance.

The restoration of absolutism in Spain was the cause of political discord among the royalist leaders in Peru.[1] Viceroy La Serna, Canterac, and Valdés, Spanish commanders of the greatest influence in the army of Lower Peru, professed constitutional principles. Olañeta, the commander of the provinces of Upper Peru, was an extreme absolutist, and he engaged in numerous controversies with those of the liberal

[1] In 1823 Ferdinand VII was able to eliminate the Cortes and to regain absolute power with the help of a French army sent by Louis XVIII. —Ed.

faction. He accused the liberals of lukewarmness in the cause of Ferdinand and of God. La Serna, for his part, charged the commander of Upper Peru with insubordination and rebellion and finally resorted to force to punish his disobedience. General Valdés crossed the Desaguadero River with five thousand men and, after various encounters, finally triumphed over Olañeta's troops at La Lava on August 17. Then he recrossed the Desaguadero to join the viceroy, who was concentrating his forces on the right bank of the Apurímac River.

Bolívar was unable to profit from these events as advantageously as he might have desired because of the state of his army. He did, however, issue repeated orders to the corps commanders to redouble their activity in order to hasten the preparations needed to place them in a position to take the offensive. So great were the difficulties that had to be overcome that it seemed wise to abandon the undertaking or at least to make an immediate withdrawal. Although the conduct of most of those charged with executing the Liberator's orders was worthy of the highest praise, there were some among them who were remiss in their duties. The Liberator was saddened when he saw that even though the country was in a death struggle there were men who were so corrupt they would sacrifice every noble patriotic sentiment for the sake of making a fortune by appropriating the revenues of the state. Whenever he discovered it, he became terribly angry, but even on these occasions he let the law take its course.

In the months of May and June he went out from his headquarters in Huaraz and Caraz to visit all the places where the various units were quartered. On June 15, after receiving the reinforcements brought from Colombia by José María Córdova and Miguel Antonio Figueredo, he ordered all the units to break camp and to cross the cordillera at different points to Cerro de Pasco. There, on August 2, he reviewed the united army, which amounted to 7,700 men of all branches, not including the guerrilla bands. This was all that he could put on the field as a result of his ceaseless efforts. The discipline of the troops and their zeal inspired the greatest confidence in the success of the campaign. The Colombian troops, who made up the main force of the army, idolized the Liberator, who had led them to victory so many times. The Peruvian units were anxious to restore to their arms the

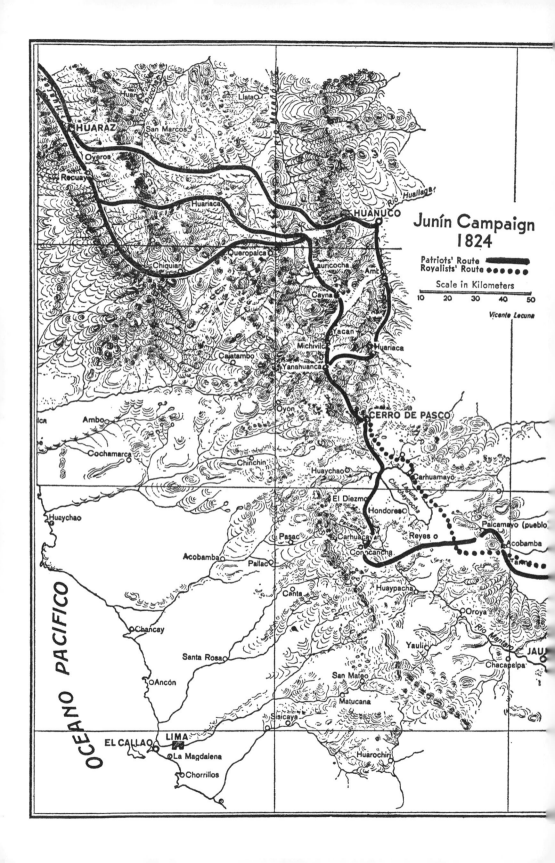

luster that had been dimmed by repeated defeats. The veterans whom San Martín had brought from La Plata were equally anxious to recover their former reputation, which had been blackened by the treason of their disloyal comrades at Callao. If anything further was needed to bolster the army's morale, Bolívar accomplished it with a proclamation in which he told the soldiers that they were about to complete the great task of freeing a whole world from slavery and that Peru and all America looked to them to bring peace, for they were invincible.

While the Liberator was preparing to march to Jauja, General Canterac assembled his own army and marched on Cerro de Pasco to reconnoiter the patriots' position. Upon arriving near Pasco, he learned that the patriots were moving on Jauja along the western bank of Lake Reyes. He thereupon countermarched at a rapid pace along the opposite bank, intending to take his stand between the patriots and Jauja. On August 6, at two o'clock in the afternoon, the two armies came within sight of each other. Canterac continued his withdrawal, and the Liberator advanced with the cavalry, which was under the immediate orders of Necochea, and overtook him at five o'clock on the plain of Junín. Canterac, who was thoroughly familiar with the terrain, skillfully wheeled about and attacked the patriots before they were able to correct their difficult position. So furious was the attack that the columns on the right gave way and retreated in confusion, but Major Philipp Braun, at the head of a few cavalrymen from his Granaderos a Caballo Squadron, withstood the enemy's charge and then put to flight those who were bearing down upon him. Thanks to the firm stand made by the Húsares del Perú Regiment, commanded by the courageous Lieutenant Colonel Manuel Isidoro Suárez, the patriot squadrons being pursued were able to rally. Then, led by the gallant William Miller, commander of the Peruvian cavalry, and the Colombian Colonels Laurencio Silva and Lucas Carvajal, all these units attacked the Spanish squadrons. Their courage and skill changed the tide of battle and decided the outcome of this memorable feat of arms. The royalists were completely routed and forced to seek the protection of their infantry, which was withdrawing hurriedly.

During the battle, which was like the combats of the knights of olden times, there was not a single shot fired. The terrible silence was broken only by the piercing call of bugles, the clash of swords and lances, the galloping and stamping of horses, the curses of the vanquished, and the moans of the wounded. The Spanish losses were 240 dead and a like number wounded; the patriot losses amounted to only a third of this number. This brilliant feat of arms broke the spell that seemed to link victory to the standards of Castile and showed the Peruvians that their oppressors were not invincible. In a letter to General José Ramón Rodil, governor of Callao, Canterac stated that despite insignificant losses in terms of manpower, the effect of his cavalry's flight and the numerical superiority of the enemy infantry would oblige him to fall back to an undetermined point in the provinces to the rear. All efforts, he said, must be devoted to the task of assembling sufficient forces to crush Bolívar.

The royalist withdrawal and the abandonment of the fertile valley of Jauja were the immediate consequences of the battle of Junín. The Liberator had to fit his movements to the circumstances and limit himself to dispatching cavalry pickets and several guerrilla bands in pursuit of the royalists in order to harass them and pick up the stragglers. Despite his enterprising nature, he was obliged to devote himself above all to keeping his small army intact. Canterac, in his withdrawal, cut the bridge at Iscuchuca, leveled the crops, and destroyed everything that might be useful to the patriots.

After two days of rest in Reyes, the troops continued their march on August 9. From Tarma instructions were sent to Colonel Urdaneta to organize a unit consisting of convalescents and stragglers in Trujillo and the guerrilla bands of Canta and Huarochiri. This force, together with a Colombian unit expected to arrive soon from Guayaquil, was to blockade Callao. On the thirteenth the headquarters staff arrived in Huancayo, where the first news was received about the real state of the quarrel between Olañeta and the viceroy. In the month of May the Liberator had written to Olañeta urging him to associate himself with the good cause of America, which was bound to win. The Spanish liberals who were active in Peru were astonished when they saw that the champion of South American independence had entered into correspondence with his ultraroyalist opponent. Even greater was their astonishment when, in a proclamation addressed to the Peruvians on the advantages gained from the battle of Junín, Bolívar declared that Olañeta was worthy of America's gratitude for having thrown off the yoke of Spanish tyranny in Upper Peru. This proclamation filled the patriots with confidence and brought consternation to the royalists.

When the army reached Huancayo, the Liberator was obliged to take measures to increase its size. One of the most extraordinary of these measures was that of commissioning General Sucre to assemble the stragglers and convalescents to the rear and send them to headquarters. Sucre, who never refused any personal service that would contribute to the welfare of the army, did not make the slightest objection and performed the task with his customary diligence and zeal. Once it was completed, however, he complained in a letter to the Liberator about having been reduced to a role that had occasioned derogatory remarks from some people and surprise among his friends. Since, as he put it, he had not been fortunate enough to be a good soldier, he wanted to be a good citizen in Colombia. He said that he would choose Bolívar to be his adviser in the dilemma confronting him. The Liberator's letter in reply honors him as much as Sucre is honored by his. He assured Sucre that this commission was a proof of preference rather than a humiliation. He went on to say that glory consisted in being great and in being of service and that if Sucre wanted to come and place himself at the head of the army, he would go behind. With human beings of that temper, could there be any doubt about the success of the enterprise that had been undertaken? After these mutual and satisfactory explanations Sucre once more assumed the post that his talents and courage fitted him for.

In the meantime the army pushed ahead as far as Huamanga, and the Liberator arrived there on the twenty-eighth after having received, in all the towns on the way from Jauja, the honors and respect that he deserved as a victor and as a benefactor of humanity. The army's progress had been delayed by the necessity of waiting for the auxiliaries being brought by Sucre and the troops who had recently arrived from Guayaquil. The enemy had already crossed the Apurímac and destroyed all the bridges except the one at Ocopa. The recruits stationed beforehand along the line of march were more than sufficient to replace the losses suffered in the hasty withdrawal. Every stopping place brought the enemy closer to his base of operations, while the patriots, in their advance, moved farther away from their own and had to cross territory devastated by the enemy.

Despite all these obstacles, the Liberator ordered Sucre to advance to Challhuanca. While making a reconnaissance of the Apurímac River territory with his staff, he received several dispatches containing important news that affected the subsequent operations of the army and even his own personal plans. The negotiation of the loan sought in London by the Peruvian government had been completed, leaving three million pesos immediately available to him. Other pleasant news was that three thousand of the twelve thousand men being organized in Colombia were already on their way to Peru. On the other hand, he learned of the arrival of Spanish warships in Peruvian waters and of the termination of the disputes between the royalists of Upper Peru, which left General Jerónimo Valdés free to join forces with the viceroy. This latter news offset the pleasing news and demanded serious consideration.

From the beginning of the campaign Sucre had constantly opposed the march toward the departments of Cuzco without the reinforcements expected to arrive from Colombia. Another who held the same opinion was Colonel Heres, who also believed that the Liberator's presence in Lima was absolutely necessary in order to further the war effort and to direct political affairs. After giving the matter serious consideration, the Liberator first thought of sending La Mar or Sucre to the coast. La Mar absolutely refused to accept such a commission, and Sucre did not want to accept it, because he believed that only the Liberator, with his prestige, could master the inevitable difficulties arising from the very unsettled state of the country. Since Bolívar did not want to remain idle during the rainy season, he decided to return to the coast. The authority he gave Sucre was broad enough to cover all circumstances; that is to say, he might choose between continuing active operations and quartering the troops.

Leaving Sañaica on October 7, Bolívar reached Andahuailas on the tenth. Here he established definite governments for the liberated provinces and appointed governors to enforce the laws and dictatorial decrees. The latter were to foster harmony and union among all the factions and classes, to make a formal inventory of state property, to appoint justices of the peace, and to establish hospitals. Besides these measures, Bolívar ordered schools to be founded in the towns through which he passed. He honored the town of Reyes with the name of Junín, which he also gave to the whole province of Jauja. The appointment of the principal magistrates was made by the municipalities, thus placing the agents of the executive in direct contact with the people, by whom they were chosen. A distinguished Peruvian has said that the laws of Peru were never so well respected as when Congress permitted Bolívar to consign them to oblivion. This observation, which does more honor to the Liberator's government than does the astonishing success attained by it, certainly did not lack foundation.

Upon his arrival in Huancayo on October 24, the Liberator received dispatches from Colombia that disturbed him considerably. The government informed him that Congress had repealed the law of October 9, 1821, which granted him extraordinary faculties in any territory that was a theater of war. Even when Congress gave him permission to go to Peru, it made no attempt to revoke these faculties. To do so at the present time, when he was confronted by huge obstacles, was a despicable course of action that did not fail to make a profound impression on his sensitive nature, especially since the vice-president assured him that the measure was the exclusive work of Congress. The truth of the matter is that this measure was adopted at the suggestion of Vice-President Santander himself, who regarded with envy Sucre's deserved advancement in the army and feared that the Liberator would confer upon him the rank of general in chief should he be victorious in Peru. This is not mere conjecture on my part, for I base my opinion on facts and authentic documents.

In no period of his life did Bolívar give greater proof of the purity of the intentions governing his political conduct than he did on this occasion. The spirit of the law of July 28, 1824, and the decree of August 2 not only deprived him of the authority that he had exercised until then in the southern departments of Colombia and of the power to promote deserving army officers, but it also removed him from command of the Colombian troops serving in Peru. The latter was the most grievous blow that could have been struck against him and the one that hurt him the most, for he was the creator of that army of veteran soldiers who had followed him from the farthest reaches of Colombia and who regarded him more as a father than a commander. The very day on which he received the decrees, he wrote to General Sucre, ordering him to notify the troops about them with the greatest caution, so that they would not have any adverse effect on discipline and do harm to the service. At the same time he delegated to Sucre the immediate command of the Colombian army, because he was "the most distinguished commander in Peru and had, moreover, been previously appointed general in chief of that army."

Bolívar thus gave an example of obedience to the laws of his country, when a single word on his part would have been all that he needed to ensure the most wholehearted obedience of the army and the people of Colombia. Despite the prudent manner in which Sucre communicated to the army the decrees and the Liberator's decision, the effect produced can be estimated from the tenor of the petition signed by the division generals and commanders. Expressing their deep sorrow over Bolívar's decision, they urged him to suspend his decision, at least until after he had presented the petition they had addressed to Congress, so that he might lead the army to a final glorious victory in the campaign that he had begun.

Despite these petitions, the Liberator would not change the decision he had made in Huancayo. Neither would he allow their petition to be sent to Congress. He did, however, try to check the army's increasing dissatisfaction with very sound advice. The only sign of displeasure that he showed over the imprudent action of the chief executive of Colombia was to stop his personal correspondence with Santander. Then he left Huancayo for Jauja, where he stayed until October 29. In less than two weeks he succeeded in assembling three hundred veterans and some seven hundred recruits, and in the course of the following month he sent Sucre a thousand more, as well as horses and supplies. Before departing from Jauja, he wrote to Sucre, especially calling his attention to the necessity of keeping the army units together, and concluded his letter as follows: "This promising state of affairs requires the greatest prudence in all operations. When we have hopes of obtaining large and excellent reinforcements, it would be madness to risk an outcome that can be secured in the natural course of events."

Wherever the Liberator went, he seemed destined to encounter unforeseen difficulties. From the summit of the Andes he saw the storm that was brewing over toward the coast, and he quickened his pace, moved by an eager desire to avert it. Colonel Luis Urdaneta had succeeded in assembling about fifteen hundred men, with whom he marched from Trujillo on Lima. After passing through the city on November 3, he was suddenly attacked on the road to Callao by a squadron of enemy cavalry that was lying in ambush. His body of untrained recruits were so completely disorganized that they could not be regrouped, with the result that there followed a shameful rout and a great slaughter. The Liberator received news of this disaster on November 5 when he reached Chancay, twenty leagues to the north of Lima, and it made him so angry that he immediately prescribed justifiably stern measures. A permanent court-martial was set up, and the individuals whose cowardice had been most pronounced were sentenced to death and shot. Then he ordered Urdaneta to withdraw to Chancay, where he himself reorganized the remnants of the unit in a few days, putting it on a better footing than ever, so that by the beginning of December the coast division was ready to march against the enemy. The approaches to Callao were occupied beforehand by the guerrilla bands from Huarochiri and Canta, and on the night of December 7 the Liberator personally passed through Lima with an escort, on his way to reconnoiter the area around Callao.

The capital had the appearance of a deserted city, for the inhabitants had shut themselves up in their homes in order to avoid the savage Manuel Ramírez. But as soon as it was known that the Liberator was in the vicinity, throngs of people gathered at the places where they thought he would pass again on his way to the granary, where his troops had their camp. When he appeared, they surrounded him, took him bodily from his horse, and carried him to the house they had hastily prepared for his reception. Loud cheers, shouts of joy, and the gay ringing of the bells announced to the City of the Kings that the American hero was within its walls. Never, perhaps, was he welcomed with greater demonstrations of enthusiasm and joy.

During the previous year Lima had suffered under the despotism of Ramírez, a brutal soldier who was the abject tool of his commanders. In addition to his cruel and savage tyranny, bands of marauders terrorized the inhabitants, and neither persons nor property was safe from their depredations. The garrison served only to terrify the peaceful citizens, not to protect them. Urdaneta's defeat intensified their sufferings and increased the insolence of the merciless Spanish rulers. For a month they suffered no end of anguish, which the unexpected arrival of the Liberator made them forget. Bolívar had not intended to establish his headquarters in Lima, but the pleas of thousands of people were so urgent that it was impossible for him to refuse to do so. The very name of Bolívar, they said, would be enough to keep the royalists inside the Callao fortress. And that is what happened, for the commander of the stronghold, respecting the Liberator's prestige, never dared to sally forth beyond the range of his batteries.

When some of the three thousand troops expected from Colombia arrived in December, the Liberator added them to the force placed under the orders of General Salom for the blockade of Callao. He called this force the Army of the Coast. The fleet, which under the command of the courageous Admiral Guise had defeated the Spanish seamen, despite inferior forces, in an engagement near Callao on October 7, had to withdraw shortly thereafter to Guayaquil for repairs. Only one corvette remained to prevent the transportation of supplies into the stronghold. The Liberator improved the facilities of the neighboring port of Chorrillos in order to remedy the damage done to Lima's commerce after the occupation of Callao by the enemy.

Having ensured the country's defenses in that section, the Liberator devoted himself to organizing the government of the capital and the free provinces. He re-established it under the previous form in conformity with the constitutional regime. Dr. José Sánchez Carrión was appointed first secretary of state, and Dr. Hipólito Unanue resumed charge of the Department of the Treasury. Colonel Tomás de Heres became head of the Department of War and the Navy. Then the Liberator re-established the high court of justice. This was the second time that it was set up in Peru, and the second time that the amazed world beheld something that is a marvel in the political order: the iron hand of a dictator opening the temple of Astraea in order to give greater liberty to a people, while keeping his own authority within the ordinary limits.

After he had organized the government in Lima, the Liberator once more busied himself with the project of confederating the republics of South America. His vivid imagination presented it to him in the most optimistic light and enabled him to foresee the great advantages to be gained by America from the confederation. Soon after the new cabinet was formed, he wrote to the governments of Colombia and Mexico, requesting their cooperation. They were bound by treaties to promote the meeting of the congress in Panama. While he was thus using his time for the benefit of Peru and all America, the news of a great victory came as a pleasant surprise to him.

Retracing my steps, I shall describe the movements of the patriot army prior to the battle of Ayacucho. As I have already indicated, Sucre had established his headquarters in Challhuanca and quartered the army units in the neighboring towns and ranches. This position, protected by the Pachachaca River, was a threat to the rear-guard of the royalists, who were concentrating their forces in Cuzco. The selection of Sucre for the supreme command was most fortunate, being justified by his great military talent, his devotion to duty, and his unselfishness. Although La Mar had a higher rank as grand marshal of Peru, he consented to serve under the orders of a younger commander, remaining in charge of the Peruvian division. The first of the two Colombian divisions was commanded by General Jacinto Lara, an energetic soldier who was precise in the exercise of his authority. At the head of the second division was General Córdova, a young Granadine who was as brave as a lion but careless and despotic as a commander. The commander of the cavalry was General William Miller, an Englishman who had won distinction during the war in Chile and Peru. The regiments were led by officers tested in a hundred battles, and among them there were some foreigners from England and other nations. When the Liberator gave the command to Sucre, the army consisted of seven thousand combatants.

While in the Mamara area reconnoitering the enemy positions, Sucre received definite information on October 16 that Valdés and Canterac had joined forces and that the viceroy had taken command of the army.

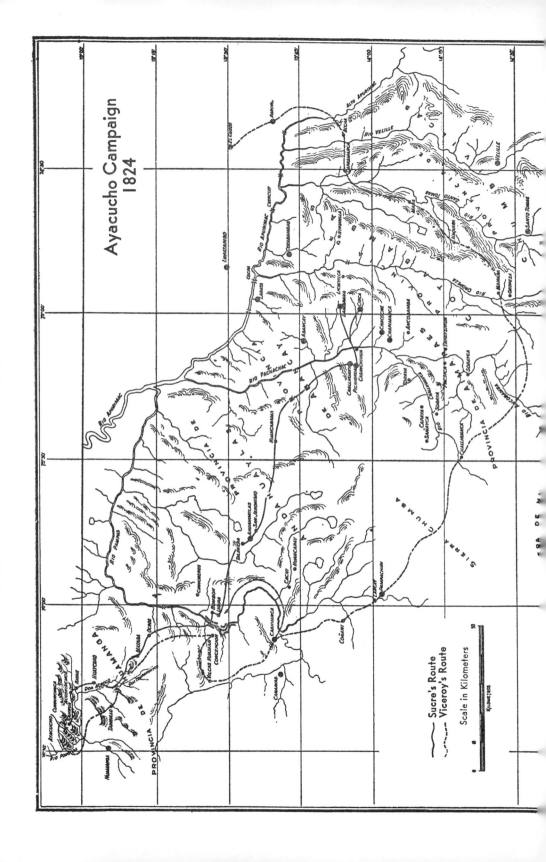

Ayacucho Campaign
1824

——— Sucre's Route
– – – Viceroy's Route

Scale in Kilometers

When the royalist outposts fell back, he was led to believe that the viceroy had no intention of advancing. On the twenty-fourth he quartered the army units in accordance with instructions from the Liberator, except for some battalions that were moving about with Miller, making a reconnaissance. On November 2, while on the way to Lambrama, Sucre received a report from General Miller, which stated that all the enemy forces were moving rapidly and that a battle would soon be inevitable. After quickly assembling his forces near Lambrama, he moved to Pichirgua, which has good pasture land and the only fairly good position for a battle. The enemy, in the meantime, passed through Challhuanca in order to penetrate to the rear of the patriots and march on Huamanga. Instead of being disconcerted, Sucre saw this move as a serious mistake, costly to the enemy in man and horses because of the rough roads. Despite everything, the enemy succeeded in hiding from Sucre the true state of his forces, which the latter supposed could not exceed eight thousand men.

On November 11, Sucre moved toward Andahuailas, and after his arrival he camped there until he learned that the enemy had occupied Huamanga on the sixteenth and was already marching toward him. He had the army advance in that direction, and on the twentieth the entire royalist army came into view after some of its companies of chasseurs were dislodged from the heights of Bombón. After scaling these heights with his troops, Sucre stayed there until the thirtieth, when he observed that the enemy was trying to flank his position. He therefore recrossed the Pampas River and advanced toward Matará, where he arrived on December 2, at the same time that the royalists appeared on the heights opposite. Sucre's position there was so poor that he decided to continue withdrawing toward Huamanga, which necessitated crossing the Corpahuaico ravine. After the patriot vanguard and center divisions had crossed, the infantry of the rearguard division was attacked while marching across by the royalist General Valdés. The infantry managed to withdraw after offering stubborn resistance. Sucre admitted that he lost three hundred men, in addition to the baggage train, the artillery, and some ammunition, which fell into the hands of the enemy.[2]

[2] See account of General Jacinto Lara in *Narración*, II, 295–296. In order to form

As Sucre moved along the Huamanga road, the enemy made a parallel move. On the eighth the royalists took up a position in front of the patriots on the heights of Cundurcunca (Condorkanki), within cannon range of the latter's positions. On the morning of December 9 both armies made ready to decide the fate of the campaign. Both camps were equally enthusiastic, but their forces were not equal in number. The royalists had nearly ten thousand men, whereas the patriots numbered less than six thousand.

As Sucre himself describes the battle scene, the Spaniards were supremely confident of victory, for they were completely dominating the small plain of Ayacucho with forces about twice as large as his own. Although his position was exposed, the flanks were protected by ravines, and the enemy cavalry could not operate freely to the front. In his summary report of the battle we learn how he was able to win a great victory against superior forces. Taking the offensive and skillfully deploying his forces in such a way that he could exert pressure wherever needed, he was able to rout the enemy squadrons as they began to enter the plain. A rapid pursuit resulted in the enemy's being cut off in every direction. The final comment in his report is that the Peruvian campaign was finished and that the trophies won by the army in the victory of Ayacucho were an offering worthy of acceptance by the Liberator of Colombia. The battle of Ayacucho brought Sucre a crown of immortal glory, which he deserved, but he did not show any signs of conceit. No boastful words or mean insults came from him to aggravate the misfortune of the humiliated royalists. The terms of surrender that he granted to them are an eternal monument to his generosity.

The news of the victory that brought an end to Spanish domination in Peru was applauded throughout the country, but Lima was where it received the warm welcome that the event deserved, for the presence of the Liberator helped to heighten the demonstrations of joy. But

---

an accurate opinion of Lara's personal version, see Vicente Lecuna, *Crónica razonada de las guerras de Bolívar,* III, 455–456. —Pedro Grases.

Lara states that he was able to save the division, though left alone. According to Lecuna, Sucre had not abandoned the rearguard, but had ordered the Rifles Battalion to climb a hill and open fire on the enemy, a light column rather than a division.—Ed.

had done, so great was his eagerness to do much more. The first money he used from the fund allocated for the benefit of his country was the twenty thousand pesos that he sent to the famous Lancaster, in order to foster the education of the young people of Caracas, and he offered him another larger sum if needed. At a later date he had to pay this money out of his private funds, because the Peruvian agents in London were unable to cover his drafts. Just at this time Don Simón Rodríguez, his former teacher, arrived in Lima. When the Liberator learned that he had returned to Colombia after a long absence, during which he had visited many European countries, he invited him to come to his headquarters, supplying him with funds for the trip. I saw the humble pedagogue dismount at the door of the government palace. Instead of being rudely turned away, as he perhaps feared he would be, he received a warm welcome as a friend, with all the respect due his age and his long friendship. His arrival was really timely, occurring just when the Liberator was preparing to travel through the southern departments of the Republic, where he wanted to establish schools. Now he would place them under the immediate direction of his friend, making them conform to the Lancaster system as improved by Rodríguez. With this in view, he hastened to invite Rodríguez to accompany him on his trip.

The Peruvian Congress was dissolved on March 10. Scarcely had the Liberator received the authority granted him by Congress when he decided to delegate the exercise of the executive power to Señores La Mar, Sánchez Carrión, and Unanue. Because of La Mar's absence and the illness of Sánchez Carrión, it was necessary, much to the Liberator's dislike, to make some changes. Don José María Pando, a native of Lima who had recently returned to Peru after serving Spain in the field of diplomacy, replaced Unanue in the Treasury Department, and the latter took Carrión's place in the Department of Foreign Relations, becoming vice-president of the council. General Heres took over the vacant post in the War Department. Bolívar delegated the president's authority to this council in the northern departments, reserving for himself the approval of any measures taken and the supreme direction of affairs in the departments of Arequipa, Cuzco, and Puno. The in-

Francisco de Paula Otero to brigadier general, he wrote to Sucre that "without the devotion to duty of Colonel Otero, it would perhaps have been impossible to undertake the campaign that has brought liberty to Peru and peace to America."[3]

[3] Before the battle of Junín the Argentine Colonel Otero had thoroughly scouted part of the route to be followed by the patriots. After the battle he had followed Canterac's army and had reported back to headquarters that the royalist army was massing in Lima Tambo. —Ed.

CHAPTER NINETEEN

AFTER THE LIBERATOR HAD SUMMONED the Congress of Peru to meet on February 10, 1825, he issued many useful decrees to promote the welfare of the country. Special mention should be made of the decree establishing an economic society to promote the prosperity of the state and of another decree by which a commission of prominent jurists was appointed to draw up a tentative civil and criminal code of laws. But his most remarkable accomplishment was the establishment in the capital of each department of a normal school based on the Lancaster system.[1] Moved by his great desire to extend education to all

---

[1] According to the system promoted by the famous English educator Joseph Lancaster, brighter or more proficient children, under the direction of an adult teacher, would aid in teaching other children. —Ed.

social classes, he ordered that the children of the poor should receive free instruction at the expense of the government.

These useful labors were interrupted by the discovery of what was thought to be a royalist plot to assassinate the Liberator. Bolívar became convinced of this as a result of the revelations made by the assassin of Colonel Don Bernardo Monteagudo, whose violent death occurred on the night of January 28, 1825. The assassin's confession and the subsequent findings revealed that the crime had been the result of a royalist plan suggested and directed by General Rodil. Nevertheless, General Heres, who was intimately concerned with the affair, was of the opinion, as were many other people, that there was no such conspiracy. Colonel Belford Wilson, the Liberator's aide, who was in Lima at the time, was of the same opinion; he declared that he "became convinced that Monteagudo died at the hands of a thief, who murdered him in order to rob him." I should add that I witnessed the interrogation of the criminal, Candelario Espinosa, at the villa in Magdalena where the Liberator resided. Espinosa stood by the declaration he had made previously, but nothing was proved, either then or later.

General Rodil refused to accept the Ayacucho capitulation. Revealing a tenacity that does him honor, he rejected every proposal made to him. The Callao garrison was declared to be a violator of international law, and a tight blockade of the stronghold was therefore established. This disappointment did not prevent the Liberator from climaxing his administration as dictator with a great act of clemency, revoking the decree of July 9, which had branded as traitors those who, while in government service, had gone over to the royalists or had remained in Lima after the royalists occupied it.

The day marking the anniversary of the dictatorship arrived, and Congress was installed. No glory ever equalled the glory that was Bolívar's on that day. In less than a year he had accomplished wonders, and then, after his triumph, he called together the representatives of the people and returned to them the authority with which they had vested him, without any bloodstains, without a single crime to dishonor it. The nation that he delivered into their hands was no longer a humble slave, victimized by treachery, but a free and independent lady. What dictator has ever done anything comparable?

On the very day of the installation, Congress sent a committee of its own members to inform the Liberator of their fears that previous mistakes might be repeated. In his reply he pointed out how dangerous it was to entrust unlimited authority to one man, and especially to a foreigner. Immediately thereafter the Liberator proceeded, amidst the loud cheers of the townspeople, to the hall where Congress held its sessions. In his message he reviewed what had happened during his year of dictatorship and pointed out that much remained to be done. Then he emphasized the value of a close federation of the new states, which could be achieved in Panama at the assembly to which he had invited all the states in the name of Peru. Now that he was returning the supreme power to the Congress, the nation should not allow anything but the rule of law to remain. He concluded with the remark that, after assisting as an auxiliary soldier in the liberation of Upper Peru and in the capture of Callao, he would hurry back to his country to inform the representatives of his mission in Peru.

The members of Congress showed sincere and profound horror at the very mention of his return to Colombia. The president, in the name of Congress, thanked Bolívar for the liberation of Peru and added that the country would return to its former state of servitude if he abandoned it. He replied that once he had completed his military mission, there would be nothing left for him to do in Peru, because he was a foreigner and the president of Colombia. New arguments were adduced to make him desist from the noble resolve that he seemed so determined to keep. When the Liberator retired from the hall, thousands of voices begged him, as he passed along the streets, not to abandon Peru.

A heated discussion thereupon ensued in Congress, and it was unanimously agreed that Bolívar should remain in order to organize the government and that he should continue to exercise power as a dictator. The final result was that a large delegation from Congress, headed by its president, placed in the Liberator's hands a decree, voted unanimously, which entrusted him with supreme authority until the Congress met in 1826 and empowered him to delegate any powers at his own discretion. Believing any further resistance to be inopportune, the Liberator finally gave his assent, but with the condition that he would keep this authority only if the Republic of Colombia permitted him to do so. Immediately taking advantage of the power conferred upon him, he delegated part of his authority to a council, to which he appointed General La Mar as president and Secretaries Carrión and Unanue as voting members. His decision to remain in Peru was not only approved but applauded by the government and the people of Colombia, and this approbation was his only consolation for the sacrifice he had made.

Moved by a spirit of liberality, Congress then proceeded to show its gratitude for the Liberator's splendid services. In addition to giving him a solemn vote of thanks and declaring him Father and Savior of Peru, it decreed that a medal be struck in his honor, that an equestrian statue be erected on the Plaza de la Constitución, that a tablet expressing gratitude be placed on the main squares of the department capitals, that his portrait be hung in the municipal buildings, and that the sum of one million pesos be placed at his disposal. In his reply to the president of Congress the Liberator stated that he could not possibly accept this splendid gift. Though Congress insisted once more on its offer, there was no way to overcome his determination. This conflict between gratitude and unselfishness was resolved when the president requested the Liberator to devote the million pesos to works that would be of benefit to his native city and to any other section of the Republic of Colombia. The Liberator finally yielded and communicated to the Congress his gratitude and that of his fellow citizens of Caracas for the way in which it had chosen to end its noble contest with him.

The liberality of Congress did not stop there. It gave the name of Bolívar to the capital of the department of Trujillo, and it decreed a vote of thanks to the united liberating army. Then again, the members of the Colombian army were declared native Peruvians, and a million pesos were made available to the Liberator for the purpose of rewarding the army. General Sucre received a fitting reward for the splendid success he had obtained: he was given the title of Grand Marshal of Ayacucho and the sum of 200,000 pesos. Sucre was duly grateful, but what pleased him most of all was a sketch of his life, the work of his illustrious chief. Amidst the cares of public life, Bolívar found time to devote some moments to his friends, and his "Brief Sketch of the Life of Sucre," though written hastily, bears the impress of genius, as do all the writings of its author.

Those were glorious days in the life of the Liberator. From all quarters came glowing tributes to his genius and his great talents, and even his enemies suspended their attacks and calumnies for the time being. The Colombian Congress decided to award the honors of victory to the Liberator as soon as he returned to the country, and a platinum medal was ordered to be struck especially for him. It also issued an order for the immediate payment to him of his back salary of 150,000 pesos, which he had never collected. The executive power delegated to him the authority to grant promotions in the army—authority it had taken from him in more difficult and more pressing circumstances. Caracas, his native city, voted in his honor an equestrian statue, to be placed on the square where the house in which he was born was situated. This house was to bear his name. The Constitutional Congress of the United Provinces of La Plata also honored him by sending a delegation to congratulate him and to thank him for his services to the New World. This unexpected tribute was most pleasing to him, especially in view of the invidious policy of the previous administration and Rivadavia's absurd rivalry.

What brought Bolívar the greatest satisfaction of all was the hope that his great project of confederating the republics of South America would soon come true. Colombia, Mexico, Guatemala, and Chile had replied in a satisfactory manner to his invitation, which led him to believe that these states would promptly agree to meet at the Isthmus of Panama. His fiery imagination made him picture this assembly as the forerunner of the future greatness and happiness of his own country. If he deceived himself, it was because, carried away by his patriotism, he preferred to heed its promptings rather than the cold logic of political life. The ideal benefits expected by Bolívar from the Congress of Panama were to disappear in the face of stark reality. But why anticipate the period that was to bring bitter disappointment to his bright hopes and darken the last days of his life with the shadow of ingratitude?

All the tributes and the praise did not succeed in dazzling Bolívar. He believed that he did not deserve so much admiration for what he how must Bolívar have felt? Comparing the sad situation of the past with the brilliant future he now glimpsed, he must have been stirred by strong emotions. His first act was to manifest his gratitude to the illustrious companions of his labors. The most precious honor for them was the approbation of their leader, and that approbation was made evident to them in proclamations addressed to the soldiers and the Peruvians. He told the soldiers that both Colombia and Peru were indebted to them and that they would be rewarded as they deserved. Addressing the Peruvians, he declared that the valor of the Colombian army had accomplished everything despite the disunity that had existed on all sides. Then he informed them that the day their Congress convened would be the day his most ardent wishes would be fulfilled —not to rule any more.

Acting in accordance with his vow not to rule any more, he issued a call for the convocation of the Peruvian Congress on February 10, 1825, and presented his resignation from the presidency of Colombia in a communication addressed to the president of the Senate. In it he declared that the time had arrived for him to keep the promise he had so often made not to continue in public life once there were no enemies left in America. Furthermore, he said that he was constantly tormented by the idea his enemies had that his devotion to liberty was motivated by personal ambition. The acceptance of his resignation would, he said, be the reward for his services in the two republics. This decision would have saved him great grief had he carried it out, but his friends succeeded in proving to him that his retirement was incompatible with the happiness of these two republics.

Having attended to these affairs, the Liberator busied himself with the matter of giving rewards to the army that had so gloriously ended the campaign, and on this occasion he outdid himself in liberality. No spirit of miserliness or ingratitude deprived a single individual of what he deserved. Bolívar voluntarily gave up the well-deserved title of Liberator of Peru in order to transfer it to the fortunate general who had succeeded in ending the war. With this intention, he suggested to Congress the classical idea of rewarding Sucre with the name of the field that had been the scene of his glory. But it was not to Sucre alone that he acknowledged his indebtedness, for upon promoting Colonel structions given to the council were extremely liberal and reveal the statesman.

On April 3, 1825, the council was solemnly inducted into office, and on the tenth the Liberator, accompanied by his secretary-general and his staff, left for Arequipa by way of the coastal road. The Peruvian coast is an unpleasant and forbidding desert interrupted at intervals by streams that form wide ravines, where the land is generally fertile. Here and there one sees ruins that attest the degree of civilization attained by the native inhabitants under the rule of the Incas. The great paved highway has survived the fall of their empire. All along the way the Liberator was given a most enthusiastic reception. The desolation caused by the war was everywhere visible, but not a single town or hamlet failed to receive benefits from the Liberator. Nothing escaped his penetrating glance, whether it was burdensome taxes, poor sanitary conditions, or destroyed government property.

As he approached Arequipa on May 14, the city officials and a great many citizens came out to welcome him, bringing him a magnificent horse with splendid gold trappings. The most pleasing welcome he received in the city was that of the victors at Ayacucho, the beloved comrades of his sufferings and his glory. Banquets and balls were held in his honor, but in the midst of these festivities he tirelessly pursued his task of organizing the department and introducing pertinent reforms. Thus, in less than a month's stay, he extended his beneficial influence to all branches of the administration and established the foundations of the prosperity and civilization that soon developed.

On June 10 he left for Cuzco, crossing the cordillera in easy stages. Even on the very peaks of the Andes there were triumphal arches erected in honor of his passage. His progress through the southern departments was like the march of a conqueror; but it was really only the visit of a philosopher, who saw with profound regret that the growth of one of the richest parts of the earth had been paralyzed because of the niggardly policy of the Spanish overseers and the natural indolence of the inhabitants. The department of Cuzco, though well populated and rich in natural products, was almost completely isolated from the coastal provinces because of the lack of roads. Bolívar therefore ordered two highways to be opened in the departments of Cuzco and Puno. He himself outlined the route, but this magnificent project was never carried out, because the genius that conceived it was wanting for its execution.

On June 21 the Liberator was welcomed at the boundary of the department of Cuzco by the prefect and the authorities of the capital. Nothing can be compared to the magnificence that the ancient capital of the Incas displayed when he entered it on June 25. On seeing the triumphal arches and the fronts of the houses adorned with rich tapestries and gold and silver ornaments, one would have thought that the city had suffered very little during the course of the revolution. As in Arequipa, the municipal authorities gave the Liberator a horse with gold trappings, and the keys of the city presented to him were of the same metal. At the municipal building the most prominent women were waiting for him with a civic crown of gold covered with diamonds and pearls. Although he could not refuse to accept these costly gifts, I am certain that he did not keep any of them for himself. He distributed them among his staff officers and some of the army commanders, and even among the soldiers, giving preference to those who had won the most distinction in the campaign. I had the honor of receiving the keys of the city as a gift from him.

The Indians themselves, despite their abject state of degradation, shared in the general enthusiasm, welcoming their regenerator to the capital city of the ancient empire with all the pomp and courtesy with which their ancestors received the emperors. Even though they had been raised as serfs, they knew the value of liberty and realized that it was he who had freed them from the unjust tribute of serf labor and compulsory service that the *repartimientos* and the *mita* entailed.[2] The spirit of Las Casas seemed to live again in Bolívar, judging from the laudable zeal he displayed in promoting the regeneration of the In-

[2] In early colonial days the *repartimiento* was the assignment of Indians to the care of the conquistadors and their descendants. At the time of the revolution it was the periodic distribution of goods to the Indians, who were often forced to pay whatever the crown official demanded. The *mita* was a system of forced labor requiring the Indians to work in the mines, on public construction, or for individuals who hired them from the crown. —Ed.

dians. He not only freed them from all kinds of oppression and from poverty, but he also procured for them every possible convenience and individual parcels of land, enabling them to lead a productive life. He even flattered their pride with exquisite kindness by ordering the preservation of the ruins of their monuments that had withstood the ravages of time and Spanish avarice. The city of Cuzco can truly be called the Rome of America. Its history, its legends, and its ruins are fascinating.

Great as were the benefits received by the other departments on the occasion of the Liberator's visit, the department of Cuzco was the recipient of much greater ones. He founded Cuzco Academy and an academy for girls, endowing them with sufficient revenue. He established an asylum for orphans and foundlings and a home for old people and the poor. With the approval of the ecclesiastical authorities, he reduced the number of convents and devoted their buildings and revenue to purposes that rendered a service to the public. He ordered the construction of a vast cemetery and of an aqueduct to supply the city with water, which had been very scarce up to that time. Most of his time was spent on administrative reforms, and all his measures were essentially just, economical, and beneficial to the state. His departure on July 26 caused general regret.

From Cuzco he went on to the capital of the department of Puno, where he arrived on August 6 after receiving along the way tributes of patriotic enthusiasm equal to those previously given to him. Puno, in its turn, promptly received benefits similar to those he had lavished on Arequipa and Cuzco. The Liberator left the capital of Puno to visit the principal towns and Lake Titicaca and its island, which is famous as the birthplace of Manco Cápac, the founder of the empire of the Incas. Titicaca was the Mecca of the ancient Peruvians, and their descendants still regard it with a certain degree of religious veneration. Bolívar, in a pensive mood, was deeply moved when he beheld the ruins that avarice had caused in Peru. There are few places that do not show vestiges of the power of the Incas alongside the barbarism of the Spanish invaders.

The Liberator had already completed the task he had set for himself upon leaving Lima, that of visiting the southern departments of the Republic and providing them with the provisional organization they needed, in conformity with the most liberal principles. An illustrious Peruvian, Javier Luna Pizarro, who had just returned from exile, which he had voluntarily imposed upon himself out of a rigid sense of patriotism, declared in a letter to the Liberator that his soul was filled with the purest joy when he saw in his own country the measures adopted to establish order. He described Bolívar as Washington's worthy rival, who would undoubtedly occupy the first page in the annals of South America. For his own glory the Liberator had still another duty to fulfill: to constitute a new state, the creation of his heroic deeds, which, expressing its gratitude in a splendid manner, had taken his name. It is, however, time for us to turn our attention now to the liberating army, which we left on the field of its glory.

The war in South America should have ended with the victory at Ayacucho, but the persistence of the Spaniards made it necessary that the epilogue, as well as the prologue, of their domination in Peru be written in blood. Once the capitulation was arranged, Sucre lost no time in occupying the towns and provinces south of Huamanga. After La Serna had been taken prisoner, Don Pío Tristán assumed the title of viceroy in Arequipa, but this incident was of such short duration that it scarcely deserves mention. A more dangerous enemy was to be found in General Olañeta, head of the absolutist party in the provinces of Upper Peru. Since it seemed only natural to Sucre to think that consideration for his own interests would lead Olañeta to accept the honorable conditions offered him, he sent Antonio Elizalde to confer with him.[3] At the same time he asked the Liberator for instructions, inasmuch as he did not wish, for diplomatic reasons, to precipitate the invasion of Upper Peru.

The provinces of Upper Peru had formed part of the political jurisdiction of Buenos Aires prior to the revolution, and since the uti possidetis was recognized as the basis for the territorial division of the new states, Sucre did not believe he had any authority to violate this arrangement. The Liberator ordered him to invite the Spanish general to declare himself in favor of American independence or to allow the

[3] Elizalde was a Granadine colonel serving as adjutant general in Sucre's army. —Ed.

people to decide their future fate. In case of a refusal, however, Sucre was to occupy the country by force. Olañeta's ambiguous behavior and his hostile attitude removed all doubt from Sucre's mind, and he therefore undertook the campaign.

Olañeta, abandoned by the people and his troops, withdrew before the approaching patriot forces, which occupied the entire country as far as Potosí, where they made their entrance on March 29, 1825, without firing a shot. Colonel Medinaceli, who was in command of a unit of Olañeta's army in Chichas, declared himself in favor of independence. On April 1, in Tumusla, he met his former commander, and in the battle that ensued Olañeta sealed with his blood the sincerity of his convictions and his honest allegiance to a hopeless cause. Colonel José Valdés, nicknamed Barbarucho, surrendered on April 9 with the small column under his command, and with him the last enemies in Upper Peru disappeared. From Ayacucho to Potosí over eighteen thousand men of the Spanish army had been defeated, scattered, taken prisoner, or incorporated into the liberating army.

Upper Peru, an area of about 105,000 square leagues with one million inhabitants, includes the provinces of La Paz, Potosí, Chuquisaca, Cochabamba, and Santa Cruz. On July 16, 1809, La Paz had the honor to be the first among all the peoples of South America to raise the glorious standard of revolt, but the efforts of the patriots were too weak to uphold their independence. The unsuccessful attempt served only to tighten the bonds of Upper Peru. Help sent from the provinces of La Plata was of no avail, for the army from Buenos Aires was destroyed. The enthusiastic reception given the troops of General Santa Cruz when they occupied La Paz and Oruro in 1823 was unmistakable proof of the fervent love for liberty that ever burned in the hearts of the inhabitants.

The position of General Sucre after he crossed the Desaguadero River was all the more delicate because the political situation of the country involved serious complications. Several of the provinces had declared themselves independent, but there was no uniformity of opinion among them or among the inhabitants. Mindful of the necessity of avoiding all the horrors of anarchy, Sucre decided to convoke an assembly of representatives from the provinces, who would be chosen by the municipalities, to deliberate about the future state of the provinces. He did, in fact, issue a decree to this effect on February 9, 1825, appointing the day of April 19 for the meeting of the assembly in Oruro and declaring the country to be subject, meanwhile, to the supreme authority of the liberating army. The incidents of the campaign, however, made it impossible to hold the elections, which finally had to be canceled.

After General Sucre had notified the Liberator of his action, he learned that the Congress of the United Provinces of La Plata had been installed in Buenos Aires on December 16 of the previous year. Without losing any time, he sent the same information to that government, inviting it to enter into negotiations with the Liberator. The action taken by Sucre, which was liberal and moderate, did not, however, satisfy the Liberator, as he made clear when he disapproved the decree of February 9. He judged it to be untimely and detrimental to the rights of Río de la Plata: untimely because the country was at war, and detrimental to Río de la Plata because of the recognition given to the sovereignty of certain provinces to which it had an incontestable right. As he stated in his private correspondence with Sucre, the only mission of the latter was to occupy the country in a military sense and not to take any unnecessary action.

The agreement of the government of Buenos Aires, which was then the instrument of the General Congress of that republic, to the step taken by Sucre, and the mission of the delegate, General Juan Antonio Alvarez de Arenales, to express the assent of Río de la Plata to having the provinces determine their own fate, resulted in the suspension of the Liberator's prudent plan to reconcile the various parties and led him to confirm the decree of February 9, with the reservation, however, that any decisions he should make at the time would be subject to approval by the Congress of Peru. This solution was approved by the interested parties, who manifested to the Liberator their desire that he should visit the territory of Upper Peru. But he did not accept their invitation, for fear that his intentions might be misinterpreted and his presence might be an obstacle to complete freedom of public debate. Moreover, he issued orders for the troops to withdraw from the meeting place of the assembly.

Despite the fact that the Liberator postponed his trip to Upper Peru, he did not neglect the welfare of those provinces. He instructed General Sucre to relieve the people of the burden of contributions and taxes to the extent permitted by the army's needs. Sucre therefore abolished many of them and cut in half war excise taxes established by the Spaniards. In pursuance of these instructions he also introduced economic reforms in all branches of the administration and rooted out a great number of abuses found in all of them.

The assembly of the representatives of Upper Peru was installed in Chuquisaca on July 10, and its first act was to implore the protection of the Liberator. These illustrious citizens did not rush headlong into imprudent debates; they calmly discussed the interests of the provinces with the necessary circumspection. It was not until August 6 that the independence of Upper Peru was formally proclaimed. This very solemn declaration marked the completion of the first great act indicative of the majesty of a people about to assume the position of a free and sovereign nation.

In order to reward Bolívar with all the glory due him for his services as the first champion of the liberty of South America, they gave his name to the first people in that region to raise the banner of independence. Proclaiming him Father of the Country, they vested him with supreme executive authority for the period of his residence in the state, and during his absence he would enjoy the honors of protector and president. Orders were given for his portrait to be placed in all the public buildings, and an equestrian statue was to be erected in the capital of every department. He was assigned a million pesos to be used to reward the army. Anxious to receive the fruit of his experience, the representatives to Congress requested him to draw up a basic code of laws that would assure them of the blessings of liberty to which they aspired.

The Liberator was on the way from Cuzco to Puno when he received the sealed documents notifying him of the resolutions and decrees of the Chuquisaca assembly and of the honors granted him. He decided not to defer his visit to the new state any longer. He departed from Puno to go to Copacabana on September 15, met General Sucre in Zepita on the following day, and, after crossing the Desaguadero, entered La Paz on the eighteenth. The welcome given him here was no less enthusiastic and magnificent than the one he had received in Cuzco. A richly caparisoned battle charger and solid gold keys to the city were given to him by the municipal government. One of the prominent women presented him with a civic crown of gold studded with diamonds. "This reward belongs to the victor," said the Liberator, handing it to Sucre, "and that is why I am turning it over to the hero of Ayacucho." He was deeply moved by the overwhelming manifestations of devotion and confidence that he received from the people.

The Chuquisaca assembly requested the immediate recognition of the independence of Bolivia by the Liberator himself, in the name of Peru, but he had no choice but to oppose this measure, since his authority was limited by the decree of the Peruvian Congress to the establishment of a provisional government. He did, however, assure the assembly that he would use his influence and his good offices to obtain the independence to which the provinces so rightfully aspired. But the independence of the country had been virtually recognized from the moment when the adjoining states, to which these provinces had been subject in times past, sanctioned the installation of the assembly for the purpose of deliberating upon their fate.

Since the representatives were anxious to take advantage of the Liberator's stay among them to further their goals, they requested him to devote part of his time to drawing up the constitution for their government. He acceded to this request, although he modestly expressed doubt concerning the adequacy of his qualifications. At his instance the assembly appointed a permanent commission of five representatives to help him in obtaining the information needed for the organization of the various branches of the administration. The assembly closed its sessions after putting off its next meeting to May 25 of the following year and after sending commissioners to Río de la Plata, Peru, and Colombia to seek recognition of the country's independence.

Wishing to acquaint himself with the local needs of each section, the Liberator convened, through the authorities of La Paz, a council composed of one hundred of the most able citizens from all the professions. They were to draw up a report listing all the complaints and common evils and suggest to him the most effective way to eliminate them. After several sessions the Liberator dissolved the council because it showed signs of a regrettable spirit of antiliberalism and vengeance. Despite this opposition to his plans for regeneration, he did not fail to attend to the needs of the departments, and he was successful in his efforts to root out the abuses and ingrained evils. In order to eliminate smuggling, he organized military patrols on the coast of Arequipa. Approval by a diocesan synod of the schedule of fees presented by him relieved the people of La Paz from ecclesiastical oppression. By his order a thorough investigation was made of irregularities in the fiscal administration, and the penalties sanctioned by law were applied to those found guilty.

On September 20 the Liberator left La Paz to continue his visit to the southern provinces and to receive in Potosí the delegation that the government of Río de la Plata had sent to congratulate him and to initiate other negotiations. After three days of rest in Oruro he proceeded to Potosí, which he entered on October 5 to the accompaniment of loud cheers from the people. General Miller, who was serving as prefect of the department, received the illustrious visitor with a wonderful display of fine hospitality. The municipal government decided to honor him by changing the name of the city to Bolívar, but he refused to sanction the resolution because he had no authority to do so. Moreover, he suggested the impropriety of depriving the city of its original name, which was universally famous as a symbol of immense wealth and fabulous riches.

Shortly after his arrival the Liberator, accompanied by General Sucre, the prefect of the department, the plenipotentiaries from Río de la Plata, and his staff, visited the lofty mountain for which the city is named. The ascent is almost perpendicular, and mules can be ridden only two-thirds of the way up. The rest of the way must be traveled on foot, and the going is anything but easy because of the rugged terrain and the difficulty of breathing. Upon reaching the top, one sees a barren, desolate paramo devoid of all vegetation. On that famous peak the Liberator unfurled the flags of Colombia, Peru, and La Plata. As he looked northward, his thoughts went back to the glorious life he had led, the hardships he had endured, the great work he had completed—fifteen years of trials, of necessary decisions, of defeats, and of victories, alternating between disappointment and success. That notable day on which he climbed the celebrated peak of the gigantic Andes, whose grandeur was rivaled by his own when he reached the pinnacle of fame, must certainly have been the happiest day in Bolívar's life.

Even though he had achieved the military goal he had in view, his political desires were still not fully satisfied. He aspired, with all the ardor of his fiery nature, to gather the republics that he had emancipated into a great confederation bound by the closest ties and to give these creations of his triumphs the appearance, as he expressed it, "not of nations but of sisters indissolubly united." America's prosperity was, in his opinion, completely dependent upon the realization of that plan, and those of us who heard him talk that day about the advantages of confederation could hardly fail to agree with his plan, so solid were his arguments and so brilliant the eloquence with which he stated them. Ah! He did not realize then that ingratitude would create obstacles that would spell the failure of his patriotic proposals, nor did he foresee the host of enemies that envy and evil passions were organizing against him.

The Liberator found the public treasury of the new state in the greatest disorder. The people were burdened with heavy taxes, and the revenue was insufficient to cover expenses. One of his concerns was to organize this important branch of the administration. The Congress of Upper Peru had authorized the government to contract a loan for the purpose of rewarding the services of the army, but he refused to approve the decree, declaring that a loan of this kind was contrary to his policy. He did his best to establish a balance between expenses and ordinary revenue, and he succeeded in doing so through the strictest economy.

CHAPTER TWENTY

W HEN THE LIBERATING ARMY occupied the provinces of Upper
Peru, the Constituent Congress of the United Provinces of La
Plata had just been installed. Unlike the government of Buenos Aires,
the majority of that assembly admired Bolívar's exploits and respected
his ability. Motivated by these sentiments, the Congress ordered the
executive to send a duly accredited commission to congratulate him
for his distinguished services and to let him know how grateful the
provinces of the Union were for all that the liberating army had done
to maintain order in Upper Peru, thus making it possible for that country to organize a government. The exercise of the executive power of
the confederation and the government of the province of Buenos
Aires had just been temporarily entrusted to General Las Heras, who

immediately communicated to the Liberator the appointment of General Don Carlos Alvear and Dr. Don José Miguel Díaz Vélez, two of the most distinguished citizens of the Republic, as plenipotentiaries.

It so happened that at that time the government of Buenos Aires was involved in discussions with Brazil that would eventually result in a war between the Empire and the Republic over the territory of the Banda Oriental and Montevideo. A decision was reached to propose to the Liberator the formation of an offensive and defensive alliance between Río de la Plata, Peru, and Chile in order to demand from the Emperor, in the name of the allies, the restoration of the Banda Oriental. An occurrence in the province of Chiquitos gave the government of Buenos Aires reason for hoping that the Liberator would have no objection to giving his assent to the plan.

When the provinces of Charcas and Cochabamba rose in rebellion as a result of the march of the united army, thus causing a disruption of communications between General Olañeta and the eastern provinces of Upper Peru, Colonel Don Sebastián Ramos, governor of Chiquitos, sought the protection of the imperial authorities of Mato Grosso, a border district of Brazil. On March 28, 1825, he signed a treaty with them, according to which he recognized the Emperor's authority and ceded the territory under his jurisdiction to the Empire. Immediately afterward a detachment of imperial troops invaded the illegally ceded province without previous warning. Senhor Araujo e Silva, the officer in charge, demanded that Don José Videla, independent governor of the department of Santa Cruz de la Sierra, evacuate the province without delay. He also had the imprudence to threaten the general in chief of the united army, admonishing him in an insolent manner to refrain from any act of hostility designed to recover the province of Chiquitos.

Such extraordinary and unjustifiable conduct could not help but cause concern and spread alarm among the republicans. Loud and indignant protests were voiced in the Colombian army, and Sucre, who was so temperate and prudent in all his acts, shared the feelings of his subordinates. On May 11 he angrily answered Araujo e Silva, reminding him that the province of Chiquitos was already under the protection of the liberating army and threatening not only to drive him out but also to invade Brazilian territory if he did not immediately evacuate the province. He immediately dispatched a small body of veteran troops under the command of Colonel López to the aid of the invaded province, with orders to repel the aggression. Upon informing the Liberator of the measures he had adopted, Sucre asked him for advice concerning the necessity of invading Brazil. But Bolívar, who was more diplomatic than his lieutenant, considered the matter from the point of view of the statesman and replied through his secretary-general that there must be no invasion of Brazilian territory and that only regular troops led by experienced officers should be used to retake the occupied territory, in order to show the world that the patriots of America recognize "no course other than that of justice and honor."

Although the Liberator disapproved Sucre's zeal and issued prudent instructions, he gave the matter all the importance it deserved. In view of the doubt as to whether the invasion was a spontaneous act or whether it had resulted from direct orders issued by the court in Rio de Janeiro, he decided to prepare for every eventuality. He informed the governments of Mexico, Colombia, and Chile of the event, calling attention to the urgent need to contain the growing ambition of the Emperor and pointing out once more the necessity of assembling a federal congress in Panama, which he believed would be the best judge to decide such matters.

Meanwhile, Sucre's hostile attitude and the strong language in which he addressed the Brazilian commander alarmed the authorities of Mato Grosso, making them realize how unjustly they had acted. Terrified at the thought of the difficult situation in which their rash conduct would place their government, they canceled the pact by which Chiquitos had been annexed to the territory of Brazil and offered satisfaction for the illegal acts that had been committed. Araujo was immediately deposed, but this officer gave new grounds for complaint by plundering the towns through which he effected his withdrawal. Later on, the court of Rio de Janeiro fully satisfied the government of Bolivia by repudiating the conduct of its agents and removing them from the positions of trust they occupied.

The delegation chosen by the Congress of the United Provinces of La Plata to negotiate with the Liberator arrived in Potosí on October

7, 1825. It was not until the twenty-fifth of the same month that the decree was issued in which the Congress solemnly declared that the provinces of the Banda Oriental were being incorporated into the territory of the Republic. This decision had been delayed until it was determined that the British government did not approve the annexation of Montevideo to Brazil, which the Emperor so eagerly desired. When, on October 8, General Alvear and Dr. Díaz Vélez notified the Liberator's secretary-general of their arrival, they were told that the Liberator would give them an audience on the sixteenth, but that he could not deal with them officially, since the minister of foreign affairs resided in Lima, the seat of the government. Greatly upset by this reply, the plenipotentiaries requested a private conference, which the Liberator immediately granted to them.

They were received with the courtesy that the Liberator could display whenever he wished to please, especially when Colombia's interests were concerned. When General Alvear expressed his great regret over the Liberator's decision not to enter into negotiations, the latter replied that he was eager to contribute to the favorable outcome of the present mission, but that by virtue of the decree of February 24 he had delegated to the Council of Government in Lima all the authority with which Congress had vested him. After emphasizing the vital importance of their mission and pointing out their well-founded fears that such a refusal might be misinterpreted by the enemies of the Confederation, the plenipotentiaries reiterated their request that he change his mind or suggest some remedy to them. The Liberator assured them again that the decision he had communicated to them was irrevocable, but that he might receive them as plenipotentiaries and hear their proposals, form his opinions on the proposals, and submit them to the governments of Peru and Colombia.

The plenipotentiaries willingly accepted the proposal and pledged their government to the observance of the strictest secrecy concerning the matter. Then they informed the Liberator that, though the only object of their mission when they left Buenos Aires was to congratulate him for his recent victories, they had received on the way formal instructions to discuss with him the subject of war with Brazil and to seek the protection of the great Bolívar for their country, since he was regarded as the person most capable of bringing the war to a successful conclusion. They spoke at length of Dom Pedro's ambition and of the danger of allowing an empire to exist in America, and they suggested to the Liberator that his return to Colombia by way of Rio de Janeiro, after having assured forever the independence of America, would be a fitting climax to his glorious career. These considerations impressed the Liberator, for whom the very word glory had an irresistible appeal, and he would not have been able to keep from acceding to the wishes of the plenipotentiaries had it not been for the great respect he sincerely professed for the institutions of Colombia and for his obligations toward Peru. He did, however, approve the decision to retain possession of the Banda Oriental by armed force, and he assured them that he was ready to help them if Peru and Colombia allowed him to do so.

The Liberator did not hide the fact that great obstacles were bound to arise. He pointed out, however, that one way he could overcome them was to create a diversion for the benefit of the Republic by invading the province of Paraguay through Bermejo in order to compel Dr. José Gaspar Rodríguez de Francia[1] to allow the inhabitants to decide their own fate or, failing this, to incorporate them by force into the Confederation of La Plata, to whose jurisdiction that territory belonged. Alvear and Díaz Vélez not only approved but applauded the idea, and they added that they would lose no time in bringing the matter to their government's attention. The truth is that the plenipotentiaries had received definite instructions to avoid this proposal. This was not the only point on which the Argentine government acted with duplicity in these negotiations, for it had already requested the mediation of Great Britain. But thanks to his admirable prudence and circumspection, Bolívar escaped the trap that was being set for him, despite the cunning methods used to catch him off guard.

On October 16 the plenipotentiaries were received in a public audience. On such occasions the Liberator did not forget the dignity of the high post he occupied, nor did he dispense with the ceremonies that he usually omitted on ordinary occasions. When he received the delegation, he was surrounded by his staff, the generals of the army who were

---

[1] Dictator of Paraguay.—Ed.

in Potosí, and the civil authorities of the department and the city. After presenting his credentials and those of his colleague, General Alvear officially congratulated the Liberator in the name of the Argentine nation for his outstanding service to the cause of the New World and urged him to assume the leadership in the efforts to compel Brazil to desist from its attempt to take over the province of the Banda Oriental. In his reply the Liberator declared that it was truly surprising that an American prince, who seemed destined to be friendly, should occupy a province not belonging to him and allow his troops to invade Chiquitos. He added that these flagrant violators of the rights of nations had gone unpunished, but that the people of America should be grateful for events that strengthened the ties that bound them so that they might reclaim their rights simultaneously.

The delegation from La Plata repeated officially what they had said in the private conference of the tenth. They also suggested the desirability of adopting resolutions to ask the Emperor to make reparation for the invasion of Moxos and Chiquitos and to leave Montevideo free to decide its future fate, to invite Brazil to make a definitive treaty with the republics of Colombia, Peru, and La Plata, and to have these republics make a secret treaty obligating themselves to cooperate in a war against Brazil in case of a refusal. The Liberator, in his reply, declared that he was convinced of the justice of the claims made by the Argentine Republic against Brazil, and he expressed regret that his obligations prevented him from taking an active part in the recovery of the rights of a government that he respected. He added that he was definitely convinced that nothing would be more conducive to the security and prosperity of America than for all the republics to unite in order to assert and to defend their respective rights.

The Liberator was more than a little pleased when he saw that the arguments he had vainly used to induce the new American states to enter into a common league for mutual defense were now being repeated. Furthermore, he experienced a real sense of triumph when he recalled that the representatives of the government that had most bitterly opposed these arguments were forced to cite them now; he did not stop to consider that his patriotic proposals had been disregarded by an Argentine minister who, with more vanity than foresight, pretended to believe, or perhaps did believe, that Colombia needed La Plata more than the latter republic did the former.

On November 1 the Liberator left Potosí for Chiquisaca, where he arrived on the third. In the capital of Bolivia he was given the same kind of patriotic welcome that he had received from the inhabitants of the entire region through which he had traveled, from Lima to Pilcomayo, in a trip of nearly seven hundred leagues. The Argentine plenipotentiaries followed him there and with the most fervent zeal continued their efforts to oblige him to take part in the pending struggle with Brazil and through his influence to bring Colombia and Peru into the alliance. When they realized that it was useless to continue to insist on seeking his assistance for the political aims of Buenos Aires, they proposed to him that a treaty of alliance for offensive and defensive action against Brazil be made between La Plata and Bolivia. The Liberator promised to submit this proposal to the Bolivian Congress, and he accompanied this promise with words of great encouragement.

Apart from the question of his respect for the institutions of Colombia, the Liberator was not in a position to embrace the cause of La Plata, because of the uncertainty concerning the attitude of the English government toward the struggle with the Emperor; for the South American states regarded Great Britain with the same terror with which imperial Rome was regarded by her allies. This deference served at the time as a shield for the throne of Dom Pedro, because there would not have been the slightest doubt about the outcome of the struggle if Bolívar had directed it, helping Buenos Aires with the auxiliary forces at his command. He once more declared to the plenipotentiaries that all he could do in the existing circumstances was to assume the obligation, of subduing the unruly province of Paraguay and returning it to the Confederation. He would also send his first aide-de-camp, Colonel O'Leary, to Rio de Janeiro to request an explanation for the territorial violation resulting from the invasion of Chiquitos. Finally, this officer would receive instructions to suggest privately to the ministers of His Imperial Majesty that the restoration of the Banda Oriental would assure the peace of the continent and the good will of the republics toward the Emperor. The last part of this proposal was immediately accepted, but the plenipotentiaries were very careful to avoid the offer concerning Paraguay.

Since the plenipotentiaries were now convinced that it was not as easy as they had imagined to make Bolívar change his mind or to win his assent to the plans of the government of La Plata, General Alvear decided that they should return to Buenos Aires. But he was still eager to involve Bolívar in the matter. Knowing that the latter was less circumspect in his private conversations than in his official correspondence, he therefore sought, by means of a confidential note bearing only his own signature, Bolívar's opinion in writing on important points they had discussed. The Liberator saw no objection to answering the questions asked, but when he did so, he made it clear that he was expressing his opinions as an individual performing an act of courtesy that involved no public responsibility and no obligation for the national interests. The prudent and carefully chosen words in which his reply was expressed did not fail to vex General Alvear and to dash every hope that he had formerly harbored of obtaining his consent to having Bolivia, at least, take part in the war against Brazil.

With regard to the other objectives of his mission, Alvear met with a more prompt response from the Liberator, who, basing his policy on justice and moderation, consented to everything that was not contrary to these principles. The province of Tarija, which was a considerable part of the state of Salta, had withdrawn from the Confederation and joined the new republic. Now that the Argentine envoys were claiming it, he ordered it to be restored to its former allegiance. He also made the same concessions to the commerce of the Confederation that he had made to that of Peru.

The government of La Plata did not return this very generous treatment. It acted deceitfully in making its promises to Bolívar, for the section of the press most immediately under its control never stopped its attacks on his reputation, including the insistent charge that his plans and his aims sprang from a desire for power. After Rivadavia's return to Buenos Aires these public manifestations of spite became much more pronounced. The Liberator could have taken revenge on his gratuitous enemies in that country by offering his protection to the other provinces of the Confederation, many of which detested the influence that Buenos Aires exercised among them. They would have dissolved the Union and joined Bolivia, which, since it comprised the greater part of the territory of the former viceroyalty, had some justification for recognizing their claims. But the Liberator scorned to resort to such means, since he knew very well that the party then dominant in the capital could not do any harm to his reputation. He was also convinced that the great majority of the people of that state esteemed his ability and services.

General Alvear said good-bye to Bolívar in a public audience on January 2, 1826. The Liberator, replying to his speech, said to him, among other things: "General, you can assure the Argentine government of my sincere affection for a sister republic that should always be one of the most interesting parts of American society. I am pleased to believe that its differences with Brazil will be successfully resolved, for justice must triumph in the end." The plenipotentiary left shortly afterward for Buenos Aires, where the minority political party, which opposed the government's ideas concerning Bolívar, accused him of having served as a blind party tool in order to worm his way into Bolívar's confidence, discover his secrets, and then betray him.

Later on the Liberator had very good reason for being highly satisfied with the prudent conduct that he had observed in the matter of the dissension between La Plata and Brazil. The imperial government disapproved the actions of its agents, and he merited the plaudits of the governments of Peru and Colombia. Furthermore, he received the highly esteemed commendation of the great man who then headed the British Cabinet. In a letter to him Mr. George Canning spoke of his satisfaction over being the one to announce the recognition by his sovereign of the independence of Colombia; then he went on to say that the forbearance shown by the Liberator in the Chiquitos affair had given eminent proof of his peaceful sentiments. He expressed the hope that the Liberator would cooperate in recommending the termination of hostilities between Brazil and Buenos Aires and would continue to abstain from intervention in this struggle. In order not to interrupt the narration of matters related to this important mission, I have purposely carried it to the end of the year, putting aside other events to which I shall now return.

There were many important matters requiring the Liberator's attention in Chuquisaca, since he found all the branches of the administration in the greatest disorder. Though respecting the old Spanish laws and the time-honored practices, he believed it necessary to revoke some of them and to revise others. He ordered the more liberal system of judicial proceedings adopted by the Spanish Cortes of 1812 to be observed in the courts until a more suitable civil and criminal code could be promulgated.[2] He also established judgeships and courts of justice in the departments needing them and greatly improved this shamefully neglected branch of the administration.

Giving special attention to public funds, he established the most rigid economies and succeeded in establishing a balance between expenditures and revenue. At the same time he abolished the extraordinary taxes recently imposed by the royalists. Proposing to do justice to the Indians, he abolished the ancient tribute and granted them full rights as citizens. The Indians of Upper Peru are the most abject of all the members of this unhappy race, completely broken in spirit as a result of enforced labor and innumerable types of extortion. The Liberator also replaced the objectionable taxes of the past with a small poll tax of three pesos a year or with an income tax. Though intended as only temporary measures, they produced satisfactory results in practice.

Eager to promote public education as much as possible, the Liberator issued a decree for the establishment of an academy in each department and of primary schools in the capitals of the provinces, and he founded a military school in Chuquisaca. In addition, he extended his protection to needy children whom crime or misfortune had deprived of their parents. Don Simón Rodríguez was appointed director of public education and supervisor of the charitable institutions. Since

---

[2] The Constitution of 1812 provided for quicker trials and simpler appeal procedures. Defendants were no longer required to make any statement under oath pertaining to their guilt or innocence. Arbitration proceedings were established, and town mayors were allowed to serve as mediators in legal disputes. —Ed.

the seminaries of Chuquisaca, La Paz, and Santa Cruz had scanty resources, the Liberator endowed them with sufficient income and established seven professorships to take care of modern advances in the field of learning. Finally, he recommended the prompt execution of these measures to General Sucre, who, despite the cares of government and the demands of public service, worked very hard to repay the confidence placed in him.

Although the Liberator was not able to give all the public needs the attention they required, he did not neglect to provide regulations to stimulate agriculture, to which little attention was naturally paid in a country whose mines constituted most of the wealth. To this end he ordered a detailed survey to be made by competent men of the rural estates then under cultivation. In the very fertile department of Santa Cruz he ordered an equitable distribution of land among those willing to cultivate it. In districts lacking water and woodlands he gave privileges and inducements to those who would settle there. He also did his best to advance the mining industry, abolishing all special taxes and establishing schools of mining in Potosí and La Paz.

The Liberator was equally solicitous about the construction of roads and the improvement of the existing ones, which, as in almost all of South America, were little more than footpaths over impassable mountains. Commerce was in dire need of this improvement, as well as of the protection he actually granted it by reducing the duties on imports and eliminating the widespread smuggling. In Chuquisaca he established an "Economic Society" to promote national prosperity by furthering the plans that he had proposed. The decrees that he had issued in matters involving public utility were submitted to a permanent commission set up at his suggestion by the assembly of Upper Peru. He ordered the opening of a port in the province of Atacama and called it La Mar, in honor of the general of the same name.

Since the revolution had left vacant many of the government offices and posts, the Liberator had to make new appointments. In his assignments he always gave preference to merit and civic virtue, and he conferred lucrative posts and positions of trust only on persons who possessed those qualities. There were frequent cases in which he promoted to high places individuals whose opinions did not coincide with his own but whose talents and reputation for honesty gave them preeminence over other aspirants.

From Lima, just about this time, came Colonel Salazar, who had been sent by the Council of Government to present to the Liberator and General Sucre the magnificent gold swords and the handsomely embroidered uniforms that the municipality of that city was offering to them as a sign of its affection and gratitude—a costly gift, which that body called a "small token." In his reply to the municipality the Liberator said that the beautiful sword would be the most satisfying reward for his devotion to the defense of Peru and that the grand marshal had received from his hands, on the anniversary of the battle of Ayacucho, the sword they had sent him, for which he was most grateful.

Despite the many pressing affairs, the Liberator had time to draw up the fundamental law, which the Chuquisaca Assembly had requested him to do because of his knowledge and experience. Much has been said and written about the Bolivian Constitution. I do not consider myself competent to pass judgment on the merits or the defects of this document, but it is my duty to testify to the sincerity of the motives that led its illustrious author to suggest innovations in the political system that was so popular in America.

Profoundly versed in the history of the human race and well instructed in the theories of political science, the Liberator had acquired a well-rounded knowledge of the world such as few individuals have had more or better opportunities to acquire. Moreover, there have probably been few men with keener insight or a more delicate sense of tact. The peculiar circumstances of his tragic life and the extraordinary events of his public career had brought him into contact with all classes of society and enabled him to gain firsthand knowledge of man in all his aspects and conditions, and those whom he knew best were his fellow citizens of South America. He was familiar with every place and its products, and even with its individuals and their habits, from the northernmost boundary of Colombia to Potosí. In his constant travels he strove with insatiable curiosity to acquaint himself with even apparently insignificant matters, inquiring about everything from the inhabitants whose profession or position best qualified them to furnish him with satisfactory information.

The political outlook for Spanish America did not appear very promising to the eyes of an observer as keen as Bolívar, who had played the leading role in the drama and knew its deepest secrets. The various sections of the continent had absolutely severed all ties with the mother country. The provinces of Buenos Aires, the only section to achieve this status with little bloodshed, offered the best norm for judging other countries, for all that they had to do was organize themselves. But the promoters of their revolution sought, with their blind zeal, to set up a political system that would assure them of what they called their natural rights. The result was an obvious clash between the opposing ideas, followed by popular uprisings, military insurrections, and continual alarms, battles, and sacrifices. The consequences have been the same in all the other sections of America where the establishment of such a system as been tried.

Bolívar gazed with awe upon the terrifying scene confronting him, and he made plans to turn the lesson thus learned to good use. He had too much greatness of soul to sacrifice on the altar of popularity the convictions he held. That is why he did not hesitate in deciding upon his course of action—to look for a system capable of controlling revolutions, rather than for theories that might foment them. The unfortunate spirit of ill-conceived democracy, which had already produced so many evils in America, had to be curbed if its effects were to be prevented. In view of all these considerations he composed the draft of the Bolivian Constitution, some of whose principal features I shall endeavor to outline.

The government was a popular representative government, with four principal divisions of power: electoral, legislative, executive, and judicial. The first one, an innovation in the field of legislation, provided definite protection for civil liberty. Every ten citizens appointed one elector, resulting in an electoral branch composed of one-tenth of the total number of citizens. The electors named the members of the legislative chambers and proposed the candidates for offices in the departments, provinces, and cantons. The exercise of the legislative power resided in three chambers: the Chamber of Tribunes, the Chamber of Senators, and the Chamber of Censors. The latter body, whose members held office for life, served as an arbiter in case of disagreement between the other two, and it also exercised a certain amount of moral power, seeing to the observance of the constitution and protecting the freedom of the press. The exercise of the executive power resided in a president elected for life, whose authority was much like that of the president of the United States of America. He was not responsible for the acts of his administration, for this responsibility rested with the vice-president and the secretaries, who endorsed them. The judiciary was absolutely independent, being entirely separate from the executive branch. The electoral branch presented the candidates to the legislative branch, which elected the judges from among those presented. Civil liberty, in the broadest sense, was guaranteed by this constitution. No recognition was given to titles, privileges, or the ancient entailments of landed estates.

This is an incomplete outline of the draft that the Liberator submitted to the Bolivian people. Zealous republicans may criticize the president's term of office and the transmission of his power to a successor appointed by him, but if they take into account the character of the people for whom he was legislating and all the evils that frequent elections produced in the neighboring countries, perhaps they will be inclined to be more indulgent in judging a document that in all other respects should merit their approval. The authority conferred upon the electoral college is the greatest concession ever made to the people. In order to avoid the evils of corruption or bribery to which small groups are exposed, Bolívar chose to extend the base of the representation, despite the dangers arising from ignorance and base motives. He offset this latter evil up to a certain point by requiring the ability to read and write as an indispensable requisite of the right to vote. The complete abolition of slavery and the moral power granted to the censors are ideas worthy of a philosopher. A spirit of real liberality is clearly evident in the entire document, whatever its partial defects may be. Posterity will do the author the justice he deserves, even though his contemporaries have denied it to him.

The address that the Liberator sent with the Bolivian Constitution to Congress is a masterpiece of eloquence, in which he explains and analyzes many of the novel provisions of this document. He dictated it to an amanuensis during the final days of his stay in Chuquisaca, but he did not present it until the following month of May, when he sent it with his aide-de-camp, Colonel Belford Wilson. This famous message will doubtlessly be read by the lovers of liberty with pleasure, and this pleasure will be heightened by the realization that the one who wrote it fought for the cause of liberty from his study with extraordinary eloquence, after having been its most renowned champion on the field of battle. The passages in which he speaks of slavery and religion are exceedingly brilliant. He calls slavery the negation of all law, a shameless violation of human dignity whereby an image of God is coupled to the yoke like a beast. In speaking of religion, he declares that a political constitution should not prescribe any particular religion, for religion is the law of conscience. To apply compulsion to conscience is to destroy the value of faith, which is the very essence of religion and cannot be legislated.

After promulgating the decree in which he convoked the Bolivian Congress for May 25, 1826, he delegated the supreme command to General Sucre and said good-bye to the Bolivians before leaving to open the Peruvian Congress. After his departure from Chuquisaca on January 6, 1826, he visited Misque and Cochabamba before going on to Arica, where he boarded the Colombian brig of war *Chimborazo* on February 2. He reached Chorrillos on the night of the seventh and went immediately to his Magdalena residence.

CHAPTER TWENTY-ONE

THE COUNCIL OF GOVERNMENT OF PERU, whether with the personnel it had when the Liberator left Lima the previous year or with the changes that were made in it later, did not completely enjoy the respect that the government needed in order to achieve good results. It would have been difficult, however, to find better qualified men to replace the members of this body. When Sánchez Carrión, who had presided over it in the absence of General La Mar, retired because of illness some three months before his death, his post was filled by Don Hipólito Unanue, whose forceful character was mistakenly attributed to the irritability of old age. Don José María Pando, another member who possessed excellent qualifications, was unpopular among his countrymen because he was a recent convert to the cause of independence. When he was sent by the Liberator in May, 1825, to represent Peru in the Panama Congress,[1] his place was filled by Don José Larrea y Laredo, a more likable person with a better claim to the title of patriot but lacking the former's experience in the management of affairs. Nevertheless, his appointment was received by the nation with general applause. The third member of the council was General Heres, a native-born Colombian who, despite his talent and great experience, was regarded with suspicion by the Peruvians because of the hatred that his nationality aroused in the country and the rumors that were spread about his being involved in political intrigue.[2] Convinced of the false position he occupied, he had repeatedly offered to resign his post as minister of war, and, when his resignation was finally accepted, he handed over the portfolio of the ministry to General Salazar, whose only merit consisted in his adherence to his country's cause and in the influential position of his friends and relatives.

One month after the Liberator's departure a young man named Cabero, a former army ensign, conceived the daring plan of taking over the reins of government. Since the government, however, had been promptly notified of the intended revolt, he and his sole companion, a police lieutenant named Manuel Milán, were imprisoned, tried, condemned to death, and executed. This was the only disturbance of public order in the capital, but another conspiracy, headed by some former royalist officers, was discovered in Ica a few months later. They also suffered the appropriate legal penalty. An incident of another type at the beginning of June caused some alarm in the capital and gave rise to intrigue and further trouble. After the supreme court reversed a sentence pronounced by the superior court of justice, the members of the superior court were suspended from the exercise of their duties by virtue of a clause of the decree issued the year before by General Bolívar as dictator of Peru. Everyone was greatly surprised, because the case was trivial and there was no precedent for this kind of action. The

---

[1] The Congress of Panama convened in June, 1826. —Ed.

[2] Colonel J. Gabriel Pérez, who alternated with General Heres as the Liberator's secretary, was also very much hated in Lima. "You are as bad as Pérez [Eres tan malo como Pérez]" became a proverbial expression in the city. The pun on the phrase "Heres as bad as Pérez [Heres tan malo como Pérez]" is really clever.

Council of Government, limiting its action to the literal interpretation of the law, ordered the sentence to be executed. One of the suspended justices, Don Mariano Alvarez, made a political issue out of the matter, and the subsequent elections gave him ample opportunity for his machinations.

The election period had already arrived, with the consequent factional agitation and party strife. The indifference of the government party stood out in contrast to the activity displayed by the opposition party. Of the four deputies to the next Congress elected in October by the canton of Lima, only one, Dr. Galdiano, could be considered a government man. On the other hand, Alvarez, the instigator of the opposition after the council confirmed the sentence of the supreme court of justice, was also elected to Congress, as was Carrasco, a man without distinction chosen by the friends of former President Riva-Agüero.

Prudent men looked upon this partial victory of the malcontents as the beginning of a new storm that threatened to vent all its evil fury on Peru. For this reason they did not hesitate to disapprove of the excessive political delicacy that had led the Liberator to give unnecessary proof of the liberality of his aims by convoking the legislature seven months ahead of the date set by Congress. There were no disturbances in the northern provinces, because the deputies elected declared themselves in favor of the existing state of affairs. Such was not the case in Cuzco, where the clergy, displeased over the reforms introduced by the Liberator in ecclesiastical affairs, condemned the government's policy as irreligious. The enemies of independence made the most of the discontent produced by the fanatics. Dr. Eugenio Mendoza and Dr. Pedro Leiva, priests from Tinta and Sicuani who were well known for their loyalty to the royalists, triumphed in the elections. Nevertheless, the majority of the deputies were more inclined to favor the government, and in the neighboring department of Puno all of those chosen favored it.

But the place where the opposition displayed its full strength was Arequipa, which it selected as the scene for its most determined election campaign against the administration. The administration's defeat, though foreseen, was not thereby less regrettable. During his visit there the Liberator had found the department stirred up by opposing factions.

The royalist partisans were bending every effort to retain their former preponderance, while the patriots, in their turn, were seeking to wrest control from them. The royalist party was led and supported by the bishop of the diocese, Don Sebastián Goyeneche, a native of Arequipa and a brother of General Goyeneche, who, after having dishonored himself, retired to the Peninsula with the American plunder he had gathered. The royalists also found a hidden protector in General Don Pío Tristán, the viceroy for a day, despite his submission to the constituted authorities. The Liberator acted this time with the greatest indulgence, making every possible effort to lessen the tense state of both parties. He suggested to the bishop the necessity of addressing a pastoral letter to the priests of his diocese in order to point out to them that there was not the slightest incompatibility between Catholic dogma and republican institutions. The bishop, despite his offer to put the Liberator's suggestions into practice, reverted to his secret intrigue, which helped to prevent the establishment of public tranquillity.

The government, with the object of remedying the evil, appointed Dr. Manuel Córdova, a learned priest who had served the country well, to be rector of the cathedral of Arequipa and granted him ample authority for the administration of the diocese. Goyeneche consented without protest, since he could still keep intact the privileges that enabled him to satisfy his greed, the sordid passion that dominated him. The rector introduced some reforms and removed from their parishes the priests most in favor of the old system, a measure that naturally made more than a few enemies for him. Arequipa was, then, a center of intrigue as the time for the elections was approaching.

By this time Dr. Javier Luna Pizarro, a patriot and formerly a distinguished member of the Constituent Congress, had returned after a long absence in Chile, where he had retired after Riva-Agüero assumed supreme authority. Upon his return he found that Bolívar had rewarded him for his patriotism by promoting him to a prebend. A learned man endowed with superior talent and sound judgment, Luna Pizarro well deserved this promotion, but he had more ambition than befitted the life of self-denial he had led since his youth. Furthermore, he was probably less sincere than a person of his austere manner should have been. Grateful for the favors received from Bolívar personally and for those dispensed to his country, he reacted at first in a highly generous manner and wrote to Bolívar to urge him to continue his stay in Peru, which needed him more than Colombia did because of the lack of political development. In view of the soundness of his opinions concerning the state of his country and the knowledge he apparently had of the machinations of the enemies at home, it seems very strange that so able a man should have become involved in the difficulties that he himself had believed it necessary to avoid.

The elections were held a few weeks after the date of Luna Pizarro's admirable letter, and he was chosen to represent the province in the future Congress. When it came to the departmental elections, party strife broke out in all its fury. General Tristán was presented in opposition to Dr. Córdova, the rector. Dr. Córdova was elected in spite of the eloquence of Luna Pizarro, who backed Tristán, and the effrontery of Tristán's supporters. These elections left implanted the seed of future discord. Luna Pizarro was unable to hide his resentment over the advancement of Córdova and over the unlimited confidence that the government bestowed upon him. This was the real reason for his opposition. Therein lies the explanation of his affiliation with the "enemies at home," whom he had described so vividly in his letter to the Liberator, and of his subsequent behavior.

The results of the elections in the various provinces of the Republic were communicated to the Liberator in Chuquisaca at a time when the correspondence he received painted the domestic disturbances in Peru in such dark colors that he became deeply alarmed. Respectable men from all the parties begged him in their letters to return immediately to Lima in order to save Peru from the calamities that directly threatened her existence. On the other hand, there were very plausible rumors circulated and supported by the political cabal concerning probable hostile acts on the part of France. In view of these circumstances the Liberator decided to leave Bolivia and return to Lima. Now his Ixion-like troubles were about to begin, for no sooner did he reach the goal of his dreams than his wheel of fortune started to turn in the opposite direction. His popularity, however, continued to gain ground in Peru, for ingratitude had not yet injected all its poison into the contemporary generation.

General La Mar arrived in Lima at the beginning of January, 1826, and took over the presidency of the council on the fifth of the same month. This appointment, which Bolívar had suggested the previous year, caused special satisfaction in Peru. La Mar's camaraderie while fighting in the field, as well as his obedience to the Liberator and his affection for him, had restored him to the good graces of the zealous patriots, who formerly were always inclined to be suspicious of his conduct.

The fortress of Callao finally had to surrender, despite the stubborn stand made so courageously by its garrison and its heroic general. On January 11, 1826, General Rodil requested the suspension of hostilities, which was granted to him by General Salom in compliance with the humane instructions he had received from the Liberator. Although the garrison had been reduced to a wretched state in its struggle with disease and hunger, Rodil agreed to surrender only after being convinced by honest and impartial persons that he could expect no help. During the ensuing negotiations the royalists showed extreme concern over everything related to military honor, protesting at times that Rodil would blow up the fortress, with himself in it, rather than sign any clause reflecting on his heroic defense during the siege. The republican commissioners acceded to all their proposals because they had been ordered to do so. On January 23 the garrison marched out of the fortress with the honors of war, whereupon the last Spanish flags left flying on the American continent were lowered over the last bit of territory still occupied by the successors of Pizarro. The honor of bringing this final act of the war of independence to a glorious close fell to a Colombian general at the head of the united forces of Colombia and Peru.

The rejoicing over this event had scarcely ended when announcement was made of the Liberator's arrival at the villa in Magdalena, four miles from Lima. He had sent me from Chuquisaca to announce his return and also to communicate to the government his decision to open the sessions of Congress in person and not to consent to any preparations being made for a public welcome, because he wished to enter the city as a private citizen. The members of the council and of the other corporations begged him to come to the city, which he consented to do with great reluctance. When he made his entry on February 10, he received a spontaneous and hearty welcome from the people. What a sublime spectacle it was to see the entire population of one of the principal cities of America burst into wild applause and demonstrate in such civilized fashion and in such a variety of ways the gratitude it felt toward its worthy liberator!

This splendid triumphal welcome stirred him deeply, because it showed that the friction between the parties had resulted in the formation of a nonpartisan group, which all the really patriotic individuals seemed eager to join. After a solemn Te Deum in the cathedral, the Liberator went on foot to the palace, where he answered, with his characteristic easy eloquence, all the prepared speeches addressed to him. When one of the orators alluded to the vehement desire of the people to see him once more at the head of the Republic, he replied that it would be an insult for him to occupy the seat of honor, in which Grand Marshal La Mar should sit for many reasons. Taking La Mar by the arm, he had him sit down in the seat reserved for the first magistrate in public ceremonies. La Mar declared that he was now in poor health and lacked the ability to govern people. Upon hearing these words, the Liberator replied that it was up to the national assembly to consider La Mar's excuses, that all he had done was to place him in a position he believed should be his. Those present applauded the idea, realizing that Bolívar was making this noble gesture in order to show his impartiality. General La Mar continued to head the government until ill health forced him to retire, whereupon Unanue took charge of the administration, as he had done previously during the absence of the Liberator. Bolívar kept only his military command.

Magdalena became the center of political interests in the South. Although the political agitation that had previously caused alarm had apparently ceased, intrigue and suspicion continued to thrive. Magdalena was open to all parties, and people called there to promote and protect their various interests. Everyone seemed anxious to find out the Liberator's ideas. With his characteristic frankness and sincerity, he told all those he saw that he had returned to Peru with the object of re-establishing the supreme authority of Congress and helping the government with his influence, in order to promote the prosperity of the country.

Various projects related to the future welfare of the nation in particular, and of South America in general, were discussed at Magdalena. Some influential members of the next Congress expressed the opinion that Peru and Bolivia should be united into a single republic, bearing the latter's name, and that General Sucre should be appointed president of it. Other members demanded an energetic government for those countries, with the Liberator at the head. Still others hastened to point out that only the adoption of a monarchical system would prevent the evils to which the recently emancipated colonies were exposed. The members of the administration formed part of the circle that supported this idea, and especially Unanue, who had the courage to proclaim his opinions publicly. Luna Pizarro, who arrived in Lima shortly after the Liberator, seemed to favor the union of Peru and Bolivia, and he considered the Liberator's proposed constitution to be more suitable for the country than the existing one. The Liberator himself was not adverse to this plan, but he maintained that nothing should be done until solemn treaties had been made between both nations.

The period designated for the installation of Congress had already arrived, but there was still not a sufficient number of deputies on hand. At a preliminary meeting held on May 29 by the sixty-five who were already in the capital, a long and violent debate ensued about the nature and duties of the assembly. The majority brought the debate to an end by declaring that the preliminary assembly had no national authority. But those who were to preside over Congress were chosen previous to this declaration, and it was agreed that the deputies should present their credentials to a commission appointed by the president. There was a second session in which the debate was resumed. The Council of Government had conferred upon the supreme court of justice the right to examine the records of the electoral colleges and the credentials of the deputies. Some deputies questioned the assumption of such authority by the government and proposed that the assembly itself should exercise it. The debate occasioned by this incident was marked by the most alarming symptoms of factional spirit. The deputies from Arequipa, led by Luna Pizarro and aided by Dr. Alvarez and a few others of the ultraradical group, were most violent in their opposition to the government, but a considerable majority decided in its favor when the question was finally voted.

The capital was in a constant state of anxiety during these debates, and it was not long before party hatreds were awakened. As soon as the Liberator learned what had happened in Congress, he decided to leave the country and ordered General Salom to prepare transports and have the troops ready to embark. News of these measures filled the capital with consternation. The deputies to Congress met on April 2 and unanimously resolved to send a delegation to Magdalena to assure the Liberator that the wishes of the people of Peru and their representatives were that he should remain in the Republic and exercise the same authority that the Constituent Congress had conferred upon him. The powerful and conclusive arguments of the delegation were irresistible, and the Liberator acceded to the wishes of the preliminary assembly. When his decision was known, there was no end to the rejoicing that this happy outcome occasioned in the capital.

On April 6 the sessions were suspended by agreement of the majority of the deputies. Some fifty-two of them then decided to request the government to hold new elections and to postpone the meeting of Congress until the following year, in view of the uncertain state of the country and the irregularities that affected the election proceedings in the various provinces. The Council of Government considered this petition to be of a delicate nature and consulted the Liberator about it. In his reply he expressed his approval of the plan of these deputies because they wanted to refer to the original source of their authority, which was in keeping with democratic principles. This approval coincided with the opinion of the council, which therefore decided in favor of the plan.

Not long afterward this decision was maliciously used as a pretext for accusing the Liberator of having employed deceit and intrigue to dissolve Congress in furtherance of his own ambitious aims. His detractors overlooked the fact that he had convoked Congress five months before the date set by law, that he had absented himself during the elections, that he had a great majority in that body, and that the deputies still to arrive were all supporters of the government. Thus, whatever the aims attributed to him, it would have been difficult to find a Congress more willing to help him to realize them. Furthermore, if unlimited power were his object, anyone with the most inordinate ambition could not have aspired to greater power than what he already held, for never was there authority so broad as that which the representatives of the nation had conferred upon him. The most vociferous members of the opposition were those who insisted most on the approval of the recent measure of Congress and who were most eager about visiting him as usual in Magdalena. Luna Pizarro was the one person who was sent away without an interview, despite his appeals to the Liberator's generosity and sense of justice and despite his protests that persons interested in prejudicing the Liberator against him had misinterpreted his words and harbored unjust suspicion concerning the motives of his conduct.

On April 15 General Don Juan de Berindoaga and Don José Terón were executed, in fulfillment of the sentence passed by the courts having jurisdiction in the case. I have already related how the former, together with the Marqués de Torre Tagle, joined the Spaniards in February, 1824, and took refuge in Callao, from where he encouraged the enemies of independence with his writings and private letters. Early in October of the following year he succeeded in escaping from Callao, but he was seized in a launch with Miranda, Rodil's aide. Great efforts were made in Lima to save the unfortunate Berindoaga and his companion Terón, and even the municipality sent a petition to the Liberator requesting commutation of the sentence. But Bolívar allowed the sentence to be carried out, for the enormity of the crime and the high position of the transgressor, who had been minister of war and a brigadier general in the Peruvian army, required an exemplary punishment. As he stated in a note dictated to his secretary-general, it would be in accord with his feelings to exercise clemency, but leniency and impunity for such great crimes would bring fatal consequences, opening the door to similar crimes.

CHAPTER TWENTY-TWO

S CARCELY HAD THE EXCITEMENT caused by this event begun to subside when Don José M. Pando arrived from Panama, where he had gone with Don Manuel de Vidaurre to represent Peru in the great American congress, and from where he had been called by the Liberator to take charge of the Ministry of Foreign Affairs. The news brought back by Pando was as alarming as it was exaggerated, but the Liberator, who had the greatest confidence in him, gave complete credence to his reports. Pando stated that the Spaniards, who had already gathered a large force in Cuba, were preparing to attack some point on the coast of Colombia, with the backing of the Holy Alliance and the financial help of France. According to him, Mexico was planning to negotiate a separate peace, and Great Britain would not oppose the aims of the continental powers with respect to America. In addition to these alarming reports, Pando brought back other equally gloomy and unfortunately accurate information about the situation in Colombia.

The Liberator was deeply upset over this overwhelming mass of discouraging information, especially when he realized that such circumstances could nullify the sacrifices of fifteen years. Pando was of the opinion that the only way to avoid these evils was to temporize with Europe, and he fervently advocated the establishment of an empire extending from Potosí to the mouth of the Orinoco. Some Peruvians of great influence, among them General Gamarra, wrote to the Liberator about the matter, beseeching him to put aside personal scruples and save America. Other circumstances, which I shall explain later, made the plan seem practical, but Bolívar never supported it. He believed, and rightly so, that it was not in keeping with his own sense of honor and the laws of his country, and that even though its adoption might assure America of Europe's protection, it would inevitably bring on a bloody war between the supporters of democracy and those of monarchy, which would ultimately degenerate into a class war.

The plan that the Liberator found more consistent with his own ideas and principles was the one for the confederation of the republics of Colombia, Peru, and Bolivia by means of a close alliance in which each republic would retain its own laws and its general government and would be represented in a federal congress. Only the direction of foreign affairs and the defense of the country would be the particular concern of the federal government. He was of the opinion that such an imposing national body would have all the vigor and stability of a monarchy without offending the susceptibilities of the people, to whom the name of king was as hateful as it had been to the citizens of republican Rome. The organization of the executive power in his draft of a constitution for Bolivia was applicable to this system, and its adoption would make the whole structure solid. On the other hand, it would facilitate the reconciliation of Europe to the South American revolution. As Bolívar explained the plan in a letter to General La Fuente, there would be a general federation more closely knit than that of the United States and directed by a president and vice-president. The three houses of the federal congress, together with the vice-president and the secretaries of state, would govern the federation. The capital would be a central point, and there would be one flag, one army, and one single nation with whatever name the people wished. Colombia would be divided into three states, as would Upper and Lower Peru once they were united.

The plan was magnificent in theory but difficult to put into practice. It is true that the South American continent was united by a common background, religion, and language, and by the habit of obedience to a central authority, but it is also true that there was no real cohesion between the various states, subject as they were to inveterate antipathies that divided them morally. Furthermore, the insurmountable difficulties that stood in the way of concerted action, because of the fact that the sparse population was scattered over vast stretches of territory, eliminated all hope of carrying out this magnificent plan. There would have been, however, one point of contact between the confederated republics. Even though they had diverse ideas and interests in other respects, they all felt the same way about Bolívar, and each one wanted to retain him. If the infernal spirit of discord had not made such frightening inroads in Colombia since the beginning of the revolution and distracted Bolívar's attention, his genius might have overcome the obstacles that stood in the way of that plan and that seemed insurmountable to ordinary minds. We shall soon see to what extent domestic disagreements had developed.

When the glory of a man is so pre-eminent that it deprives his most ambitious compatriots of the hope of rivaling him, they then strive to bring him down to their own level, to repudiate his claims to merit, to destroy his influence, and to make him an object of suspicion, imputing to him selfish aims, no matter how patriotic his motives may be. This was Bolívar's lot. If a Colombian Saint-Pierre had conceived the idea of confederating two or more South American states under one government, those who scoffed at the practicability of such a plan would have, at most, considered it as "the dream of an honest man." But Bolívar had the misfortune—for that is really the word for it—to be a many-sided public figure, who combined in admirable harmony the special talents of the soldier and the keen insight of the politician, together with the brilliance of his military exploits. The sterling traits evident in his excellent writings, where he revealed himself as a statesman and a philosopher, usually awakened the foolish envy of those who rashly aspired to emulate him.

This happened particularly in Chile and in Buenos Aires, where the governments, unlike the people, criticized the acts and even the words of the Liberator with excessive severity and strove to stir up suspicion concerning his conduct. The time was rapidly approaching when the dictates of reason and justice would be disregarded and the treacherous insinuations of envy and the frenzied appeal of demagogy would be heeded. The advent of this period of confusion was hastened as a result of the publication of the Bolivian Constitution.

The assiduous visitors to Magdalena considered, or at least pretended to consider, this proposal to be the key to the future well-being of America in general and of Peru in particular. The Liberator listened with great pleasure to the praise they lavished on the constitution, but he did not for this reason avoid discussing it or fail to express a sincere desire to have them point out its faults to him. The truth is that in Magdalena he heard only a full measure of applause for the work. The people of Bolivia, for whom it was originally intended and to whose representatives, meeting as a congressional body, the Liberator submitted it, received it with gratitude, but they did not make haste to adopt it as their own. Only with great caution did they proceed to ratify it as the fundamental law of the nation. A committee appointed by Congress recommended its adoption, with slight modifications, after twenty-four days of conscientious debate. On July 12, 1826, the report was read in Congress, and the discussion continued without interruption for three and one-half months. The modifications made in the original constitution were insignificant, except for the article introduced recognizing the Roman Catholic religion as the state religion. The emancipation of the slaves was approved in conformity with the Liberator's recommendation and with the consent of the owners. The most influential citizens of Bolivia applauded the constitution as a masterpiece of political wisdom and as the best safeguard of the people's rights.

Even in Buenos Aires and Chile it had admirers and supporters, but

Rivadavia, as was his custom, vented all his wrath against the Liberator in the daily press, using another name. The only revenge that the
latter took against his irascible adversary was the humorous review,
which appeared in *El Peruano Independiente*, of the inaugural address
that Rivadavia delivered after taking the oath as president of the Argentine Republic at the beginning of the year. This address is the most
extraordinarily ridiculous piece ever spoken or written by anyone who,
like Rivadavia, aspired to public recognition as a statesman. Bolívar,
a master of all the elements of satire, therefore used this weapon against
him in a critical article that was a most amusing caricature of his address.[1]

As in all the South American nations, opinions were divided in Colombia concerning the merit of the Bolivian Constitution. Only in the
southern districts was it received with enthusiasm. In the central section a few competent judges exerted a favorable influence on public
opinion. They believed that the Bolivian arrangement of the executive
power could also be applied to Colombia and that it was necessary for
her preservation. Other men, on the contrary, although they approved
certain articles, criticized the life tenure for the president and the succession of the vice-president as a barefaced imitation of monarchical
government. Furthermore, they regarded the electoral power as an
invitation to anarchy. Nevertheless, neither group at that time attributed
its adoption to unworthy motives on the part of the Liberator. Even
General Santander, who later distinguished himself by the virulence
of his opposition to both the author and the constitution itself, said in
a letter to Bolívar that he considered it to be "liberal and popular,
strong and vigorous."

I have believed it necessary to make the preceding observations in
order to have a basis for comparison with later events and to show
fully the vicious conduct of Bolívar's opponents and the almost complete lack of honest principles of logic in the hostile criticism later
aimed at his reputation. The very same men who had been most lavish
with their praise in the days of Bolívar's splendor were the first ones
to berate and slander him when fortune no longer favored him. If the

---

[1] Bolívar received a copy of Rivadavia's address while at the theater, and, after
reading it, he dictated the article to an aide-de-camp.

Bolivian Constitution deserved the severe criticism to which it has been subjected recently, why was there not a single patriot in Peru who would point out its defects? I am convinced that if any of the individuals who visited Magdalena daily had had the frankness to declare that the constitution was not suitable for America, the Liberator would have limited himself to submitting it to the scrutiny of the Congress of Bolivia, thus complying with what he believed to be his duty. He never showed any of the sensitiveness characteristic of writers, which was depicted so realistically by Lesage in the Archbishop of Granada of his famous novel, *Gil Blas*. In no case was he more eager for the opinion of the public and of individuals than he was in the matter of this proposed constitution. He invited criticism even from beyond the confines of America. In a letter to his friend Don José Joaquín de Olmedo, who was on his way to England as diplomatic agent for Peru, he asked Olmedo to read the constitution and the address and to tell him frankly what he found wrong. He also requested him to have it translated into French and English and published in daily newspapers.

Although quiet was restored in Lima and in the provinces, thanks to the Liberator's willingness to defer his departure, the political prospects of the Republic were not promising in the least. The Constitution of 1823, which had very little to recommend it, was despised by all the parties, some of whose members repeated daily that Bolívar's departure from Peru would be the signal for a revolution unless there were an administration vigorous enough to enforce the laws without fear or favoritism. As Vidaurre expressed it to Bolívar, "I wish Peru to be free, to have a constitutional government, to occupy its proper place in the world, but I will never side with any anarchistic demagogues whose last thought is the welfare of the country." What was there left for Bolívar to do? The deplorable state of his own country, where everyone was desperately clamoring for his presence, would not allow him to prolong his stay in Peru.

The favorable reception given his proposed Bolivian Constitution gave him the idea of consulting the people about its adoption. The idea was applauded by the Council of Government and the influential people. Since they were anxious to find an immediate solution for the existing conflicts, they decided—quite unwisely, in fact—to submit the matter to the electoral colleges, which they regarded as the most approximately popular means possible of ascertaining the will of the people. A decree was therefore issued calling for them to meet in their respective provinces and to decide about the desirability of promulgating the Bolivian Constitution as the fundamental law of Peru.

While this measure was being put into effect, the Liberator studied the means of accomplishing the confederation of Colombia, Peru, and Bolivia. His first intention was to unite the latter two into a single state, but once he became convinced of the unpopularity of such a union in Bolivia, he decided to invite the latter republic to form an integral part of the federal league. The new Council of Government therefore sent Don Ignacio Ortiz Ceballos, a well-known lawyer, to Bolivia, with the rank of minister plenipotentiary, to congratulate her on the recognition of her independence and to enter into negotiations concerning the proposed confederation. At first the envoy obtained satisfactory results in the pursuance of his mission, but this initial success was followed shortly afterward by an unfortunate turn of events.

Although the Liberator had decided to return to his native country, where his presence was urgently required, it was necessary for him to remain in Peru a little while longer in order to consolidate the government. After General La Mar's retirement from the council because of illness, Bolívar appointed General Santa Cruz to succeed him in the presidency. Santa Cruz was a very ambitious and shrewd man of a practical turn of mind who was sufficiently qualified to hold the high position entrusted to him. Under the new organization of the council the president had authority to dispatch all business that did not require more thorough deliberation. Shortly after taking possession at the beginning of July, General Santa Cruz had to leave to quell the revolt that had started following the mutiny of two squadrons of Húsares quartered in Huancayo.

This revolt, which was purely military, was headed by a sergeant named José Pedro Rivas. The excuse adopted by the rebels was that they intended to free Peru from the oppression of Colombia and her troops. After having committed many outrages, these Huancayo rebels were crushed by Colonel Benavides at the head of four companies of the Pichincha Battalion. Rivas and many of his companions were taken prisoner. This event had a most painful effect on Bolívar, who feared that the accusation hurled at the Colombians would be seized upon later by the other units of the Peruvian army and that, in the end, his own enemies would find a way to make him appear responsible for the calamity. He therefore had his secretary address a communication to the Council of Government requesting that steps be taken to transport the Colombian troops to their native land. This communication aroused in the members of the council the same feelings that the Liberator had: sorrow and great fear for the future of Peru.

Scarcely had this seditious uprising been quelled when a widespread and dangerous conspiracy was discovered in the capital. The government was fortunately able to bring it to an end on July 28. The conspirators were planning to surprise the Colombian unit commanded by Colonel Prieto and force the others to surrender, with the object of driving the Liberator and the Colombian troops out of the country, under the pretext that they were the oppressors of the people. Their program had a definitely mercenary basis, involving the distribution of the lucrative positions as a reward. The high government posts were reserved for the principal leaders. Generals Necochea and Correa of Buenos Aires were the instigators and principal proponents of the plan. Generally speaking, the Peruvian people took no part in the movement. After the conspirators were tried and convicted of treason, they were condemned to exile, but this punishment was not imposed upon them until after Bolívar had left Peru.

Tired of war, revolutions, and disorders, the masses longed for peace, and they regarded Bolívar as the guardian of public order. He, for his part, was only awaiting the return of General Santa Cruz before starting on his way. Petitions flowed into the office of the Liberator's secretary from all the provinces of the Republic, beseeching him not to abandon them. Finally, the electoral college met on its own initiative, and, making one last effort to detain him, it voted unanimously for the Bolivian Constitution and declared Bolívar president of the Republic for life. The Liberator could not help being moved by such definite proof of esteem and popularity, but the disasters of his own country had first claim on his attention.

The time finally arrived for Bolívar to take his leave of the Peruvians. The date was September 3, 1826, a day of real, general mourning among the inhabitants of the capital. The streets and the road to Callao were crowded with people, and the air was filled with prolonged and enthusiastic cries of "Hurrah for Bolívar" and "May he return soon." After Bolívar reached the shore where he had landed three years before, he took off his hat upon entering the boat and waved to the crowd accompanying him. Then he left the country, having fulfilled the promise he had made upon accepting the dictatorship "of returning to Colombia without even a grain of sand from Peru, leaving her free." That night he set sail for Guayaquil in the Peruvian brig of war *Congreso*.

He bade farewell to Peru with a proclamation in which he told the Peruvians that Colombia was summoning him and that he had to obey, even though parting from them occasioned him deep sorrow, especially since their generosity had put him under obligation to them. He was really not leaving them, he said, because they would have his devotion and his political ideas in their government. He warned them to be ever fearful of the dreadful evil of anarchy.

Since Bolívar's stay in Peru after the battle of Ayacucho has been strongly criticized, it will probably not seem irrelevant to recapitulate the principal reasons for his prolonged stay and to add others that I have not previously noted. The complete confusion into which the country had fallen as a result of the war and the revolution required the help of an expert hand to set matters right. Unfortunately for Peru, there was no one among her native sons who had sufficient prestige to undertake the herculean task. The situation in Upper Peru was distressing, for the war had not yet ended there, but more to be feared was the horrible specter of anarchy. Such considerations and the repeated entreaties of the Peruvian Congress and the most eminent citizens prompted Bolívar to change his original decision to withdraw from Peru. If, then, the assent that Bolívar finally gave was a mistake, Bolívar was the one who made it, but it was the kind of mistake that deserved to be classed as a fortunate one, in view of the official approval it received from the government of Colombia. Santander, in a private letter, said to him that his decision to remain there relieved the Colombians of a great worry, for the organization of Peru without his presence seemed very difficult, if not impossible.

There were even more compelling reasons for the presence of the Colombian army in Peru. The country had really had no army until after Ayacucho, when General Sucre incorporated a considerable number of the defeated soldiers into the native units. Though Peruvians, they had no love for the national colors, and there was reason to doubt their loyalty in case it were put to the test. Moreover, it was not until after the surrender of Callao at the beginning of 1826 that the entire country was free of danger. The Congress of Peru requested that the auxiliary troops be allowed to stay, and General Santander frequently urged the Liberator to keep them there, declaring that Colombia had no way to maintain them. Nevertheless, once the campaign in Upper Peru ended, Bolívar began sending some of them home, and after the surrender of Callao a large contingent left for Guayaquil and Panama. Thus it was that when he departed from Peru he left behind only the Third Division, composed of the Rifles, Vencedor, and Caracas battalions.

In order to pay his personal debts before leaving that country, which he had served with glory for three years, Bolívar had to borrow from Colonel Belford Wilson and other officers of his staff the money they had available or were able to obtain from their friends. Even though his expenses were reasonable, his liberality was so great that he needed more funds than those he had set aside for his expenses and the comforts of his home. The Peruvians bestowed upon him magnificent gifts, but the only gift that he kept for himself was the sword presented to him by the municipality of Lima.

CHAPTER TWENTY-THREE

WHILE THE EVENTS I HAVE RELATED were taking place in Peru, the American congress was meeting in Panama. Bolívar is the only one recognized as the initiator of the plan to confederate the new states of the American continent. He conceived the idea soon after the beginning of the revolution, but at first it seemed like one of those visionary theories that the capricious imagination of idealistic statesmen adorns with beautiful colors. The natives of the various sections of South America lived in complete ignorance of each other as a result of the system of government that Spain applied to her colonies. Thus it was that when most of the continent rose up in rebellion, all the states thought only of their own security.

While wandering in exile on an island in the Caribbean, Bolívar spoke for the first time about the great confederation of all the states in America. He wrote to a friend in Jamaica in 1815 that it was a grand idea, and he even envisioned the Isthmus of Panama as a meeting place of all the nations of the world to discuss peace and war. With the war claiming his entire attention, he did not speak of the idea again until he officially presented it to the government of Buenos Aires in 1818. When victory finally favored his armed forces, he returned to his favorite idea and obtained, as the first fruit, the union of Venezuela and New Granada. At his suggestion, after Colombia was established in 1821, Don Joaquín Mosquera was sent to the governments in the South to invite them to join forces with Colombia against Spain and to send their representatives to Panama for the purpose of forming a general congress. Don Miguel Santamaría was sent to Mexico with identical instructions.

In both Peru and Chile, Mosquera succeeded in negotiating treaties for an offensive-defensive alliance with Colombia and in obtaining an agreement to send representatives to Panama for a federal congress. Then Mosquera went on to Buenos Aires, where the government was controlled by Don Bernardino Rivadavia. Failing to foresee that some day his country would need Colombia's assistance, Rivadavia refused to take part in the congress of plenipotentiaries and contented himself with negotiating an insignificant treaty of friendship. Mexico, more loyal to her own interests and to the American cause, warmly welcomed the idea proposed by Bolívar and solemnly pledged to participate in the great congress. The treaty negotiated by Santamaría was substantially the same as those Mosquera had negotiated with Peru and Chile. These negotiations were carried on during the years 1822 and 1823, and at the end of this period there still remained the question of ratification by the legislatures of the states that were the contracting parties.

Once Bolívar's military duties allowed him a slight respite, he devoted himself once more to this magnificent project. After leading the army as far as the Apurímac River, he returned to the coast, entered Lima on December 7, 1824, and on the afternoon of that same day addressed a circular letter to the governments of the American republics, inviting them to send their representatives to the Isthmus of

Panama and expressing to them the urgent necessity of hastening the meeting of the great assembly in order to concentrate the power of the great political body of American republics under a superior authority.

This letter was well received by the governments to which it was addressed. The Colombian government in particular appeared eager to further the Liberator's aims, and it had anticipated his wishes by taking steps to hasten the convocation of the congress. The vice-president of Colombia instructed the chargé d'affaires in Buenos Aires to attempt to persuade the new administration of the value of sending plenipotentiaries to the Isthmus. He also proceeded to make the same proposals to the Emperor of Brazil and to Guatemala, once it was recognized. Furthermore, he ordered Señor Salazar, the Colombian minister in Washington, to sound out the intentions of that government regarding the great assembly and, should it be disposed to support the idea, to invite it formally to send plenipotentiaries to Panama. Upon expressing Colombia's compliance with the Liberator's wishes, the vice-president submitted for his consideration a list of proposals concerning efforts to be made by the plenipotentiaries of Colombia and Peru to effect an early meeting of the assembly and to select a suitable place on the Isthmus. The Colombian government also proposed a list of essential objectives of the congress.

These proposals were readily approved by the Council of Government of Peru, which, in turn, invited the governments of Chile and Buenos Aires to participate in the congress. Though Chile was then bordering on anarchy, General Freyre gave his word that he would urge the legislature, which he expected to assemble within two months, to take the matter into consideration and to send plenipotentiaries immediately. The government of Buenos Aires, still influenced by the attitude of petty jealousy that characterized the Rivadavia administration, regarded, or pretended to regard, the plan with less favor than had the director of Chile. The Constituent Congress, which was more liberal than the government, authorized the government to appoint the plenipotentiaries. Guatemala quickly accepted Colombia's invitation, and so did the Emperor of Brazil and the government of the United States, although the latter two declared that they would observe strict neutrality toward the belligerent parties. The assent of the various nations of North and South America was finally obtained, thus permitting the realization of the hopes entertained by Bolívar since 1815.

These developments awakened the suspicion of the continental powers of Europe, and even England let it be known that she was suspicious. It was feared that the Congress of Panama would outlaw monarchy in America and spread exaggerated principles of liberty. The suspicion harbored by Mr. Canning was not allayed until the Colombian minister to the Court of St. James assured him that Colombia, far from having the intentions attributed to her by her enemies in Europe, had invited the Emperor of Brazil to take part in the deliberations of the proposed congress and that she would likewise be glad to have a British envoy accredited to it. Although the Liberator had already suggested to General Santander the advisability of obtaining the protection of Great Britain for the confederation, he was not unaware of the danger of admitting such a powerful ally into the league. In a reply to several letters from Señor Revenga, minister of foreign affairs of Colombia, he voiced his fear that such a powerful nation might become the arbiter of the decisions of the assembly. He also expressed doubt that Chile and Río de la Plata would join the confederation in good faith or accept the plan in its present form.

When Bolívar left Lima in April, 1825, he indicated to the Council of Government that Don José María Pando and Don Manuel Vidaurre were the men he considered best fitted to represent Peru in the federal congress. When Pando was summoned by his government to take over the Ministry of Foreign Affairs, Don Manuel Pérez de Tudela replaced him in Panama. Six months elapsed before the Peruvian ministers were joined by their Colombian colleagues, Dr. Pedro Gual and General Pedro Briceño Méndez. The representatives from Guatemala, Don Antonio Larrazábal and Don Pedro Molina, landed in Panama on March 18, 1826, and those from Mexico, General José Mariano Michelena and Don José Domínguez, reached the meeting place on June 4, a year later than the delegates from Peru. The government of Great Britain sent Mr. Dawkins to assist with his advice but without taking part in the discussions. With similar instructions, Colonel Van Veer attended the assembly as the representative of Holland.

Finally, on June 22, 1826, the Congress of Panama was solemnly installed, with the plenipotentiaries from Colombia, Guatemala, Mexico, and Peru in attendance. There was such perfect agreement from the beginning that the most cordial harmony was maintained during the course of the deliberations. But I should point out that Peru, the section of the continent that had contributed least to the victory of the American cause, was the country that made the most exacting demands and showed evidence of ambitious designs. On various occasions its plenipotentiaries laid claim to Guayaquil as part of Peru. The Mexicans, though more cautious, made it clear that they would like to try to regain possession of a province belonging to Guatemala, and they even sought the annexation of Cuba to their already vast territory.

The meetings ended on July 15, 1826, with the plenipotentiaries of the four states signing in the name of their respective governments: a treaty of union, alliance, and perpetual confederation; an agreement to meet every two years in time of peace and every year in time of war in the town of Tacubaya, one league from Mexico City; a pact fixing the quota each state was to contribute toward the common defense; and a military pact determining the bases for the use of the contingents. The other American states would be allowed to join the confederation if they endorsed the treaty within a year after ratification. This treaty, without usurping the sovereignty and independence of the contracting parties, embraced everything that a wise man could desire in order to avoid civil war and preserve peace in America. This was substantially the result of the labors of the Congress of Panama. When the sessions ended, one delegate from each group left to report what had transpired to his respective government and took with him a copy of the treaties to be ratified.

From the brief account that I have given of the decisions of the assembly, it can be seen that the noble aims of the initiator of this grand idea were not realized nearly as completely as he had hoped they would be. The absence from the congress of the representatives of several states and the reasons therefor greatly lessened the hopes that the Liberator had conceived of the usefulness of the decisions of that body in the future. The petty and jealous attitude of the government of Río de la Plata prevented it from appointing the plenipotentiaries, despite the authorization granted by Congress. Chile, despite Freyre's laudable intentions, was unable to send her representatives, because of the domestic disturbances that troubled the country at the time. The plenipotentiaries from Bolivia were not able to reach Panama in time to take part in the deliberations. Neither was Brazil represented in the congress. The government of the United States appointed Mr. J. Sergeant and Mr. Richard C. Anderson, who, as minister plenipotentiary to Colombia, was in charge of the legation in Bogotá, but neither were these delegates able to take their seats in the assembly. Anderson died in Cartagena on the way to Panama, and when Sergeant arrived the delegates from the other states had already left for Tacubaya.

This delay on the part of some of the American governments was a great disappointment to the Liberator. For many years he had cherished the hope that the Congress of Panama, should it ever become a reality, would bring immense benefits to the new republics, confirm their independence, and, by placing them in contact with each other and strengthening their ties, create a spirit of union and patriotism that would ensure harmony in their domestic affairs and bring them prestige abroad. Once he was sure that the meeting of the assembly would actually take place, he abstained from intervening further in the matter, for he believed that he had explained his position satisfactorily in official documents. Influential members of the confederated states, the delegates to the congress, and especially General Santander urged him repeatedly to visit the Isthmus during the sessions, but he refused to accede to their entreaties because he feared, and rightly so, that his presence there might cause suspicion and arouse distrust among the individuals and the governments that were not acquainted with his character and showed a lack of confidence in his policy. This refusal on his part is all the more praiseworthy in view of the fact that there is no doubt that he could have exercised great influence on the deliberations of that assembly. If his intentions at that time had been as perverse as later charges made them out to be, he could have directed the deliberations to his own advantage.

After reading the treaties signed at the Panama sessions, Bolívar wrote from Guayaquil to the vice-president of Colombia expressing the disappointment he had suffered. In a letter to General Pedro Briceño Méndez on the same day, he stated frankly that the convention respecting troop contingents was futile and ineffective because it enabled the enemy to act with full knowledge of the facts and to invade with double the number of forces.[1] He expressed his fear that the transfer of the assembly to Mexico would bring it under the influence of that country and the United States. He therefore requested that ratification of the treaties be deferred until he reached Bogotá and examined them with Briceño Méndez and others.

The Congress of Panama accomplished little good, and even this was not of practical value. Even though it turned out to be, according to the poetic expression of its initiator, "like the mad Greek who, perched on a rock, pretended to direct the ships that were sailing in the area," this does not detract from the magnificence and the usefulness of the plan as it was conceived. Perhaps at some future date, after the various American nations have become stronger and have attained a higher degree of civilization, their representatives will meet there again under more favorable auspices. Then they will take satisfaction and pride in recognizing that the path that led them to national independence, that gave them political stability, and that raised them to the rank of nations was blazed by Bolívar.

[1] The convention stated the specific number of troops and amount of money that each nation was to contribute for the common defense. —Ed.

CHAPTER TWENTY-FOUR

W HEN THE LIBERATOR LEFT THE SHORES of Colombia to assume charge of the glorious enterprise of liberating Peru, the entire national territory, with the exception of the single stronghold, Puerto Cabello, was free of enemies. Despite the severe damage caused by the war to the national economy, the spirit of enterprise had begun to revive the devitalized forces of the nation. The fiscal measures adopted by the Constituent Congress were not, it is true, appropriate for increasing revenue, but there was the hope that the experience of the executive would suggest needed reforms to the legislators. The first Constitutional Congress, which rejected federalism, fulfilled the nation's hopes to a certain extent. The army, which had to be maintained on a war footing because of Spain's continued hostility, observed the law and was obedient to the government, despite the fact that it was poorly requited. The foreign relations of the Republic were in an excellent state. Bolívar's fame, the splendor of his victories, and an illusory reputation for wealth had given Colombia an aura of respectability such as had never been attained by her sister republics. The United States had formally recognized the independence of the Republic, and treaties of offensive-defensive alliance had been made with almost all the other states of the American continent.

Such was, in brief, the political situation of the Republic in August, 1823, when the Liberator embarked in Guayaquil. I shall now describe the events that occurred during his absence and the state in which he found Colombia upon his return. In order to give a better idea of the course of events, I shall have to depart from the chronological order and divide my narration into separate sections, according to where the events took place.

The inhabitants of Pasto, in their semibarbarous ignorance and fanaticism, waged war continually in the territory between the Juanambú and Guáitara rivers, keeping the southern departments in a continual state of alarm. Military rule therefore had to be maintained in this area at all times. Their vigorous resistance was accompanied by the most ferocious deeds of bloodthirsty barbarism ever found, even in the most inhuman kind of society. It is necessary to point out, however, that the republican troops carried out horrible reprisals, thereby bringing dishonor upon themselves. Some of the commanding officers employed in the pacification of the natives of Pasto appeared to have set for themselves the inhuman task of rivaling Boves himself in the commission of horrible, bloodthirsty acts of vengeance.

The South suffered other evils of an unavoidable nature during the Liberator's absence. The war in Peru required great sacrifices, which were willingly made, for a noble spirit of patriotism still prevailed among the inhabitants. The interior departments of the South had devoted themselves largely to the manufacture of cloth, but they had to give up this profitable enterprise when the laws of the Republic established free trade. Unable thereafter to compete with the goods imported from Europe, their factories closed and the capital invested in them was lost. Agriculture might have benefited from free trade, but the exportation of agricultural products was extremely difficult and costly because of the poor condition of the roads. The new laws abolished the tribute and the sales tax, to which the people were accustomed and which they gladly paid, and replaced them in 1825 with a direct tax. These reforms decreased public revenue and aroused discontent among the taxpayers. The salaries of civil employees were not paid for months at a time, and even the daily rations of the troops were supplied only with great difficulty and sometimes in scanty amounts. If the inhabitants of Ecuador had not had the hope that the Liberator would apply some remedy upon his return to Colombia, it is likely that their suffering would have driven them to take matters into their own hands.

Although the central part of the Republic was definitely affected by some of these ills, it received some benefits that helped to offset them, since it was most directly under the influence and protection of the supreme government. The head of the government was a Granadine. Since New Granada had a larger population and more territory than the other sections, it had a large majority and a great deal of influence in the legislature. Nevertheless, except for the capital, its provinces did not thrive very well in the years 1824 and 1825. Various municipalities, including all those of Antioquia, even had to appeal to the personal generosity of the Liberator, who was in Peru, in order to establish elementary schools.

The provinces of old Venezuela were the ones that had suffered most from the war of independence. Agriculture was almost completely ruined as a result of the revolution, the emancipation of the slaves, and taxation. When Caracas, the capital, protested against the Constitution of Cúcuta, the executive of Colombia charged that the protest was seditious, but the grand jury declared that there was no ground for action. These incidents helped no little to promote disunity. Caracas considered itself, with some justification, to be the most cultured city of the Republic, but it constantly opposed the enforcement of the laws instead of supporting the government's policy. To tell the truth, not all the laws were in harmony with the basic elements of the nation. The direct tax was never put into effect or collected, for few people would pay it, and the poorly administered sales tax on tobacco was likewise unproductive. The domestic tranquillity of the northern part of the Republic, like that of the South, was endangered because of the tax situation.

When General Soublette vigorously enforced in Venezuela the law calling for the expulsion of Spaniards and Canary Islanders, a faction that continually antagonized the government raised its intemperate voice against the measure and the agent of the supreme government. General Soublette, despite his very impassive nature, requested his own removal in order not to have to endure the accusations aimed at him. He was succeeded as head of the civil government by General Toro, the former marquis of the same name, who resigned at the end of seven months. Toro was replaced by General Escalona, who was also a worthy individual but who was not thereby more fortunate.

The principal leader of this faction was Colonel Francisco Carabaño, who had recently returned from the Peninsula, where he had been sent by the Spanish authorities in 1812 because of the active part he had played in the fight for independence. Although taken back into the army of the Republic at his former rank upon his return in 1822, he expressed dissatisfaction with the constitution then in force and proceeded to seek followers in Caracas and the provinces in order to promote the federal system. He was joined by some old federalists and other individuals who were considered to be averse to independence. A newspaper, El Venezolano, ostensibly edited by Colonel Hall, was the organ of this party's opinions. All the laws and all the government's actions were criticized in its columns with excessive severity. But since the newspapers are rarely the organ of public opinion in South America, the people, in spite of this urging, continued to obey the government. This paper acquired its principal importance from the fact that the head of the government himself did not hesitate to answer its articles through the medium of the Gaceta de Gobierno. Within a short time the newspaper war became a personal feud between the collaborators of El Venezolano and General Santander.[1]

Toward the end of the year 1824 a conspiracy discovered in Petare, a town three leagues from Caracas, caused considerable alarm; it was

[1] "I wrote Article 115 against El Venezolano." Letter from Santander to the Liberator, January 6, 1824. Memorias, III, 135.

said that the Negroes and the people of mixed blood were attempting to revolt against the government and that they were being spurred on by the remnants of the Spanish party and by some of the priests. The speed with which General Páez, the commandant general of the department, moved to put down the uprising proved most effective, but all his measures were bitterly criticized by the opposition. There were also intermittent disruptions of the public peace by armed bands, which committed outrages in the King's name in the neighborhood of Caracas and Los Güires.

When the time for the constitutional elections arrived, the growing oppositionist party, which already had in its ranks General Mariño and other worthy military men, became most active. The publisher of *El Argos*, Antonio Leocadio Guzmán, became an enthusiastic supporter of the liberal party and boldly attacked the government. Carabaño was presented by this party as a candidate for the vice-presidency in opposition to Santander. There was no question regarding the presidency, for Bolívar was the idol of the populace. The elections took place, and the federal party did not win, even in Venezuela. The defeated group did not, however, abandon the field; but since the people had taken no part in these events, everything seemed quiet. But this calm was due in large measure to the influence of General Páez, who was able to check every attempt at insubordination with a strong hand. Having been accustomed for years to the exercise of unlimited power, he was never able to conform to the restraints of constitutional government, for which reason he was wont to commit injustices. Nevertheless, all the parties courted his favor.

Such was the situation of the northern part of the Republic about the middle of the year 1825. Before this year was over, conditions would be ripe for the explosion that rocked the Republic of Colombia to its very foundations. We shall now return to the center of authority, because from there came the spark that was to ignite the combustible elements already on hand.

If the state of affairs in the various sections, such as I have briefly outlined it, was not very promising, neither was that of the Republic in general, though the government was able, with the aid of exaggerated reports, to maintain an illusion of prosperity that was of advantage to it for the moment. Great Britain had recognized the independence of the Republic and signed a treaty with it. Although the treaty was extremely prejudicial to Colombia's interests, this fact went unnoticed amidst the general rejoicing over its ratification, the reason being that it seemed likely to provide some security against the hostile acts constantly committed by France and the other powers as allies of Spain. Unfortunately, Spain constantly rejected the kindly efforts made by the governments friendly to Colombia to persuade her to recognize the latter's independence. In other respects, foreign relations, under the able direction of Don Pedro Gual, were on an excellent footing.

Fiscal requirements compelled the government in 1823 to resort to extraordinary measures in order to maintain its political existence. A thirty-million-peso loan authorized by Congress was obtained in 1824, subject to conditions that were burdensome to the state, all because of the bad faith and inexperience of the commissioners. These millions were dissipated, however, shortly after they were received. Public opinion has accused General Santander, Don Manuel J. Hurtado, and the negotiators of the loan, Señores Montoya and Arrubla, of having defrauded the Republic in this transaction. From all parts of Colombia bitter complaints were heard about the matter, and the most impartial and upright citizens raised their voices and made them heard even in the distant residence of the Liberator. Señor Joaquín Mosquera, then a senator, wrote to him in May, 1825, that he was sorely needed in Colombia because of the increasing misery of the nation. There were, however, a few less honest or less generous citizens who offered different advice. Among the latter was the chief executive, whom many people regarded with suspicion. In a letter dated August 21, 1825, Santander said to the Liberator: "As long as I live I shall continue to advise you never, under any circumstances, to govern during a period of peace. No, my dear General, no one can be a real friend of yours if he advises you to govern ignorant people." Since this insidious advice had prevailed in the mind of the Liberator, who had faith in the honesty and friendship of the vice-president, the evils of the country increased.

Despite the receipt of the "accursed millions," the public treasury was relieved only for a short while. When the legislative body of a nation is a focal point of corruption and selfish desires, the entire foundation of public morality is weakened, and the condition of society becomes sad indeed. This was what was happening in Colombia. Though there were some exceptions, most of the men in the legislature were dominated by a despicable desire for personal gain. I have already stated that the first Constitutional Congress fulfilled the nation's hopes to a certain extent, which is to say that it did not make the mistakes people feared it would make. The subsequent legislatures were less wise. Congress began to show suspicion concerning the soldiers, and the House of Representatives voted disfranchisement. That measure was not passed, but the harm was done. In the elections of the year 1825 the right of the soldiers to vote was questioned. By authority of Congress, the soldiers' pay was reduced one-third, but they did not complain. The interests, revenue, and privileges of the clergy were also attacked, and the latter were insulted in the courts. A fanatical people never views with indifference what it considers to be insults directed at men whom it is accustomed to respect blindly and whom it regards as invulnerable.

The united command, which produced such fine results during the war, was dissolved. This measure was motivated by a petty spirit of jealousy rather than by a desire for justice. The civil authority began to clash immediately with the military authority, and deep-seated enmities resulted. The civil courts were given authority to decide cases involving military matters, as though the army personnel were not worthy judges of their own controversies. In every session of Congress the army was dealt severe blows, until it became depressed in spirit.

In view of these factors— a dissatisfied people, a demoralized army, a despairing clergy, a depleted public treasury, an executive who had a part in the dissipation of public funds, and a corrupt legislature—it was not surprising that domestic tranquillity was in a precarious state. Only a single spark was needed to ignite all these explosive elements. The crisis was already near at hand.

I have said that in Colombia the individual was everything and that the institutions meant nothing. One or two examples will suffice to prove the truth of this assertion, and I shall select one that had no little part in hastening the clash between the opposing forces that were attacking the stability of the government. Near the end of the year 1824 an officer named Francisco Perdomo was assassinated in Bogotá, and the crime was generally attributed to Colonel Leonardo Infante, a colored man, who had been promoted to the rank he held because of his extraordinary bravery and who had made himself odious by reason of his notorious evil conduct. After charges were preferred against him, he was tried by a military court and condemned to death on the basis of grave suspicion, for lack of a single witness to the deed of which he was accused. Among those who testified against him there was not a single respectable person. A deadlock resulted when the case was reviewed by a court-martial, but capital punishment was then imposed on the basis of a law prescribing only a relative majority.

The president of the high court of justice, Dr. Miguel Peña, refused to sign a sentence that he considered to be notoriously illegal, despite the executive's order. He was therefore suspended from his post after the impeachment charges brought against him in the House of Representatives were admitted by the Senate. Infante's sentence was confirmed, and this unfortunate colonel was executed on March 25, 1825. He protested his innocence up to the very moment of his death. After the execution the vice-president appeared on horseback and there, before the corpse, delivered a speech to the troops. More than anything else it seemed like a show of vanity unbecoming to the head of the government. If to this is added the fact that the vice-president was generally reputed to be a personal enemy of the victim, we can understand why this step was regarded as an ignoble act of vengeance.

The Senate refused to give Peña a hearing previous to the consideration of the charge. Though appearing before a tribunal from which he could expect no consideration, he showed no fear. He defended himself brilliantly, and even though he did not succeed in convincing his judges, he astonished his audience. The Senate, which was prejudiced against Peña, sentenced him by a great majority to be suspended from his post and to pay the interim appointee out of his own salary. Miguel Peña was no ordinary man. He had been insulted, persecuted, and dishonored, but he carried away with him a desire for vengeance and plans for achieving it when he departed from the capital, where men readily became instruments of a government they scorned.

We have arrived at the year 1826, a year that bears out what I have already said about the tranquillity of a country being in a very precarious state when the laws are not in consonance with the other essential elements of the nation. In his message to Congress the vice-president painted a bright picture of the public affairs of the country. He pointed out that Colombia had won esteem among the nations and was on friendly terms with two strong nations, that the people enjoyed political and civil liberty, that the constitution and the laws were based on public opinion and freedom of the press, that the spirit of free enterprise was beginning to gain hold, and that the groundwork had been laid for populating and cultivating large areas. These were the illusions with which General Santander, seeking a fictitious reputation, always deceived the people, foreign nations, and the Liberator himself, whenever it was to his advantage. In a private letter dated January 6, 1826, he said to the Liberator that his message was "written with *frankness and simplicity*" (O'Leary's italics) and that he would be very glad if it pleased him.

The state of the Republic was really very different from the picture presented by the vice-president. The people were discouraged, for their condition had not improved, and they were tired after so many years of sacrifices and hardships. A huge debt hurt the credit of the state, and the national revenue did not cover one-half of the expenses. No matter requiring the attention of Congress was more urgent than the examination of the factors that had a depressing influence on national credit and made bankruptcy imminent. Charges were filed twice in the House of Representatives against Señores Montoya and Arrubla, the government commissioners, concerning their evil manipulations in arranging the loan in London, but on both occasions they were absolved in a few days. Their most zealous defender was Santander, and his influence, together with some gold skillfully distributed among the most needy, or the most venal, representatives, obstructed the course of justice. After this profitable victory was won, the vile spirit of greed inspired the speculators to strike another blow. The government proposed to Congress another loan of twenty million pesos. "The speculators had bought up huge quantities of national bonds at a fifth or a sixth of their value in order to sell them at their face value to the government, which would pay for them with the fateful loan."[2]

The Republic was in dire financial straits at this time, and its misfortunes grew with the failure of Goldschmidt's banking house, in which Colombia became involved through the stupidity or the greed of Hurtado, minister of the Republic in England. After being called back for an extraordinary session, Congress passed a law advancing the date of the direct tax, which could not yield anything until the end of the year, if even then, because the obstacles that had made this tax futile had not been removed. The amount due for the previous year had not yet been collected. And of what use was it to pass laws to ensure a yield from taxes if the government agents either did not carry them out or defrauded the treasury? General Santander wrote to the Liberator that all the customs officials on the Atlantic coast, except one, were abusing their positions.

In its sessions of 1826, Congress had to decide about the elections for the president and the vice-president of the Republic. The office of chief executive went to Bolívar by an almost unanimous vote of the electoral colleges while he was in Peru. He presented his resignation as soon as he was notified of his election. There was a contest for the vice-presidency, but Santander received a majority of the votes, thanks to the influence exercised by the Liberator. Nevertheless, neither the Liberator's influence nor all the zealous efforts of the candidate himself won a sufficient number of popular votes for him. Congress met on March 15 to review this election, and Santander was elected vice-president of the Republic by seventy votes.

The Liberator's resignation was unanimously rejected. Santander, who had repeatedly declared that he would not accept the vice-presidency if he were not elected by popular vote, made only one effort to resign. Congress did not accept this resignation, but even this decision was not unanimous. The most important question confronting Congress arose from a petition presented by the municipality of Caracas in

[2] Letter from Joaquín Mosquera to the Liberator, dated April 21, 1826. *Memorias,* IX, 31.

protest against the conduct of General José Antonio Páez, commandant of the department of Venezuela. Since his conduct caused great confusion in the nation, precipitated a revolution, and dealt Colombia a mortal blow, it should be described in great detail.

CHAPTER TWENTY-FIVE

I N AUGUST, 1824, the government of the Republic issued a decree for the general enlistment in the militia of citizens from sixteen to fifty years of age, with the exception of persons usually exempt because of their profession or employment. This surprisingly antiliberal decree was regarded in Caracas with great repugnance and was severely criticized by the press. When General Páez informed the government of the alarming state of public opinion, all that it did was to order him "to avoid *as far as possible*" (O'Leary's italics) any incident that might require the use of armed force. In its first session Congress had passed a law more in consonance with the republican system, but this law had not been approved by the executive and had therefore not been published.

In the meantime General Páez refrained from enforcing the conscription decree. Finally, near the end of 1825, the military commander of the province of Caracas reported to him the defenseless state of the city and his fear of a conspiracy being hatched by the Negroes. Páez decided to call out the militia to meet the emergency, should the conspiracy turn out to be true. Unfortunately, the civil and military authorities were not in agreement. Civil authority was then exercised by General Juan de Escalona, a man of many good qualities, but hated by the soldiers. Furthermore, there had been serious quarrels between him and Páez, which had a pronounced effect on later events.

When a call was issued for the citizens to enlist, in compliance with the terms of the decree, it was ignored, even though repeated. General Páez thereupon had another call issued, ordering the citizens to present themselves at the San Fernando barracks at nine o'clock in the morning on January 6, 1826. Since the great majority failed to appear, the general ordered detachments of regular troops from the garrison to bring into the barracks any men they found on the streets. The troops told all those they met to go to the barracks or they would take them there themselves; but no house was broken into, nor any person harmed. Nevertheless, the action caused great consternation in Caracas, and the citizens apprehended were held for many hours. When the intendant was advised by General Páez of what was going on, he requested him to have the troops withdraw, assuring him that everyone would appear voluntarily, to which Páez assented.

On the following day the intendant, Escalona, made a report to the supreme government in which, evidencing his personal resentment, he echoed rumors like the one that "General Páez had issued an order to fire on those who fled and to search houses if necessary." Even more exaggerated, however, was the petition sent by the municipality to the representative body of the nation, though it is worth noting that this illustrious corporation complained more about the militia law than about the commandant general. The accusation made against the latter is not very clear.

The chief executive asked General Páez for a report on the affair, and the House of Representatives requested information from the executive. With his reply, which was favorable to General Páez, the vice-president enclosed not only Escalona's report but also another communication from the intendant that had nothing to do with the matter in question and that was highly offensive to the honor of the general. Although the vice-president stated in his reply that there was no proof that the outrages mentioned by the intendant had been committed by order of the commandant general, his observations made no impression on the minds of the representatives, among whom were some from Venezuela who were personal enemies of Páez. Outstanding among the latter was Santos Michelena, who was noted for his lack of loyalty to the cause of independence and whose brother had had a serious quarrel with General Páez.

The discussions occasioned by the petition were remarkable for the reckless ardor and the complete lack of prudence displayed. The orators forgot about everything, and, acting with great speed, they and their colleagues brought charges against the commandant general without having on hand any document other than the simple petition of the municipality, in which there was no explicit request that proceedings be instituted against him. One could conjecture that the measure was not dictated by zeal for the public interest but by a thirst for vengeance on the part of the personal enemies of General Páez. It also led thoughtful men to anticipate the approach of legislative tyranny, because of the manifest abuse by Congress of the preponderance that the constitution gave it over the other branches of the government.

Dr. Eusebio Canabal was entrusted with the presentation of the charges to the Senate, where Páez also had enemies and where, more important, General Santander had a great deal of influence. As in the House of Representatives, all the latter's friends in the Senate manifested hostility toward the accused. Francísco Soto, who had prosecuted Infante and voted against Peña, displayed all the perversity of his nature against Páez. A very close friend of Santander, he was reputed to be the mouthpiece for the latter's opinions. It was not, then, venturesome to conjecture that the vice-president favored the charges, since Soto advocated them so energetically. Contrary to all the dictates of prudence, and perhaps contrary to justice, the Senate admitted the charges, and General Páez was therefore suspended from his post. General Escalona, his personal enemy who had brought the charges, was appointed by Santander to succeed Páez in the post of commandant general.

With the exception of Congress and the government, there was but one opinion with respect to the hasty action of the assembly. All those who had a clear understanding of the state of affairs not only disapproved this action, but also looked forward with dread to its consequences. The opinion most commonly held was that General Páez could not expect even strict justice and that, refusing to appear, he would appeal for support to the forces that he had at his disposal and in which he had blind confidence. Furthermore, it was held that he would encounter little difficulty in persuading a great part of the people to follow him if he promised them separation from Cundinamarca. This was the substance of the opinions communicated to the Liberator by men of great respectability. General Santander did no more than tell him that "the Senate had admitted the charges introduced against Páez by the House of Representatives for *petty mistakes* made by him when forming the militia" (O'Leary's italics).[1]

Now it is necessary to return to Venezuela and to follow the course of events in that country, starting with the period of the elections in 1825. The elections had taken place without causing any great disturbances, and some persons believed that the constitution had had its severest test. People refused to believe, however, that the stability of the government depended upon the men who had established independence rather than upon the intrinsic goodness of the institutions.

When the supporters of federalism in Venezuela saw their cherished hopes of success thwarted by the results of the elections, they changed their tactics. The very people who had worked for years to discredit the centralist system suddenly went to the other extreme. They actually considered the establishment of a monarchy to be the only remedy for the evils that threatened the Republic because of European pressure and the legislative anarchy they pretended to foresee. To achieve success with its new plan, the Caracas faction had to seek support from the very man who had previously made it observe law and order. Though the undertaking seemed difficult, it was easy to take advantage of

[1] Letter of May 28, 1826, one day after the hearing. *Memorias*, III, 250.

Páez, and the idea of monarchy flattered his ambition. He welcomed the plan, and then he decided to find out how the Liberator felt and to inform him of the need for the plan, at the same time sounding out public opinion and making ready to put it into effect. There is not the slightest doubt that the first reaction was favorable when he spoke of it in Caracas and in the departments, and that many important and influential people gave their support to it.

In his letter to the Liberator, Páez gave an adequate idea of the aims of the new party, and it may well be that the picture therein presented of the political situation in Colombia was not exaggerated. He deplored the damage caused by intrigue under a government dominated by lawyers who openly attacked and humiliated the army, to which they owed their very lives, and who managed the elections as they pleased while the people remained indifferent to governmental activity. In his opinion the country certainly needed a system different from the present one. Describing the calamity that would ensue if the Liberator were to abandon the country, he urged him to complete his work by destroying the domestic enemies. On the twenty-first of the same month (October 21, 1825) Páez wrote to the Liberator again, saying that the bearer of the letter and of a duplicate of his previous one would supply all the information that could not be stated in a letter.

The bearer of these letters was Antonio Leocadio Guzmán, the publisher of *Argos,* who was the one chosen to carry out this important plot. He also carried letters from some of the principal actors in the plot and from individuals who had previously been fanatical demagogues. One of those who wrote was General Mariño, who, ever since the beginning of the revolution, had gotten himself into the most absurd situations through his futile attempts to compete with the Liberator. In his letter he told the Liberator that the one from General Páez expressed his own feelings, and he invited him to save the country, since no sacrifice should be avoided to make independence secure.

While Guzmán was pursuing his mission, the monarchists were winning adherents in the army and among the people, but public order was not disturbed until after the occurrence of the event that gave rise to the prosecution of General Páez. A friend of the general in the House of Representatives kept him informed of the course of the hearing and of the presentation of the charges in the Senate. Since Páez was not accustomed to tolerating any opposition, the first news that he received made a deep impression on him, and he immediately expressed great dissatisfaction. On April 26, 1826, there arrived in Valencia, where he was at the time, the official letter from the government informing him of the Senate's decision, of his suspension from his post, and of the order to turn over his command to General Escalona. He was already prepared for the Senate's verdict, but not for the appointment of a successor so little to his liking. This news cut him to the quick, and rage and resentment instilled in him a desire to destroy all his enemies.

At that time there was in Valencia, enjoying the confidence of Páez, a man who considered himself to have been insulted by Congress and the government and who had also been summoned for trial on the charge of having defrauded the Republic of a sum of money. This was Dr. Miguel Peña, who had conceived in Bogotá the unpatriotic plan of taking revenge on his public enemies at the expense of the public welfare. Suave of manner, astute, and ingenious, Peña did not take long to acquire over Páez the ascendancy that a man endowed with intellectual vigor generally achieves over those who owe their prominence to the exercise of their physical advantages. Susceptible to flattery, like all men of this type, Páez allowed Peña to rule him completely, and, from the time of the first news of the charges, he consulted him frequently. The latter took advantage of his confidence to further his own desires for vengeance. With this dishonest aim in mind, he cited the example of his own trial and reminded Páez of his previous brilliant career, of the envy it had aroused in Santander, of the constant efforts of the members of Congress to humble the military class, and of the little justice that he could expect from such men. Finally, standing up in front of Páez, who was listening to him in silence, he took the government note from the table, opened it, read it, and, holding it out in his two hands, said: "No matter which way you look at this paper, it means only one thing—revolution." This revolution had already been decided upon, and the means to accomplish it had been adopted.

With the pretext of seeking means for the maintenance of the troops, permission was obtained from the governor of the province of Carabobo, Fernando Peñalver, to ask the citizens of Valencia for a loan. For this purpose Jacinto Mujica, the second civil authority in the province, summoned the citizens to a meeting, which was held at the city hall on April 27, 1826. After discussing the loan, they took up the matter of Páez's suspension, which was the real reason for the gathering. After Dr. Peña and other lawyers expressed their opinion that there was no legal way to set aside the order for his suspension, the municipal council passed a resolution in which it expressed its regret and that of the entire population over the charges brought against the commandant general. This wise decision did not satisfy the aims of those who wanted to create a disturbance, and they succeeded in having the meeting adjourned until the twenty-ninth, with the excuse that the amount subscribed on that day was not sufficient to satisfy the army's urgent needs. Páez, meanwhile, consented to recognize Escalona as commandant general of the department.

When Governor Peñalver was informed of the events of the twenty-seventh, he notified Mujica that he would not consent to the meeting on the twenty-ninth. His laudable conduct irritated the agitators, among whom were a number of officers, including two members of General Páez's staff. On the twenty-ninth a large number of soldiers and civilians gathered in the main square, where they noisily demanded the suspension of the government's order and made seditious and threatening remarks, with the object of intimidating the governor and the peaceful part of the population. The governor, accompanied by the city councillors and Dr. Peña, in his capacity as adviser, appeared in the council hall, where there was a group of citizens, among them many of the agitators. Undeterred by the shouting of the latter, Peñalver took the floor and declared that the meeting was illegal, having been promoted by a faction. His speech was greeted by some with signs of displeasure and answered with shouts and insults, but nothing was accomplished in the council meeting.

That same day Páez answered the official communication he had received from the government informing him of his suspension. In his reply he stated that he would turn over his command to his successor as soon as the latter arrived at headquarters. He also wrote on the same date to the vice-president, expressing to him his willingness to accept the Senate's decision, which he hoped would be favorable to him.

The agitators, who became desperate as a result of the unexpected firmness shown by the illustrious Peñalver, decided to use terror to achieve what they had not been able to gain through less objectionable means. Some soldiers in disguise and a group of civilians, fanning out through the area around Valencia, alarmed the peaceful inhabitants and insulted those whom they encountered on the way. Then they murdered three hapless farm workers who had not in any way provoked or opposed them. The bloody corpses of these unfortunate victims were taken to Valencia and placed before the city hall door on the morning of the thirtieth. Such a horrible spectacle could not help but alarm the inhabitants, and it was obvious that the intention of the murderers was to threaten with the same punishment those who opposed the faction's plans. The municipal council, spurred to action by the disorderly activity of the agitators, met in an extraordinary session and decided to summon the governor so that he might arrange with it the measures needed to maintain public order.

After the governor appeared, a long and heated discussion arose concerning whether or not General Páez should be restored to his post. Peñalver declared that this did not lie within the sphere of his authority and that no human consideration would induce him to violate his oath. Entreaties and threats were alternately used to win him over or to intimidate him, but to no avail. How fortunate Colombia would have been if she had had many native sons like this illustrious friend of Bolívar! The municipal councillors did not have the same strength of character. Frightened by the shouts of the agitators, who acclaimed Páez head of the department and led him to the hall where the corporation was meeting, they yielded and decreed that he should be restored to his command.

Páez informed the Liberator of these events in his letter of May 25. After reviewing the actions leading up to his suspension and his decision to obey the Senate's orders, he went on to say that he finally assumed the responsibility of protecting the people against the common enemies and any imprudent action of the Bogotá government. His concluding words were a plea to the Liberator to come and take command. Páez accepted a command founded on the violence and the threats of a faction that included some of his most intimate friends, and he thereby committed an act of rebellion against the Republic. The resolution in which his compromises with lawlessness and crime are recorded also preserves the memory of Peñalver's sublime act of courage, which inspired such great respect among the very ones who trampled the laws under foot that they requested him to continue in office. After a lengthy struggle with himself, he yielded, "in order to repay the favor shown him by a city that acclaimed him and protested its confidence in him."[2]

The disorders and uprisings came to an end when Páez was restored to power, since the agitators had already achieved their first objective. The municipal council of Valencia sent word of the event to the other councils in the province and to the authorities of the departments of old Venezuela. This circular letter, dictated by Peña, announced the restoration of General Páez to the full authority he had exercised in the post of commandant general.[3] The agitators had already included in their plans the whole territory of old Venezuela, perhaps without consulting General Páez. The main concern of Peña and Carabaño was now to persuade him that he would be lost if he turned back.

The news of General Santander's re-election and of the charges against Páez did not fail to arouse in Caracas some fear as to the consequences. Fortunately, the civil authority of the department was in the hands of Dr. Cristóbal Mendoza, a citizen who had acquired the respect and confidence of his compatriots. His prudent conduct might have prevented any incident likely to arise if the unfortunate happening of April 30 in Valencia had not stirred up the people of Caracas. Everything remained quiet, however, until May 5, when considerable alarm was noted among the people as a result of rumors spread by the agitators that troops were approaching Caracas under the command of General Mariño in order to compel the inhabitants to make common cause with Valencia.

At an extraordinary session of the municipal council, Domingo Navas Spínola, as political chief, explained the reason for the meeting

[2] Valencia resolutions of April 30.

[3] Governor Peñalver, president of the municipal council, protested against the circular letter.

and expressed the opinion that it was necessary to enter into correspondence with General Páez, the municipal council of Valencia, and
General Mariño. Señor Iribarren, an old supporter of federalism, proposed the explicit recognition of General Páez as commandant general.
When the intendant, Mendoza, realized that any opposition on his part
was futile, he retired after declaring that any decision coming from
that body was illegal. Not in the least intimidated, the agitators approved Iribarren's proposal and immediately appointed two commissions, one to inform General Mariño of the deliberations and the other
to present to General Páez the resolution recognizing him and conferring upon him full power to arrange a settlement.[4]

These proceedings were, without a doubt, the product of intrigue
and threats, for it is incredible that the same men who four months
previously had sent to Congress the petition that gave rise to the charges
against Páez should now violate the law in order to place above it the
very man about whose arbitrariness they had complained. The individuals appointed to the commissions by the municipal council of Caracas,
as well as those who took an active part in sponsoring the resolutions of
this city, were a threat to Colombia's institutions. It is pleasing, however, to find that there were some men who had no part in this story
of weakness.

The resolution that appeared in Valencia on May 12 dealt a more
terrible blow to the social order and completely revealed the aims of
the agitators. The delegates from Caracas and the municipal councillors
of Valencia placed Páez in supreme command of the department, with
the title of superior civil and military chief and with authority "to raise
armies to defend the territory from any foreign invasion or other hostile
acts." They declared that "his authority shall last as long as required
by the circumstances, which, it is hoped, will change upon the arrival
of the Liberator President." The people of Venezuela would then be
convoked to discuss the form of government most suitable for their
situation. It was also decreed that an envoy should be sent to the Liberator to request him to visit his native land. On May 14, Páez took a
formal oath "to observe and enforce the established laws, but not to
obey the new orders from the Bogotá government."

[4] Caracas resolutions of May 5.

It was not considered necessary even to pretend that the people had had a part in this final usurpation of sovereignty. A great step forward was thus taken in the plan to separate Venezuela from the rest of Colombia and to gain control of public affairs. At the instigation of these same men of the faction, the municipal council of Caracas ratified the Valencia resolutions, with the result that the general government was actually no longer recognized in the department of Venezuela. The municipal councils of San Fernando de Apure and Achaguas abided by the Valencia resolutions and sent their delegates to Valencia so that a manifesto justifying the rebellion might be formulated. This assembly met on June 29 and drew up resolutions containing a list of excuses offered to justify the illegal proceedings. Venezuela's troubles were attributed for the most part to the "abuses and usurpations with which the vice-president of the Republic, Francisco de Paula Santander, had curbed the happiness of these inhabitants." Although several of these abuses really had been committed, it must be admitted that the guardians of public liberty in Venezuela did not avail themselves of their right to accuse that magistrate through the legal channels afforded by the constitution.

After his authority was recognized in Caracas, Páez appeared there, accompanied by Dr. Peña, whom he had made his secretary, and other leaders of the revolt. Although urged to remove Mendoza from his intendancy, he did not dare to do so, because of the popularity enjoyed by the latter. Mendoza, for his part, decided to remain in office and to be as friendly as possible with Páez in order to discover his real intentions. The latter general, who might not have acted thus if he had been better advised, tried to flatter all the parties. He protested to the enemies of the Union that he had no personal interest at stake and that he wanted to have all desired reforms made through the great convention. The good patriots felt most optimistic about his statement that he was interested only in the public welfare, having accepted the post that he held in order to preserve domestic order and keep the nation intact until the Liberator arrived. Since almost everyone shared the same opinion concerning the Liberator, there was not much opposition to the progress of the revolt in Caracas.

Acting in accord with the general wishes, Páez sent a commission to the Liberator to request him to come quickly and to assure him that the people desired some reforms and would like to have him suggest them. In his official note he stated that without the Liberator there could be no peace, for civil war was inevitable. He complained that the insidious character of General Santander had poisoned the very wellspring of his administration and that the legislative body had followed his whims. The commisson was entrusted to Dr. Diego B. Urbaneja and Colonel Diego Ibarra. The former was a well-educated and judicious patriot who had held distinguished positions and was thoroughly aware of the real state of public opinion in Venezuela. The latter was a valiant soldier and former aide of the Liberator who had unfortunately acquired prejudices that prevented him from being an impartial judge. His attachment to the Liberator bordered on fanaticism, and Páez, knowing this, completely won his sympathy by vehemently declaring his own loyalty to the chosen idol.

Through Ibarra, General Páez renewed the offer that he had previously made to the Liberator through Briceño and Guzmán, to use all his influence in establishing a monarchy in Colombia. In a letter confided to Ibarra, he said that no one could make him change his mind except the Liberator and that the latter could count on him, for he had not been disloyal, nor did he have any desire to be.[5] Perhaps these were Páez's real sentiments at that moment, but it was difficult for him to adhere resolutely to his purpose, surrounded as he was by scheming men who had the assistance of a press that was now spreading seditious ideas without any restraint. For fear that the government might use force to make him obey, he quickly took every possible measure to ensure security: military preparations were hastily made, new units were raised, the militia was called into service, and detachments were stationed at the border of Cundinamarca.

The events in Valencia and Caracas made a painful impression in the adjacent departments of Maturín and Zulia, and they were generally disapproved. General Páez sent commissioners from Caracas to inform the authorities in the other sections of the recent occurrences and to solicit their cooperation. General Bermúdez, who was then in Barcelona, learned of the Valencia affair through Dr. Francisco Aranda, a

[5] Mariño also wrote on this occasion, repeating his opinions in favor of monarchy.

young lawyer who had been named legal adviser of the intendancy of Cumaná. An old rival of General Páez, Bermúdez warmly welcomed the opportunity to ruin him. Without waiting for official news, he hastened to declare his own department in a state of emergency. Despite the poverty of the people, he extracted from them unnecessary sacrifices, thus sowing the seed of discord. Even though Bermúdez's zeal was imprudent, he did no more than anticipate the orders of the supreme government. General Urdaneta, the commandant general of Zulia, who was more discreet and farseeing, adopted conciliatory measures that kept his department quiet for some time. Páez respected Urdaneta, and he tried to win him over. Urdaneta did not adopt any hostile measures, nor did he declare his department in a state of emergency, until he received express orders from the government. The esteem in which he was held enabled him to maintain order, but this situation came to an end when he took more energetic measures.

A communication from the intendant of Venezuela, which reached Bogotá on June 3 by way of Cartagena, contained exact information about the conflict in Valencia on April 30. When General Santander invited a few influential people and various members of Congress to give him their opinions concerning the alarming event, they suggested the desirability of convoking an extraordinary session of congress and of immediately summoning the Liberator President to head the government. Santander's pride did not permit him to follow this prudent and patriotic advice. He recalled that at an earlier date he had informed the Liberator in an official note that "the territory of the Republic was quiet as far as the war was concerned and was not disturbed by domestic factions, either." He probably concluded, not without reason, that the inaccuracy of that information might lead to the accusation that he was a man of little foresight or a man of bad faith. He first thought of ordering an invasion of the rebel territory, but General Soublette, secretary of war, succeeded in convincing him of the imprudence of this plan and of the inability of the government to execute it.

More suitable orders were then issued in order to prevent the contagion from spreading to the adjacent departments, but none of these measures had the effect intended by the executive power, because General Santander's personal activity was not in accord with his official conduct. Forgetting the dignity of his position, this magistrate seized control of the press and, through the medium of the *Gaceta Oficial* and other newspapers, tried to awaken the spirit of provincialism and to sow discord between Venezuelans and Granadines. All his secret efforts tended to produce greater bitterness and to make reconciliation more and more difficult.

Finally stirred to action by the extent of the evil and the clamors of the people, Santander wrote to the Liberator and revealed to him the true state of the country, which he alone had tried to hide from him. In these letters Santander blamed the untimely liberality of Congress, the indiscreet use of the freedom of the press, and the confusing mass of laws for much of the trouble. People were not paying the taxes and fraud was being practiced on all sides. In his opinion the presence of the Liberator in Colombia had become absolutely necessary, for he was the only one who could save the country from anarchy or civil war.

The dark tones of this picture do not exaggerate the situation in the least. New events were yet to cast further gloom over the political scene and to set in motion all the elements of discord before Bolívar could arrive to calm the tempest with the magic of his prestige. It is worth noting that instead of urging the Liberator to take the helm from the beginning, General Santander had used every effort to dissuade him from taking this step and to strengthen by all the means within his power the aversion that, as he well knew, Bolívar had to administrative tasks. In a confidential letter of July 19, he had suggested to the Liberator that he should not come to head the government, because in that position he would be involved in a thousand difficulties and would win enemies, thus damaging his moral prestige, without which Colombia could not prosper. It was at a later date, on October 6, 1826, when the entire Republic was bordering on anarchy, that Santander pointed out to the Liberator that "the domestic tranquillity of the Republic and its security abroad require your presence in the capital." In order to comprehend the full significance of this demand, it is necessary to take into account the effects caused in other departments by the event of April 30 in Venezuela.

CHAPTER TWENTY-SIX

O NCE THE CRY OF REVOLT had been raised in the northern part of the Republic, its echo resounded at the opposite end, and its evil influence spread in every direction. In another chapter we saw evidence of the lack of harmony between the laws passed by the congresses and the needs of the southern departments of Colombia in the sad state to which they were reduced. The Goldschmidt failure and the subsequent protest of the drafts drawn by the government, which were bought in Guayaquil, were a fatal blow to the commerce of that city. News of this misfortune was followed shortly by news of the movement in Venezuela. On July 6, 1826, the municipal council met and drew up resolutions in which it expressed profound regret over the events in Venezuela and announced its adherence to the law, its hopes that the

Liberator would stop the separatist movement, and its opinion that the time had arrived to revise the constitution. The resolutions were approved by the citizens, but for the factions that Guayaquil harbored in its midst they were only a signal for action. The federalists, above all, believed that the moment had arrived to advance their claims in earnest.

When Lieutenant Colonel Cipriano Mosquera, newly appointed intendant of the department, arrived in the city on July 9, he was welcomed with shouts of "Death to Congress" and "Long live the federation." On the following day the disturbance was repeated, and the municipal council met in an extraordinary session, which was attended by Mosquera. He was recognized, as the government had ordered, after being required to declare himself in favor of the federation. The disturbances ceased upon the arrival of an individual who announced that the Liberator was leaving Callao for Guayaquil on July 12. Despite the attempts of some agitators to upset the public order by means of a subversive pamphlet, a truce was tacitly established between monarchists, federalists, centralists, and independents—the parties causing division in the city.

Soon after word was received in Quito of the events of April 30 in Valencia and of the disturbance in Guayaquil, the people enthusiastically took advantage of the occasion thus presented. The municipal council invited the intendant, Pedro Murgueytío, to an extraordinary session at which there was a discussion of the dangerous situation of the country. A proposal was made to substitute the former financial system of the Spanish government for the present system of direct taxes. Although the great majority of the assembly gave its support to this measure, the intendant, after a lengthy discussion, succeeded in preventing adoption of the measure and in having the resolutions limited to an expression of agreement with the Guayaquil resolutions. The assembly also decided to send Colonels Aguirre and Payares to the Liberator to express its wishes to him.

Since, however, the municipal council of Quito was not satisfied with the resolutions that it had signed, it sent a confidential statement to the Liberator on July 19, 1826. This document is of the greatest importance. It reveals the state of misery to which the country had been reduced by the premature adoption of a system for which the people were not ready, the unlimited confidence of these same people in Bolívar, and the opportunity they afforded him to give further proof of his disinterestedness by constantly resisting the temptation of a crown. The council deplored the prohibitive and oppressive laws, the lack of revenue and the opposition to paying taxes, and the miserable condition of Ecuador's manufacturing industry, which was the only hope of wealth. In view of this situation, the council resolved "that His Excellency the Liberator President of Colombia should have a permanent position in the supreme government, either as president for life *or in whatever capacity he deems best.*"

The third southern department, like the other two, was thrown into turmoil. On July 30 a group of agitators paraded through the streets of Cuenca cheering the federation and cursing the existing constitution. The intendant, General Ignacio Torres, asked General Jesús Barreto, the military commander, for help, which the latter refused to give, asking in turn for an open meeting of the municipal council. Trouble was avoided through the mediation of the municipal council, which requested and received permission from the intendant to hold an extraordinary session. The council met on the following day and was able to avert the terrible storm that was threatening Azuay by expressing adherence to the decision of the other departments and invoking the name of Bolívar, which was the rallying cry for all the parties.

The state of the South in those days was truly sad. Society was divided in opinion, and the army was dissatisfied and wanted to destroy the existing system in order to raise a throne on the ruins for the leader to whom it was devoted. Letters to the Liberator from General Juan J. Flores, commandant general of Ecuador, and Lieutenant Colonel T. C. Mosquera, intendant of Guayaquil, indicated that most of the army was in favor of a constitutional monarchy. The clergy made common cause with the military, while the lawyers spoke in favor of federalism. A demand for reforms was being made by everyone. The official letter from the Liberator's secretary-general, in reply to the Guayaquil municipal council's communication of July 10, helped to calm the general excitement. He stated that the events in Valencia had not disrupted the Colombia pact of union and that the reasons given by Guayaquil for a revision of the constitution would be carefully considered by the national representative body. He added that the Liberator had expressed his political beliefs in the constitution presented to Bolivia. A few days after this letter was received, Señores Demarquet and Antonio Leocadio Guzmán arrived in Guayaquil, where they had been sent by the Liberator to announce his impending return to Colombia.

Upon his return to Lima from Bolivia in February, 1826, the Liberator met Guzmán, who had been commissioned by General Páez to propose to him the establishment of a monarchy in Colombia. At almost the same time he received communications filled with the gloomiest predictions from distinguished persons who stressed the fact that the only way to save the country was for him to return. The vice-president alone advised the Liberator to remain in Peru and described the situation of the Republic in glowing terms. Bolívar did not doubt the truth of this information, because he had great confidence in Santander and because he was reluctant to suspect a friend whom he had every right to believe sincere.

Bolívar considered Páez's proposal alarming and rejected it without a moment's hesitation. His ideas and decision in this respect are eloquently expressed in several letters written during this period. In a letter to Briceño Méndez on February 27, 1826, he said that the best remedy would be to send Páez his draft of a constitution for Bolivia and to tell him that reform could be effected in 1831. Writing to Santander on February 21, he declared that the proposed plan for a monarchy hurt him more than all the insults of his enemies, since it presupposed that he was capable of descending to the level of an Iturbide.[1] In his reply to General Páez on March 6, he declared that nothing could justify the course proposed, for Colombia was not France and he was not Napoleon. For him the title of Liberator was superior to any other. As a basis for the future revision of the constitution, he recommended

[1] General Agustín Iturbide was a royalist officer who joined the patriot forces in Mexico and played a prominent role in the fight for independence. In 1822 he was proclaimed Emperor Agustín I, but he was soon forced to abdicate. He was shot upon his return to Mexico in 1824. —Ed.

the plan of a constitution he had designed for Bolivia. His final advice to Páez was not to do for himself what he, Bolívar, would not permit to be done for him.

Every day the Liberator's position became more and more difficult because of the unusually rapid sequence of events. The accusation against General Páez, which he learned about from Pando upon his return to Peru, was the event that he considered most important. The accuracy of the forecast that he had made concerning the prospects for Colombia, even before he knew with certainty the state of public opinion in Venezuela and what would happen in Peru after his departure, can be seen in his letter to General Santander on May 7. Commenting on the report of an imminent Spanish expedition backed by the Holy Alliance, he ventured the opinion that if the idea of an empire were accepted, there would be peace with the outside world and civil war at home. On the other hand, if the Republic were defended, there would be war abroad and anarchy at home. If he were to go to Colombia, he said, his presence would only increase the anger of the factions, with each one claiming that he had come to support it. As he saw it, whether General Páez obeyed or disobeyed, the latter being more likely, the Spaniards would be expected to benefit from the general confusion. Then again, if he were to leave Peru before a real authority had been created, all the factions would throw off every restraint and fight each other. As against the idea of an empire from Potosí to the Orinoco, he stated that he favored the proposal of a true federation composed of the three sister republics with himself as protector. He added that the position of Venezuela and Cartagena was doubtful.

Weeks and months passed, and the head of the Colombian government still remained silent about the perils that the Liberator's other correspondents declared were inevitable. Convinced, however, that the Senate had admitted the charges against General Páez, and fearful of the consequences of this step, the Liberator decided to send me to Colombia to determine the real state of the country and to inquire about public opinion with respect to reform. I was to come to an understanding with the vice-president concerning what it would be best to say to Páez on behalf of the Liberator, and, above all, I was to inform Páez that the Liberator would be deeply distressed were he to do anything to disturb the public peace. I carried letters written by the Liberator to Santander, Páez, and all the most influential persons in Venezuela, calling upon them to prevent the spread of an evil that gave him great concern. It was already late, for the evil had by now grown and spread.

Near the end of June the Liberator received by way of Panama the first news of the disturbances in Valencia. This news, which was vague and confusing, was sent from Caracas by Dr. Cristóbal Mendoza, intendant of Venezuela, and by one of Bolívar's own sisters. This sister forwarded to him a letter written to her by General Páez a few days after the event, in which he said that "General Bolívar's name was engraved on his heart and he invoked it with every breath." When the Liberator received the Guayaquil resolution of July 6, he felt somewhat reassured, because the exaggerated news he had received from that department had led him to fear the worst consequences. The letters from Páez and Mendoza also helped to set his mind at ease. In a letter written after receiving these communications, he said: "I see a ray of hope piercing the frightful darkness in which I imagined that territory to be enveloped, and I am confident that I shall be able to reorganize Colombia and save the work for which so many sacrifices have been made."

The prolonged and unexplainable silence of General Santander prevented the Liberator from coming to a definite decision. He therefore decided to wait in Lima for communications from the government and in the meantime to send Guzmán to Colombia to announce his impending return and to inform the persons of influence about his opinions. These opinions were expressed in letters to be delivered by Guzmán. This choice was not a very happy one in view of the particular circumstances that unfortunately pointed toward Guzmán as one of the leaders of the Venezuela faction, but the Liberator wished to take advantage of the influence that he supposed Guzmán would have over General Páez. Be this as it may, feelings had been aroused to such a point in Colombia that even the mission of an angel would have been unsuccessful.

In one of the letters mentioned above, a circular letter written in Lima on August 3, 1826, the Liberator noted that not only Colombia, but all the republics of South America, wanted reform in order to eliminate the weakness of their political structure. He contended that the draft constitution he had submitted to Bolivia could become the keystone of unity and stability for these governments, since it combined all the advantages of federalism, all the firmness of centralized government, and all the stability of monarchical regimes, at the same time that it allowed for the most direct participation of citizens in the exercise of sovereignty. He concluded this letter with a recommendation that the Bolivian code of laws be examined and adopted in Colombia, with whatever modifications deemed suitable. In another letter, this one to General Briceño Méndez on August 8, he spoke of his great uneasiness over the danger threatening Colombia and of the plan that Guzmán would describe to him in detail. After urging Briceño Méndez to write to Venezuela about the matter, he emphasized the need to keep everything in its present state until his return to Colombia, since any imprudent outburst or separation from the government would mean the loss of reputation, morale, the army, and the very existence of the nation. He said that he had everything ready and packed for his trip and that he would have departed already had they called him back to Colombia. He noted, however, that General Santander had always described the internal situation of the Republic in the most glowing terms and that the latter's latest communication said only that he would summon him should the need be urgent. In a letter to General Páez the Liberator declared that a great volcano lay at their feet and that he had very little hope of seeing order restored in Colombia, for its fate was sealed the day that Páez was summoned by Congress. The idea of a prince under a federal constitution was, he added, visionary and absurd, as his poor delirium of a constitution might also appear to be. Even so, he just had to say something in the midst of so much conflict. Expressing the wish that the Bolivian code could be adapted to small states within a vast confederation, he told Páez that Guzmán would give him his ideas on the subject. He advised Páez that the most sensible thing to do at the moment was to keep public authority strong in order to check abuses. This letter would seem to have been dictated by the genius of prophecy, for everything in it has come true.

Once Guzmán had been sent on his way, the Liberator made ready to carry out his decision to return to Colombia. He undertook the trip despite the urgent pleas repeatedly voiced by the Peruvians in their efforts to keep him among them. In the meantime, however, extraordinary events occurred that made the state of affairs in the South and the general situation of Colombia even more complicated. It is essential to relate them for a complete understanding of the difficulty involved in undertaking the reorganization of the latter country.

Anarchy had made formidable progress in the southern departments, and the exaggerated reports frequently received about the advances made by the spirit of disunity in other sections and about the threats of foreign enemies increased the alarm of the people. In Cuenca the quarrel between the civil and military authorities kept the inhabitants split into two sharply divided factions. The Masonic societies, on the other hand, were a source of great annoyance to the fanatics, who, in their turn, incited the people against them. All Azuay felt the evil influence of these disturbances. A military uprising in Quito on August 22 filled the city with consternation. Part of the Araure Battalion, which had received orders to march to the capital, staged a revolt outside the city. The personal bravery of General J. José Flores prevented the city's being looted or even burned and saved the inhabitants from the annoyances to which they would have been exposed by the enraged mob of soldiers. The province of Pasto was in the most abject state, and its garrison was on the point of either perishing from hunger or taking matters into its own hands. The authorities had to exercise constant vigilance in order to prevent any outbreak on the part of the inhabitants of that turbulent district.

Such were the circumstances when Señores Guzmán and Demarquet arrived in Guayaquil. The former had been entrusted with a mission to the coastal departments of New Granada and of Venezuela, similar to the one that the latter had to the southern departments. The Liberator's ideas were enthusiastically received by all those to whom they were communicated. Motivated by a desire to anticipate the benefits that they confidently expected after the Liberator's arrival, a large number of citizens asked the intendant for an open meeting of the municipal council on August 28. The resolutions passed at this meeting stated that the people of Guayaquil were reassuming their sovereign authority and delivering it into the hands of the Liberator, that they hoped the great convention would meet as soon as possible, and that they would like to see the Bolivian Constitution adopted. No coercion of any kind was employed in the adoption of this extraordinary measure, for there was complete harmony among the group. Civilians and soldiers, office-holders and nonofficeholders, rich and poor—all voted in favor of it.

Guayaquil's example quickly spread to the neighboring departments. Quito manifested its joy in a most enthusiastic manner when it placed its fate in the hands of the Liberator by entrusting him with dictatorial power and expressing approval of the Bolivian code. The individuals in the country who were most noted for their wealth, their learning, and their influence were the ones who showed the most interest in promoting these measures. Their praise of the Bolivian code brought it great popularity in the entire South. They regarded it as a source of future benefits, inasmuch as the mere mention of it had resulted in the disappearance, for the time being, of the differences of opinion that had kept the country divided until then. When posterity passes judgment on the culpability of the authorities in promoting the resolutions that violated the constitution, it will, if its judgment is to be just, have to bear in mind that the vice-president himself said the constitution was *"the cause of all of Colombia's evils"* (O'Leary's italics).

At dawn on September 12, 1826, the brig *Congreso* dropped anchor in the Guayaquil estuary, bringing the Liberator back to his own country. Upon learning of his arrival, the intendant, the other authorities of the department, and a few private citizens went on board to pay him their respects. It was then that the Liberator learned in detail of the ills produced in Colombia by inadequate institutions and an inexperienced and corrupt administration. It was then also that he was given to understand that General Santander, dazzled by power and consumed by greed, was more attentive to his own interests than grateful to the benefactor who had placed him in eminent posts. The pride of the patriot and the sensibilities of the man were wounded by these revelations, but Bolívar turned a deaf ear to the insinuations about hatred and ingratitude and thought only of alleviating the distress of the people.

Never had such enthusiasm been displayed in the city as that which the people showed when they saw on their shores the man whom everyone wanted. From that moment the country's wounds were considered healed. In a proclamation to his compatriots the Liberator announced that he had come, bearing an olive branch, to offer his services again and that he alone was to blame for their strife, since he had not come in time. He urged his compatriots to put an end to the crime of their disunity, to be Colombians rather than inhabitants of Cundinamarca or Venezuela. This eloquent document would have quieted the uneasiness had words sufficed to stem the tide of revolution that had already smashed all the bulwarks of society in its rapid advance.

The Liberator gave his entire attention to the resolutions adopted in the South. Even though he himself was of the opinion that only a dictatorship could save the country, he bowed before the law and ordered the re-establishment of constitutional order. Vesting himself then with the powers prescribed by the constitution, he made some improvements in the departmental administration and alleviated the misery of the garrison. With his characteristic generosity he remedied the hardships of a few private individuals out of his own funds. Furthermore, he promoted the intendant, Mosquera, to the rank of colonel and gave other promotions to officials who had had a part in formulating the popular resolutions. These latter measures were criticized, and perhaps rightly so, but since he had disapproved the southern resolutions, he believed that it was advisable to give positive evidence of the fact that the reconciliation he planned admitted of no distinctions. Consequently, in accordance with this principle of impartiality, Obando, governor of Pasto, whose province had remained loyal to the established government, was rewarded in common with Mosquera, the promoter of the Guayaquil resolution.

After six days in Guayaquil the Liberator left for Quito, where he arrived on September 28. He spent seven days in the capital, acquainting himself with the state of affairs in the South and providing some measures to remedy in part the ills of the people. He was sorry to see that the nature of the reforms needed was such that he could not take appropriate action in the time at his disposal. He therefore appointed special commissions for each department to consult the people themselves about their complaints. He left his secretary, General José Gabriel Pérez, in Quito to assemble the data to be submitted to him by the commissioners. He asked him to inquire into the causes of the insolvency of the public treasury, to determine what kind of taxes would yield the largest revenue with the least burden for the people, to propose a method for developing the agriculture and the manufacturing industry of the country, to improve the roads and protect commerce, to indicate the public offices that could be abolished, and, finally, to make a careful investigation of all matters related to the southern departments. He would wait until he had received this information before taking appropriate action.

On October 5, Bolívar left Quito for Pasto, where the welcome given him exceeded his expectations. Instead of a city desolated by war and factions, he found a city whose streets were crowded with people who had come from all the surrounding area to see him. His one day's stay proved beneficial to the city. Public education had been completely neglected by the government of this province, and the Liberator, assuming responsibility for it, applied part of the national revenue to its development. Wishing to put an end to the war in this section, he offered full amnesty to the rebels who had fled to the mountains, provided that they presented themselves to the authorities within two months, and he specified rewards for the citizens who apprehended any of those who failed to appear prior to the expiration of this period. The governor of Pasto, Colonel José María Obando, did not, however, wait to see how this laudable measure would work. A former royalist himself, he had Lieutenant Colonel Joaquín Paredes, who had served the King's cause for years, trick his former comrades into joining him in a supposed revolt in the canton of Túquerres. After the rebels had assembled, Paredes surprised them and turned them over to Obando, who had them shot. Colonel José María Benavides, twelve officers, and thirty-one soldiers were victims of this dishonorable and treacherous deed. Paredes received a reward, but he did not live long to enjoy it. At a later date, after he had joined Obando in a revolt headed by the latter, he was taken prisoner and shot by General Flores.

On October 15 the Liberator resumed his trip, and he reached Popayán on the twenty-third. On the way he had crossed the mountains of Berruecos, which became so well known later because of the assassination there of a great man, Antonio José de Sucre. In Popayán, as in all the other capitals through which he had passed, the inhabitants greeted him with a most enthusiastic display of affection and gratitude.

It was there that Colonel Ibarra, one of the envoys sent by General Páez, joined him after a long roundabout trip. His companion, Dr. Urbaneja, was unable to go that far, and Bolívar was thus unfortunately deprived of the impartial account of a dependable eyewitness to the events in Venezuela, which would have been useful to him and which he needed to rectify his own opinions. Leaving Popayán on the thirtieth, the Liberator traversed the frozen wastes of the paramo of Guanacas, passed through the city of La Plata, and crossed the burning plains of Neiva before arriving in the capital of the province of Neiva on November 5. The following night he continued on his way, and on the eleventh, in Tocaima, he met the vice-president of the Republic and the secretaries of war and of foreign affairs. On the fourteenth he entered the capital.

The events in Venezuela had made a deep impression in Bogotá. The centralization of the Republic had been beneficial to the capital, which, thanks to it, had advanced in civilization and wealth under the protection of the constitution. The laws were enforced there, and the taxes that impoverished the other sections of the state were not felt there, because the government, fearful of making itself unpopular, overlooked the slowness of the collectors in putting them into effect. Medieval in appearance in 1819, Bogotá was superior to most of the cities on the South American continent at the beginning of 1826. Since it had received such definite benefits from the centralist system, Páez's act of rebellion naturally produced an unfavorable impression there. The press immediately expressed its disapproval, but instead of giving prudent advice to those who had directed the movement, it turned the people against Venezuela, whose natives had never been very popular in Bogotá. Although Bolívar's great services had made the inhabitants forget that he had conquered them in 1814, they never forgot that his army was composed of Venezuelans. It was therefore not difficult to revive the former local resentment; nor was the head of the government a man who would fail to take advantage of such an opportunity.

Santander, who was subtle, astute, and ambitious, immediately conceived the idea of profiting from the disasters that he saw approaching. All the resolutions and all the newspapers of Venezuela blamed him for the evils besetting the nation, and he chose to seek personal vengeance rather than to try in good faith to relieve the nation's woes. Fearful of the result of the measures that he had adopted upon hearing of the events in Venezuela, he summoned to his side a few individuals whom he himself had shortly before charged with being perverse and rebellious. Making use of them, he started to arouse the latent spirit of provincialism that had been so damaging to the common cause in previous periods.

A new faction was formed with the vice-president at its head, and although its apparent object was to support the established institutions, it very quickly showed that it was really opposed to unity. *La Bandera Tricolor* was the organ of this party, and its editor was Dr. Vicente Azuero, a headstrong lawyer who not long before had been a fiery opponent of Santander and had opposed his re-election. The *Gaceta de Colombia*, under the immediate supervision of the vice-president himself, expressed the same ideas. The disunity sown by those who should have worked only for harmony was already beginning to have pernicious effects. Although it is true that the same means had been employed in Venezuela by a faction that was striving to further dishonest aims, it was, on the other hand, neither lawful nor proper for the head of a nation to widen the breach that that faction had opened or to imitate a course of action that was unreasonable and unpatriotic. Under the mask of liberty and its sound principles, absurd theories were proclaimed, and even the name of the Liberator, which on all sides was pronounced with reverence and invoked with fervor, was made the target of insidious and malicious attacks by the very men who a short time before had been calling upon him to save them.

The reply made by the Liberator to the municipal council of Guayaquil, when the latter proclaimed the federation, though extremely discreet, uncompromising, and written expressly for the purpose of preventing the dismemberment of the Republic, was taken as a pretext for those attacks. The vice-president's friends pretended to detect a hostile attitude toward the law in this communication and therefore proceeded to spread the most alarming rumors. Santander, meanwhile, acted with great dissimulation and succeeded for a time in deceiving the true patriots and Bolívar's best friends. He employed hypocrisy in his correspondence with Bolívar. In one letter he wrote that Bolívar should give careful consideration to the course he was to follow. If, he said, Bolívar gave in to the agitators or hotheads, he would be striking a deadly blow at the constitution and consecrating the principle of perpetual anarchy. But if, on the other hand, he did not give in, they might have civil war or rising discontent leading to a very violent explosion.

Such was his manner of speaking before the resolutions arrived from the southern part of the Republic. It was after their arrival that he revealed in part his sinister intentions. These resolutions spoke of dictatorship and expressed a preference for the Bolivian code, but at the same time they complained about the evils of the administration and the inadequacy of the laws. Santander himself had done as much, praising the Constitution of Bolivia while attributing all the ills of Colombia to the Constitution of Cúcuta and the existing laws. Nevertheless, he could not tolerate having the people declare themselves in favor of the former and against the latter. This was a sad effect of party spirit and the blindness of ambition. The *Gaceta de Colombia* criticized these resolutions, and rightly so, though more harshly than an official newspaper should. On the other hand, *La Bandera Tricolor* threatened their authors with the gallows, reviled entire groups of people, and defended tyrannicide.

The insinuations against Bolívar became more direct from day to day, and the criminal intentions of the faction more evident. Santander, without even waiting to hear the Liberator's decisions and believing his plan for separation to be sufficiently advanced, dared to remove his mask and to write to him personal letters containing paragraphs like the following: "Now with respect to the new Quito and Guayaquil resolutions, I can state with almost complete certainty that neither the Magdalena department nor Cauca nor Cundinamarca nor Boyacá is *now* in favor of the Bolivian code. This large segment of the population, governed by men of influence in the respective departments, would rather be a single republic, separate from Venezuela and Quito, if the existing institutions are not to be upheld until the time set for their revision in our code." "If the authority to advance the date for the convocation and meeting of the great convention for the revision of our institutions is upheld, I can say to you right now that there will be no

Colombian Union and that efforts will be made to re-establish the Republic of New Granada of 1815. Many men of influence think this way, and I am of the opinion that it is better to go alone rather than in bad company" (O'Leary's italics).[2] This declaration was one of the severest blows that Bolívar had received until then, inasmuch as it revealed to him the whole perilous situation in the center of the Republic and the secret dealings of those who had boasted of being supporters of the established institutions.

In the following proclamation he announced to the Colombians his return to the capital of the Republic, not to rest after so much arduous work, but "full of zeal to do the will of the people":

Colombians! Five years ago I left this capital to march at the head of the liberating army, from the banks of the Cauca River to the silvery peaks of Potosí. A million Colombians and two sister republics have obtained independence under the protection of your banners, and the world of Columbus has ceased to be Spanish. This is what we have done during our absence.

Your misfortunes have brought me back to Colombia. I come full of zeal to do the will of the people. It will be my code, for being sovereign, it is infallible.

The vote of the nation has obliged me to assume the supreme command. I utterly detest it, for it is the cause of my being accused of having ambitious aims and of attempting to set up a monarchy. So! Do people think that I am so foolish that I am anxious to lower myself? Do they not know that the position of Liberator is more sublime than a throne?

Colombians! I shall again subject myself to the intolerable burden of the magistracy, because indifference on my part in time of danger would be cowardice, not moderation. But count on me only until sovereign authority is restored to the law or to the people. Allow me, then, to serve you as a simple soldier and true republican, as a citizen bearing arms in defense of the beautiful trophies of our victories: YOUR RIGHTS.

[2] Letters of October 8 and 18, 1826. —Pedro Grases.

INDEX

Achaguas: ix, 138, 147, 148, 149, 150, 350
Addison, Captain: 250
Adlercreutz, Friedrich de: 203
Agualongo, Agustín: 233
Aguirre, Guillermo: 11
Aguirre, Vicente: 355
Aix-la-Chapelle, Congress of: 136
Alacrán: 98, 106
Alava, Miguel Ricardo de: 11
Aldama, Juan: 111, 117, 125
Aldao, Manuel: 133
Alvarado, Felipe Antonio: 225
Alvarado, Rudecindo: 226, 247
Alvarez, Manuel Bernardo: 76
Alvarez, Mariano: 304, 310
Alvarez de Arenales, Juan Antonio: 282
Alvear, Carlos: 288, 290, 291, 292, 294, 295
Alzaga, Félix: 246
Alzuru, Isidro: 104
Amador, Juan de Dios: 79
Amestoy, José Félix: 90
Andahuailas: 260, 267
Anderson, Richard C.: 327
Angostura: O'Leary goes to, ix, 137, 139; siege of, 110, 111, 112; occupied by Bermúdez, 114; Piar executed in, 119–120; Congress of, 135, 143, 144–146, 165, 170, 171–173, 174, 178, 179, 196; mentioned, 108, 118, 121, 122, 136, 138, 152
Antioquia: x, 85, 93, 164, 331
Anzoátegui, José Antonio: in Aux Cayes expedition, 101, 103, 106; wounded at Semen, 129; commands infantry at Cojedes, 133; and O'Leary, 139; in Apure campaign, 143, 146, 147, 149, 152; reputation of, 154; in Boyacá campaign, 159, 163; death of, 169–170
Apure (province): 112, 137, 143, 147, 150, 151, 174, 191
Apure River: 50, 116, 118, 133, 146, 148, 150, 152, 191
Apurímac River: 238, 255, 259, 260
Aragua, battle of: 68
Araguaquén: 137, 147

Aramendi, Francisco: 123
Aranda, Francisco: 351
Arauca River: 146, 147, 148, 149, 150, 154
Araujo e Silva, Senhor: 288, 289
Araure, battle of: 60
Arequipa: occupied by Sucre, 238; welcomes Bolívar, 277; viceroy in, 280; patrols on coast of, 285; election campaign in, 304–306; mentioned, 276, 278, 279
Argentina: 244 n. 1, 316. SEE ALSO Buenos Aires; Río de la Plata, United Provinces of the
Arica: 301
Arismendi, Juan Bautista: routed by Rosete, 63; sacrifices Spanish prisoners, 64; opposes royalists on Margarita, 84, 94; welcomes Bolívar, 101; leaves for mainland, 107; constructs *flecheras,* 112; hated by Morillo, 117; as vice-president of Venezuela, 170–171; commands Army of the East, 171
armistice: negotiated between Bolívar and Morillo, 178–184; and regularization of the war, 182–183; Bolívar's opinion of, 189; termination of, 190–191
Arrubla, Señor: 334, 337
Asanza, José de (Viceroy): 11
Asunción: 102, 113, 117
Atacama: 297
Atahuallpa: 205
Atrato River: 211
Aury, Luis: 101
Aux Cayes, expedition of: 101–105
Ayacucho: 281
Ayacucho, battle of: prologue to, 265; described by Sucre, 268; mentioned, 280, 298, 320, 321
Aymerich, Melchor: 213
Aymerich, Ramón: 36
Azuero, Vicente: 366
Azuola, Luis Eduardo: 196

Banda Oriental (Uruguay): attempted annexation of, by Brazil, 288, 290, 291, 292, 293

Bárbula, battle of: 56, 57
Barcelona: surrender of, to royalists, 68; guerrillas in llanos of, 96; occupied by patriots, 106, 107, 109, 110; occupied by royalists, 109, 112, 117; irregular warfare in, 146; mentioned, 37, 53, 120, 136, 351
Barinas: held by Tizcar, 48; captured by Bolívar, 50; safety of, ensured by Morillo, 117; Bolívar returns to, 191; mentioned, 54, 125, 150, 151, 153, 184
Barquisimeto: 34, 51, 60, 71, 181, 191, 198
Barranca: 42, 80, 176
Barranquilla: 82, 83
Barreiro, José María: opposes advance of Bolívar in New Granada, 159–162; defeated by Bolívar at Boyacá, 163; death of, 165–166; mentioned, 164, 169
Barreto, Jesús: 95, 97, 356
Bello, Andrés: 11, 22
Benavente, José María: 244
Benavides, José María: 318, 364
Beresford, William Carr: 5 and n.
Berindoaga, Juan: 246, 247, 248, 251, 311
Bermejo: 291
Bermúdez, José Francisco: returns from exile, 53, 54; in Maturín area, 70; escapes from Margarita, 84; succeeds Castillo in Cartagena, 86; rejects Bolívar's authority, 101, 105; occupies Angostura, 114; in Cumaná, 120, 122, 134, 136, 204; occupies Güiria, 135; commands Army of the East, 152, 153; in Caracas area, 193, 195; and Páez, 351–352
Berruecos: 213, 364
Blanco, José Félix: 113
Blanco Encalada, Manuel: 217
Bocachica (New Granada): 86, 203
Bocachica (Venezuela), battle of: 65
Boconó: 193
Bogotá: occupied by Bolívar, 76, 163–165, 168; made capital of New Granada, 77; plots in, 92; occupied by La Torre, 93; prisoners executed in, 165–167; named capital of Cundinamarca, 172; Bolívar arrives in, 175, 187, 365; named capital of Colombia, 200, 202; Francisco Perdomo assassinated in, 336; factions in, 365–367; mentioned, 5, 157, 170, 177, 188, 196, 198, 204, 229, 230, 327, 328, 352. SEE ALSO Colombia, Greater Republic of; Cundinamarca; New Granada
Bolívar, Juana (sister of Bolívar): 9
Bolívar, Juan Vicente (brother of Bolívar): 9

Bolívar, Juan Vicente (father of Bolívar): 9 and n. 1
Bolívar, María Antonia (sister of Bolívar): 9, 359
Bolívar, Simón: and O'Leary, ix–x, xi, 139, 209, 234 n. 2, 244, 286, 293, 307, 358–359; burial of, x, xv; ancestry and birth of, 8–9; boyhood of, 10–11; education of, 10–11, 12, 16, 18, 23, 141–142; character of, 10, 11, 40, 43, 49, 52, 55, 58, 66, 73, 74–75, 89, 120, 130, 139–142, 158, 184, 197, 201, 204, 209, 221–222, 248, 262, 290, 298–299, 321, 327; military ranks of, 11, 21, 27, 41, 58, 78, 240; travels to Spain, France, and Italy, 11–20; on government, 14, 15–16, 17, 19, 23, 27, 28, 41, 55–56, 61, 74, 88–89, 229, 298–301, 313–314, 318, 358, 359–360; marriage of, 14; death of wife of, 15; sent on mission to England, 21–23; and Miranda, 23 and n. 1, 24, 27, 28, 33, 36, 37–38; military ability of, 27, 43, 73–74, 125, 126; and earthquake, 30–31; assigned to Puerto Cabello, 34 and n. 1, 36; and Monteverde, 39–40; defeats royalists in New Granada, 40, 42–44; Venezuelan campaign of (1813–1814), 48–66; and war to death, 49–50, 103, 124, 125–126, 133, 165, 182; on union of Venezuela and New Granada, 56, 89, 144, 168, 171, 172, 175, 323; given title of Liberator, 58; given absolute power, 62; orders sacrifice of Spanish prisoners, 64–65; retreats and returns to Cartagena, 67–68, 72, 75; Santa Marta expedition of, obstructed by Castillo, 78–82; in Jamaica, 83, 87–90; attempted assassination of, 90; in Haiti, 91–92, 99, 101, 105, 107; Aux Cayes expedition of, 100–105; on slavery, 103, 145, 199–200, 315; liberates Guayana, 107, 110–115; establishes administration of Guayana, 118–119, 121; and execution of Piar, 119–120; campaign of 1818 of, 120–133; convokes Congress of Angostura, 135, 143, 144–146; sketch of, 139–142, 150, 176–177; presents constitution of 1819, 144–145; elected president of Venezuela, 145; Apure campaign of, 146–152; Boyacá campaign of, 152–165; returns to Angostura, 171; elected president of Colombia, 173; negotiates armistice with Morillo, 178–184; Carabobo campaign of, 191–196; re-elected president of Colombia, 198, 200–201; and Congress of Panama, 206–207, 265, 273, 275, 289, 292, 322–325,

327–328; Bomboná campaign of, 211–213, 215; takes charge in Guayaquil, 218–219, 223–224; meeting of, with San Martín, 220–221, 221 n. 1, 224–225; prepares expedition to Peru, 231–233, 234; and the idea of monarchy, 357, 360, 368; and the accusation against Páez, 358–359; returns to Guayaquil, 362; orders re-establishment of constitutional order, 363; returns via Quito to Bogotá, 363–365; attacked by Santander faction, 366–368
—in Peru and Bolivia: arrives in Lima, 239; and Riva-Agüero, 239–240, 241–243; given supreme authority, 240–241; visits northern provinces, 243, 245; ill in Pativilca, 246, 249; organizes government, 249–250; has headquarters in North, 251–255; Junín campaign of, 255–261; removed from command, 261–263; returns to Lima, 263; convokes Congress, 271; given supreme authority for another year, 273; travels to southern provinces and Upper Peru, introducing many reforms, 277–280, 283–286, 289–301; Bolivia named for, 283; discusses Banda Oriental and Brazil with La Plata delegates, 290–295; improves government in Bolivia, 296–298; draws up Bolivian Constitution, 298–301; returns to Peru, 301; receives supreme authority again, 310; declared president for life, 319; leaves for Guayaquil, 320
—writings and speeches of: letters, xi, xvi, 36, 41, 46, 77, 87–89, 107, 177, 179, 180, 189, 190–191, 195, 197, 200–201, 204, 209, 211, 220, 221 n. 1, 229–230, 234, 240, 245, 258, 259, 262, 269, 270, 274–275, 282, 289, 294, 311, 313, 323, 324, 357–358, 359, 360; speeches, proclamations, and decrees, 49, 61–62, 77–78, 83, 101–102, 103, 107, 118, 120, 135, 136, 144, 168, 171, 172, 175, 178, 184, 202, 211, 218–219, 241, 251, 257, 258–259, 269, 273, 286, 292, 298, 300–301, 320, 368; style, 140, 177; dictation, 141, 176–177; newspaper articles, 177, 316 and n. 1; Sucre sketch, 274–275
Bolivia: independence and name of, 283; Bolívar makes reforms in, 284–286, 296–298; Congress of, 293, 301, 315, 317; and Argentina, 294–295; Constitution of, 298–301, 315, 316, 317, 318, 319, 357, 358, 360, 362, 367; and confederation, 318; and Congress of Panama, 327; mentioned, 289, 294,

306, 357. SEE ALSO Chuquisaca; Upper Peru
Bolivian Constitution. SEE Bolivia
Bombón, heights of: 267
Bomboná, battle of: 212, 215
Bonaire: 104
Bonaparte. SEE Napoleon
Bonpland, Aimé Goujaud: 17
Bonza: 160, 161, 162
Borrás, Miguel: 105
Boves, Benito: 227, 228
Boves, José Tomás: leads royalist guerrilla troop, 59–60; appearance of, 60; victories and defeats of, 63–70 passim; death of, 70; mentioned, 74, 94, 186, 227, 330
Boyacá: 367
Boyacá, battle of: 162, 163, 164, 165, 170, 188, 235
Braun, Philipp: 257
Brazil: and invasion of Upper Peru territory, 288–289; and Banda Oriental dispute, 288, 290, 291, 292, 293, 295; and Congress of Panama, 324, 325, 327; mentioned, 228
Briceño, Antonio Nicolás: 41, 48–49
Briceño Méndez, Pedro: aids O'Leary, xv; accompanies Bolívar to Jamaica, 83; testimony of, 104; at council of war in El Mantecal, 152; as minister of war, 177; description of, 178; authorized to negotiate armistice, 179, 182; as Colombian delegate to Congress of Panama, 325, 327, 328; letters to, from Bolívar, 357, 360; mentioned, 126, 202, 351
Brión, Luis: furnishes ship to Bolívar, 91; in Aux Cayes expedition, 101, 103, 104–105; with Bolívar on Margarita and in Barcelona, 107; and Congress of Cariaco, 113; takes ships to the Orinoco, 114; appointed to Council of Government, 121; operates with Bermúdez, 135, 136; receives Bolívar's instructions, 153; ordered to convoy expedition of Irish legionaries, 173
Brisel, Mr. ———: 103
British legionaries: 134, 137, 138, 143, 146, 147, 161, 194
Buenaventura: 207, 211
Buenos Aires: Bolívar's predictions for, 88; concludes separate treaty with Spain, 243, 244; army of, crushed in 1909 revolt, 281; and Banda Oriental dispute, 288, 293; political problems of, 299; opposed to Bolívar, 315; invited to Congress of Panama, 324; mentioned, 222, 242, 287, 290, 294, 295.

SEE ALSO Argentina; Río de la Plata, United Provinces of the

Cabero, Ensign: 303
Cachirí, battle of: 92
Cádiz: 84
Cádiz, Constitution of: 52, 175 and n. 3, 178
Cagigal, Manuel: succeeds Monteverde as captain general, 62; defeated at Carabobo, 66; and Boves, 69; mentioned, 65, 74
Caicara: 122
Cajamarca: 245, 249
Calabozo: cleared of royalists, 60; Boves's troops from, 65; royalist headquarters in, 118, 123, 137; patriot headquarters in, 130, 131, 132; mentioned, 35, 61, 143, 195
Calabozo, battle of: 123–126
Caldas, Francisco José: 187
Cali: 187, 206
Calibío, battle of: 76
Callao: San Martín in, 222; Bolívar goes to, 235, 239; patriot government moves to, 237; revolt of garrison in, 247; Torre Tagle takes refuge in, 249, 311; royalist ships destroyed at, 250; patriot blockade of, 263, 272; surrender of, 307, 321; Bolívar leaves from, 320; mentioned, 244, 245, 257, 258, 264
Calzada, Sebastián de la: defeats patriots, 71, 92, 93; commands division in Barinas, 125; withdraws after battle of Boyacá, 164; occupies Popayán, 174
Camacho, Joaquín: 187
Camaguán: 132
Campo Elías, Vicente: clears royalists from Calabozo, 57, 60; defeated by Boves at La Puerta, 63; death of, 64
Canabal, Eusebio María: 342
Cañafístolo: 122
Cancino, Colonel: 211
Canning, George: 295, 325. SEE ALSO England
Canta: 245, 258, 263
Canterac, José de: arrives from Spain with expedition, 95, 117; plunders Lima, 237–238, 241; professes constitutional principles, 254; defeated at Junín, 257–258; joins Valdés, 265; mentioned, 246, 248, 270 n. 3
Caraballero, ranch of: 150
Carabaño, Francisco: 41, 332, 333, 348
Carabaño, Miguel: 38, 41
Carabobo: 66, 194, 346
Carabobo, battle of: first (May 28, 1814), 66; second (May 24, 1821), 194–195, 197, 230

Caracas: deposes captain general, 6, 20 n. 8; earthquake in, 29–31; occupied by royalists, 38–39, 69, 95, 118, 193; royalists flee from, 51–52; Bolívar arrives in, 53, 55, 195–196; sufferings of inhabitants of, 68; named capital of Venezuela, 172; votes statue in Bolívar's honor, 275; education in, 276; protests against constitution, 229, 331; protests conduct of Páez, 338–339; and conscription decree, 340–341; and monarchy, 343–344; recognizes Páez as commandant general, 348–351; mentioned, 21, 22, 27, 28, 36, 37, 61, 64, 131, 152, 153, 173, 174, 190, 191, 274, 332, 333, 359
Carache: 181, 182
Caraz: 255
Carbonell, Pedro: 36
Cariaco: 117, 136
Cariaco, Congress of: 112–113
Cariaco, heights of: 211
Caroní River: 110, 113
Carrasco, Representative: 304
Carrillo, Cruz: 152, 193
Cartagena: insurrection in, x; makes Bolívar a colonel and approves his progress, 40–43; welcomes Bolívar, 72, 75; division in, 75, 79, 83; asks Bolívar for recruits and money, 80; besieged by Bolívar, 81–82; besieged and captured by Morillo, 85–86; besieged by patriots, 176, 179, 180; surrenders to patriots, 203–204; mentioned, 5, 90, 91, 188, 327, 352, 358
Carúpano: 72, 102, 103, 117
Carvajal, Lucas: 257
Carvajal, Luis: 212
Casacoima: 114
Casanare: 93, 135, 151–159 passim, 173
Casariego, Colonel: 248
Casas, Bartolomé de las: 172 and n. 2, 278
Casas, Juan de las: 5, 6
Casas, Manuel María de las: 38
Castillo, José María: 202
Castillo, Manuel del: as commander of Pamplona, 43; and Bolívar, 47; as member of Cartagena's moderate party, 75; accuses Bolívar, 78; made brigadier general, 79; refuses to help Bolívar, 79–82 and n. 4; death of, 84; accused of treachery and deposed, 84, 86; mentioned, 90
Cauca: 206, 209, 211, 367
Cauca River: 368
Cauca Valley: 187
Caura River: 108
Cautaro: 109

Cautaro, battle of: 134
Ceballos, José: as governor of Coro, 32, 34, 35; in battle of Araure, 60; and siege of Valencia, 63, 65; mentioned, 74
Cedeño, Manuel: leads guerrilla band, 94, 96, 97; and Piar, 108, 114, 119; appointed to Council of Government, 121; joins Bolívar, 122, 130; in battle of Calabozo, 124; various activities of, 126, 131, 132, 143; on operations, 128; routed by Morales, 133; commands division at Carabobo, 193; death of, 195; mentioned, 136, 137
Central America: 89
Cerinza: 160
Cerro de Pasco: 255, 257
Cerruti, Nicolás María: 111
Cerveriz, Francisco Javier de: 54
Chacabuco, battle of: 222
Chaguaramas: 106, 120
Chala: 238
Challhuanca: 260, 265, 267
Chancay: 263
Charcas: 288
Charles IV (king of Spain): 12 n. 3
Chichas: 281
Chile: independence of, 222; troops from, in Peru, 223, 226; expedition from, abandons Peru, 244–245; and Congress of Panama, 275, 289, 323, 324, 325, 326–327; government of, criticizes Bolívar, 315; mentioned, 88, 224, 242, 250, 254, 265, 288
Chiloé: 245
Chimborazo, Mount: 215
Chiquitos: 288, 289, 292, 293, 295
Chiriguaná: 42
Chita: 153, 174
Chitaga, battle of: 92
Choroní: 105
Chorrillos: 264, 301
Chuquisaca: assembly of, proclaims independence and gives country Bolívar's name, 283; requests Bolívar to draw up constitution, 284, 298; as capital of Bolivia, 293; administration in, improved by Bolívar, 296–298; sets up permanent commission, 297; Bolívar departs from, 301; mentioned, 281, 306, 307. SEE ALSO Bolivia; Upper Peru
Cires, Tomás de: 102–103
Clarines: 109
Cochabamba: 281, 288, 301
Cojedes, battle of: 132–133
Colombia, Greater Republic of: people and geography of, 4–5; establishment of, 172; government of, moves to Cú-

cuta, 196; and Guayaquil, 205, 217–219; and Peru, 221, 231, 245, 250, 260; situation of, in 1823, 236, 329–330; and Congress of Panama, 289, 323, 324, 325, 326; discord in, 314, 330, 331–333, 344–353; and Bolivian Constitution, 316, 360; situation of, during Bolívar's absence, 330–339, 344; conscription decree of, 340; mentioned, 290, 291, 292, 293, 295, 312, 313, 318, 358, 368
—First Constitutional Congress of: installation of, 173, 196–197; re-elects Bolívar president, 198, 201–202; constitution (of Cúcuta) ratified by, 198–200, 229, 230, 236, 331; moves capital to Bogotá, 200; accepts Bolívar's gift of salary, 204; loan authorized by, 334; permits Bolívar to go to Peru, 234 and n. 2; removes Bolívar from command, 261–262; awards honors to Bolívar, 275; success of, 329; mentioned, 232, 233, 335, 367
—Second Congress of: reduces soldiers' pay, 335; suspends Miguel Peña from court, 336; absolves government commissioners, 337; elects Santander vice-president, 338; admits charges against Páez, 342, 343, 344, 345, 347, 349, 360; mentioned, 340, 341, 352
Columbus: 172, 368
Copacabana: 283
Coquimbo: 244
Cordero, Colonel: 245
Córdova, José María: 164, 176, 227, 255, 265
Córdova, Manuel: 305, 306
Coro: occupied by Miranda, 20 n.; as royalist stronghold, 26, 32, 190, 230; occupied by Urdaneta, 193; mentioned, 29, 35, 62, 191
Corpahuaico, ravine of: 267
Correa, Cirilo: 319
Correa, Ramón: invades Mérida and Cúcuta, 43; defeated by Bolívar, 44; replaces Morillo, 129; joins La Torre and given command, 132, 133; ordered to respect lives of prisoners, 133; mentioned, 190
Cortés Campomanés, Manuel: 41
Cortés Madariaga. SEE Madariaga
Creole, the: 4, 139
Cuba: 86, 312, 326
Cuchivero River: 97
Cúcuta: occupied by Correa, 43; captured by Bolívar, 44; La Torre arrives in, 169; Bolívar arrives in, 175, 188, 189, 198; Bolívar rests in, 176, 178, 179; patriot army in, 180; designated capi-

tal of Colombia, 196; capital moved from, 200; mentioned, 46, 47, 48, 152, 153, 162, 164
Cúcuta, Congress of. SEE Colombia, Greater Republic of
Cúcuta, Constitution of. SEE Colombia, Greater Republic of
Cuenca: 205, 215, 225, 227, 356, 361
Cumaná: abandoned by Bolívar, 68; occupied by royalists, 69, 102, 117, 190, 196; patriot guerrilla warfare in llanos of, 95, 96; Mariño repulsed in, 109; attacked by Bermúdez, 134; surrenders to Bermúdez, 204; mentioned, 37, 53, 120, 146, 352
Cumanacoa: 109, 117
Cunaviche: 147
Cundinamarca: differs with federal Congress, 75; recognizes Union, 76; made department of Colombia, 172; Santander's administration of, 201; indifference of government of, 209; and Venezuela, 343; mentioned, 175, 363, 367
Cundurcunca (Condorkanki): 268
Curaçao: 40, 57
Cuzco: royalists concentrate forces in, 265; Bolívar directs affairs of, 276; conditions in, improved by Bolívar, 277–279; clergy of, condemn government's policy, 304; mentioned, 169, 238, 260, 283, 284

Dawkins, Mr.: 325
Delgado, Francisco: 189
D'Elhuyar, Luciano: 57
Demarquet, Carlos Eloy: 357, 361
Desaguadero River: 238, 255, 281, 283
D'Evereux, John: 173
Díaz Vélez, José Miguel: 288, 290, 291
Domínguez, José: 325
Ducoudray-Holstein, H. L. V.: 101

Echeverría, José Tiburcio: 188
Ecuador: 201, 202, 355, 356. SEE ALSO Cuenca; Guayaquil; Ibarra; Quito
El Alacrán, battle of: 98, 106
El Altar Mountain: 51, 191
El Argos: 333, 344
El Azuay: 215, 361
El Banco: 42
El Caujaral: 146
El Cerrito de los Patos, battle of: 133
El Chaparro: 112
El Chocó: 93
Elizalde, Antonio: 280 and n. 3
El Juncal, battle of: 106
El Mantecal: 152
El Pao: 111, 112, 130, 131, 132, 195

El Pao de Zárate: 104
El Peñol: 212
El Pilar: 109
El Rastro: 124, 130, 131
El Rincón de los Toros: attempted assassination of Bolívar at, 131–132, 140
El Rosario de Cúcuta. SEE Cúcuta
El Socorro: 93, 160, 163, 174
Elsom, George: 137, 143
El Sombrero: 124, 125
El Tocuyo: 51, 71
El Venezolano: 332
El Yusepe, heights of: 212
Emparan, Vicente de: 6, 20 and n.
England: recruitment in, ix, 134 and n., 137, 143; and Venezuelan independence, 22–23; mediation proposal of, 25; attitude of, toward South America, 91; helps Colombia, 236; and Banda Oriental, 290, 291; deferred to, in South America, 293; recognizes independence of Colombia, 295, 334; and continental powers, 312–313; and Congress of Panama, 325
English, James T.: 143, 146
Escalona, Juan de: 332, 341, 342, 345
España, José María: 5 and n. 8
Espinar, José Domingo: xv
Espinosa, Candelario: 272

Ferdinand VII (king of Spain): authority exercised in name of, 6, 20 and n. 8, 205; chooses Morillo as peacemaker, 84; marriage of, 118; requests mediation by Holy Alliance, 136; accepts Cádiz Constitution, 175, 178; asked by Bolívar to recognize independence, 189; restored to absolute power, 250, 254 n. 1. SEE ALSO Spain
Fernández Madrid, José: 77, 93
Fierro, Antonio: 51–52
Figueredo, Miguel Antonio: 255
Flores, Juan José: aids O'Leary, xv; appointed governor of Pasto, 229; defeated in Pasto, 233; as commandant general of Ecuador, 356; saves Quito during revolt, 361
France: influence of revolution of, 5; and Napoleon, 14, 15, 91; probable hostile acts of, 306; reported helping Spanish expedition, 312; compared to Colombia, 357
Francia, José Gaspar Rodríguez de: 291
Freyre, Ramón: and Chile's offer to aid Peru, 244–245; and Congress of Panama, 324, 326–327

Gaceta de Colombia: 366, 367
Gaceta de Gobierno: 332

Gaceta Oficial: 353
Galdiano, José María: 240, 304
Galindo, Fernando: 131
Gamarra, Agustín: 238, 313
Gámeza, battle of: 160
Gámeza River: 160
García, Basilio: 211, 212, 213
García de Ortigosa, Salvador: 57
García Robira, Custodio: 71, 92–93
García Toledo, José María: 75
Genoy: 187
Gibraltar, Island of: 189
Girardot, Atanasio: leads patriot force to Barinas, 50; assigned to watch Puerto Cabello, 51; death of, 57; funeral honors for, 73
Godoy, Manuel: 12 and n. 3
Gómez, Francisco Esteban: 117
González, Vicente: 213
Gorrín, Salvador: 97
Goyeneche, General: 305
Goyeneche, Sebastián (bishop of Arequipa): 305
Great Britain. SEE England
Guachi, battle of: first (1820), 205; second (1821), 206
Guadarrama: 132
Guaica Pass: 34, 35
Guáitara River: 208, 216, 227, 330
Gual, Manuel: 5 and n. 2
Gual, Pedro: heads Cartagena government, 79; heads Department of Foreign Affairs, 202, 334; as delegate to Congress of Panama, 325
Guamacho: 117
Guanacas, paramo of: 365
Guanaguanay, José Miguel: 96
Guanare: 193
Guardatinajas: 127
Guárico River: 124
Guasdualito: 48, 153
Guatemala: 275, 324, 326
Guatire: 193
Guayana: in royalist hands, 54, 62; liberated by patriots, 108–115; mentioned, 117. SEE ALSO Angostura
Guayana la Vieja: 111, 138
Guayaquil: independence of, 185; aided by Colombia, 205–206; and annexation, 206, 207, 216–219, 223–224, 326; Bolívar and Colombian troops arrive in, 218, 230; Bolívar and San Martín meet in, 220–221, 224–225; expeditionary army embarks at, 231, 232; Bolívar departs from, 234–235, 330; Bolívar returns to, 320, 362–363; resolutions of municipal council of, 354–355, 356–357, 359, 361–362, 363, 366, 367; mentioned, 5, 209, 213, 215, 233,

243, 254, 258, 259, 264, 321, 327, 354, 356
Güiria: patriots land in, 53; Bolívar's authority in, rejected by Mariño and Bermúdez, 105; Morillo sends column against, 117; occupied by Bermúdez, 135
Guise, Martin George: commands Peruvian fleet, 243; recognizes Bolívar's government, 245; destroys ships in Callao Bay, 247, 250; places obstacles in Bolívar's path, 254; defeats Spanish seamen, 264
Gutiérrez de la Fuente. SEE La Fuente, Antonio Gutiérrez de
Guzmán, Antonio Leocadio: as publisher of *El Argos*, 333; carries letters to Bolívar, 344, 351; sent by Bolívar to announce his return to Colombia, 357, 359, 360, 361

Haiti: patriot refugees in, 91, 94; Bolívar and refugees in, 99–101; Bolívar returns to, 105, 107
Hall, Colonel: 332
Heres, Tomás de: joins patriots, 213; favors Bolívar's presence in Lima, 260; heads War Department, 264, 276; on assassination plot, 272; and Peruvians, 303 and n. 2
Herrera, José María: 178
Holland: 325
Holy Alliance: 136 n. 3, 312, 358
Honda: 163, 164, 165
Huamachuco: 253
Huamanga: 259, 267, 268, 280
Huancayo: 258, 259, 261, 262, 318
Huanchaco: 245
Huanuco: 250
Huaraz: 249, 255
Huarochiri: 258, 263
Huáscar: 205
Huayna Cápac: 205
Humboldt, Alexander von (Baron): 17, 23
Hurtado, Manuel J.: 334, 338
Hyslop, Maxwell: letter to, from Bolívar, 87–88; lends Bolívar money, 89, 90

Ibarra (Ecuador): 228
Ibarra, battle of: 233–234
Ibarra, Diego: 195, 196, 351, 365
Ibarra, valley of: 215
Ica: 303
Iglesias, Rafael: 101
Ilo: 238
Incas, the: 277, 278, 279
Inchauspe, Francisco: 36
Indians, the: location of population of,

4; political awareness of, 65; pursue patriot refugees, 96; Bolívar's treatment of, 213, 278–279 and n.2, 296; mentioned, 139, 198
Infante, Leonardo: 106, 132, 336, 342
Intermedios: 237, 244
Iquique: 227
Iribarren, Guillermo: 124–125, 152, 349
Irish legionaries: 173, 176
Isabel de Braganza (queen of Spain): 118
Iscuchuca: 258
Iturbe, Francisco: 40, 204
Iturbide, Agustín: 357 and n. 1
Izquierdo, Julián: 51
Iztueta, Jacinto: 36

Jacmel: 105, 107
Jalupana: 215
Jamaica: O'Leary exiled in, x, xv; Bolívar exiled in, 87–90; mentioned, 323
Jauja: 237, 244, 250, 257–262 passim
Jefferson, Thomas: 17
Jerez y Aristeguieta, Juan Félix (relative of Bolívar): 9
Jimena, Rafael: 216, 223
Jiménez, Francisco: 117, 163
Juanambú River: 76, 187, 206–216 passim, 227, 330
Juan Griego: 101, 118
Junín: 261
Junín, battle of: 257, 258, 259, 270 n. 3
Jurubamba: 215

La Aguada: 44
La Bandera Tricolor: 366, 367
Labatut, Pierre: 42, 43
La Cabrera: 35, 103
La Fuente, Antonio Gutiérrez de: joins San Martín's army, 222; and capitulation of Riva-Agüero, 242; arrests Riva-Agüero, 243; letter to, from Bolívar, 313
La Gamarra: 148
La Grita: 47, 48
La Guaira: Bolívar arrives in, 14, 23, 36, 37, 38; Miranda seized in, 38; royalist officials embark at, 52; Spanish prisoners sacrificed in, 57, 64; royalist garrison in, 95; surrenders to patriots, 195; mentioned, 173
La Hogaza, battle of: 121
La Lava: 255
La Madera, battle of: 134
La Mar, José de: joins San Martín's army, 217, 222; heads Peruvian junta and council, 225, 226, 231, 274, 276, 302, 307; commands Peruvian division, 250,

265; refuses Lima commission, 260; retires from council, 308, 318
La Mar (Bolivia): 297
La Mata Casanareña: 146
Lambrama: 267
Lancaster, Joseph: educational system of, 271 and n. 1, 276
La Paz: occupied by Santa Cruz, 238; first revolt of, 281; welcomes Bolívar, 284, 285; school of mining in, 297
La Peña de Tópaga: 160
La Plata. SEE Argentina; Buenos Aires; Río de la Plata, United Provinces of the
La Plata (Colombia): 187
La Puerta, battle of: first (n.d., 1814), 63; second (June 15, 1814), 67
Lara, Jacinto: aids O'Leary, xv; brings news from Casanare, 151; collects arms and stragglers in Tunja, 159; occupies Valle de Upar, 175, 176; commands Colombian division, 265; account of, on attack at Corpahuaico ravine, 267 n. 2
Larrazábal, Antonio: 325
Larrea y Laredo, José: 303
Las Casas. SEE Casas
La Serna, José de (Viceroy): joined by Valdés, 238; Riva-Agüero corresponds with, 242; professes constitutional principles, 254; accuses Olañeta, 255, 258; takes command of army, 265; route of, in Ayacucho campaign, 266; taken prisoner, 280; mentioned, 246
Las Heras, José Rafael: 189, 190, 195
Las Heras, Juan Gregorio: 287–288
Las Queseras del Medio, battle of: 148–149
Las Trincheras, battle of: 57
La Tacunga: 215
La Torre, Miguel de: occupies Bogotá, 92, 93; defeated at San Félix, III; evacuates Angostura, 114; defeated at Macuritas, 116; assigned to defend Guayana, 117; reinforces Morillo's army, 125; replaces Correa, 129; attacked by Bolívar, 130; wounded by Cojedes, 133; assembles army in Calabozo, 137; enters Cúcuta, 169; proposes suspension of hostilities, 179; succeeds Morillo, 186; protests occupation of Maracaibo, 189, 190; defeated at Carabobo, 194, 195; tries to regain territory, 230; mentioned, 178, 193
La Urbana: 122
La Uriosa: 124, 125
La Victoria: 35, 37, 52, 128
La Victoria, battle of: 64, 65
Leiva, Pedro: 304

Liberator, the. SEE Bolívar, Simón
Liberators, Cross of: 162
Liberators, Order of: 58, 73, 149
Lima: San Martín arrives in, 213 and n. 2, 222–223; Sucre departs from, 237; royalists take possession of, 237–238, 249; welcomes Bolívar, 239; La Fuente sees Bolívar in, 242; Buenos Aires mission in, 246; Necochea named commander of, 248; Bolívar returns to, 263–264, 306, 307, 308, 323, 357; celebrates Ayacucho victory, 268; royalist plot in, 272; Bolívar departs from, 277, 325; Heres and Pérez hated in, 303 and n. 2; efforts in, to save Berindoaga, 311; mentioned, 205, 207, 232, 234, 238, 243, 247, 260, 290, 293, 298, 302, 317, 359
Lima Tambo: 270 n. 3
llaneros: under Boves, 60, 66; under Páez, 108, 116, 151; as soldiers, 147, 158; rewarded by Bolívar, 149; praise Morillo, 186; mentioned, 128, 138, 139, 140, 148, 150, 161
Llona, José Leocadio: 218
Loja: 215, 225, 227
London: Bolívar on mission in, 22–23; Wilson expedition formed in, 137; Colombia loan arranged in, 337
López, Manuel Antonio: 289
López, Rafael: controls Barinas llanos, 95; attacks Rojas, 97; defeats Monagas, 98; routed by MacGregor, 106; joins La Torre, 130; attacks patriots, 131; death of, 132
López Méndez, Luis: 21, 22
Lorenzo, battle of: 222
Loriga, Juan: 246
Los Aguacates, battle of: 103
Los Corrales de Bonza: 159
Los Frailes (islands of): 101
Los Güires: 333
Los Horcones, battle of: 51
Los Molinos de Tópaga: 160
Louis XVIII (king of France): 254 n. 1
Luna Pizarro, Javier: returns from exile, 280, 305; chosen for Congress, 306; favors union of Peru and Bolivia, 309; opposes Peruvian government, 310; refused interview with Bolívar, 311

MacGregor, Gregor: heads march to Choroní and Barcelona, 98 and n. 3, 105–106 and n. 3; in Aux Cayes expedition, 101; in battle of El Juncal, 106
Mackintosh, John: 147, 175
Macuchíes: 49
Macuchíes, battle of: 71
Macuritas, battle of: 116

Madariaga, José Cortés: 6, 112
Madrid, José Fernández. SEE Fernández Madrid
Magdalena (Bolívar's residence near Lima): as political center in South, 308, 309, 310, 311, 315, 317; mentioned, 272, 301, 307
Magdalena (Colombia): 367
Magdalena River: 42, 43, 79, 82, 83, 85, 176
Maipú, battle of: 222
Mallo, Manuel: 12
Mamara: 265
Manco Cápac: 279
Manrique, Manuel: 112, 152
Maracaibo: proclaims separation from Spain, 189; La Torre protests patriot occupation of, 190; occupied by Morales, 230–231; mentioned, 54, 62, 176, 182
Maracaibo, Lake: 189, 198
Maracay: 26, 35, 128
Marañón River: 228
Margarita (Island of): Bolívar arrives on, 72; captured by Morillo, 81, 84; patriot revolt on, 94–95; Aux Cayes expedition arrives on, 101–102; defended against Morillo, 117–118; British legionaries land on, 146; Arismendi's insubordination on, 170; Irish legionaries arrive on, 173
María Luisa (queen of Spain): 12, 13
Marimón y Enríquez, Juan: as mediator in Cartagena, 79, 80, 81; in Aux Cayes expedition, 101
Mariño, Ignacio: 155
Mariño, Santiago: in exile, 53; as dictator in the East, 60; in battles of Bocachica, Carabobo, and La Puerta, 65–67; departs from Venezuela, 68; arrives in Cartagena, 72; in Aux Cayes expedition, 101–102; rejects Bolívar's authority, 105; success of, in Barcelona and Cumaná, 108, 109; defection of, 111 and n. 6; and Congress of Cariaco, 112–113; dissension of, 133; in Cariaco, 134; reconciled to government, 136; summoned to Congress, 152, 153; as adjutant general, 193; in oppositionist party, 333; invites Bolívar to save country, 344; mentioned, 54, 188, 348, 349
Martí, José: 51
Martínez, Enrique: 247, 248
Matará: 267
Mato Grosso: 288
Maturín: taken by Morales, 70; patriot guerrilla activity in, 95; Bolívar and

Mariño confer in, 136; mentioned, 53, 68, 96, 119, 171, 351
Mayz, Francisco Javier: 113
Maza, Hermógenes: 49
Medinaceli, Colonel: 281
Mendoza (Argentina): 221 n. 1, 222, 242
Mendoza, Cristóbal: as intendant of Venezuela, 348; declares illegal recognition of Páez, 349; decides to remain in office, 350; writes to Bolívar about conflict, 352, 359
Mendoza, Eugenio: 304
Mérida: Bolívar arrives in, 48, 180–181; Morales invades the province of, 230; mentioned, 47, 49, 50, 153
Meta River: 174
Mexico: Bolívar's visit to, 11; Bolívar's opinion of, 89; and Congress of Panama, 207, 275, 289, 323, 326, 328; territorial rule of, 224; invited to assist Bolívar in Peru, 250; separate peace of, 312; and Iturbide, 357 n. 1
Mexico City: 11, 326
Michelena, José Mariano: 325, 342
Michelena, Santos: 342
Micura: 98
Milán, Manuel: 303
Miller, William: in battle of Junín, 257; as commander of the cavalry, 265; makes reconnaissance, 267; as prefect of Potosí, 285
Miranda, Francisco de: Coro expedition of, 5 and n. 2, 20 and n. 7; returns to Venezuela, 23 and n. 1; appointed lieutenant general, 24; captures Valencia, 27; protests against constitution, 28; evacuates Valencia, 34; repulses Monteverde, 35; negotiates San Mateo pact, 37; imprisonment and death of, 38; mentioned, 36, 39, 40, 188
Miranda (General Rodil's aide): 311
Mires, José: with Bolívar at Puerto Cabello, 36; helps plan to seize Miranda, 38; marches to Obando's aid, 174; reinforces Albión Battalion, 175; at battle of Guachi, 206
Misque: 301
Missions of the Caroní River: 110, 113
mita: 278 and n. 2
Miyares, Fernando: 32, 38
Molina, Pedro: 325
Mompox: Bolívar commands in, 42, 43; welcomes Bolívar, 79; Marimón meets Bolívar in, 80; taken by royalists, 82, 83; occupied by Córdova, 176
Monagas, José Tadeo: leads guerrilla band, 94, 95, 96; learns about Bolívar

in Carúpano, 97–98; joins MacGregor, 106; sent to Barcelona, 120; joins Bolívar, 122, 128, 137; in battle of Calabozo, 124; checks Morales, 129
Monet, Juan Antonio: 246
Monteagudo, Bernardo: deposed in Lima, 223; visits Bolívar, 228; assassination of, 272
Montes de Oca, Julián: 121
Monteverde, Domingo: leads royalist forces, 32–37; treachery of, 38–39; and Bolívar, 39–40; advances in Venezuela, 43; plans invasion of New Granada, 50; flees to Puerto Cabello, 51; flees to Maturín, 54; refuses to ratify capitulation, 54, 57; defeated at Bárbula and Las Trincheras, 56–57; badly wounded, 57; removed from command, 62; mentioned, 72, 112, 204
Montevideo: 288, 290, 292. SEE ALSO Banda Oriental
Montilla, Mariano: aids O'Leary, xv; in Cartagena, 41; appointed to command Irish legion, 173; occupies Río Hacha and advances to Cartagena, 175–176; captures Cartagena, 203–204
Montilla, Tomás: helps plan to seize Miranda, 38; in Cartagena, 41; escapes from Cartagena, 80; and Congress of Cariaco, 113
Montoya, Señor: 334, 337
Moquegua, battle of: 226, 231
Morales, Francisco Tomás: succeeds Boves and captures Maturín, 70; outrages of, 70, 86, 108; on Margarita, 84; marches to Cartagena, 85; sent to Valencia, 95; wins at Los Aguacates, 103; defeated at El Juncal, 106; relieved of command, 110; checked by Monagas, 129; threatens llanos, 132; occupies Calabozo, 133; occupies Caracas, 193; occupies Maracaibo, 230; mentioned, 94, 96
Morillo, Pablo: and O'Leary, xvi; arrives on Margarita, 81, 84, 117–118; lands in Venezuela, 84; as peacemaker, 84, 85; reaches Caracas, 85; captures Cartagena, 85–86; subjugates New Granada, 92–94; excessive cruelty of, 93, 108, 133, 155; fathoms Bolívar's plans, 95; position of, in 1817, 108–109; re-enters Venezuela, 116; retreats from Calabozo, 123–126; wounded at Semen, 129; sends La Torre to reinforce Real, 132; enlarges army, 137; crosses the Arauca, 146; in Achaguas, 147, 148, 150; defeated at Las Queseras del Medio, 149; negotiates with

patriots, 178, 179; corresponds with Bolívar, 180, 181; ratifies armistice, 182; meets Bolívar, 183–184; called to Spain, 186; comments about, 186–187; mentioned, 87, 90, 120, 134, 153, 164, 169

Mosquera, Joaquín: as president of Colombia, x; mission of, to Lima, 207; negotiates treaties in Peru and Chile, 323; writes to Bolívar, 334, 338 and n. 2

Mosquera, Tomás Cipriano: as intendant of Guayaquil, 355; asked for open meeting, 361; pays respects to Bolívar, 362; promoted to colonel, 363

Motavita: 163

Mourgeon, Juan de la Cruz: 206

Moxó, Salvador de: 95, 108

Moxos: 292

Moyano, Dámaso: 247

Mujica, Jacinto: 346

Murgueytío, Pedro: 355

Napoleon: compels Ferdinand VII to abdicate, 6 n. 3; as head of the Republic, admired by Bolívar, 14; as emperor, regarded as tyrant, 15, 16, 17, 18, 357; as usurper, 22; imprisonment of, destroys hope of aid to patriots, 91

Nariño, Antonio: defeats Sámano, 75–76; taken prisoner in Pasto, 76; chosen as vice-president, 196

Navas Spínola, Domingo: 348

Necochea, Mariano: named commander of Lima, 248; evacuates Lima, 249; in battle of Junín, 257; involved in conspiracy, 319

Negro, the: in Güiria Battalion, 102; Piar's attitude toward, 114; rumored revolts of, 333, 341; mentioned, 4, 198

Neiva: 365

New Granada: General Congress of, 41, 46, 48, 50, 75, 76, 77; threat to, 43, 44; union of, with Venezuela, 56, 89, 144, 168, 171, 172, 175, 323; Cundinamarca recognizes Union of, 76, government of, transferred to Bogotá, 77; prejudice of, against foreigners, 78; royalist invasion of, 83; subjugated by Morillo, 92–94; Bolívar's invasion of, 151–165; despotism and terror in, 155, 156; name of, abolished, 172; and jurisdiction over Guayaquil, 217 and n. 3; influence of, in legislature, 331; re-establishment of republic of, 368; mentioned, 4, 164

Niquitao: 184

Niquitao Heights, battle of: 51

Nutrias: 50, 150, 191

Obando, Antonio: 174, 175

Obando, José María: 363, 364

Oberto, Francisco: 51

Ocaña: great convention of, x; occupied by Bolívar, 42; threatened by Monteverde, 43; enemy in, dislodged by Bolívar, 79; occupied by royalists, 85

Ocopa: 259

Ocumare: slaughter of inhabitants of, 63; Bolívar's proclamation from, 103; Bolívar's hurried departure from, 104

Olañeta, Pedro Antonio de: joins Valdés pursuing Santa Cruz, 238; as absolutist, accuses liberals, 254–255; Bolívar's letter to and proclamation about, 258–259; offered honorable conditions, 280; death of, 281; mentioned, 288

O'Leary, Daniel Florencio: marriage of, ix; birth of, ix and n. 1; arrives in America, ix, xv, 137; meets Bolívar, ix, 139; as diplomat, x; family of, x; at Bolívar's burial, x, xv; in exile in Jamaica, x, xv; death of, xi; as a writer, xi, xii; collects documents, xv–xvi; comrades of, xv–xvi; visits Morillo, xvi; experience of, in Achaguas, 138; sent to Panama, 209; accompanies Bolívar to Peru, 234 n. 2, 235 n. 3; in Chile as Bolívar's commissioner, 244–245; receives keys of city from Bolívar, 278; hears Bolívar speak at Potosí, 286; as Bolívar's first aide-de-camp, 293; sent to announce Bolívar's return to Lima, 307; sent by Bolívar to Colombia, 358–359

O'Leary, Simón Bolívar (O'Leary's son): xi, xii

Olmedo, José Joaquín de: on Bolívar as poet, 177 and n. 4; as president of Guayaquil junta, 207; and independence, 216; alarm of, over flag, 219; praises Bolívar, 223; in Peruvian Congress, 225; heads mission to Bolívar, 234; letter to, from Bolívar, 317

Orinoco River: 96, 97, 108–122 passim, 136, 137, 144, 146, 147, 171, 174, 188, 313

Ortiz: 126, 130

Ortiz, battle of: 130

Ortiz Ceballos, Ignacio: 318

Oruro: 238, 281, 282

Otavalo: 215

Otero, Francisco de Paula: 270 and n. 3

Pachachaca River: 265

Padilla, José: 203

Páez, José Antonio: and O'Leary, ix; occupies Apure llanos, 108; recognizes Bolívar's authority, 112; victory of, at Macuritas, 116; defends Apure line, 120, 122; meets Bolívar, 122; description of, 122–123; in battle of Calabozo, 124; returns to San Fernando, 126, 130; letters to, from Bolívar, 127, 174, 357, 359; attacks San Carlos, 132; in battle of Cojedes, 132–133; joins forces with Bolívar, 137; and Wilson's proposal, 138; in San Juan de Payara, 143; promoted to major general, 144; follows Morillo and wins at Las Queseras del Medio, 146–149; and Bolívar's invasion plan, 151–152, 153, 162; in Carabobo campaign, 191–195; given rank of general in chief, 195; as commandant general, puts down Venezuela uprising, 333; protest against conduct of, 339; ordered to avoid incidents, 340; authority of, in central government, 341–352; proposes monarchy to Bolívar, 357–358; letter from, to Bolívar's sister, 359; mentioned, 118, 131, 136

Páez, Rafael: 90
Paipa: 162
Palacé, battle of: 76
Palacios, Carlos (uncle of Bolívar): 10
Palacios, Esteban (uncle of Bolívar): 12
Palacios, Florencio (relative of Bolívar): 83–84, 101
Palacios, Silvestre: 124, 132
Palacios y Blanco, María Concepción (mother of Bolívar): 9 and n. 1, 2
Pampas River: 267
Pampatar: 102, 107, 117
Pamplona: threatened by Correa, 43; Bolívar and Urdaneta meet in, 75; invaded by Calzada, 92; Bolívar goes to, 168–169; Anzoátegui dies in, 169; mentioned, 160, 163
Panama: becomes part of Colombia, 209; unit from, joins Sucre, 215; sea voyage from, 254; Colombian troops leave Callo for, 321; as meeting place of nations, 323; Congress meets in, 325–326; mentioned, 327, 359
Panama, Congress of: Bolívar's idea about, 206, 322–323; governments invited to, 207, 273, 275, 289, 323, 324–325; meeting of, 303 n. 1, 325–326; treaties signed at, 326; states absent from, 326–327; Bolívar on treaties of, 327–328; mentioned, 265, 292, 303, 312
Pando, José María: heads Treasury Department, 276, 302; represents Peru at Congress of Panama, 303, 325; takes charge of Ministry of Foreign Affairs, 312, 325; reports and views of, 312–313, 358
Pantano de Vargas, battle of: 161–162, 163
Pao River: 120, 122, 137
Paraguay: 291, 294
Pardo, Juan Bautista: 102
Paredes, Joaquín: 364
Parejo, Francisco Vicente: 96, 98
Paria, Gulf of: 135
Pasto: tenacity and hostility of people of, 206, 208, 213, 330; Bolívar's proclamation to people of, 211; capitulation of, 213; rebellion of, 227–229, 233–234; abject state of, 361; loyalty of, 363; welcomes Bolívar, 364; mentioned, 187, 205, 207, 212, 215, 230
Patía: deadly climate of, 206, 208; people of, 208; Bolívar's proclamation to people of, 211; mentioned, 207
Pativilca: 246, 247, 248, 249
Pavageau, Mr. ———: 90, 99
Paya: 158, 159, 160
Payares, Colonel: 355
Paz del Castillo, Juan: 226
Pedro I (emperor of Brazil): and Banda Oriental dispute, 288, 290, 291, 292, 293, 294; invited to Congress of Panama, 324, 325
Peña, Miguel: as governor of La Guaira, 38; suspended from high court of justice, 336–337, 342; rules Páez, 345; as lawyer and adviser, 346; restores Páez, 348; as secretary of Páez, 350
Peñalver, Fernando: as friend and adviser of Bolívar, 74, 135; declares Valencia meeting illegal, 345–346; protests restoration of Páez to post, 347–348 and n. 3
Peñas Negras: 96
Perdomo, Francisco: 336
Pereira, José: 195
Pérez, José Gabriel: aids O'Leary, xv; in Cúcuta with Bolívar, 177–178; negotiates armistice, 182; negotiates Pasto capitulation, 213; as Bolívar's secretary, 235 n. 3, 303 n. 2, 363; hated in Lima, 303 n.; assembles data in Quito, 363–364
Pérez de Tudela, Manuel: 325
Peru: San Martín lands in, 213 and n.; and Guayaquil, 216, 217 and n. 3, 221 and n. 1; treaty of, with Colombia, 221, 231; San Martín departs from, 223; Colombian troops leave for, 224, 231; junta of, 225, 226, 231; Bolívar

arrives in, 239; constitution of, 242, 317; government of, re-established by Bolívar, 264; Council of Government of, 274, 276, 290, 298, 302–303, 304, 307, 309, 310, 317, 318, 319, 324, 325; union with Bolivia, 309, 318; electoral college of, votes for Bolivian Constitution, 319; Bolívar departs from, 320–321; and Congress of Panama, 303, 323, 324, 325, 326; mentioned, 89, 205, 220–330 *passim,* 358
— Congress of: installation of, 223; gives junta executive power, 225; fiscal measures of, 226; and Riva-Agüero as president, 231, 237, 239; thanks Bolívar, 232–233; appoints Torre Tagle president, 239; gives Bolívar supreme authority, 240–241, 248, 251, 273, 310; and preliminary peace convention, 246; convoked by Bolívar, 269, 271, 272, 304, 307, 309; rewards Bolívar and army, 274; dissolved, 276; elections for, 304–306; wants Colombian troops to remain, 321; mentioned, 234, 238, 243, 282, 284, 290, 301, 308, 311, 320
Petare: 332
Pétion, Alexandre Sabès: helps refugees in Haiti and offers Bolívar support, 91–92, 99; welcomes Bolívar for the second time, 105
Piar, Manuel: in exile, 53; asks Monagas for aid, 98; in Aux Cayes expedition, 101, 102; takes command in Barcelona, 106; goes to Guayana, 108; arbitrary decisions of, 110 and n. 5; defeats La Torre at San Félix, 111; dissatisfaction and desertion of, 113–114; parents of, 114 n. 7; arrest and execution of, 119–120; mentioned, 54, 112
Pichincha, battle of: 215
Pichirgua: 267
Picornell, Mariano: 5 and n. 2
Picton, Thomas: 5 and n. 2
Pilcomayo: 293
Piñeres, José Gabriel: heads extremist party in Cartagena, 75; as member of government, 79; exiled, 79; in Aux Cayes expedition, 101
Piñeres, Juan Antonio: helps head extremist party in Cartagena, 75; exiled, 79; in Aux Cayes expedition, 101
Pío (former slave of Bolívar): attempts to assassinate Bolívar, 90
Píritu: 106
Pisba, Paramo of: 158
Pisco: 213 n. 2
Pitayó, battle of: 187
Pius VII: 19

Pizarro, Francisco: 205, 307
Plaza, Ambrosio: operations of, 131; at council of war, 152; commands La Guardia division, 191, 193; death of, in battle of Carabobo, 195
Popayán: royalist invasion of, 75; occupied by Calzada, 174, 175; Valdés arrives in, 187; as assembly point of patriot army, 206, 207, 208; march from, 211; Flores retreats to, 233; welcomes Bolívar, 364–365; mentioned, 164, 212
Popayán, bishop of: 208
Pore: 157
Porlamar: 117
Port-au-Prince: patriot refugees assemble in, 91; Pétion welcomes Bolívar in, 99; Bolívar returns to, 105
Portobelo: 173
Portocarrero, Mariano: sent to Bolívar to request aid, 231; returns to Peru with good news, 232; invites San Martín to return to Peru, 243
Potosí: occupied by Santa Cruz, 238; patriot forces enter, 281; Bolívar arrives in, 285; La Plata delegation arrives in, 289; Bolívar departs from, 293; school of mining established in, 297; mentioned, 169, 231, 250, 292, 313, 368
Prado, Esteban (Bolívar's chaplain): 131
Prieto, Colonel: 319
Puerto Cabello: commanded by Bolívar, 34 and n. 1; loss of, 36; Miranda and prisoners sent to, 38, 39; Monteverde flees to, 51; royalist reinforcements in, 56; royalists seek refuge in, 57; siege of, 62, 63, 195, 196; Morillo sails from, 85; as royalist stronghold, 95, 230, 236, 329; mentioned, 54
Puerto Real: 42
Puerto Rico: 204
Puno: highways in, 278; receives benefits from Bolívar, 279; Bolívar departs from, 283; mentioned, 276

Quebrada Honda, battle of: 106
Quero, Juan Nepomuceno: covers plains in the East, 95; routed by MacGregor, 106 and n. 3; rejects Bolívar's ultimatum, 123
Quito: made a Colombian department and capital, 172; independence of and surrender of, 205; liberated by Sucre, 206, 208, 209, 212, 213–216; Bolívar arrives in, 215, 229, 230, 233, 234, 363; Bolívar departs from, 218, 230, 234, 364; Agualongo marches on, 233–234; Mosquera as intendant of, 355;

resolutions and statement of municipal council of, 355–356, 362, 367; uprising in, 361; mentioned, 5, 202, 221, 227, 228

Ramírez, Manuel: 263–264
Ramos, Sebastián: 288
Rangel, Antonio: 126, 152, 195
Real, Pascual: covers plains in the East, 95; occupies Barcelona, 109; relieved of command, 110; falls back to Valencia, 132
Renovales, Tomás: 131
Restrepo, José Manuel: 202
Revenga, José Rafael: 188, 325
Reyes: 258, 261
Reyes, Lake: 257
Ribas, José Félix (Bolívar's uncle by marriage): in Cartagena, 41; heads patriot division, 47, 50; wins decisive victories, 50–51; defeats Boves at La Victoria, 64; in battle of Carabobo, 66; in battle of Urica, 70; death of, 70
Ricaurte, Antonio: 64
Rincón Hondo: 151
Riobamba, battle of: 215
Río Caribe: 136
Rio de Janeiro: 289, 291, 293
Río de la Plata, United Provinces of the: war of independence of, 222; troops from, in Peru, 223, 226; concludes armistice convention with Spain, 243, 244; discussions of, with Brazil, 288; government of, criticizes Bolívar, 294; and Congress of Panama, 323, 324, 325, 326; mentioned, 257, 281, 284, 288. SEE ALSO Argentina; Buenos Aires
— Congress of: sends delegation to Bolívar, 285, 289–295; incorporates Banda Oriental, 290; mentioned, 275, 282, 287
Río Hacha: 78, 173, 175, 176
Riva-Agüero, José de la: appointed president of Peru, 231; deposed by Congress, 237; dissolves Congress, 239; urged by Bolívar to accept his offer, 240; correspondence of, with royalists, 241, 242; arrested and exiled, 243; mentioned, 304, 305
Rivadavia, Bernardino: plan of, for peace with Spain, 244; presidential inaugural address of, 316; Bolívar's review of address of, 316 and n. 1; refuses to take part in Congress of Panama, 323; mentioned, 275
Rivas, José Pedro: 318
Roca, Francisco: 216, 223
Rodil, José Ramón: letter to, from Can-

terac, 258; refuses to accept Ayacucho capitulation, 272; agrees to surrender Callao, 307; mentioned, 311
Rodríguez, Simón: as Bolívar's tutor, 10–11; with Bolívar in France and Italy, 16, 17, 20; welcomed in Lima by Bolívar, 276; appointed director of public education in Bolivia, 296
Rodríguez del Toro, Bernardo (father-in-law of Bolívar): 13, 14, 15
Rodríguez del Toro, Fernando: urges a junta in Venezuela, 6; accompanies Bolívar to France, 15; and Congress of Cariaco, 113
Rodríguez del Toro, Francisco (third Marqués del Toro): repulsed by Spaniards, 26–27; takes Bolívar as aide-de-camp, 27; as head of civil government in Venezuela, 332
Rodríguez del Toro, María Teresa (wife of Bolívar): betrothal of, 13; marriage of, 14; death of, 15
Rodríguez del Toro, Sebastián (second Marqués del Toro): 13
Rodríguez Torices, Manuel: 40, 43
Rojas, Andrés: 94, 97, 113
Rondón, Juan José: 97, 161
Rooke, James: joins Bolívar, 137; at council of war, 152; description of, 154–155; leads unit across paramo, 160–161; dislodges enemy at Pantano de Vargas, 161
Roscio, Juan Germán: appointed vice-president of Venezuela, 173; urged by Bolívar to ship arms, 174; death of, 196
Rosete, Francisco: 63
Ruiz de Castilla, Count: 205

Sabana Larga: 182
Sabinilla: 176
Salavarrieta, Policarpa (Pola): 155–156
Salazar, Francisco: 217, 303
Salazar, Juan: 298
Salazar, Señor ———: 324
Salazar de las Palmas: 43
Salcedo, Mateo: 131
Salom, Bartolomé: aids O'Leary, xv; at Ocumare, 104; description of, 177–178; sent to occupy Guayaquil, 217, 218; in charge at Guayaquil, 225; sends Pasto citizens to Quito, 229; succeeds Sucre, 232; and Pasto rebellion, 233, 234; letter to, from Bolívar, 235 n. 3; blockades Callao, 264; captures Callao, 307
Salomón, José Miguel: 56, 57
Salta: 244 and n. 1, 294
Sámano, Juan (Viceroy): invades Po-

payán, 75; promoted to viceroy, 155; orders execution of patriots, 156, 166; flees from Bogotá, 163–164, 177

Sañaica: 260

San Antonio: 44

San Carlos: occupied by Monteverde, 34; occupied by Bolívar, 51, 60, 193; attacked by Páez, 132; Bolívar passes through, 198; mentioned, 126, 191

San Cayetano: 44

Sánchez Carrión, José: commissioned to invite Bolívar to Peru, 234; made secretary-general, 250; appointed first secretary of state, 264; appointed to Council of Government, 274; illness of, 276; death of, 302

Sánchez Lima, Vicente: 176

San Cristóbal: Antonio Briceño publishes proclamation in, 48; Bolívar receives truce envoys in, 178; Bolívar writes to Morillo from, 180, 181

Sandes, Arthur: 208, 227

San Diego de Cabrutica: Monagas defeats royalists in, 96; MacGregor arrives in, 106; Bolívar dispatches officers from, 121; mentioned, 120

San Felipe: 193

San Félix, battle of: 111

San Fernando de Apure: fortified by Morillo, 116, 117; siege of, 126, 153; occupied by Páez, 130; Bolívar returns to, 132; Morillo crosses the Apure at, 146; garrison reinforced at, 147, 149; municipal council of, sends delegates to Valencia, 350; mentioned, 50, 127, 133, 137, 180, 181

San José (Cúcuta): 44

San José de los Tiznados: 127, 130, 131

San Juan de los Morros: 129

San Juan de Payara: Bolívar stays in, 123; Bolívar's headquarters in, 137, 143; occupied by Morillo, 146, 147; Sucre sent from, 174

San Juan River: 211

San Lorenzo, battle of: 222

San Martín, José Francisco de: lands in Peru, 213; and Guayaquil, 217, 220–221 and n. 1; meeting of, with Bolívar, 220–221 and n. 1, 224–225; character of, 221–222; returns to Peru and resigns, 223; refuses invitation to return to Peru, 242–243; mentioned, 226, 228, 241, 248, 257

San Mateo: pact of, 37, 38, 41; battles of, 63–64, 65; estate of, belongs to Bolívar, 196

San Pablo, ranch of: 130

San Sebastián de los Reyes: 125

Santa Ana: 183

Santa Cruz, Andrés de: joins forces with Sucre, 213; detained in Quito, 217; joins San Martín's army, 222; returns to Peru, 224; campaign of, in the South and Upper Peru, 237, 238, 242, 244, 281; invites San Martín to Peru, 243; recognizes government, 245; appointed president of Council of Government, 318, 319; mentioned, 221

Santa Cruz (Bolivia): 281, 297

Santa Cruz de la Sierra: 288

Santa Fe de Bogotá. SEE Bogotá

Santamaría, Miguel: 323

Santa María de Ipire: 121

Santa Marta: Bolívar buried in, x, xv; proposed liberation of, 78, 80, 82; operations against, 179; units to be sent to, 198; mentioned, 173

Santander, Francisco de Paula: commands at La Grita, 47; insubordination of, 48; meets Bolívar in El Pao, 112; at El Rincón de los Toros, 131; sent to form division in Casanare, 134–135; informs Bolívar of victories, 151; in Boyacá campaign, 152–154, 160, 163; appointed vice-president, 165, 173, 200; has prisoners shot, 165–166, 336; given supreme authority, 201; character of, 201–202, 229, 261, 334, 336, 337, 350, 351, 353, 365; reports discord to Bolívar, 229, 338; Bolívar stops personal correspondence with, 262; on Bolivian Constitution, 316; approves Bolívar's stay in Peru, 320–321; and Congress of Panama, 324, 325; and dissension in Venezuela, 331–332 and n. 1, 341–343, 346, 350, 351, 352, 353; and government loan, 334, 337; message of, to Congress, 337; elected vice-president by Congress, 338; silence of, regarding perils, 343, 352, 358, 359, 360; urges Bolívar to return, 353; Bolívar has confidence in, 357; and the constitution, 362; meets Bolívar in Tocaima, 365; activities of faction formed by, 366; expresses plan for separation to Bolívar, 367–368; mentioned, 174, 234, 237, 327, 333, 345

Santa Rosa: 160

Santiago: 244

Santo Domingo River: 193

Saraguro: 213

Sedeño, Manuel. SEE Cedeño, Manuel

Semen, battle of: 129

Sepulturas: 238

Sergeant, J.: 327

Serrano, Fernando: 132

Serviez, Manuel Roergas de: 93

Setenta: 152
Sicuani: 304
Silva, Laurencio: 257
Socha: 159
Sogamoso: 159
Sogamoso River: 161, 162
Soledad: 171, 176
Soto, Francisco: 342
Soublette, Carlos: and O'Leary, ix, xv, xvi, 139; in Aux Cayes expedition, 101, 103, 104; sent to Guayana, 130; at council of war, 152; description of, 154; occupies valleys of Cúcuta, 164; ordered to join Apure army, 169; appointed vice-president of Venezuela, 191; receives Bolívar's instructions, 196; resigns as head of government, 332; as secretary of war, 352; mentioned, 174
South America: people of, 65; future of, 87–89; antipathies in, 314; lack of awareness in, 322. SEE ALSO Panama, Congress of; Spain
Spain: colonial policies of, 5, 55 n. 2, 56, 88; supreme junta of, 5, 6 n. 3; abdication of king of, 6 n. 3; Cortes of, 6 n. 3, 25, 296; blockade by regency of, 24, 25; Cádiz Constitution of, 45 and n. 1, 296 n. 2; and jurisdiction over Guayaquil, 217 n. 3; preliminary peace in convention of, 243–244; restoration of absolutism in, 250, 254 and n. 1; possible attack by, 312; refuses to recognize independence, 334
Spanish America: 4, 299. SEE ALSO South America
Suárez, Manuel Isidoro: 257
Sucre, Antonio José de: aids O'Leary, xv; in exile, 53; goes to Guayana, 113; sent to buy arms in West Indies, 174; appointed to negotiate armistice, 182; replaces Valdés in the South, 187; description of, 188 and n. 1; sent as envoy to Guayaquil, 205–206; negotiates treaty of Babahoyo, 206; and Pichincha campaign, 213–216; puts down Pasto rebellion, 227; appointed minister to Lima, 232; accepts command of army, 237; expedition of, to the South, 238; blamed by Riva-Agüero, 239; chosen commander of united army, 250, 253; complains to Bolívar, 259; given broad authority, 260, 262; in Ayacucho campaign, 265–268, 267 n. 2; rewarded by Bolívar, 269, 284; Bolívar's sketch of, 274–275; liberates South and Upper Peru, 280–283; with Bolívar at Potosí, 285; and Brazilian invasion, 288–289; hard

work of, 297; gift to, from Lima, 298; given supreme command, 301; and Peruvian army, 321; assassination of, 364; mentioned, 209, 261, 309
Sutherland, Robert: 99

Táchira River: 44, 71
Tacubaya: 326, 327
Taguanes, battle of: 51
Taindala, battle of: 227
Tamalameque: 42
Tame: 154, 157
Tarija: 294
Tarma: 258
Tarqui, battle of: x
Tasco: 160
Tello, Juan: 193, 195
Tenerife: 42, 176
Terón, José: 311
Tinaquillo: 193
Tinta: 304
Titicaca, Lake: 279
Tizcar, Antonio: 48, 50
Toca: 162
Tocaima: 365
Torices, Manuel Rodríguez. SEE Rodríguez Torices, Manuel
Toro. SEE Rodríguez del Toro
Torrellas, Andrés: 34
Torres, Camilo: supports Bolívar and approves his conduct, 42, 78; resigns as president of New Granada, 93; death of, 187
Torres, Gabriel: 180, 204
Torres, Ignacio: 220, 356
Torres, Pedro León: 121, 212
Torre Tagle, José Bernardo (Marqués de): appointed president of Peru, 234, 239; receives authority from Sucre, 238; power of, 240–241; orders Riva-Agüero's execution, 243; and preliminary peace convention, 246–247; and Callao revolt, 247; treasonable acts of, 248; takes refuge in Callao, 249; calumnies of, 251; mentioned, 311
Trapiche: 212
Trinidad: 5 n. 2, 53
Tristán, Pío: assumes title of viceroy, 280; protects royalists, 305; defeated in departmental elections, 306
Trujillo (Peru): possessed by patriots, 225, 250; Congress moves to, 237; representatives exiled from, 239; La Fuente returns to, 242; Riva-Agüero arrested in, 243; Bolívar arrives in, 245; Bolívar has headquarters in, 251; Urdaneta marches from, 263; capital

of, given Bolívar's name, 274; mentioned, 249, 258
Trujillo (Venezuela): Bolívar arrives in, 49; patriots advance to, 181; armistice negotiations in, 182; Bolívar departs from, 184; commissioners sent from, 187; Bolívar passes through, 198; invaded by Morales, 230; mentioned, 47, 50
Tumusla, battle of: 281
Tunja: General Congress meets in, 41; Bolívar arrives in, 75; proclamation circulated in province of, 158; patriot army in province of, 159; occupied by patriots, 162
Túquerres: 364
Turbaco: 179
Unanue, Hipólito: heads Department of the Treasury, 264; appointed to Council of Government, 274; heads Department of Foreign Relations, 276; made president of Council, 302, 308; favors monarchy, 309
United States: influence of revolution of, 5; indifference of, 91; shows interest in South American cause, 134; recognizes Colombia's independence, 236, 330; and Congress of Panama, 324, 327, 328
Upper Llano (Venezuela): 95
Upper Peru: Santa Cruz expedition to, 238; and the Argentines, 244 and n. 1, 281, 282; royalist rebellion in, 255; jurisdiction in, 280; liberated by Sucre, 281–283; given Bolívar's name, 283; Congress of, 283, 284, 286; and Brazil, 288–289; Indians of, 296; mentioned, 254, 259, 260, 273, 287, 314, 320, 321. SEE ALSO Bolivia; Chuquisaca
Urbaneja, Diego Bautista: 351, 365
Urdaneta, Luis: and Riva-Agüero, 240; sent to organize a unit, 258; routed by enemy cavalry, 263, 264
Urdaneta, Rafael: aids O'Leary, xv; stopped by royalists, 60; withdraws to New Granada, 71; heads division in New Granada, 75, 76; defeated at Chitaga, 92; goes to Guayana, 113; on operations, 128; wounded at Semen, 129; sent to Margarita, 146; assigned to send supplies to Casanare, 152, 153; arrests Arismendi, 170; negotiates armistice terms, 179; illness of, 181; and Maracaibo's insurrection, 189, 190; occupies Coro, 193; as commandant general of Zulia, 352; mentioned, 173, 174, 176, 191
Uriarte y Borja, José: 11

Urica, battle of: 70
Uruguay. SEE Banda Oriental; Montevideo
Ustáriz. SEE Uztáriz
Uztáriz, Francisco Javier de: 55 and n. 4
Uztáriz, Gerónimo de (Marqués de): 12, 13

Valdés, Jerónimo: routs patriot division near Moquegua, 226; attacks and pursues Santa Cruz, 238; professes constitutional principles, 254; defeats Olañeta, 255; joins forces with Canterac, 265; attacks patriot rearguard, 267; mentioned, 260
Valdés, José (Barbarucho): 281
Valdés, Manuel: in exile, 53; wounded at Semen, 129; sent to Obando's aid, 174, 175; difficulty of, in Popayán, 187; replaced by Sucre, 187, 188; in battle of Bomboná, 212; commands troops sent to Lima, 232; mentioned, 54
Valencia: captured from conspirators, 26, 27; as seat of government, 29; evacuated by Miranda and occupied by Monteverde, 34, 35; occupied by Bolívar, 51; siege of, 63, 64, 67, 69; surrenders to Boves, 69; Morillo arrives in, 125; Real falls back to, 132; Bolívar returns to, 196, 198; Páez learns of suspension in, 345; meetings in, about Páez, 346; resolutions of municipal council of, 347, 348 and n. 2; resolution of May 12 in, 349, 350; mentioned, 126, 194, 195, 351, 352, 359
Valle de Upar: 175, 176
Valles de Aragua: 103, 125, 126, 128, 130, 152
Valparaíso: 244
Van Veer, Colonel: 325
Vargas, Juan de los Reyes: 32, 181
Vásquez, Genaro: 129
Venezuela: independence of, x, 26; rebellion in, 6; junta of, 21, 24; first Congress of, 24, 25, 26, 28–29; royalist counterrevolution in, 24, 25, 26–37; first republic of, 26–37; religion in, 29–30, 110; subjugated by royalists, 37–41, 43–52, 67–71; rapid patriot advance in, 48–54; second republic of, 55–67; union of, with New Granada, 56, 89, 144, 168, 171, 172, 175, 323; patriot guerrilla bands in, 94, 95, 96–98; third republic of, 107–172; Council of State established in, 119; Council of Government established in, 121; Congress of 1819 (Angostura)

of, 135, 143, 144–146, 165, 170, 171–173, 174, 178, 196; made department of Colombia, 172; effects of war in, 331; federal system promoted in, 332; influence of Páez in, 333; idea of monarchy in, 343–344; separatist movement in, 343–353; mentioned, 4, 88, 155, 354, 358, 363, 367
Venta Quemada: 163
Veracruz: 11
Vidaurre, Manuel de: 312, 317, 325
Videla, José: 288
Vieques: 105
Vigirima, heights of: 60
Villa de Aragua: 97
Villa de Cura: 125, 128, 129
Villa del Norte: 101
Villaret, Augustín Gustavo: 103, 104
Villars, Fanny Dervieu du: 16
Vinoni, Francisco: 36

Warleta, Francisco: 93
Washington, George: 280
Washington, D.C.: 324
Wellesley, Richard (Marquis of): 22, 23
Wilson, Belford Hinton: aids O'Leary, xv; on royalist plot, 272; takes Bolívar's message to the Congress of Bolivia, 301; lends money to Bolívar, 321

Wilson, Henry: 137, 138
Woodford, Sir Ralph: 53

Yacuanquer, battle of: 227
Yaguachi, battle of: 206
Yáñez, José: captures Antonio Briceño, 48; in battle of Araure, 60; clears patriots from Barinas, 62–63

Zaraza, Pedro: leads guerrilla band, 94, 95, 96, 97; joins MacGregor, 106; ordered to form new units, 120, 122; defeated by La Torre, 121; ordered to join army, 126; flees at El Rincón de los Toros, 131
Zea, Francisco Antonio: in Aux Cayes expedition, 101; sent to ask Bolívar to return, 107; appointed to Council of Government, 121; elected president of Congress, 144; appointed vice-president of Venezuela, 145; informed of Bolívar's campaign plan, 153; reproaches Santander, 166; resigns as vice-president, 170; thanks Bolívar in the name of Congress, 171–172; appointed special commissioner, 173–174; promotes Sucre, 188; mentioned, 169
Zepita: 238, 283
Zulia: 351, 352
Zulia River: 44